Economic Growth

How can society improve its living standards? What are the conditions necessary for prosperity? These are the questions that define the essence of growth theory. In this user-friendly book, Olivier de La Grandville provides a fascinating introduction to the theory of economic growth and shows how many results from this field are of paramount importance for society. The classical mechanics of the growth process are carefully explained, with two chapters devoted to the fundamental issue of the substitution of labour for capital in the growth process (co-written with Robert M. Solow, winner of the Nobel Prize in Economics). The book also addresses the fundamental question of the optimal investment rate of an economy. In addition, La Grandville shows us that by unifying the descriptive and normative aspects of growth theory we can generate many fresh insights, including a proof of Adam Smith's "Invisible Hand" conjecture.

OLIVIER DE LA GRANDVILLE is Visiting Professor in the Management Science and Engineering Department at Stanford University, a position he has held since 1988. A Professor of Economics at the University of Geneva from 1978 to 2007, he is the author of seven books ranging from microeconomics to macroeconomics and finance. His research work has been published in international journals such as the *American Economic Review* and *Econometrica*.

OLIVIER DE LA GRANDVILLE

Economic Growth

A Unified Approach

With two special contributions by Robert M. Solow

CAMBRIDGE UNIVERSITY PRESS
Cambridge, New York, Melbourne, Madrid, Cape Town, Singapore, São Paulo, Delhi

Cambridge University Press
The Edinburgh Building, Cambridge CB2 8RU, UK

Published in the United States of America by Cambridge University Press, New York

www.cambridge.org
Information on this title: www.cambridge.org/9780521725200

First published 2009

Printed in the United Kingdom at the University Press, Cambridge

A catalogue record for this publication is available from the British Library

Library of Congress Cataloguing in Publication data
La Grandville, Olivier de.
Economic growth : a unified approach / Olivier de La Grandville ; with two
special contributions by Robert M. Solow.
    p.   cm.
Includes bibliographical references and index.
ISBN 978-0-521-89801-0
1. Economic development.   2. Economics – Mathematical models.   I. Title.
HD75.L295   2008
338.9001 – dc22   2009000339

ISBN 978-0-521-89801-0 hardback
ISBN 978-0-521-72520-0 paperback

*This book is lovingly dedicated
to my wife Ann,
to our children Diane, Isabelle and Henri,
and to their own children*

CONTENTS

INTRODUCTION

Why should you read a book on economic growth? Because the subject is important: it is about the well-being of our societies today and in the future; and because it is beautiful. It carries wonderful ideas, some exposed more than 2000 years ago, spanning all civilizations. You will certainly marvel at Ibn Khaldun's prescience, at Mo Tzu's wisdom, at Solow's depiction of transition phases, at Dorfman's incredible intuition in solving variational problems.

This book is not quite the same as other books. Economic growth has attracted, particularly in the last hundred years, countless, excellent writers who have developed the field into an immense array of topics, from theoretical to empirical. Rather than trying to cover all developments – of which you can have an idea through the bibliography – I have wanted to tell you what I found fascinating in the subject. But my hope is also that you will find here a useful introduction to this wide area of research, because a lot of the book is not only on ideas but on methodology as well.

A further reason for me to write this text was to submit personal views and present new results. For too many years I have expounded growth theory by dividing the subject, as many did, into two main strands of thought: positive, or descriptive theory on the one hand, normative on the other. I am now convinced that those two strands should be unified – hence the title of the book. For clarity's sake, I think however that both approaches to the theory should be first presented separately (parts I and II), and then unified (part III). Such unification proceeds not from any personal whim, but from logical reasons: the results of both strands of thought mutually imply each other, as will be shown.

Let me now underline the new results you will find in this book:

• A proof of one of the most important, daring conjectures ever made in economics or social sciences. We owe this conjecture, known as "the invisible hand", to Adam Smith who wrote, in his *Inquiry into the Nature and the Causes of the Wealth of Nations* (1776):

> Every individual is continually exerting himself to find out the most advantageous employment for whatever capital he can command. It is his own advantage, indeed, and not that of the society, which he has in view. But

the study of his own advantage naturally, or rather necessarily, leads him to prefer that employment which is most advantageous to the society ...

He generally, indeed, neither intends to promote the public interest, nor knows how much he is promoting it. ... He intends only his own gain, and he is in this, as in many other cases, led by an invisible hand to promote an end which was no part of his intention.[1]

Note how far reaching Adam Smith's conjecture is. Not only does the author hold that the search by individuals for the most advantageous employment of their capital stock is advantageous to society; he takes one step further by stating that this advantage is maximized.

What is then the exact benefit that Smith could have referred to in his conjecture? How is it to be measured? The answer is quite surprising. It will be shown that it is not only one, but *two* magnitudes that are simultaneously maximized for society:

(1) the sum of the discounted consumption flows society can acquire from now to infinity

(2) the benefits of society's activity at any point of time t – including today; those benefits are the sum of the consumption flows received at time t and the rate of increase in the value of the capital stock at that time.

The proof of this theorem, which you will find in the last chapter, uses the methodology and results expounded throughout this text, and draws both on positive and normative theory. If only for this very proof, there would be ample reason to justify the unified approach I am advocating.

• A thorough analysis of the importance of the elasticity of substitution in the growth process. Too often do we see growth models carrying the convenient, beloved hypothesis of an elasticity of substitution equal to 1, equivalent to the Cobb–Douglas function. We now have evidence, however, that in any economy we might consider the elasticity of substitution is significantly different from 1, with a tendency of growing – which is good news, as the reader will discover. A surprise is in store: an increase in the elasticity of substitution will be shown to have far more importance for society's future welfare than a similar increase in the rate of technical progress.

• A detailed examination of the consequences of using utility functions in optimal growth theory. Traditional treatment of the theory usually leads to a system of differential equations which does not possess analytical solutions. In my opinion, this issue, involving solving numerically such a system, has been taken too lightly, and short shrift has been given to results taking the form of exceedingly high "optimal" savings rates. It can even be read in the literature that some family of

---

[1] A. Smith, *op. cit.*, Dent and Sons, London, 1975, pp. 398–400.

utility functions can be used, although it turns out that no equilibrium point exists. Great care will be taken in analysing the optimal time-paths of the economy, both in terms of their associated initial values and their ultimate evolution.

• A formula for the optimal savings rate of an economy. Until now optimal savings rates could be calculated numerically only – no closed form was available and, as mentioned, those values often made little sense. The formula I submit is expressed in terms of the fundamental characteristics of the economy and society's rate of preference for the present, and yields reasonable, very reachable values.

• Applications and extensions of Dorfman's modified Hamiltonian. With remarkable insight, Robert Dorfman had introduced a new Hamiltonian to tackle the variational problems encountered in optimal growth theory. To honour Professor Dorfman's memory, I propose to call his concept a Dorfmanian. It will play a fundamental role in the proof of Smith's conjecture. The reader will also find here extensions of the Dorfmanian which can yield all high-order equations of the calculus of variations – including the Euler–Poisson and the Ostrogradski equations.

• The final reason why you should read this book is that Robert Solow and myself need your help: you will be invited to exercise your sagacity and try to prove a conjecture we are offering at the end of chapter 4. The conjecture, of a mathematical nature, is as formidable a challenge to prove as it is easy to express: the general mean of two numbers, considered as a function of its order, has one and only one inflection point. Why is it important? Because as a result, income per person behaves exactly like a function of production whose dependent variable is the elasticity of substitution, with a first phase of increasing returns, followed by decreasing returns, and our economies seem to be in the very neighbourhood of this point of inflection.

It is my pleasure to thank a number of persons whose role has been essential in the realization of this book. First and foremost, I would like to express my deepest gratitude to Robert Solow, who not only co-authored a large chapter (chapter 5) and the appendix of chapter 4, but also gave me invaluable advice on many other important parts of the book. Needless to say, I alone remain responsible for any remaining shortcomings, and the personal views expressed here are not necessarily condoned by him.

My colleague Ernst Hairer, of the Department of Mathematics at the University of Geneva, has used his program DOPRI for solving numerically the differential equations of chapters 9 and 10; the stunning phase diagrams – in particular the one on the cover of this book – are his work. Ernst Hairer's generosity led him also to write the program yielding the initial values leading to equilibrium for any system of parameters characterizing the economy. I am in great debt to him.

Claudio Sfreddo let us use for our regressions in chapter 6 the data he had developed on a common basis for 16 OECD countries in his PhD thesis; we are very grateful to him.

My thanks go finally to those persons who read parts of the manuscript and offered corrections or very useful remarks. I would like to thank in particular Kenneth Arrow, Eunyi Chung, Jean-Marie Grether, Bjarne Sloth Jensen, Mingyun Joo, Rainer Klump, Patrick de Laubier, Hing-Man Leung, Edmond Malinvaud, Amin Nikoozadeh, Mario Piacentini, Mathias Thoenig, Brigitte Van Baalen, Juerg Weber, and Milad Zarin-Nejadan. Jon Bilam for Cambridge University Press did a marvellous job in revising the whole text, and I am extremely grateful to him. Dave Tyler prepared the index in a masterly way; my warmest thanks to him. I would also like to express my deep appreciation to Daniel Dunlavey, senior production editor at Cambridge University Press, who supervised the whole project with great expertise. Last but not least, I want to thank heartily Huong Nguyen for her beautiful, dedicated work at typing my manuscript. It was a joy working with her.

PART I

Positive growth theory

Economics was born when some people asked the questions: How can society improve its living standards? What are the conditions of prosperity? Those questions define the essence of growth theory. It is no wonder that in the Western world they were raised – rather timidly – at the end of the Renaissance only, by Botero (1589, 1598), and then by Sully (1639) and Child (1668). Why not earlier? Because economics, as any science, is founded on observation; no sign of growth had ever appeared in the Middle Ages – and how could it have after the endless wars and plagues that ravaged Europe, particularly in the fourteenth century? Those times carried no hope, and it would have taken a bold thinker to entreat the question of development. As the French historian Pierre Gaxotte very well put it, "the man of the Middle Ages does not know of time and numbers".

It is not surprising therefore that we owe to Arab civilization the first comprehensive description of the fundamental causes of growth. In his *Muqaddimah* (*Introduction to History* (1377)), the Arab historian Ibn Khaldun went even further and set himself to explain the causes of the rise and decline of civilizations. This is a good place to recall what Arnold Toynbee had to say about Ibn Khaldun's magnum opus:

> He appears to have been inspired by no predecessors, and to have found no kindred souls among his contemporaries, and to have kindled no answering spark of inspiration in any successors; and yet, in the Prolegomena (Muqaddimah) to his Universal History he has conceived and formulated a philosophy of history which is undoubtedly the greatest work of its kind that has ever yet been created by any mind in any time or place.[1]

Ibn Khaldun's contribution encompasses not only the description of the growth process, but also what needs to be done to set it in motion. His essay therefore is not only positive or descriptive; it is normative as well, and it shares that characteristic

---

[1] Arnold Toynbee, *A Study of History*, Royal Institute of International Affairs and Oxford University Press, Vol. III, 1934, p. 321.

with Adam Smith's "*Inquiry into the Nature and the Causes of the Wealth of Nations*" that came four centuries later. In consequence, it is only fitting that these works will be presented in the final part of this book where the positive and the normative approaches are brought together.

In this first part, we will be content to describe the growth process; our first aim will be to analyse the mechanisms which make income per person grow from one period to another. In particular, we will want to answer the following question: from what we know about the growth process, is income per person bound by an upper limit?

To answer this question, we will build a simple, dynamic model of the economy. The motion of income per person – the central variable of growth theory – will be shown to be governed by a differential equation whose solution depends essentially on three sets of hypotheses. The first one summarizes the way capital, labour and technical progress define a precise production process. The second translates an important facet of society's behaviour towards its future, i.e. the amount it is willing to save and invest in order to enhance its capital stock. A final set of hypotheses will be made regarding the evolution of population and its labour force.

At the end of part I, we will deal with properties of random growth rates. In particular, we will want to determine the expected long-term growth rate of an economy as a function of the first two moments of the annual growth rate.

CHAPTER I

The welfare of society and economic growth

When I have pluck'd the rose,
I cannot give it vital growth again.
Othello

In the history of mankind, attempts to improve living conditions have only very recently superseded the struggle for survival. In all civilizations, progress has been exceedingly slow, with abrupt, unexpected downfalls. These were concomitant to natural disasters, epidemics and wars. Today, we can estimate that only one fifth of the world population enjoys a standard of life that can be considered acceptable.

The yardstick commonly used to measure standards of living is "income per person". We first show how income reflects the result of economic activity (section 1).[1] We then discuss whether income per person constitutes a proper gauge for the measurement of society's welfare (sections 2 and 3).

1 Income as a measure of economic activity

Fundamentally, nations can benefit, in the long run, only from what they have been able to produce. In turn, the amount produced within a given time span (for instance one year) can be measured from at least three perspectives.

First, we can consider the types of produced goods and services; these can broadly be distributed between consumption goods or services on the one hand, and investment goods on the other. Consumption goods and services are produced for the direct use of consumers. Investment goods (machines, factories, transportation infrastructure, etc.) are produced in order to provide ultimately, at some later date, consumption goods or services. Adding consumption to investment would measure a nation's total activity if the nation had no relations with the outside world. If

---

[1] This first section is intended for the reader who has had no introduction to national accounts.

this is not so, two major corrections should be introduced: first, one must add to consumption and investment all exports of goods and services; second, all imports should be deducted: indeed, consumption, investment and even exports include imports of goods and services, and imports are no part of a nation's activity.

From a second perspective, we may consider the output generated by the nation's various sectors of activity. We then want to determine how much agriculture or industry, or services have contributed to the nation's global activity. This can be measured by the *net* production of each sector. Net production is the sector's total production net of all purchases from other sectors. Indeed we want to avoid counting twice, or a multiple number of times, the same output. Consider two sectors: the automobile and the aluminium industries. The automobile industry uses, among many other things, aluminium. Simply adding up the production of each sector would amount to counting twice the value of the aluminium. The net production or net output is appropriately called the *value added* of the sector.

A third and final approach is to consider the income generated and distributed throughout the economy. Clearly, this income can be generated only by the value added of each sector of the economy. Three broad categories can be distinguished: labour income, capital income, and profits. Labour income is self-explanatory. Capital income is the remuneration of the (physical) capital stock that has been used in the production process, plus rentals by private individuals. Suppose that, in a given firm, this capital has been rented: the rentals are the capital remuneration. If a firm owns its capital stock, two possibilities arise: first, the firm may have borrowed in order to buy the capital it owns. The remuneration of capital is then the interest payments it pays. If the firm has financed the capital with its own resources, the remuneration of capital is the interest payments it has foregone by acquiring the capital stock instead of lending out its resources.

We will now summarize in an example each of these three approaches to the measure of economic activity within the boundaries of a given country. The global result is called the *gross domestic product*. The adjective "domestic" refers to the fact that the activity is measured within the boundaries of the country considered. The adjective "gross" reflects the fact that investment expenditures *include* amortization – or depreciation – of capital. We will explain in section 2 how to obtain other aggregates also commonly referred to, such as the gross national product and national income. Before that we will illustrate with a numerical example the three approaches to measuring the gross domestic product.

1.1 Three approaches to measuring economic activity: a simple example

1.1.1 The expenditure approach

This is the most natural and arguably the most useful approach from an informative point of view because we are interested in the nature of goods and services that will be available to society. It breaks down the gross domestic product into its constitutive parts: consumption, investment, plus exports minus imports. One point of detail: during a given year, inventories may have accumulated in the producers' hands; by definition, these have not yet been sold. They are then considered part of investment.

Consumption is usually separated into private consumption and public consumption; private consumption refers to the consumption of individuals; public consumption is that of the state (at the national or at the local level). The same distinction applies to investment. We thus have, for example:

- private consumption: 70
- public consumption: 10
- private investment: 8
- public investment: 7
- exports: 40
- *minus* imports: −35

Total: gross domestic product: 100

1.1.2   The output (value added) approach

The economy can be divided into a few – or many – sectors. If we consider the traditional three sectors (agriculture, industry, services), we may have:

- value added of agriculture: 4
- value added of industry: 30
- value added of services: 66

Total: gross domestic product: 100

1.1.3   The income approach

Retaining the classification referred to in the beginning of this section could give:

- labour income: 68
- capital income: 26
- profit: 6

Total: gross domestic product: 100

1.2   A global view of the three approaches: the input–output table

It is possible and highly useful to present in one table those three approaches. Indeed, it is by no means obvious that the three approaches amount to the same number. In fact, statisticians establishing those national accounts have to introduce sometimes large corrections to obtain the desired result.

This synthetic, global view was first proposed by Wassily Leontief[2] in a so-called "input–output" table. The table can be considered as made of three parts. In the first part (the upper-left part of table 1.1), only intermediate transactions are recorded. Those are the sales of products or services from one sector to another (for instance the aluminium sold to the automobile sector, the wheat sold by agriculture to the food industry, or the insurance premiums sold to the farmers). The table presents in its upper-left 9 squares all possible sales between the three sectors we have considered (there are 6 possible inter-sector sales and 3 possible intra-sector sales: for instance the energy sales to the aluminium industry are sales within the industry sector). The first 3 figures of column 4 (2, 9, 20) sum the sales of each sector to other sectors as well as to itself. The first 3 figures of line 4 (5, 20, 6) are the purchases of each sector from other sectors and from itself. The total of intermediate sales and purchases (31) is the 4th figure of line 4 and column 4.

The second part of the table (columns 5 to 10) breaks down the expenditure side of the gross domestic product into its components (column 5 indicates consumption goods aggregated as the sum of private and public consumption, for a total of 80; column 6 gives private and public investment, etc.). X and M designate exports and imports respectively. The total $C + I + X - M = 80 + 15 + 40 - 35 = 100$ corresponds to the gross domestic product from the expenditure approach and to the example we have given in section 1.1.

It is now possible to determine the total output generated by each sector by adding the total of intermediate goods and services (col. 4) to the column of final demand (col. 9). We thus get column 10. This will be useful to determine the value added of each sector. Indeed, just translate the numbers of column 10 into the horizontal line 9 at the bottom of the table. Just by taking the difference between the total output (line 9) and the total purchases of each sector (line 4) gives the value added by each sector (line 8). This line is the gross domestic product broken down according to value added by each sector $(4 + 30 + 66 = 100)$. In turn, each of these net contributions from each sector can be split into their components (labour income, capital income and profits). These are indicated in lines 5, 6 and 7 respectively. Their total in column 4 gives the gross domestic product from the income point of view $(68 + 26 + 6 = 100)$.

Thus the three approaches to the gross domestic product can be viewed in a single table. Two conclusions emerge. The first is that if we had to choose from those three approaches that which best reflects the welfare of society, we would probably

---

[2] Wassily Leontief (1906–99) was born in St Petersburg and received his PhD from Humbolt University in Berlin. He taught at Harvard and New York University. One of his first input–output tables divided the US economy into 500 sectors. He received the Nobel Prize in Economics in 1974 for his pioneering work on input–output economics.

Table 1.1 A simplified input–output table

		(1) agr.	(2) ind.	(3) serv.	(4) interm. output	(5) C	(6) I	(7) X	(8) -M	(9) Final demand	(10) Total output
(1)	agriculture	—	1	1	2	6	—	4	3	7	9
(2)	industry	2	5	2	9	24	15	20	18	41	50
(3)	services	3	14	3	20	50	—	16	14	52	72
(4)	interm. input	5	20	6	31	**80**	**15**	**40**	**35**	**100**	131
(5)	labour income	3	20	45	**68**						
(6)	capital income	1	8	17	**26**						
(7)	profit	—	2	4	**6**						
(8)	value added	**4**	**30**	**66**	**100**						
(9)	Total output	9	50	72	131						

The input–output table gives at once the three approaches to evaluate the Gross Domestic Product (100 in this example): the expenditure approach is the total of consumption + investment + exports − imports (80 + 15 + 40 − 35 = 100). Value added by each sector is 4 + 30 + 66 = 100. Income is distributed to labour and capital, and the remainder is profits (68 + 26 + 6 = 100).

choose the first, i.e. the expenditure approach, because we are most interested to know what kind of consumption or investment goods will be available to society. We do not care about whatever nominal income is generated if it corresponds to huge investments which will be of little use to society.

The second lesson we draw is the one-to-one correspondence between net output and income. Income will increase in an economy if and only if net production – or value added – increases.

1.3 From gross domestic product to national income

The gross *domestic* product (GDP) measures the activity taking place inside the borders of a given nation. However, it may be desirable to have a measurement leading to the revenue accrued to people actually residing in a country. This implies, in particular, adding to GDP the income received from abroad by residents and subtracting the income paid out to non residents who are working within the boundaries of the country. These corrections concern both labour and capital income. Thus we have:

Gross domestic product (GDP) + labour and capital income generated
                                   abroad and received by residents
                         – labour and capital income generated
                              domestically paid out to non-residents
                      = gross *national* product ≡ GNP

Observe that the adjective "national" is most unfortunate since it does *not* refer to the activity of national economic agents; it only refers to the activity of *residents*.

Furthermore, within one year investments may have taken place, but some depreciation of the existing stock of capital has occurred. It is important (especially in the context of economic growth) to know by exactly what amount the capital stock in existence in the economy may have increased. This is why depreciation of capital will be subtracted from (gross) investment to obtain *net* investment, and consequently *net* national product:

Gross national product (GNP) – depreciation = Net national product (NNP).

Finally, it may be interesting to know exactly what amount of income will be distributed to residents before income taxes. For that purpose, two corrections need to be introduced. First, we must deduce from the net national product *indirect* taxes – this is the sales tax paid by consumers to producers, which the latter transfer to the state. These taxes form no part of the value added that is the basis of income distribution by firms, and therefore must be deducted from net national product. On the other hand, firms may receive subsidies from the state. Together with value added these may be used to remunerate production factors such as labour or capital. Thus we have:

Net national product (NPP) − indirect taxes + subsidies = National income.

The following summarizes the various steps transforming gross domestic product (GDP) into net national income.

> *Gross domestic product* (GDP)
> > + labour and capital income received from abroad by residents
> > − labour and capital income transferred abroad to non-residents
> = *Gross national product* (GNP)
> > − capital depreciation
> = *Net national product*
> > − indirect taxes
> > + subsidies
> = *National income*

1.4 *National income at current prices and at constant prices*

Suppose that from one year to another we observe an increase in the gross domestic product, or an increase in national income. Can we conclude from this observation that the standards of living have increased? Clearly such a conclusion is not warranted since that increase might be due to the sole increase of prices. It is then important to be able to define in a precise way what part of a change in national income is attributable to a change in prices, and what part reflects an increase in output available to society. For that purpose, price indexes are constructed. We will succinctly describe here the consumers' price index.

We will use the following definitions and notations:

- p_i^t = price of good i at time t (measurement units: \$/unit of the good considered)

- $\dfrac{p_i^t - p_i^{t-1}}{p_i^{t-1}}$ = relative rate of increase in the price of good i

- $\dfrac{p_i^t}{p_i^{t-1}} \equiv X_i \equiv$ growth factor of the price of good $i \equiv$ partial price index of good i

We can note that this growth factor reflects also the growth factor of the expenditure necessary to buy one unit, or any fixed quantity, of good i.

Suppose now that between time 0 and time 1 the prices of two goods have undergone different relative increases (perhaps 10% and 30% respectively). Is there a way to define a meaningful "average" of those increases? It is obvious that considering the simple average of those rates (20%) would be of little significance if, for instance, consumers used to spend a large part of their income on one of those items. Therefore, it is natural to try to measure the consequences of such increases for a given consumer in the following way.

Consider the growth factor of the expenditure necessary for this consumer to be able to buy again the same basket of both goods which he or she had initially purchased at time 0, before the price increases.

Suppose that this basket is (q_1^0, q_2^0). Then his (or her) expenditure necessary to buy this basket at time 0, denoted D^0, is:

$$D^0 = p_1^0 q_1^0 + p_2^0 q_2^0. \tag{1}$$

When prices move to p_1^1, p_2^1, the necessary expenditure to buy the same basket becomes

$$D^1 = p_1^1 q_1^0 + p_2^1 q_2^0 \tag{2}$$

and the growth factor of the expenditure is

$$\frac{D^1}{D^0} = \frac{p_1^1 q_1^0 + p_2^1 q_2^0}{p_1^0 q_1^0 + p_2^0 q_2^0}. \tag{3}$$

It can be shown immediately that this growth factor is equal to the average of the partial price indexes of both goods $(p_1^1/p_1^0$ and $p_2^1/p_2^0)$, the weights being the shares of each good in the individual's initial expenditure, $p_1^0 q_1^0 / D^0$ and $p_2^0 q_2^0 / D^0$. Indeed, in the numerator of (3), we can make the following transformation:

$$\frac{D^1}{D^0} = \frac{p_1^1 q_1^0 + p_2^1 q_2^0}{D^0} = \frac{\dfrac{p_1^1}{p_1^0} p_1^0 q_1^0 + \dfrac{p_2^1}{p_2^0} p_2^0 q_2^0}{D^0}. \tag{4}$$

Denoting $p_1^0 q_1^0 / D^0 = \alpha_1$ and $p_2^0 q_2^0 / D^0 = \alpha_2$ the individual consumer's expenditure shares on goods 1 and 2, this growth factor is

$$\frac{D^1}{D^0} = \alpha_1 X_1 + \alpha_2 X_2, \text{ with } \alpha_1 + \alpha_2 = 1, \tag{5}$$

the weighted average of X_1 and X_2.

This generalizes of course to the case of n goods. The expenditure growth factor is

$$\frac{D^1}{D^0} = \frac{\sum_{i=1}^n p_i^1 q_i^0}{\sum_{i=1}^n p_i^0 q_i^0} = \frac{\sum_{i=1}^n (p_i^1/p_i^0) p_i^0 q_i^0}{D^0} = \sum_{i=1}^n \frac{p_i^1}{p_i^0} \frac{p_i^0 q_i^0}{D^0}$$

$$= \sum_{i=1}^n \alpha_i X_i, \quad \sum_{i=1}^n \alpha_i = 1. \tag{6}$$

We have just determined the expenditure growth factor for an individual who would have expenditure shares α_i, $i = 1, \ldots, n$. Now the same principle can be extended to a society as a whole: we just need to replace the α_i's of the individual by the *average* shares of society's consumption of each good in total consumption. Call β_i, $i = 1, \ldots, n$ those shares. The consumer price index is then defined as

$$X = \sum_{i=1}^{n} \beta_i X_i, \text{ with } \sum_{i=1}^{n} \beta_i = 1. \tag{7}$$

Needless to say, difficulties arise in practice when it comes to define "a good" – only categories of goods can be defined. But we can already surmise at this introductory stage that an individual's compensation for a rising cost of living on the basis of the index X may lead to biases. Even assuming the goods an individual buys to be exactly of the same nature as those used in the construction of the index, an individual may be under-compensated or over-compensated if her shares α_i are such that her expenditure growth factor turns out to be higher or lower than the index X. Suppose that the state, or a firm, compensates an individual for the rising cost of living by multiplying his income by the index $\sum_{i=1}^{n} \beta_i X_i$. All values of α_i and β_i such that

$$\sum_{i=1}^{n} \alpha_i X_i = \sum_{i=1}^{n} \beta_i X_i \tag{8}$$

will lead to a fair compensation of the individual if the consumer price index is used. However the inequality

$$\sum_{i=1}^{n} \alpha_i X_i > \sum_{i=1}^{n} \beta_i X_i \tag{9}$$

will lead to under-compensation of the individual, and

$$\sum_{i=1}^{n} \alpha_i X_i < \sum_{i=1}^{n} \beta_i X_i \tag{10}$$

will lead to over-compensation.

Let us now see, as an example, how to obtain a measurement of total consumption which would be independent from price changes over one year. We can think of dividing the observed consumption aggregate by the price index observed over one year and thus obtained consumption in a given year "at last year's prices". For instance, suppose that the price index over one year is 1.1 (in practice this is multiplied by 100 and quoted as 110 with a 100 basis), and that consumption has risen, in nominal terms from 1000 to 1210 monetary units, i.e. by 21%. This implies that consumption in real terms has risen only to $1210/1.1 = 1100$. In other words consumption has increased "in volume" by 10%. This example can immediately be extended to a time span longer than one year.

Such indices are constructed for the various components of gross domestic product. Lots of refinements are introduced for each of those components, and an aggregate GDP "at constant prices", or in "real terms" can thus be calculated by aggregation. Dividing GDP in nominal terms by GDP at constant prices yields the implicit price index for GDP, the so-called "implicit GDP deflator". National income at constant prices is also calculated by using such an implicit deflator.

When it comes to making inter-country comparisons, national accounts must be expressed in terms of one currency. Care must than be exerted to use exchange rates which truly reflect the purchasing power of each currency. The difficulty here lies in the fact that a currency may be over- or under-valued, and the task of the statistician is to try to evaluate the true purchasing power of any currency. Suppose that statistical methods enable us to do just this. We now have to ask a fundamental question: does income per person truly reflect the standard of living of a given society? We will address this issue in the next section.

2   Is income per person a fair gauge of society's welfare?

We have already called the reader's attention to the fact that society's income reflects the amount of goods and services that society has been able to acquire. It is only natural to examine closely, first, the nature of those goods and services. If, for instance, the production of some goods has been forced upon society, obviously these should not enter GDP if this number is to be used as a yardstick to measure society's welfare.

A significant number of corrections must be made for GDP to be used in the measure of welfare. First, some important expenditures should be excluded from GDP because they do not provide any well-being. Secondly, the simple calculation of GDP neglects a whole series of elements which may increase or decrease welfare. Those elements are either difficult to measure, or are simply not measurable. We will consider all these in turn.

2.1   Expenditures that should be excluded from GDP

We will classify such expenditures into two categories: first, we will consider expenditures decided without individuals' consent; second we will turn to expenditures chosen by individuals on their own free will, but that should be excluded from GDP because they do not enhance in any way the individuals' welfare.

2.1.1   Expenditures decided without individuals' consent

In a majority of countries, state or public expenditure is still decided without any effective parliamentary control. Those amounts which would not have been approved through a democratic process are not to be included in GDP if this statistic is to reflect welfare. In poor countries, it is almost certain that if individuals had their say, they would choose to replace unwanted public expenses by expenditure on services that they do want, namely health and education.

2.1.2 Expenses decided with individuals' consent

Individuals may very well decide upon expenses on their own free will, although they know these will never contribute to their welfare. Collective or personal security expenses are prominent examples. Suppose that, for many possible reasons, insecurity increases. This will have two major consequences, admitting that the population's work effort remains the same: first, society will have to replace goods and services which yielded some well-being by security expenses. This will be a first source of welfare decrease. It will add to the loss in welfare generated by the enhanced feel of insecurity. The same is true for the expenses generated by an epidemic, by the threat of war, or by war itself.

Other obvious expenses should be taken away from GDP because they do not reflect welfare. The cost of illnesses or accidents, or home-work commuting are obvious examples.

2.2 Fundamental factors neglected in the calculation of GDP

Working conditions are fundamental determinants of a society's welfare, but are not taken into consideration in GDP calculation. No account, furthermore, is taken of forced labour, particularly of the labour forced upon women and children.

On the other hand economic activity itself may damage the environment. We mentioned previously that depreciation of capital was accounted for when determining national income; no provision however is made for the deterioration of the environment which, contrary to the obsolescence of capital, may be an irreversible phenomenon. This factor is so important that it will prompt a major caveat in section 3 of this chapter.

Other fundamental aspects of welfare, equity and equal opportunity, are entirely omitted from national accounting. By "equity" we mean the ability for a society to reward each individual according to his own qualities and effort, and at the same time to protect those hurt by fate.

2.3 Should we, finally, rely on income per person?

It might be thought that the long list of important provisos that we mentioned, which are fundamental to the definition of our well-being, would lead us to give a negative answer. It may then come as a surprise that, despite all those reservations, income per person in our opinion *is* a useful measure of a society's welfare. We will now show why.

Table 1.2 *Hypothetical rankings*

(1) Ranking according to democracy	(2) Ranking according to income per person	(3) Coefficient of adequation of income per person to welfare	(4) Adjusted income per person (2) × (3)
1. ...	1. ...	...	...
2. ...	2. ...	...	...
3. ...	3. ...	...	...

Suppose that we established a ranking of countries according to their income per person, and compare it to a list according to welfare, built on the basis of close observations and common sense, in a way somewhat reminiscent of what travellers of the eighteenth century did when they described the "conditions of prosperity". Our view is that both lists would be very close to one another, for the following reasons.

We should first recognize that the degree of democracy has a very direct, profound bearing on society's standard of living: income per person can reach a high level only if all individuals have a freedom of choice guaranteed by the rule of law, and if public decisions truly reflect their consensus. If one could establish a list of countries according to the degree of democracy, we believe that such a list (column 1 in table 1.2) would closely match the ranking of countries according to their income per person (column 2).

Let us now turn to all amendments that must be carried out in order for income per person to reflect society's welfare. Define an adequation coefficient, between 0 and 1, as the ratio welfare/income per person. If, for instance, very few corrections have to be made, this coefficient may be, say, 0.95. On the other hand, should massive corrections be introduced, the coefficient would be much lower. Now draw up a list of those coefficents corresponding to the countries and their associated income per person listed in column 2. We can safely assume that those coefficients are proportional to the degree of democracy. Indeed, those fundamental determinants of welfare, such as working conditions, the protection of individuals, in particular women and children, the protection of the environment, the control of public policies are both the aim and the distinctive marks of democracy.

Consider now the final result of corrected income per person, obtained by multiplying column 2 by column 3. If the ranking of column 1 is the same as the ranking of column 2, it is obvious that the ranking of column 2 will be preserved in column 4. But this is only a sufficient condition; it is not a necessary one as the reader could assert by constructing an example where the rankings of 1 and 2 differ, but where the ranking in 2 is still preserved in 4 (see exercise 5).

We conclude that while income per person is definitely not an absolute measure of welfare, it can remain a valid tool for international comparisons of standards of living. This is the reason why we consider income per person as a variable of central importance, keeping in mind the adjustments that have to be made if it is to reflect the society's true standard of living.

3   A major caveat

In this chapter we have underlined that we must take into account two major corrections of GDP in order to have a sound measure of welfare: first, depreciation of capital has to be deducted from GDP for a *net* measure of economic activity. Second, we know current economic activity may be dangerous for ourselves and for future generations whenever the biosphere is harmed. The biosphere is of course part of our capital, and any depredation of it should be taken into account. Now comes a crucial problem: it is extremely difficult to gauge, from a scientific point of view, how much changes on the biosphere are due to human activity or to natural causes. In any event, it is undisputed that in the last two centuries humanity has started a process of transforming the biosphere on a new scale – unknown before – for two main, concomitant reasons: an extraordinary rise in population growth, and the industrialization of the world. Demographers estimate that between 8000 BC and AD 1900, i.e. over a period of 9900 years, the world population grew from about 5 million to 1.6 billion. This corresponds to an extremely *low* growth rate: less than 6 hundredths of one per cent per year, or 5.8 per ten-thousand per year. This exceedingly slow growth of the population was due to unending wars, epidemics and high natural mortality rates.

Suddenly, at the time scale of our history, this picture changed completely. Between 1900 and 2005 the world population increased 4-fold, from 1.6 to 6.4 billion, i.e. at a rate of 1.3% per year. Thus the long-term population growth rate was multiplied by a factor $1.3/0.058 \approx 22$. The world population now grows at a rate of 1.5% per year, i.e. at a rate 25 times higher than the long-term rate it experienced over the past 10,000 years. There is of course no reason why this rate should decrease; and if it is maintained, we will be 13.5 billion in 50 years, and 87 billion in 300 years.

The evidence is two-fold: on the one hand, world population has increased and will increase at a rate which was never witnessed in its past; on the other hand, the huge surge in population together with the industrialization process are having an unprecedented, negative, impact on the biosphere. The consequence is of course that humanity has to react, exactly as it has successfully reacted to the first, dreadful, consequences of industrialization. This will have its costs, which must be deducted from *net* national product for the measure of activity to be a measure of welfare. A new level of complexity is now reached. Our task is to understand a highly intricate set of physical, chemical and biological processes and measure what part of any deterioration of the biosphere is due to natural causes and what part is due to human activity. We then need to discover methods of counteracting the negative consequences we are responsible for; and finally we have to design institutions capable of implementing them.

In this text we are concerned with the theory of economic growth. We hold that progress means that solutions to the problems we just mentioned do exist, and that steps will be taken to implement them. In the next chapters, whenever we mention that a production function links output to factors such as capital, labour, and technical progress, we will always refer to *net* output – or *net* income, in the sense that we suppose that the cost of capital *and biosphere* depreciation has been deducted from the gross measure of output.

Appendix: A brief review of some useful concepts in economics

We start with the concepts of consumers' demand, producers' supply, the "law of supply and demand", and finally the measurement of the benefits society can derive from a given situation on a single market. This brief review is intended solely for those readers who have not had an introduction to economics.

I The law of supply and demand, and the equilibrium price

For any given good or service, demand is the relationship between the quantity q_D that consumers are willing to buy and the price p they are facing. It is denoted $q_D(p)$. Practically always this relationship is decreasing. The reason why the slope of the demand curve is negative is two-fold: when the price decreases, each consumer may have a tendency to buy more of that good; on the other hand, consumers who were not buying the good at a higher price may now be willing to do so, thus entering the market. Such a decreasing curve $q_D(p)$ is depicted in figure 1.1; for historical reasons the quantity is set on the abscissa, while the explanatory variable, the price, is on the ordinate. Notice that since the demand function $q_D(p)$ is decreasing, it can be inverted; $p(q_D)$ is then the price consumers are prepared to pay if they are to buy an amount q_D. This property will be applied soon.

Symmetrically, supply is the amount q_S producers are willing to put on the market if the price they receive is p. $q_S(p)$ is usually an increasing function of p. The positive slope of the supply curve is justified in a symmetrical way to what we have just seen for the demand curve: when the price increases, firms already in the market have a tendency to produce more; on the other hand, new firms may become profitable and enter the market. Being an increasing function of price, the supply function $q_S(p)$ can be inverted: $p(q_S)$ is the price producers want to receive if they are to put an amount q_S on the market.

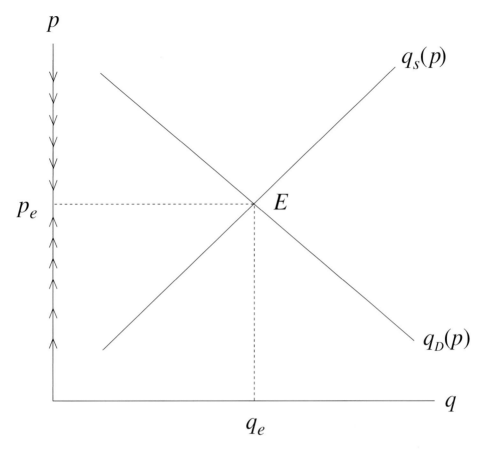

Figure 1.1 **Demand function $q_D(p)$ and supply function $q_S(p)$. The equilibrium point E: (p_e, q_e) will be reached if prices are free to move.**

When the supply and demand curves are drawn together on the same diagram as in the example shown on figure 1.1, it is obvious that for all possible prices there is always disagreement between producers' and consumers' intents, except for one price, denoted p_e. Before coming to that price and its properties, consider first the consequences of a very low price, say p_0. For such a price demand $q_0(p_0)$ is considerable higher than supply $q_S(p_0)$. We observe an excess demand, equal to the positive difference $q_D(p_0) - q_S(p_0)$. What are the consequences of such a situation? Remember that the supply and demand functions reflect only the *intentions* of producers and consumers, respectively. The producers do know that at such a low price p_0 demand exceeds supply. They realize that if they increase their price by a small amount, there will still be an excess demand. If nothing prevents them to do so, they will increase their price as long as such an excess demand still exists. At the same time, consumers may be competing for relatively scarce quantities; some consumers will be weeded out of the market; others will reduce their purchases. Producers will not increase the price beyond p_e, because that would entail an excess supply.

Choose now an initial situation where the price is way above p_e, for example at level p_1. The ensuing excess supply $q_S(p_1) - q_D(p_1)$ will induce a decrease in price, driving its value towards p_e.

Such a level p_e is called an equilibrium price because it has no reason to move if nothing else changes in the economy. We know of course that many other things may be disturbed, either on the consumers' or on the producers' side. For instance, information, tastes, income, or modifications in other prices may shift the demand curve. Production conditions, technology, prices of inputs, rates of interest may change and displace the supply curve. But fundamentally, the mechanism described above will apply again. Such adjustments in price obey the so-called "law of supply and demand", which can simply be defined as follows: a price will have a tendency to increase (to decrease) in case of excess demand (excess supply).

2   The case of fixed prices

The law of supply and demand will apply only if prices are free to move. Suppose that this is not the case. For instance, suppose that there are no laws forbidding cartels between firms, and that producers connive to fix a high price (above p_e). What will be the quantity produced and exchanged in those circumstances? Very clearly, if the fixed price is above p_e, the quantity produced will be determined by what consumers are prepared to buy at that price. For instance, if the price is fixed at $p_M(p_M > p_e)$ (denoting a monopoly price), the quantity produced and exchanged is given by $q_D(p_M)$.

On the other hand, suppose that the state imposes a maximum ceiling $\bar{p}$ (below p_e) on the price producers can charge. The quantity produced will then be determined by $q_S(\bar{p})$. A first conclusion emerges: if prices are fixed, the quantity produced and exchanged is always the *minimum* between supply and demand. We have:

quantity at society's disposal when price is fixed at $p = \min[q_S(p), q_D(p)]$.

This curve read on the abscissa in figure 1.2, has an inverted V-shape. Its fundamental property is that it goes through a maximum at the equilibrium point (p_e, q_e).

3   Fundamental properties of the equilibrium point

We have already one important result: a free (competitive) market will result in a maximum quantity available for society.

Suppose now that employment is an increasing function of production. We can picture, below the q abscissa, another horizontal axis where we indicate the corresponding employment. The relationship between production and employment

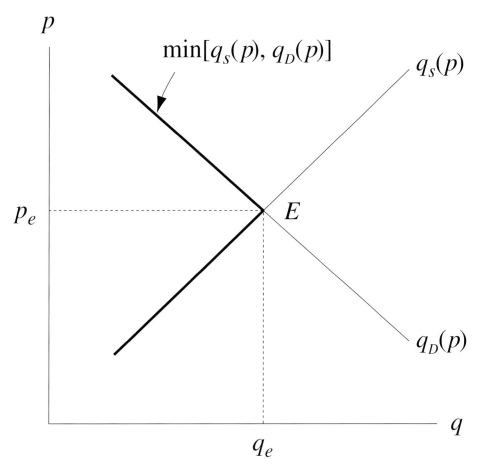

Figure 1.2   Quantity produced if prices are fixed: min[$q_S(p), q_D(p)$].

is not necessarily linear – in this text we will only suppose it is increasing and concave. It is clear nevertheless that at the equilibrium point (p_e, q_e) employment on that market will be maximized compared to any other point on the V-curve.

4   Consumers' and producers' surplus

The consequences for society can be analysed further. It is obvious that consumers that are prepared to pay some high price $p_1(p_1 > p_e)$ are better off if they pay p_e only. If they buy one unit, they are left with $p_1 - p_e$ at their disposal, which they can use to buy other goods or services, or save. This amount, called the *consumers' surplus*, is equal to the hatched area in figure 1.3, between the demand curve and the horizontal at height p_e. It is equal to the integral

$$\int_0^{q_e} [p_D(q) - p_e]dq = \int_0^{q_e} p_D(q)dq - p_e q_e. \tag{A1}$$

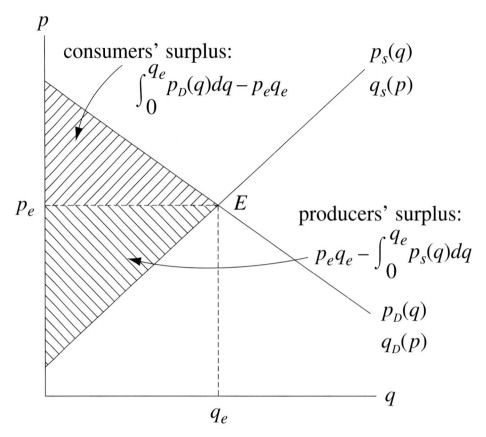

Figure 1.3   Consumers' surplus and producers' surplus when the market is in equilibrium at point $E : (p_e, q_e)$.

The integral on the right-hand side of (A1) is the valuation of q_e by the consumers: it is the total value that could be extracted from the consumers if the quantity q_e were sold to them by very small increments dq. On the other hand, $p_e q_e$ is the amount consumers actually pay.

Similarly, producers that were willing to sell one unit at $\bar{p}$ and will ultimately sell it at p_e gain a profit equal to $p_e - \bar{p}$. The producers' surplus is equal to the hatched area between the horizontal line p_e and the supply curve, and is equal to

$$\int_0^{q_e} [p_e - p_S(q)]dq = p_e q_e - \int_0^{q_e} p_S(q)dq. \qquad \text{(A2)}$$

It is not difficult to prove rigorously (see exercise 1.6) that the hatched area referred to above is exactly equal to the sum of profits made by all firms in the market.

This prompts us to consider the advantage received by society, or "society's surplus", as the sum of the consumers' surplus and the producers' profits. It is equal to the sum of the shaded areas in figure 1.3; we have:

$$\text{society's surplus} = \text{consumers' surplus} + \text{producers' surplus}$$

$$= \int_0^{q_e} [p_D(q) - p_S(q)]dq. \tag{A3}$$

It is obvious that the equilibrium point $E = (p_e, q_e)$ not only maximizes output and employment but society's surplus as well.

We will make use of these concepts and properties when we tackle some of the consequences entailed by planning or by non-competitive markets (chapter 14).

Exercises

1.1 Gross domestic product is usually measured according to three approaches, as we have seen: expenditure, value added and income distributed. Can you figure out a fourth way of measuring GDP? (Hint: consider the input–output table of an economy).

1.2 Suppose the input–output table for a given country includes the following elements:

	Sector I	Sector II	C	I	X	M	Total output
Sector I	10	100	200	10	a	60	b
Sector II	c	50	100	75	125	60	300
labour income	d	e					
capital income and profit	100	f					
Total output	b	300					

You know also that the trade balance of that country is $+20$ and that the labour income of sector II is two thirds of its value added. What are the values of a, b, c, d, e and f? (Hint: first construct the full input–output table, with lines and columns for total intermediate input and output, value added and final demand, as in table 1).

1.3 A European country started to build, over a period of twenty-five years, a nuclear super-generator. The new technology that was used turned out to be too risky for the reactor to be put in use, and it was decided to dismantle it, a process whose duration is estimated at more than two decades. Some argue that both the building of the reactor and its dismantling constitute a pure waste, or loss, for the economy. Others say that the building of the reactor and its dismantling over some 40 years generated and will generate billions of euros in income which benefit not only those directly concerned, but thousands of other sectors of activity as well. What is your opinion?

1.4 After the United States entered World War II, the highest growth rates of real national income were recorded: between 1941 and 1945 their order of magnitude was 15 to 16% per year. How do you perceive these exceptional numbers?

1.5 Think of a (theoretical) example of three countries (labelled A, B and C) ranked in order of the level of democracy. Suppose that their ranking according to income per person, however, differs: it is A, C and B. Show that their ranking according to their *adjusted* income may very well remain A, C and B. Give a necessary and sufficient condition for the ranking according to income per person to be preserved.

1.6 In this exercise, which can be considered as a project, you are asked to prove that the producers' surplus as defined in this chapter is the sum of their profits. We suggest that you proceed along the following steps.
1. Consider the supply curve on a market, $q(p)$, as the aggregate of n individual firms' supply curves, $\sum_{i=1}^{n} q_i(p)$. First, determine the supply curve of firm i as $q_i(p)$ that maximizes its profit $\pi_i = pq_i - C(q_i)$, where $C(q_i)$ is the total cost of the firm. Assume that the firm will supply some positive amount only if price is equal to, or above, the minimum of its cost per unit $\bar{c} = C(q)/q$. Notice that the supply curve will be discontinuous: it will be zero for $0 < p < \bar{c}$, and equal to the reciprocal of $C'(q_i) = p$ for $p \geq \bar{c}$ (to fix ideas, it is useful to picture $C(q)$ as a suitable second- or third-degree polynomial and to draw in another diagram, below the first one, the corresponding unit cost curve $C(q)/q$ and the marginal cost curve $C'(q)$).
2. The first-order condition will lead you to $p = C'(q_i)$; thus supply q_i is the reciprocal of the marginal cost function $C'(q_i)$, when $p \geq \bar{c} = \min(C/q_i)/q_i$, and zero for $0 < p < \min C(q_i)/q_i$. Now you have to determine, for any given price $p_0 > \bar{c}$, the integral $\int_{\bar{c}}^{p_0} q_i(p)dp$. To do so, proceed as follows. Consider profit π_i as a function of price p, compounded through the supply function q_i: $\pi_i = pq_i(p) - C[q_i(p)]$, and determine $d\pi_i/dp$. Using the first-order maximizing condition, you will end up with the result $d\pi_i/dp = q_i$, known as Hotelling's lemma, which you can use to determine immediately the value of the above-mentioned integral.

1.7 Suppose that the market depicted in figure 1.1 of this chapter corresponds to a market in autarchy – in particular, imports are simply barred from entry.

Suppose that the country opens up to external competition, allowing imports to flow in, and that foreign producers are willing to sell, at the world price p_w, smaller than p_e, the excess demand $q_D(p_w) - q_S(p_w)$. What will be the consequences of this opening up of the economy for consumers? for producers? for society as a whole?

1.8 Following the producers' complaints, the state decides to levy a tax t (in $ per unit) on imports. This implies that the price foreign producers will charge becomes $p_w + t$. Determine the consequences of this protectionist policy on consumers, on producers, and on the state (in the form of the custom duties levied). What is the net outcome of this policy on society as a whole?

1.9 Suppose that instead of levying a tax t on imports, the state decides to impose a quota in the sense that a maximum amount $\overline{m}$ can be imported. Suppose that this amount $\overline{m}$ corresponds to the amount of imports determined previously (in question 1.8) when the tax rate was t. Determine all consequences of this policy. Which of those two protectionist policies (levying an import duty or imposing a quota) is less harmful to society?

Answers

1.1 A fourth approach would be to consider the contribution of each sector (in our case agriculture, industry and services) to the final demand. In the example of this chapter, those contributions would be 7, 41 and 52 respectively.

1.2 $a = 15; b = 275; c = 10; d = 155; e = 100; f = 50$.

1.3 The building as well as the dismantling of this super-generator are indeed net losses for the economy. Remember that society manages by its work to put a number of goods or services at its disposal. For 50 years the country which decided to build and then to scrap a dangerous super-generator received a reactor which was never used, and then the service (not yet in full) of removing a device considered as dangerous. This is what society acquired, and not more. Society did not receive the reactor, its partial removal, *plus* the corresponding income. The latter was purely inflationary. It did not correspond to any welfare for society.

1.4 This is a good example of the fact that economic welfare is to be measured from the expenditure side only. Armaments in those years were a necessity; their huge volumes *replaced* civilian goods and services which would have been produced otherwise. Apart from the immense suffering due to the war itself, American society experienced a *loss* in its welfare, not an increase.

1.5 Suppose that income per person of countries A, C and B are 120, 110 and 100 respectively, and that the corresponding coefficients of adequation of income are 1, 0.9 and 0.95. The ranking according to income per person is preserved after adjustment.

(1) Ranking according to democracy	(2) Ranking according to income per person	(3) Coefficient of adequation of income per person to welfare	(4) Adjusted income per person
A	A : 120	A : 1	A : 120
B	C : 110	C : 0.9	C : 99
C	B : 100	B : 0.95	B : 95

A necessary and sufficient condition for the ranking according to income per person to be maintained is the following. Let y be B's income per person and Δy the (positive) difference between C's income per person and B's. C's income is then $y + \Delta y$. Let x be B's coefficient of adequation and Δx the (negative) difference between C's coefficient of adequation and B's. A necessary and sufficient condition for C to retain its ranking against B is that $(y + \Delta y)(x + \Delta x) > xy$, i.e.

$$\frac{\Delta y}{y} > -\frac{\Delta x}{x} - \frac{\Delta x \Delta y}{xy}.$$

This condition is met in our example.

1.6 Maximizing $\pi(q_i) = pq_i - C(q_i)$ leads to the first-order condition $\pi'(q_i) = p - C'(q_i) = 0$ and to the second-order condition $\pi_i''(q_i) = -C''(q_i) < 0$, or $C''(q_i) > 0$. The first-order condition leads to $C'(q_i) = p$. So the supply curve $q_i(p)$ is given by:

- zero if $p < \bar{c}_i = \min C(q_i)/q_i$
- the reciprocal of $C'(q_i) = p$ if $p \geq \bar{c}_i$.

The derivative of $\pi_i = pq_i(p) - C[q_i(p)]$ with respect to p is:

$$\frac{d\pi_i}{dp} = q_i + p\frac{dq_i}{dp} - C'(q_i)\frac{dq_i}{dp}$$

$$= q_i + \frac{dq_i}{dp}[p - C'(q_i)].$$

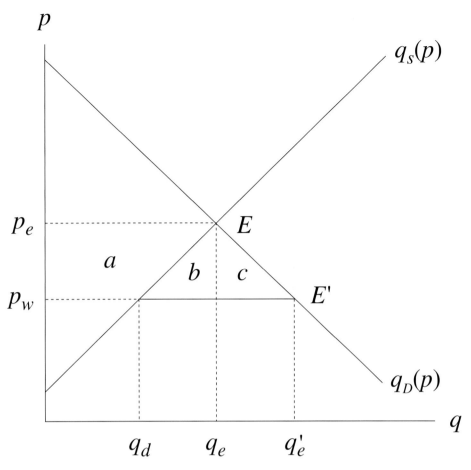

Figure 1.4   The consequences of opening up an economy to foreign competition. The equilibrium moves from E to E'; consumers gain $a + b + c$; producers' reduction of profits is a; society's net gain is $b + c$.

The first-order condition $p - C'(q_i) = 0$ entails $\pi'_i(p) = q_i$ (Hotelling's lemma). This can be used to determine our definite integral:

$$\int_{\bar{c}_i}^{p_0} q_i(p)dp = \pi_i(p_0) - \pi_i(\bar{c}_i) = \pi_i(p_0).$$

For any price p, we aggregate (we sum) all supply functions $q_i(p)$ and obtain the supply function on the market $q(p)$ (denoted in this chapter $q_S(p)$)

$$q(p) = \sum_{i=1}^{n} q_i(p).$$

Similarly the definite integral of this aggregate curve $q(p)$ between the minimum of the $\bar{c}_i$'s and any value p_0, which defines the producers' surplus, is

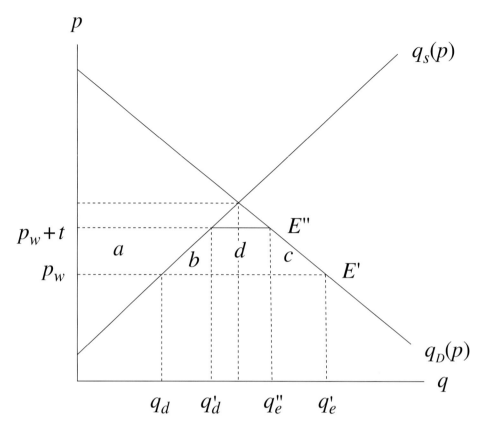

Figure 1.5   The consequences of introducing an import duty t. Consumers' loss is $a + b + c + d$; producers gain a; the state gains d in import duties. Society's net loss is $a + b + c + d - a - d = b + c$.

the sum of the definite integrals for each firm:

$$\int_{\min \bar{c}_i}^{p_0} q(p)dp = \sum_{i=1}^{n} \int_{\bar{c}_i}^{p_0} q_i(p)dp = \sum_{i=1}^{n} \pi_i(p_0)$$

and is therefore the sum of the profits of all firms.

Notice that if some firms have different cost curves, it may very well happen that the minimum of their unit cost $\bar{c}_i = \min C(q_i)/q_i$, and therefore the starting point of their supply curves, will indeed differ. When aggregating (horizontally) those curves, the resulting supply curve will have discontinuities. However, the result shown above will stand.

1.7 Since foreign competitors are willing to supply the excess demand observed at price p_w, the equilibrium point moves from E to E' (see figure 1.4). This benefits the consumers who gain $a + b + c$; $a + b$ is the amount they save on the initial quantity q_e they bought earlier at the higher price p_e; c is the surplus

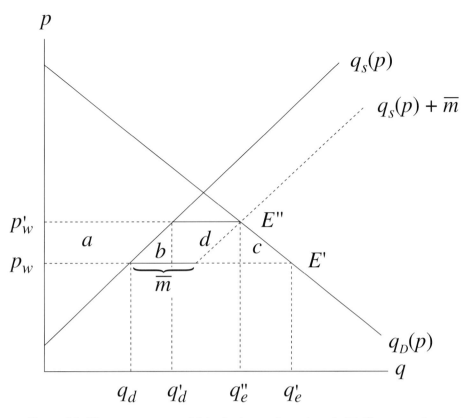

Figure 1.6 The consequences of introducing an import quota $\overline{m}$. Consumers lose $a + b + c + d$; producers gain a; d is transferred to foreign producers. Society's net loss is $b + c + d$.

they realize on the additional amount $q'_e - q_e$ they can now buy. Producers lose (in profits) a. Altogether, society has a net gain $a + b + c - a = b + c$. The amount b corresponds to a savings of costs on quantity $q_e - q_d$; c is the net gain of consumers.

1.8 After the introduction of an import duty t, the price that foreign competitors have to charge is the world price plus tax, $p_w + t$ (see figure 1.5). This enables domestic firms to sell, at that higher price, a quantity q'_d. Demand will shrink from q'_e to q''_e. Imports are reduced to $q''_e - q'_d$. The equilibrium point moves from E'' to E'. Consumers lose $a + b + c + d$; producers gain a; the state earns the customs duties d. In all society suffers a net loss $a + b + c + d - a - d = b + c$.

1.9 When a quota $\overline{m}$ is introduced, the supply curve is displaced to the right by an amount $\overline{m}$ when the world price level p_w is reached (this is the quantity foreign producers are allowed to sell on the domestic market: see figure 1.6). At the world price p_w an excess demand equal to $q_e' - (q_d + \bar{m})$ appears. This leads domestic producers to increase their price to p_w' (the supply curve becomes $q_S(p) + \bar{m}$, and the new equilibrium is E''). The amount d is now received by foreign producers. Consumers lose $a + b + c + d$; domestic producers gain a. Society's net loss is $b + c + d$, higher than in the case of an import duty. When introducing a quota, the state transfers taxes it could collect (d) to foreign firms.

CHAPTER 2

The growth process

Economic growth is simply defined as an increase of income per person. Our aim in this chapter is to explain, first without any formalization, the process by which such an increase may be achieved in a given country. The necessity for a more formal approach will emerge in a natural way.

This will lead to a precise model, from which unambiguous inferences can be made. In particular, we will be able to answer the following questions: what are the necessary conditions for an economy to grow? And if those conditions are met, will income per person always increase, or will it tend toward a limit?

1   The growth process: an intuitive approach

In a given country, at the beginning of a given year t, society has two fundamental *factors of production* at its disposal. First, it has inherited from the past a stock of capital, that we may call K_t. This is the value of all equipment that has been accumulated by society and preserved until that instant: it includes the value of land, factories, machinery, transport infrastructure, and so forth. The second production factor is labour, which we will always consider as a given proportion of population; we will thus assume that a measure of this labour force is the population itself, denoted L_t. It is endowed at time t with a given technological knowledge, also inherited from the past.

Together with the capital at its disposal, this work force will produce within a given time span (a year for instance) an output which we call the gross domestic product. Part of this product is used to replace that part of the capital stock that has decayed within the time span considered; that part is usually referred to as the depreciation of capital. The remainder is called the net domestic product, to which corresponds an equal income accruing to society. It is denoted Y_t, and called total income. Note that capital K_t and labour L_t are stocks, that is amounts observed at one point of time, in our case at the beginning of the first day of year t. On the other hand, Y_t is a flow that accrues to society within a time span, for instance in one year. Y_t is the flow of $ generated during year t. There is a definite relationship between

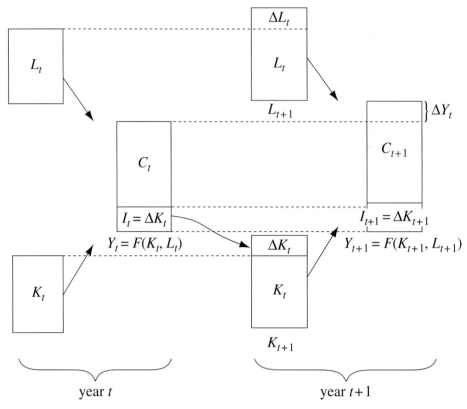

Figure 2.1 An illustration of the growth process. In year t, two factors of production (a capital stock of size K_t and a labour force L_t) are required to produce a net amount of output Y_t – net of depreciation of the capital stock. Part of this output is consumption C_t; part is net investment $I_t = \Delta K_t$ which adds itself to the existing stock K_t. A capital stock $K_{t+1} = K_t + \Delta K_t$ is thus available in year $t+1$, jointly with a labour force which may have increased by ΔL_t. Together, those factors can be combined to yield a product Y_{t+1}, higher than Y_t by ΔY_t, and the process might be repeated.

the amounts K_t and L_t, on the one hand, and the production Y_t, on the other. That relationship is given by a two-variable function called a production function, and denoted $F(K_t, L_t)$. More will be said later about the precise characteristics of that function. For the time being, we will just suppose that it depends positively upon each variable K_t and L_t, so that $\partial F/\partial K_t > 0$ and $\partial F/\partial L_t > 0$.

During that year t, the net domestic product Y_t is divided essentially into two parts: the first part is made of consumption goods and services (C_t). By far it constitutes the larger part (often 85%) of Y_t. This is not surprising, since the main purpose of economic activity is to produce goods and services that are of immediate use to society. The remainder of the product, $Y_t - C_t$, is made of investments I_t, by which we mean new capital goods that are added to the capital stock in existence at the beginning of year t (see figure 2.1).

By the end of year t (equivalently, at the beginning of year $t + 1$) two major events related to the factors of production have happened in this economy. First, the amount of capital at society's disposal has increased by an amount equal to the investment just mentioned, I_t; on the other hand, the labour force may have increased within that same year. So at the beginning of year $t + 1$, K_{t+1} and L_{t+1} are larger than K_t and L_t, respectively. In consequence, $Y_{t+1} = F(K_{t+1}, L_{t+1})$ will be larger than Y_t.

Previously, we had defined growth as an increase of income per person. Now the following questions arise: will Y_{t+1}/L_{t+1} be larger that Y_t/L_t? In other words, do we have a growth process? Under which conditions will that be the case? And will income per person increase forever, or will it tend toward a limit? The reader at this point senses that in order to answer these all-important questions, we need to be much more precise with our hypotheses; namely, we should know the characteristics of the production function $F(K, L)$, and the way K and L evolve through time.

2 A more precise approach: a simple model of economic growth

2.1 Hypotheses

We will now rely on four simple hypotheses. All of them are important in their own right.

2.1.1 Hypothesis regarding the production function

We suppose here that the production function $Y = F(K, L)$ is homogeneous of degree one. It implies that if both K and L are multiplied by a positive number λ, Y is then multiplied by λ. So we have:

$$\lambda Y = F(\lambda K, \lambda L).$$

For instance, if K and L are multiplied by $\lambda = 1.3$ (K and L both increase by a growth rate $\lambda - 1 = 30\%$), then Y is multiplied by $\lambda = 1.3$ (it increases in the same proportion). This simple hypothesis is justified by countless empirical observations.

2.1.1.1 Geometric construction of production functions homogeneous of degree one
Multiplying K and L by λ means that in a horizontal plane (K, L) we are moving from any given point (K_0, L_0) along a ray joining the origin to (K_0, L_0), either away from the origin (if $\lambda > 1$), or toward the origin (if $\lambda < 1$). If the factors increase by 30%, for instance, we move from A to B (see figure 2.2a). If, on

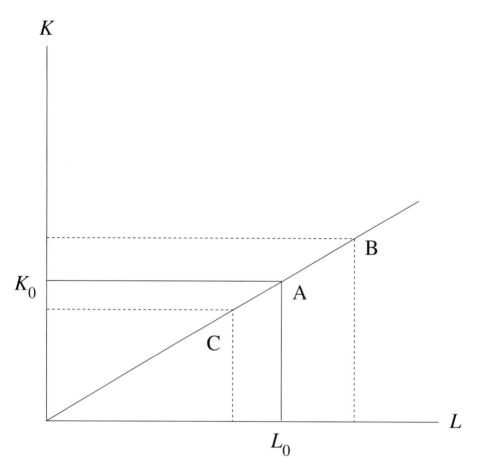

Figure 2.2a **From A we move to B with $t = 1.3$ (K and L both increase by 30%); we move from A to C with $t = 0.8$ (K and L decrease by 20%).**

the other hand, $\lambda = 0.8$, K and L decrease by 20% and we move from A to C. Now in the 3-dimensional space (Y, K, L) where we can represent the production function, homogeneity of degree one means that we will also move in the same proportions along a ray joining the origin to point (Y_0, K_0, L_0).

This property can be used to construct geometrically a production function that is homogeneous of degree one. Consider any curve γ in space (Y, K, L) that would belong to some (unknown) surface $Y = F(K, L)$. Such a curve is represented by the undulating curve in figure 2.2b. Now join the origin to that curve by a series of rays. We will be generating an undulating surface which will be homogeneous of degree one. We can see, indeed, that any point of the surface constructed in this way has the aforesaid properties: moving away from any point (K_0, L_0) by a factor λ will change Y by the same factor. We chose

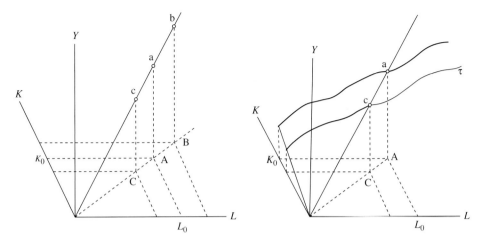

Figure 2.2b If the production function is homogeneous of degree one, Y moves also along a ray from the origin: if K and L are multiplied by t, Y is also multiplied by t.

this example to stress the fact that a homogeneous of degree one function may very well be concave and convex on various intervals in the direction of one of the axis, although both in theory and in practice it is usual to consider concave production functions, exhibiting diminishing marginal productivities, i.e. negative second partial derivatives: $\partial^2 Y / \partial K^2 < 0$ and $\partial^2 Y / \partial L^2 < 0$.[1]

A particular case is of interest: had our waving curve γ been a straight line, we would have generated a plane through the origin and our production function would have been a linear function. We can thus see immediately that a linear function is a homogenous of degree one function, but that the converse is not necessarily true. In other words, linearity is just a particular case of homogeneity of degree one.

2.1.1.2 Properties of homogeneous functions

A fundamental property of homogeneous functions is summarized in Euler's theorem, which applies to the general class of functions homogeneous of degree m. Those functions are such that if K and L are multiplied by λ ($\lambda > 0$) then Y is multiplied by λ^m. In other words, a function $Y = F(K, L)$ is homogeneous of degree m if and only if

$$\lambda^m Y = F(\lambda K, \lambda L).$$

---

[1] An important point to note: $\partial^2 Y / \partial K^2 \leqq 0$ and $\partial^2 Y / \partial L^2 \leqq 0$, although necessary conditions for concavity of $Y = F(K, L)$, are not sufficient; a necessary and sufficient condition for such concavity is that, in addition, $(\partial^2 Y / \partial K^2)(\partial^2 Y / \partial L^2) - [\partial^2 Y /(\partial K \partial L)]^2 \geqq 0$ (see Appendix 3 of chapter 7).

Homogeneity of degree $m = 1$ is just the particular case we have just seen, and $\lambda Y = F(\lambda K, \lambda L)$. In the general case, Euler's theorem states that

$$mY = \frac{\partial F}{\partial K}(K, L)K + \frac{\partial F}{\partial L}(K, L)L \tag{1}$$

(the proof is offered as exercise 2.1 at the end of this chapter).

In the case of homogeneity of degree one, Euler's theorem implies the identity

$$Y = \frac{\partial F}{\partial K}(K, L)K + \frac{\partial F}{\partial L}(K, L)L. \tag{2}$$

This identity is of great importance; we will use it often. In particular it entails

$$1 = \frac{\partial F}{\partial K}(K, L)\frac{K}{Y} + \frac{\partial F}{\partial L}(K, L)\frac{L}{Y} \tag{3}$$

or

$$1 = e_{Y,K} + e_{Y,L} \tag{4}$$

where $e_{Y,x}$ designates the partial elasticity[2] of Y with respect to x; $e_{Y,x} \equiv \frac{\partial Y}{\partial x}\frac{x}{Y} = \frac{\partial \log Y}{\partial \log x}$. Equivalently, it implies that if the remuneration rate of each factor is equal to the factor's marginal productivity, the shares of each factor in the total product add up to one, as they should. Now why should the remuneration rate of each factor be equal to the factor's marginal productivity? The reason comes from profit maximization on the producers' part, as can be easily shown. If producers are profit maximizing, they want to choose K and L such that

$$\underset{K,L}{\text{Max}}\, \pi(K, L) = pF(K, L) - qK + wL$$

where q is the nomimal rental rate of capital, and w is the nominal wage rate. A first-order condition is

$$\frac{\partial \pi}{\partial K} = pF'_K - q = 0$$

$$\frac{\partial \pi}{\partial L} = pF'_L - w = 0$$

A second-order condition is that π is concave in K, L. This is indeed the case since $\pi(K, L)$ is an affine transformation of the concave function $F(K, L)$.

From $pF'_K - q = 0$ we can write $F'_K(K, L) = q/p$; this is a fundamental equality: the marginal productivity of capital should be equal to the *real* rental rate of capital (q/p).

An important point is to be noticed: homogeneity of degree one of $F(K, L)$, or Euler's theorem (equation (2)) and the above equalities imply that

---

[2] For a definition and properties of the concept of elasticity, see appendix 1.

$pY = qK + wL$, i.e. that the total product is exhausted by the remuneration of the factors of production – equivalently that the firm's profits are maximized although they are equal to zero. This is the outcome of perfect competition. Indeed, with such a hypothesis – that we will carry throughout – any profit on a given market is supposed to induce new firms to enter that market, driving down the price to an equilibrium level corresponding to zero profit.

Average and marginal productivities as well as elasticities of homogeneous of degree one production functions have some very useful properties which can be briefly reviewed here.

If the number of variables of the function is n, these quantities are just functions of $n − 1$ variables (see exercise 2.2). If $n = 2$ (our case), they depend just on one variable. For instance, the all-important income per person variable, $y = Y/L$, is a function of the sole variable $r = K/L$, and so are the marginal productivities with respect to K and L, and the partial elasticities.

Indeed, if $Y = F(K, L)$ is homogeneous of degree one, we have $tY = F(tK, tL)$ and we can replace t by $1/L$. Then

$$\frac{Y}{L} \equiv y = F\left(\frac{K}{L}, 1\right) = f(r). \tag{5}$$

From a picture of the surface representing the function $F(K, L)$, we can immediately deduce the curve representing income per person y. Indeed, if $L = 1$, $F(K, 1) = F(K/L, 1) = y$. So y is just the section of the surface by a plane perpendicular to the L axis, at point $L = 1$. For instance, if $Y = K^\alpha L^{1-\alpha}$ (this power function is called the Cobb–Douglas function), $y = Y/L = K^\alpha L^{-\alpha} = (K/L)^\alpha = r^\alpha$, which also can be obtained by setting $L = 1$ and replacing K and Y by r and y respectively. Figure 2.2c give such a production function and its vertical section at point $L = 1$.

Also,

$$Y = Lf(r);$$

this shows that any production function homogeneous of degree one can be obtained by simply multiplying any one-variable function $f(r)$ by L. But a caveat will soon be in order.

Let us now consider the marginal productivities. We have:

$$\frac{\partial Y}{\partial L} = f(r) + Lf'(r) \cdot \left(-\frac{K}{L^2}\right) = f(r) - rf'(r) = y - ry', \tag{6}$$

using the short-hand notation $f(r) = y$, $f'(r) = y'$, which will become very useful.

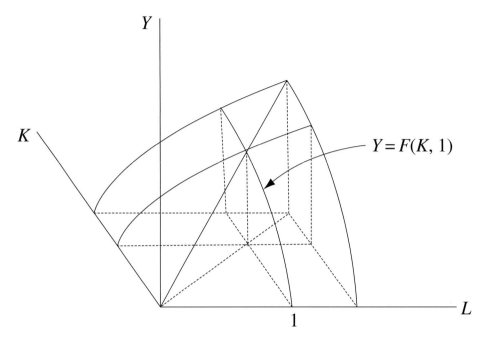

Figure 2.2c A Cobb–Douglas function $Y = K^\alpha L^{1-\alpha}$ and its vertical section $Y = F(K,1)$ giving $y = f(r) = r^\alpha$.

Similarly

$$\frac{\partial Y}{\partial K} = Lf'(r) \cdot \frac{1}{L} = f'(r) = y'. \tag{7}$$

The partial elasticities are

$$e_{Y,L} = \frac{\partial Y}{\partial L} \cdot \frac{L}{Y} = \frac{y - ry'}{y} = 1 - ry'/y \tag{8}$$

and

$$e_{Y,K} = \frac{\partial Y}{\partial K} \frac{K}{Y} = y' \cdot r/y \tag{9}$$

(Note that these elasticities do add up to one, as they should because of Euler's theorem).

It can be very useful to represent geometrically all these concepts. In figure 2.2d, we have drawn a curve $y = f(r)$ with positive and decreasing marginal productivity of capital (the second derivative is, from $\partial Y/\partial K = f'(r)$, equal to $\partial^2 Y/\partial K^2 = f''(r)/L$. Hence for $\partial^2 Y/\partial K^2$ to be negative it is necessary and sufficient that $f''(r)$ be negative). Notice that we have also chosen $f(0) > 0$, which does not preclude homogeneity of degree one of $F(K, L)$ (any function

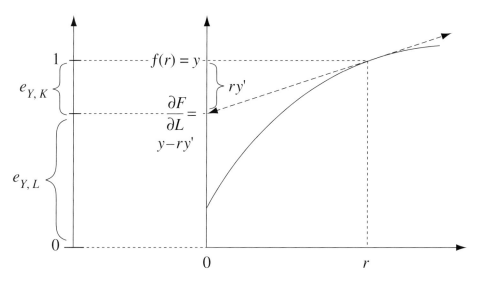

Figure 2.2d A geometrical construction of the marginal productivities and partial elasticities if $F(K, L)$ is homogeneous of degree one. At point (r, y), $\partial Y/\partial K$ is just the slope of the curve $y = f(r)$, i.e. y'; $\partial Y/\partial L$ is the length $y - ry'$. Normalizing y to one on the vertical axis to the left of the diagram yields the elasticities $e_{Y,K} = ry'/y$ and $e_{Y,L} = \frac{\partial F}{\partial L} \cdot \frac{L}{Y} = \frac{\partial F}{\partial L}/y = (y - ry')/y = 1 - ry'/y$.

$y = f(r)$ corresponds to such a function; indeed, $Y = Ly = Lf(r)$ is homogeneous of degree one).

We know that the marginal productivity of capital, $\partial Y/\partial K$, is just $y' = f'(r)$, i.e. the slope of the curve at any point (r, y). Consider the point of intersection between the tangent to the curve and the ordinate. On the vertical axis, the distance between the height $f(r) = y$ and this point is the differential $f'(r)r = ry'$. So the marginal productivity of labour, $\partial Y/\partial L = y - ry'$, is the ordinate of that point. The partial elasticities $e_{Y,K}$ and $e_{Y,L}$ are represented on the vertical axis on the left of the diagram, where y has been normalized to 1. The elasticity $e_{Y,K} = y' \cdot r/y$ just becomes ry', and $e_{Y,L}$ is $1 - ry'$.

A caveat is now in order. As we have seen, any curve $y = f(r)$ in (r, y) space corresponds to a production function $Y = F(K, L)$ homogeneous of degree one. Care must be exercised, however, when drawing such a function. Drawing an increasing concave curve $f(r)$, for instance, will not guarantee that the marginal productivity of labour will be *positive* (see exercises 2.2 and 2.3). Not only have we to be careful to have $\partial Y/\partial L > 0$, but the partial elasticities $e_{Y,K}$ and $e_{Y,L}$ should have magnitudes observed in reality – those are about $1/3$ and $2/3$, respectively. We will understand the importance of this caveat when we analyse in section 2.2.3 the stability properties of the equation of motion.

2.1.2 Hypothesis regarding the investment behaviour of society

We will suppose that society invests – and therefore saves – each year a constant proportion s of its income Y. Investment, denoted I, is the rate of increase of the capital stock. So we have

$$I \equiv \frac{dK}{dt} = sY. \tag{10}$$

Later we will ask the question: how much *should* a nation save? We will want to determine an optimal savings rate, according to an optimality criterion. This will be at the core of the theory of optimal growth. For the time being, we just take the savings rate as exogenous.

2.1.3 Growth of population

Population will be supposed to be increasing at the constant rate n. So

$$\frac{1}{L}\frac{dL}{dt} = n, \tag{11}$$

or, equivalently (solving the above differential equation with the initial condition $L(0) = L_0$),

$$L(t) = L_0 e^{nt}. \tag{12}$$

2.1.4 Technical progress

At this introductory stage, we will suppose that the know-how of the population is constant through time: technological progress will be introduced in the model only at a later stage. Let us mention here that it will have the effect of adding a third variable, time, to the arguments K and L of the production function.

2.2 The equation of motion of the economy

We are now in a position to obtain the time path of the economy, as expressed by its central variable, income per person, which will be denoted $y \equiv Y/L$. The analysis is very simple because the evolution of y depends upon one variable only, the capital–labour ratio $r = K/L$, as we have seen earlier.

2.2.1 A fundamental property

We can now immediately show that income per person y will increase (decrease, remain constant) if and only if the capital–labour ratio r increases (decreases, remains constant). This is also due to the very fact that the production function is homogeneous of degree one and that the marginal productivity of capital is positive. Remember that from equation (7) we have

$$\frac{\partial F}{\partial K} = L f'(r) \cdot \frac{1}{L} = f'(r). \tag{7}$$

This relationship is fundamental. It tells us that the marginal productivity of capital is equal to the derivative of income per person with respect to the capital–labour ratio. Since we will always consider production functions such that their partial derivatives (and in particular $\partial Y / \partial K > 0$) are strictly positive, it implies that $y' = f'(r) > 0$. So the sign of variation of y will always be that of r, and in order to know whether y increases or decreases, it suffices to focus on the possible variations of r. Formally, we have $y = f[r(t)]$ and $\dot{y} = f'(r)\dot{r}$; since $f'(r) > 0$, y will increase (decrease, stay constant) if and only if r increases (decreases, stays constant).

2.2.2 Deriving the equation of motion of the economy

We are thus led in a natural way to consider the rate of change of r through time, $\dot{r} = dr/dt$:

$$\dot{r} = \frac{d}{dt}\left[\frac{K(t)}{L(t)}\right] = \frac{\dot{K}L - K\dot{L}}{L^2} = \frac{\dot{K}}{L} - nr \tag{13}$$

(since $(1/L)dL/dt = n$). We know that $\dot{K} = sY$ and that $sY/L = sy = sf(r)$. So $r(t)$ is governed by the differential equation

$$\boxed{\dot{r} = sf(r) - nr.} \tag{14}$$

This is our first important equation. It can be called the fundamental equation of positive, or descriptive growth theory, because it is the equation that governs the movement of $r(t)$, which in turn determines the time path of income per person, equal to $y(t) = f[r(t)]$.

Notice that the right-hand side of (14) does not depend explicitly upon time t; this allows for a geometrical representation of $\dot{r}$ as a function of r. Once we know $f(r)$, s, and n, we can immediately draw $\dot{r}$ as the difference between $sf(r)$ and nr. Suppose for instance that the production function is Cobb–Douglas, of the type

$$Y = AK^\alpha L^{1-\alpha}$$

(we have set $K_0 = L_0 = 1$, and have considered a multiplicative constant A to allow later for the introduction of technical progress).

Then $y = Ar^\alpha$, and the equation of motion is

$$\dot{r} = sAr^\alpha - nr. \tag{15}$$

This is a Bernoulli differential equation which can easily be solved. What is notable here is that we can see immediately, by constructing geometrically the right-hand side of (15), under which conditions r – and therefore y – will increase or decrease, and whether they will ultimately tend toward fixed values. We do this in figure 2.3; we represent first $y = f(r) = Ar^\alpha$, (where we set $A = 1$), a power function such that its slope tends to $+\infty$ when $r \to 0$, and to 0 when $r \to \infty$. Then we take $sf(r)$, with $s = 0.1$ for instance. Finally, we build the ray nr with $n = 0.015$.

A number of conclusions immediately emerge, whatever the (positive) values of the parameters A, s and n we have chosen for our geometrical construction. First, sy ($= sf(r)$) will remain a power function with the same characteristics as those of $f(r)$: the slope $sf'(r)$ tends to infinity when $r \to 0$, and tends to zero when $r \to \infty$. Hence the ray nr defined for strictly positive values of r will intersect once and only once the curve $sf(r)$, at a point r^* (defined by $sf(r^*) = nr^*$). For values of r smaller than r^*, $\dot{r} > 0$ and r increases toward r^*; the contrary is true if $r > r^*$; then $\dot{r} < 0$ and r decreases towards r^*. Whatever the initial value of $r(0)$ (we have chosen in the diagram two such values, denoted r_0 and r_0'), we can see that r will converge toward a unique value r^*. We then say that there exists a globally stable equilibrium value of r (denoted r^*). This implies that income per person will ultimately tend toward $y^* = f(r^*)$; investment per person will tend toward $sf(r^*)$ and consumption per person will go to the limit $c^* = y^* - sy^* = (1 - s)y^*$.

The simple geometric representation of the differential equation carries a wealth of information that we will now exploit to the fullest. From the properties of power functions, we can see immediately that, if the initial value r_0 is sufficiently small (as depicted on the diagram 2.3a) the slope of $\dot{r}(t)$ is increasing, going through a maximum[3] (at point $\bar{r}$) and finally decreasing toward zero. This implies that the time path $r(t)$ is convex until $\bar{r}$, goes through an inflection point at $\bar{r}$, and ultimately becomes concave. On the other hand, we can see that if the initial value of $r(t)$ is above r^*, $r(t)$ decreases at a speed which is itself decreasing in absolute value, implying a convex time path $r(t)$ throughout.

There is however one question that the phase diagram cannot answer. Will the equilibrium value r^* ever be reached? Just looking at the diagram, we might be tempted to say that, with $r < r^*$ for example, as long as r^* is not reached, the positive speed of r will force it to reach r^*. On the other hand, we might argue that when r approaches r^* its speed becomes so very small that its advance toward r^* is hampered in such a way that r^* will never be reached. This is where the phase diagram fails to give us an answer, and why we must solve equation (15).

---

[3] This maximum is reached for $d\dot{r}/dr = sf'(r) - n = 0$; in the case of figure 2.3a, it is $r = (s\alpha/n)^{1/(1-\alpha)} \approx 2.7$. Because of scaling on figure 2.3b, the corresponding inflection point of the lower trajectory, close to the origin, is difficult to pinpoint.

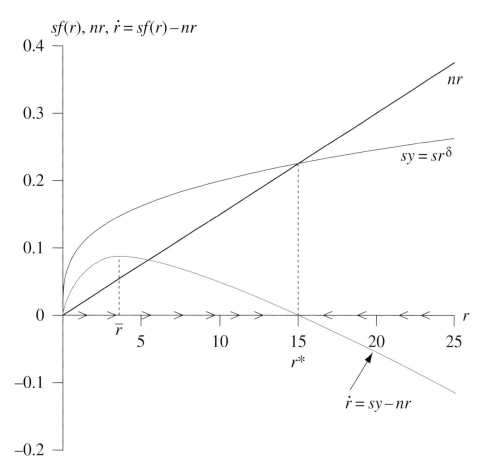

Figure 2.3a   The phase diagram in the case of the Cobb–Douglas function $Y = K^{0.3}L^{0.7}$; $s = 0.1$; $n = 0.015$. The equilibrium capital–labour ratio is $r^* = (s/n)^{1/(1-\alpha)} \approx 15.02$.

This equation, of the Bernoulli type, can be solved in a number of ways; we will indicate that which seems to be the easiest.[4] We first transform (15) into a linear differential equation through the change of variable $x = r^{1-\alpha}$.

Divide both sides of (15) by r^{α};

$$r^{-\alpha}\dot{r} = sA - nr^{1-\alpha}. \tag{16}$$

---

[4] The equation bears Bernoulli's name because we owe its solution to Johann Bernoulli who found in fact two ways to solve it (1697). The first one is described above. The second consists in looking for a solution in the form of a product $y(t) = u(t)v(t)$, following the same idea he had for solving the first-order linear equation (see appendix 2). On this, see Ernst Hairer and Gerard Wanner, *L'analyse au fil de l'histoire*, Springer Verlag, Berlin, Heidelberg, New York, 2000, p. 140.

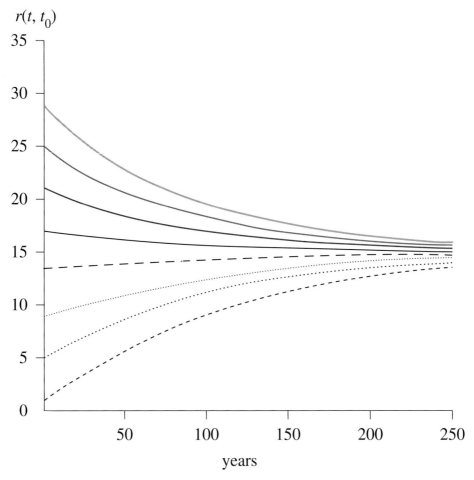

Figure 2.3b   The actual time paths $r(t;r_0)$ for initial values r_0 ranging from 1 to 29 by steps of 4.

Observe that the derivative of x with respect to time is

$$\dot{x} = (1 - \alpha)r^{-\alpha}\dot{r}; \qquad (17)$$

using the change of variable $x = r^{1-\alpha}$ and (17) yields

$$\frac{1}{1 - \alpha}\dot{x} = sA - nx \qquad (18)$$

or

$$\dot{x} + n(1 - \alpha)x = sA(1 - \alpha) \qquad (19)$$

the solution of which is immediate (see appendix 2):

$$x(t) = Ce^{-n(1-\alpha)t} + \frac{sA}{n} \qquad (20)$$

where C is a constant of integration which can be identified as follows: when $t = 0$, $r(0) = r_0$ and $x(r(0)) = x_0 = r_0^{1-\alpha}$. So we have

$$x_0 = C + \frac{sA}{n}, \tag{21}$$

and

$$C = r_0^{1-\alpha} - \frac{sA}{n}. \tag{22}$$

Replacing this value of C into (20) and $x(t)$ by $[r(t)]^{1-\alpha}$, we finally get:

$$r(t) = \left[\left(r_0^{1-\alpha} - \frac{sA}{n}\right) e^{-n(1-\alpha)t} + \frac{sA}{n}\right]^{\frac{1}{1-\alpha}}. \tag{23}$$

The equilibrium value of $r(t)$ can be determined by setting $\dot{r} = 0$ in (15). This yields

$$r^* = \left(\frac{sA}{n}\right)^{\frac{1}{1-\alpha}}. \tag{24}$$

We can see from (23) that this value will never by reached. Only at infinity does $r(t)$ have r^* as a limiting value. We have $\lim_{t \to \infty} r(t) = \left(\frac{sA}{n}\right)^{\frac{1}{1-\alpha}}$. In turn we can derive immediately the limiting value of $y = f(r)$. It is $y^* = \lim_{t \to \infty} f[r(t)] = A\left(\frac{sA}{n}\right)^{\frac{\alpha}{1-\alpha}}$. Notice how this equilibrium value of income per person is modified when any of the parameters A, α, s or n undergoes a change. y^* is an increasing function of A, s and α, and a decreasing function of n, which of course makes good economic sense since A and α are efficiency parameters, and increasing the savings rate implies more income in the future.

2.3 An economic interpretation of the equation of motion

The phase diagram is highly useful in understanding how the economy will move, given any initial conditions. However, we have not yet given the economic significance of each of its constituent parts, i.e. of each part of the right-hand side of the equation of motion (14). Once we do this, we will understand why an economy behaves as it does.

We start with the easiest part of the right-hand side of (14), sy or $sf(r)$. We know that $sy = sY/L$. Since sY is investment, $sY/L = sf(r)$ is simply investment per person, which is itself an increasing function of r. The second part of the right-hand side, nr, is a wee more tricky to read.

Suppose we want to increase K such that $r (= K/L)$ remains constant. If the growth rate of L is n, then the rate of increase of K should be nK; this is the investment required for K/L to stay constant; so $nr = nK/L$ is the investment per person necessary to maintain r constant.

With more formality, we could say: if $r = K(t)/L(t)$ is to remain constant, we must have

$$\frac{\dot{r}}{r} = \frac{\dot{K}}{K} - \frac{\dot{L}}{L} = \frac{\dot{K}}{K} - n = 0 \tag{25}$$

or

$$\dot{K} = nK \tag{26}$$

and hence the investment per person necessary and sufficient to achieve that goal is: $\dot{K}/L = nK/L = nr$.[5]

So the ray from the origin nr is the investment per person which is both necessary and sufficient to maintain r constant. It is then clear that r will increase (decrease) if and only if the actual investment per person $sf(r)$ is higher (lower) than the investment per person nr needed to keep r at its current level.

2.4 The speed of convergence toward equilibrium

While it is clear from the phase diagram and its economic interpretation that the capital–labour ratio and the corresponding income per person will tend toward equilibrium, we have no clue as to the speed at which this will come about. In particular we have no idea of the magnitude of the growth rate of those variables. We only know that both growth rates are linearly dependent and that they are decreasing : since $y = r^{\alpha}$, $\dot{y}/y = \alpha \dot{r}/r = \alpha(sr^{\alpha - 1} - n)$. In order to know more about the speed of convergence, we must put some numbers on the analytic solution (23).

The surprise is how slow the convergence is. Suppose that we normalize A to 1, and that $s = 0.1$; $n = 0.015$; $\alpha = 0.3$. The resulting equilibrium value is $r^* = (sA/n)^{1/(1-\alpha)} \approx 15.03$. Figure 2.3b gives the actual time paths corresponding to values of r_0 ranging from 1 to 27, by steps of 4. Consider for instance an initial value $r_0 = 9$. It would take about 174 years for the capital labour ratio to grow to $r = 14$. Such slow growth of r, implying even slower growth rates of income per person (see figure 2.3c) does not square with facts: in these last 210 years, the American economy has grown at a real yearly average rate of 2.1% with a standard deviation of 5.3% – see chapter 6.[6] Therefore growth is definitely driven by other forces than the mere increase of a homogeneous stock of capital per person; one

---

[5] We can verify this result by considering equation (14) itself. In the right-hand side, sy and nr are measured in the same units; and $sy = nr$ if and only if $\dot{r} = 0$; so nr is investment per person if and only if the capital–labour ratio is constant.

[6] We will be careful to make the distinction between the *average* of 215 yearly growth rates, and the long-run, compounded rate that transforms a given value into a new one 215 years later. Both rates are random variables, and we will have a close look at their links in chapter 6.

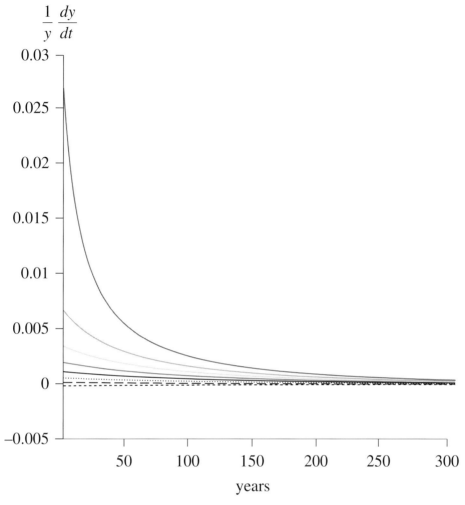

Figure 2.3c **The growth rates of income per person corresponding to the time paths of** $r(t; r_0)$**. The upper curve corresponds to** $r_0 = 1$ **and** $y_0 = 1$**.**

of those forces is technical progress, to be introduced in section 3 of this chapter. Before doing this, however, we should discuss other shapes of production functions and their impact upon the dynamics of the economy.

2.5 Alternate production functions and stability analysis

From the phase diagram just depicted in figure 2.3a, we can immediately see the all-important dependency of the evolution of the economy on the shape of the production function. For instance, we might think that multiple equilibrium points $(r^*, f(r^*))$ are possible, some being stable and others unstable. Figure 2.4a presents some of those possibilities.

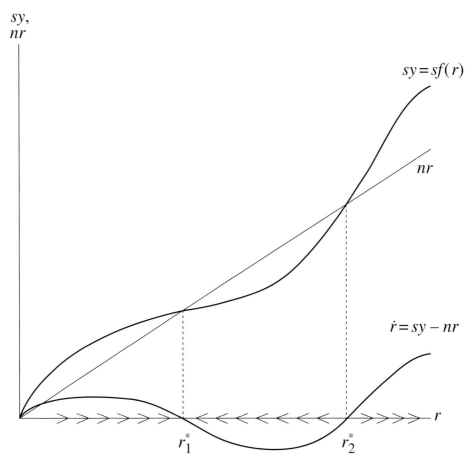

Figure 2.4a The production function $Y = F(K, L)$ can be homogeneous of degree one and be concave and convex on various intervals, entailing both concavity and convexity for $f(r)$. This may result in a number of equilibrium points, some stable (as r_1^*), some unstable (as r_2^*). However, an unstable point implies a negative marginal productivity of labour and an income share of capital larger than one; such configurations are therefore dismissed (see text and figure 2.4b).

We will show however that such locally unstable points are not admissible because they imply a negative marginal productivity of labour at those points (throughout our analysis we suppose as before that s and n are constants).

THEOREM 1   *An unstable equilibrium point $(r^*, f(r^*))$ such that $sf(r^*) = nr^*$ and $sf'(r^*) > n$ implies that the marginal productivity of labour is negative at that point.*

PROOF   If $sf'(r^*) > n$, there is a neighborhood around r^* such that to the left of r^* we have $sf(r) < nr$, while to the right of r^*, $sf(r) > nr$, entailing

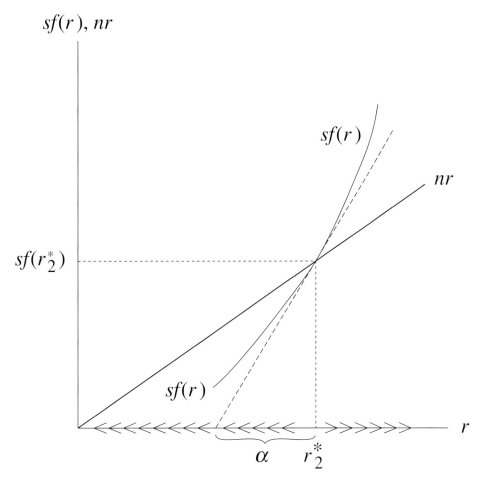

Figure 2.4b **An unstable equilibrium point implies a negative marginal productivity of labour. At that point r_2^* the partial elasticity of production with respect to capital is $e_{Y,K} = r_2^*/\alpha > 1$; because of Euler's theorem, $e_{Y,L}$ must therefore be negative, implying $F_L' < 0$.**

disequilibrium. Furthermore, if $sf'(r^*) > n$ and $sf(r^*) = nr^*$, then $n = sf(r^*)/r^*$ and $sf'(r^*) > sf(r^*)/r^*$, implying $f(r^*) - r^*f'(r^*) = \frac{\partial F}{\partial L}(r^*) < 0$.

Therefore such a point should be dismissed. We are then led to the following important theorem.

THEOREM 2 *If a neoclassical economy has an equilibrium point $(r^*, f(r^*))$, this equilibrium is stable and unique.*

PROOF $\frac{\partial F}{\partial L}(r) > 0$ for any r implies $\frac{\partial}{\partial L}(Lf(r)) = f(r) - rf'(r) > 0$ and $rf'(r) - f(r) < 0$. If an equilibrium point $(r^*, f(r^*))$ exists, its abscissa r^* is given by the solution of

$$\frac{\dot{r}}{r} = \frac{sf(r)}{r} - n = 0$$

or $sf(r)/r = n$. The slope of $sf(r)/r$ is

$$\frac{d}{dr}[sf(r)/r)] = \frac{s}{r^2}[rf'(r) - f(r)].$$

Since $rf'(r) - f(r) < 0$, the slope of $sf(r)/r$ is negative everywhere, including at r^*. If point $(r^*, f(r^*))$ exists, it is therefore unique, and it is a stable equilibrium point.

We therefore conclude that with the hypotheses an economy cannot have an unstable equilibrium point, and that if an equilibrium point exists, it is stable and unique.

It is a good point to emphasize that Robert Solow, in his fundamental "Contribution to the Theory of Economic Growth" had very precisely described the evolution of income per person in three major cases:

(a) the so-called Harrod–Domar, or Walras–Leontief case: $Y = F(K, L) = \min \left(\frac{K}{a}, \frac{L}{b}\right)$

(b) the Cobb–Douglas case: $Y = AK^\alpha L^{1-\alpha}$
(c) a third case: $Y = (aK^{1/2} + L^{1/2})^2$.

We have already covered the second case as an illustration of the growth model. We will now take up cases (a) and (c). Their outcomes are fundamentally different. While case (a) nearly always ends up in disaster for the economy, case (c) holds the promise of a possible ever-lasting growth of income per person.

2.5.1 The Walras–Leontief, or Harrod–Domar case

Suppose that the production function corresponds to the corner of a pyramid: it will be given, analytically, by the minimum of two planes, each of those planes passing through the axes L and K. Let $\frac{1}{a}K$ be the plane going through axis L; it has slope $\frac{1}{a}$ in the direction of K and slope 0 in the direction of L. Let $\frac{1}{b}L$ be the plane going through axis K; its slope in the direction of L is $\frac{1}{b}$; its slope in the direction of K is zero. Both planes intersect along an edge whose projection on the horizontal plane (K, L) is given by the set of points (K, L) such that $\frac{K}{a} = \frac{L}{b}$, i.e. it is the ray $K = \frac{a}{b}L$ (see figure 2.5a). Also, the analytic expression of the corner of the pyramid is

$$Y = \min\left(\frac{K}{a}, \frac{L}{b}\right). \tag{27}$$

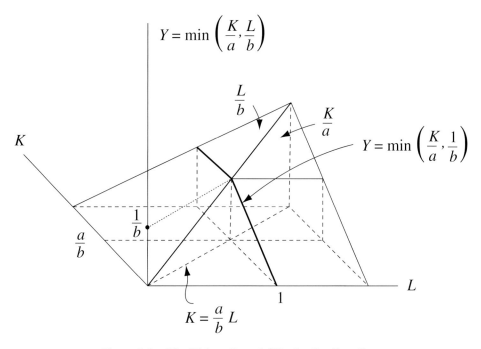

Figure 2.5a   The Walras–Leontief Production Function

$$Y = \min\left(\frac{K}{a}, \frac{L}{b}\right)$$

and its section $Y = \min(\frac{K}{a}, \frac{1}{b})$ giving $y = \min(r/a, 1/b)$.

The function is homogeneous of degree one; multiplying K and L by λ will result in Y being multiplied by λ. From a geometrical point of view, the corner of a pyramid may be considered as generated by a ray from the origin, touching everywhere any of the curves on the surface – such as, for instance, any horizontal section.

Let us now consider our central variable, income per person $y = Y/L$. If we divide each variable K, L by L, we obtain

$$\frac{Y}{L} = y = \min\left(\frac{K/L}{a}, \frac{1}{b}\right) = \min\left(\frac{r}{a}, \frac{1}{b}\right), \tag{28}$$

In (r, y) space this is the minimum between a ray from the origin with slope $1/a$ and a horizontal line at height $1/b$. This result could have been obtained immediately from a geometrical point of view by applying a result mentioned earlier: for any production function homogeneous of degree one, income per person is the vertical section of the surface $F(K, L)$ at point $L = 1$ of the L-axis. Considering figure 2.5b, we get indeed the kinked line $y = \min(r/a, 1/b)$.

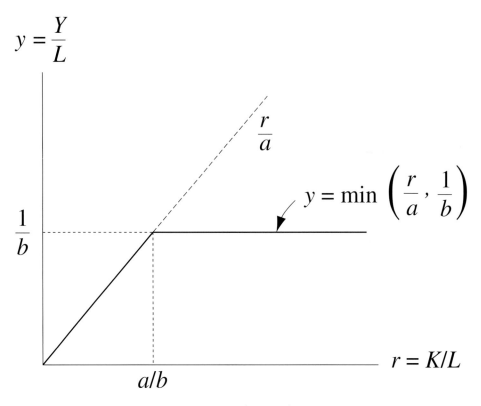

Figure 2.5b Income per person $y = \min \left(r/a, 1/b \right)$ in the case of the Walras–Leontief production function $Y = \min \left(\dfrac{K}{a}, \dfrac{L}{b} \right)$.

The equation of motion of the economy thus becomes

$$\dot{r} = sy - nr = s \min \left(\frac{r}{a}, \frac{1}{b} \right) - nr$$

$$= \min \left(\frac{s}{a} r, \frac{s}{b} \right) - nr. \qquad (29)$$

Since the equation is autonomous (independent of time), the qualitative behaviour of the solutions is easy to derive from the phase diagram. Three cases must be distinguished, corresponding to various values of the population growth rate: $n_1 > s/a$; $n_2 = s/a$; $n_3 < s/a$. In figure 2.5c, the upper diagrams are the phase diagrams corresponding to each of those situations. The lower diagrams are the time paths $r(t, r_0)$ corresponding to various initial values of the capital–labour ratio r_0.

Consider for instance case $n_1 > s/a$. This implies $\dot{r} = \min \left(\frac{s}{a} r, \frac{s}{b} \right) - n_1 r < 0$; the growth rate of the population n_1 is so high that, for any capital–labour ratio r, the investment per person necessary to maintain r constant ($n_1 r$), is always

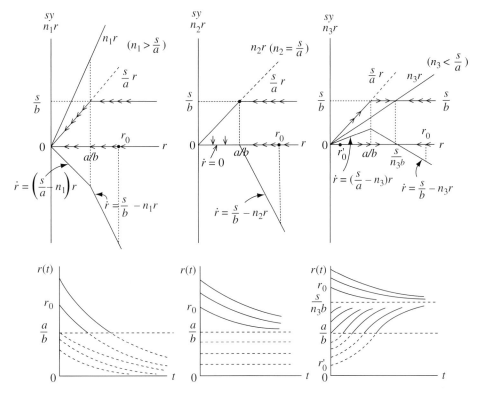

Figure 2.5c   The phase diagrams and the corresponding time paths $r(t, r_0)$ in the Walras–Leontief case

$$y = \min\left(\frac{r}{a}, \frac{1}{b}\right); \quad \dot{r} = sy - nr = \min\left(\frac{sr}{a}, \frac{s}{b}\right) - nr.$$

higher than the actual investment per person $sy = \min\left(\frac{s}{a}r, \frac{s}{b}\right)$. Therefore r will be diminishing forever. We will now describe the motion of $r(t)$ through time.

If $r_0 > a/b$, $r(t)$ will first be governed by the differential equation

$$\dot{r} = \frac{s}{b} - n_1 r \tag{30}$$

whose solution is, with initial condition $r(0) = r_0$:

$$r(t) = \left(r_0 - \frac{s}{n_1 b}\right) e^{-n_1 t} + \frac{s}{n_1 b}. \tag{31}$$

At a time t_1, $r(t)$ reaches a/b; t_1 is the solution of $r(t) = a/b$; it is equal to

$$t_1 = -\frac{1}{n_1} \log\left(\frac{\frac{a}{b} - \frac{s}{n_1 b}}{r_0 - \frac{s}{n_1 b}}\right) \tag{32}$$

(we are sure that $t_1 > 0$ because $r_0 > a/b$ and therefore the parenthesis is smaller than one).

From t_1 onward, $r(t)$ is governed by the second differential equation

$$\dot{r}(t) = \left(\frac{s}{a} - n_1\right) r(t) \tag{33}$$

whose solution is, using the initial condition $r(t_1) = a/b$,

$$r(t) = \frac{a}{b} e^{\left(\frac{s}{a} - n_1\right)(t - t_1)}. \tag{34}$$

Hence $r(t)$ will decrease toward 0 at a (negative) growth rate equal to $s/a - n_1$.

All other cases can be analysed in a similar way (see exercises). Only if $n \leq s/a$ can we expect r to converge toward a positive value (a/b if $n_2 = s/a$, or $\frac{s}{n_3 b}$ if $n_3 < s/a$), as can be seen from the diagram.

2.5.2 The "third" case

In 1956, Robert Solow had chosen to analyse a production function which constituted a "third example"; it was

$$Y = (aK^{1/2} + L^{1/2})^2. \tag{35}$$

Income per person is now given by $Y/L = y = (ar^{1/2} + 1)^2$ (this is obtained by factoring $L^{1/2}$ in the parenthesis of (35)), and the marginal productivity of capital is:

$$f'(r) = a(a + r^{-1/2}).$$

Hence $\lim_{r \to \infty} f'(r) = a^2$. Contrary to what we noted in the first two production functions we examined (Cobb–Douglas and Walras–Leontief) the marginal productivity of capital does not tend to zero when $r \to \infty$. It tends toward the constant a^2. On the other hand, $\lim_{r \to 0} f'(r) = +\infty$.

The slope of $f(r)$ starts at $+\infty$ and always decreases towards a^2 when r increases; thus the slope of $sf(r)$ decreases toward sa^2. If it happens that sa^2 is equal to or larger than n, $sf(r)$ will never reach the level of nr: investment per person ($sf(r)$) will always be larger than investment per person required to maintain r constant (nr). We will always have:

$$\dot{r} = sf(r) - nr > 0.$$

On the other hand, if $s < n/a^2$, there will be an equilibrium point. Therefore, two cases must be distinguished when drawing the phase diagram: $s < n/a^2$ and $s \geq n/a^2$ (figures 2.6a and 2.6b). Consider first the case $s < n/a^2$; then there exists an equilibrium value r^*, which is the solution of

$$\dot{r} = s(ar^{1/2} + 1)^2 - nr = 0 \tag{36}$$

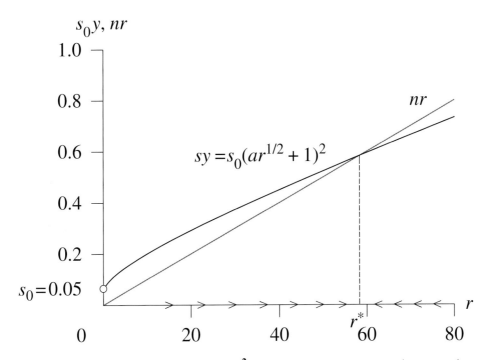

Figure 2.6a For s_0 such that $s_0 < n/a^2$, a stable equilibrium point r^* exists: $r^* = \left[\dfrac{1}{(n/s)^{1/2} - a} \right]^2.$

equal to

$$r^* = \left[\frac{1}{(n/s)^{1/2} - a} \right]^2, \tag{37}$$

and, whatever the initial conditions, income per person will converge toward

$$y^* = (a\sqrt{r^*} + 1)^2. \tag{38}$$

On the other hand, if the investment ratio s is sufficiently high (if $s \geq n/a^2$), the economy will grow forever. We will always have

$$\dot{r} = sf(r) - nr > 0. \tag{39}$$

Note that the differential equation

$$\dot{r} = s(ar^{1/2} + 1)^2 - nr \tag{40}$$

does not allow a solution in closed form; however, numerical methods are available today in softwares such as MAPLE 9. We will have recourse to those in chapters 9 and 10.

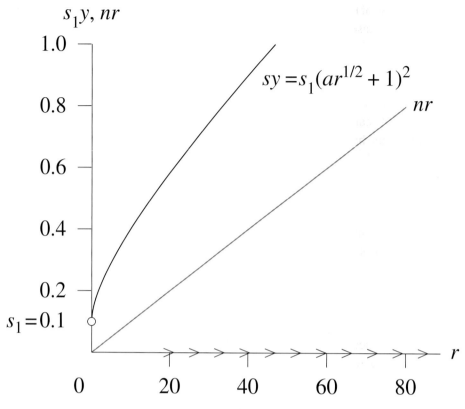

Figure 2.6b For s_1 such that $s_1 \geq n/a^2$, no equilibrium point exists, r increases indefinitely.

For the time being, observe that we have here a possibility of permanent growth without introducing technical progress in the model. Our task is to understand why the perspectives of the economy systematically improve when we go from the Walras–Leontief case to the Cobb–Douglas, and finally to the "third case".

To that effect, we now introduce the function which generalizes these three cases. We owe it to Ken Arrow, Hollis Chenery and Bagicha Minhas and Robert Solow (1961); it is the "constant elasticity of substitution (or CES) production function". We must first define the concept of the elasticity of substitution, indicate its fundamental properties, and then show how the CES function was derived. This will be done in chapter 3.

3   Introducing technical progress

Until now we have considered mainly two possible outcomes for the economy. Either the capital–labour ratio r and income per person $y = f(r)$ tend toward equilibrium values r^* and $y^* = f(r^*)$, or they tend to increase for ever. (Here we dismiss the case of the Walras–Leontief production function). Consider, indeed, the Cobb–Douglas case: we have seen that in the limit, whatever the initial conditions of the economy, $\lim_{t \to \infty} r(t) = r^* = (sA/n)^{1/(1-\alpha)}$. In that case, it means that in the limit $K(t)$ grows at the same rate as $L(t)$, i.e. its ultimate growth rate is n. In turn, since Y/L is constant at $y^* = f(r^*)$, Y grows also at rate n. (There would be another way of showing this: if K and L grow at the same rate n, Y grows at the same rate because $Y = F(K, L)$ is homogeneous of degree 1).

On the other hand, we have seen in the special "third example" that, when $Y = (aK^{1/2} + 1)^2$, there were possibilities for r and y either to tend toward limits (given by equations (37) and (38), respectively; case $s < n/a^2$) or to grow indefinitely (case $s \geq n/a^2$). In this last case, it means that total income will always increase more rapidly than population. But of course, such a favourable outcome is much more commonly due to another factor, now to be introduced, which is technical progress.

Suppose that, for some reason, capital and labour are fixed. Capital is fixed if gross investment is just equal to depreciation. In our text we have always considered *net* investment, net of depreciation; so in our terms the capital stock will be constant if (net) investment is zero. Labour is constant if $n = \frac{1}{L}\frac{dL}{at} = 0$. In those circumstances, it is quite possible that income will still grow, due to the fact that both factors of production are, over the years, used in a more efficient way.

It is logical to imagine that in fact both K and L may be used in an increasingly efficient way. One possible formulation of the effect of technical progress is that each factor is multiplied by functions of time that may increase through time at some growth rate g_K and g_L, respectively; g_K and g_L could be constants, or be themselves functions of time. We say in such cases that technical progress is "capital-augmenting" and "labour-augmenting". Supposing that the growth rates g_K and g_L are constants, the formulation of the production function would be

$$Y = F\left[Ke^{g_K t}, Le^{g_L t}\right]. \tag{41}$$

As an example, consider that F is of the Cobb–Douglas type. We would have

$$Y = A(Ke^{g_K t})^\alpha \left(Le^{g_L t}\right)^{1-\alpha} \tag{42}$$

Let us suppose that $A = 1$ and $g_K = 0$, and just keep g_L at some positive value (perhaps 1.5% per year). Since $L_t = L_0 e^{nt}$, we have:

$$Y = K^\alpha \left(L_0 e^{(n+g_L)t}\right)^{1-\alpha}. \tag{43}$$

If, as before, we suppose that $I_t = \dot{K}_t = sY_t$, we will be led to a Bernoulli differential equation in K_t. If we are interested in the long-run behaviour of the economy we would like to be able to infer this behaviour from a phase diagram, and thus avoid any unnecessary calculations. That will not be possible if we remain in $(\dot{r}, r)$ space, because the differential equation governing the motion of r, determined by calculating $\dot{r} = \frac{d}{dt}[K(t)/L(t)]$, depends explicitly on time.[7] The trick will be to make a change in variables such as the structure of the basic differential equation is preserved. In particular it should be autonomous, i.e. independent of time.

We thus make the change in variables

$$\hat{L} = L_t e^{g_L t} = L_0 e^{(n+g_L)t} \tag{44}$$

Labour is now expressed in so-called "intensive" units. So Y can be written as

$$Y = K^\alpha \hat{L}^{1-\alpha} \tag{45}$$

which has the same structure as the traditional Cobb–Douglas function. In particular, it is homogeneous of degree one in $K, \hat{L}$. Finally, set $Y/\hat{L} = \hat{y}$ and $K/\hat{L} = \hat{r}$.

Consider now the derivative of $\hat{r}$. Denoting $\hat{L}'$ as the time derivative of $\hat{L}$, we have

$$\frac{d\hat{r}}{dt} = \frac{\dot{K}\hat{L} - K\hat{L}'}{\hat{L}^2} = \frac{\dot{K}}{\hat{L}} - \frac{K}{\hat{L}}\frac{\hat{L}'}{\hat{L}} = \frac{sY}{\hat{L}} - (n+g_L)\hat{r} = s\hat{y} - (n+g_L)\hat{r}. \tag{46}$$

Replacing $\hat{y}$ by $\hat{r}^\alpha$, our basic differential equation is

$$\frac{d\hat{r}}{dt} = s\hat{r}^\alpha - (n+g_L)\hat{r}. \tag{47}$$

We observe that our two goals are accomplished. First the differential equation is autonomous: we will be able to deduce immediately the existence of an equilibrium point in the phase diagram (this is just the same diagram as before). Secondly it has the same structure as our former equation (15). The only difference comes from the magnitude of its coefficients: sA is replaced here by s (because we have normalized A to one) and n is replaced by $n + g_L$; in other words, n is augmented by the rate of technical progress g_L.

We can immediately conclude, applying formula (24), that $\hat{r}$ will converge toward

$$\hat{r}^* = \left(\frac{s}{n+g_L}\right)^{\frac{1}{1-\alpha}}. \tag{48}$$

Now let us not forget that $\hat{r}$ is not the capital–labour ratio; it is the capital–labour ratio r *divided* by $e^{g_L t}$. Indeed, we have

$$\hat{r} = \frac{K}{\hat{L}} = \frac{K}{L_0 e^{(n+g_L)t}} = \frac{K}{L_0 e^{nt} \cdot e^{g_L t}} = r(t)e^{-g_L t}, \tag{49}$$

---

[7] It is $\dot{r} = sr^\alpha e^{(1-\alpha)g_L t} - nr$. See exercise 2.7.

so that in the limit, when $t \to \infty$, we have

$$\lim_{t \to \infty} \hat{r}^* = \left(\frac{s}{n + g_L}\right)^{\frac{1}{1-\alpha}} = \lim_{t \to \infty} r(t)e^{-g_L t} \qquad (50)$$

and consequently

$$\lim_{t \to \infty} r(t) = \left(\frac{s}{n + g_L}\right)^{\frac{1}{1-\alpha}} e^{g_L t}. \qquad (51)$$

This means that the asymptotic behaviour of $r(t)$, when $t \to \infty$, is an exponential with a growth rate equal to the labour-augmenting rate of technical progress g_L.

From this we can infer the ultimate evolution of capital, income and total income per person. Since $\hat{r}$ tends to a constant, the growth rate of K tends toward the growth rate of $\hat{L}$ which is $n + g_L$. Y being homogeneous of degree one in K and $\hat{L}$, $\hat{Y}$ will ultimately grow at the same rate $n + g_L$, and the growth rate of income per person will tend to g_L.

It is useful to verify those results by determining the actual time paths of $r(t)$ and $y(t)$ corresponding to the chosen parameters of our growth process. There are two ways to proceed. One is to take advantage of the fact that the same structure of the Bernouilli differential equation (15) has returned in the form of (47). The other one is to solve the differential equation in $(r, \dot{r}, t)$ space by setting, as before, $x = r^{1-\alpha}$ (see exercise 2.7). Using the first method, we can directly apply (23), where r_0, r_t, sA and n are replaced by $\hat{r}, \hat{r}_0, s$ and $n + g_L$ respectively.

We thus obtain:

$$\hat{r}(t) = \left[\left(\hat{r}_0^{1-\alpha} - \frac{s}{n + g_L}\right)e^{-(n+g_L)(1-\alpha)t} + \frac{s}{n + g_L}\right]^{\frac{1}{1-\alpha}}. \qquad (52)$$

Since $r(t) = \hat{r}(t)e^{g_L t}$, we have, with $\hat{r}_0 = r_0$

$$r_t = e^{g_L t}\left[\left(r_0^{1-\alpha} - \frac{s}{n + g_L}\right)e^{-(n+g_L)(1-\alpha)t} + \frac{s}{n + g_L}\right]^{\frac{1}{1-\alpha}}; \qquad (53)$$

and, factoring on $e^{-g_L(1-\alpha)t}$ from the bracketed term,

$$r_t = \left[\left(r_0^{1-\alpha} - \frac{s}{n + g_L}\right)e^{-n(1-\alpha)t} + \frac{s}{n + g_L}e^{g_L(1-\alpha)t}\right]^{\frac{1}{1-\alpha}}. \qquad (54)$$

From (43), $Y = K^\alpha L_t^{1-\alpha}e^{g_L(1-\alpha)t}$, so that $Y/L = y = r^\alpha e^{g_L(1-\alpha)t}$. Using (54):

$$y(t) = \left[\left(r_0^{1-\alpha} - \frac{s}{n + g_L}\right)e^{-n(1-\alpha)t} + \frac{s}{n + g_L}e^{g_L(1-\alpha)t}\right]^{\frac{\alpha}{1-\alpha}} e^{g_L(1-\alpha)t}. \qquad (55)$$

We can verify from (54) that $\lim_{t\to\infty} \dot{r}/r = g_L$, and from (55) that $\lim_{t\to\infty} \dot{y}/y = \frac{\alpha}{1-\alpha} g_L(1-\alpha) + (1-\alpha)g_L = g_L$.

A final remark is in order. The reader may have noticed that the easiest way to solve a time-dependent differential equation is not necessarily to transform it into an automonous equation as is usually done (see also exercise 2.7). In the above case, it is simpler to work with the original equation. However, when we have systems of equations it can be very useful to make those systems autonomous because it is then possible to illustrate solutions (each depending on initial conditions) in a phase diagram and, in particular, to understand their fundamental instability, for instance. This will be done in chapters 9 and 10.

Appendix 1: The concept of elasticity, its use in economics, and its applications to growth rates

One of the great inventions of mathematics at the end of the seventeenth century was the concept of derivative. While the rate of increase of a function, denoted $\Delta y/\Delta x$, is easy to conceive, it has its drawbacks: indeed, it is usually dependent upon the size of the increase given to the variable x. Therefore, at any given point of a function $y = f(x)$ there may be an infinite number of values corresponding to the rate of increase $\Delta y/\Delta x$ of a function; some of those may be positive, zero or negative; worse, some may even not be defined. Therefore, in order to characterize by one and only one number the tendency of a function to increase or decrease at any of its points, mathematicians decided to consider the limit of $\Delta y/\Delta x$ when $\Delta x \to 0$, if such a limit exists. The name "derivative" (rather unfortunate, because little revealing its meaning) was then attached to

$$\lim_{\Delta x\to 0} \frac{\Delta y}{\Delta x} = \frac{dy}{dx} = \frac{df}{dx} = f'(x) = y',$$

and the concept was immediately extended to functions of several variables. The partial derivative of $y = f(x_1, \ldots, x_i, \ldots, x_n)$ with respect to x_i was defined as

$$\lim_{\Delta x_i\to 0} \frac{\Delta y}{\Delta x_i} = \frac{\partial y}{\partial x_i} = \frac{\partial f}{\partial x_i} = f'_{x_i} = f_{x_i} = f_i.$$

The derivative itself, however, has some drawbacks. Consider two functions $u = f(x)$ and $v = f(y)$, and suppose that u, v, x and y are measured in different units. We will not be able to compare the derivatives of u and v, precisely because they are expressed in different units. However, we might still be quite interested in knowing whether u is more sensitive to a change in x than v is to a change in y. The same applies for the partial derivatives of a given function, if the variables are expressed in different units. Fundamentally, we want to be able to gauge the sensitivity of any function to a change in its dependent variable(s).

The natural answer to these questions is to consider *relative* changes, both for the independent variable and the function. Thus the elasticity (another poorly chosen name) of a function $y = f(x)$, denoted $e_{y,x}$, is defined by the following limit:

$$e_{y,x} = \lim_{\Delta x \to 0} \frac{\frac{\Delta y}{y}}{\frac{\Delta x}{x}} = \frac{x}{y} \lim_{\Delta x \to 0} \frac{\Delta y}{\Delta x} = \frac{x}{y} \frac{dy}{dx} = \frac{x}{y} f'(x) = \frac{x}{y} y'$$

assuming that $x \neq 0$ and $y \neq 0$. One very useful notation of the elasticity of y with respect to x is

$$e_{y,x} = \frac{dy/y}{dx/x}$$

because it reveals directly the geometric interpretation of the concept. At any point (x, y), the elasticity of y with respect to x is the relative increase of the tangent to the curve $y = f(x)$, divided by a given relative increase in x. An example will be helpful. Consider the power function $y = ax^b$ $(a > 0)$. Its derivative is abx^{b-1} and its elasticity is $e_{y,x} = f'(x) \cdot x/y = abx^{b-1} \cdot x/ax^b = b$. Notice that $e_{y,x}$, as a concept independent of measurement units, does not depend upon a – contrary to the derivative abx^{b-1}. Notice also that the elasticity of the power function is independent of x – also contrary to its derivative. The fact that the elasticity of a power function is equal to its power (b in this case) means that if x, at *any* point, increases by 1% then the function increases in linear approximation by $b\%$. For instance, a parabola ax^2 is such that if x is increased by 1% at any point (except at $x = 0$), the tangent to the parabola increases exactly by 2%.

Observe also that since $dy/y = d \log y$ and $dx/x = d \log x$, the elasticity can be defined and calculated as the derivative of $\log y$ with respect to $\log x$:

$$e_{y,x} = \frac{dy/y}{dx/x} = \frac{d \log y}{d \log x}.$$

For instance, we could have written, from $y = ax^b$, $\log y = \log a + b \log x$ and obtained directly its elasticity as $e_{y,x} = d \log y/d \log x = b$.

We have shown that the elasticity of a power function is a constant (it is its power). We can easily show that the converse is true: the only function with constant elasticity is the power function. Indeed, suppose we have

$$e_{y,x} = \frac{dy/y}{dx/x} = b \text{ (a constant)}.$$

Table 2A.1 *Elasticity of a few common functions*

function $y = f(x)$	derivative $f'(x)$	elasticity $e_{y,x} = f'(x) \cdot \frac{x}{y}$
$ax + b$	a	$\dfrac{ax}{ax+b}$
ax^b	abx^{b-1}	b
$\log x$	$\dfrac{1}{x}$	$\dfrac{1}{\log x}$
e^x	e^x	x
$u(x) + v(x)$	$u'(x) + v'(x)$	$e_{u,x}\frac{u}{u+v} + e_{v,x}\frac{v}{u+v}$
$u(x)v(x)$	$u'(x)v(x) + u(x)v'(x)$	$e_{u,x} + e_{v,x}$
$g[f(x)]$	$g'[f(x)] \cdot f'(x)$	$e_{g,f} \cdot e_{f,x}$

If $x > 0$ and $y > 0$, we can integrate both sides and write

$$\int \frac{dy}{y} = b \int \frac{dx}{x}$$
$$\log y = b \log x + \log a$$

where a is a constant, or

$$y = ax^b$$

which is the power function.

Table 2A.1 indicates the elasticity of a few common functions; it also gives the elasticity of a sum and a product of functions, as well as the elasticity of composite functions. Those results, which can be easily verified, will be very useful in this text.

Notice that the elasticity of a sum of functions is the weighted sum of the elasticities, the weights being the shares of each function in the sum. The elasticity of a product of functions is simply the sum of the elasticities; and the elasticity of a composite function is the product of the elasticities.

Reading the elasticity of a function from its graph

A nice property of the elasticity is that we can evaluate its order of magnitude just looking at the graph of $f(x)$, without knowing the measurement units on the axes – contrary to the derivative, which is unit-dependent. Figure 2A.1 shows that drawing the tangent at any point of the curve immediately yields the value of the elasticity of the function at that point. Let α be the distance between x and the

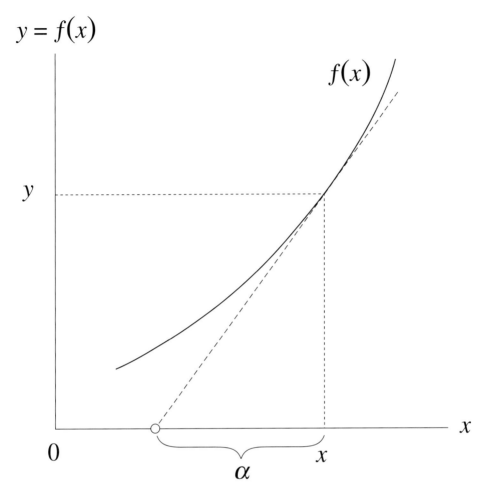

Figure 2A.1   A geometrical construction of the elasticity of $y = f(x)$ at point (x, y). The elasticity is equal to $e_{y,x} = \dfrac{dy/y}{dx/x} = \dfrac{dy}{dx} \cdot \dfrac{x}{y} = \dfrac{y}{\alpha} \cdot \dfrac{x}{y} = \dfrac{x}{\alpha}.$

intersection of the tangent with the abscissa. Assuming $f'(x) > 0$, we get

$$e_{y,x} = \frac{dy}{dx} \cdot \frac{x}{y} = \frac{y}{\alpha} \cdot \frac{x}{y} = \frac{x}{\alpha}$$

(if $f'(x) < 0$, we would have $e_{y,x} = -x/\alpha$).

On figure 2A.1, the elasticity at the chosen point, x/α, is about 1.7. It implies that if x increases by 1%, y will increase in linear approximation by 1.7% (this is the relative increase measured on the tangent to the curve at the chosen point).

Growth rates and elasticities

Suppose now that y is a composite function of time t through a variable x:

$$y = f[x(t)].$$

Thus y is a function of time. Let us consider its growth rate $\dot{y}/y$:

$$\frac{\dot{y}}{y} = \frac{1}{y}\frac{dy}{dt} = \frac{1}{y}\frac{df}{dx}\frac{dx}{dt} = \frac{x}{y}\frac{df}{dx}\frac{1}{x}\frac{dx}{dt} = e_{y,x}\frac{1}{x}\frac{dx}{dt}.$$

Thus the growth rate of y is just the growth rate of x multiplied by the elasticity of y with respect to x.

These concepts extend immediately to functions of several variables. Let the function $y = f(x_1, \ldots, x_i, \ldots, x_n)$ be differentiable at least once. We define the *partial elasticity* of y with respect to x as

$$e_{y,x_i} = \lim_{\Delta x_i \to 0} \frac{\Delta y}{\Delta x_i} \cdot \frac{x_i}{y} = \frac{x_i}{y}\frac{\partial y}{\partial x_i} = \frac{x_i}{y} f'_{x_i}.$$

The total differential of f is:

$$dy = \sum_{i=1}^{n} \frac{\partial f}{\partial x_i} dx_i$$

and the relative increase of the function in linear approximation is given by

$$\frac{dy}{y} = \sum_{i=1}^{n} \frac{\partial f}{\partial x_i}\frac{1}{y} dx_i.$$

Multiplying and dividing each term by x_i, we have

$$\frac{dy}{y} = \sum_{i=1}^{n} \frac{\partial f}{\partial x_i}\frac{x_i}{y}\frac{dx_i}{x_i} = \sum_{i=1}^{n} e_{y,x_i} \cdot \frac{dx_i}{x_i}.$$

The relative increase of the function in linear approximation is thus equal to the sum of the individual relative increases of the x_i's, weighted by the partial elasticities of y with respect to the x_i's.

As an application, let us determine the growth rate of a function of several variables. Suppose that each x_i is a function of time $x_i(t)$. We have

$$y = f[x_1(t), \ldots, x_i(t), \ldots, x_n(t)].$$

The total derivative of y with respect to t is

$$\frac{dy}{dt} = \sum_{t=1}^{n} \frac{\partial f}{\partial x_i}\frac{dx_i}{dt}.$$

The growth rate of y is

$$\frac{1}{y}\frac{dy}{dt} = \sum_{i=1}^{n} \frac{1}{y}\frac{\partial f}{\partial x_i}\frac{dx_i}{dt}.$$

Multiplying and dividing the right-hand side by x_i, we have

$$\frac{\dot{y}}{y} = \frac{1}{y}\frac{dy}{dt} = \sum_{i=1}^{n} \frac{x_i}{y}\frac{\partial f}{\partial x_i}\frac{1}{x_i}\frac{dx_i}{dt} = \sum_{i=1}^{n} e_{y,x_i} \cdot \frac{\dot{x}_i}{x_i}.$$

Thus the growth rate of the function is the sum of the growth rates of each variable, weighted by the partial elasticities of the function with respect to each of the variables x_i. All these relationships will prove very useful in this text.

As an example, consider the function

$$Y = A K_t^{\alpha} L_t^{\beta} e^{gt}$$

where K and L are functions of time. Applying the last formula as well as one of the properties we have just seen (the elasticity of a power function is its power) we get immediately

$$\frac{\dot{Y}}{Y} = \alpha\frac{\dot{K}}{K} + \beta\frac{\dot{L}}{L} + g$$

(the easiest way to verify this result is to take $\log Y$ and determine $d\log Y/dt = \dot{Y}/Y$).

Appendix 2: Solution of the first-order differential equation

$$a(x)y' + b(x)y = g(x). \tag{A1}$$

2.1   Solution in indefinite form

Let us first solve the differential equation

$$a(x)y' + b(x)y = 0. \tag{A2}$$

Denoting $a(x) \equiv a$ and $b(x) \equiv b$ for simplicity, this differential equation can be written

$$y' = -\frac{b}{a}y.$$

The variables are separable. We can write

$$\frac{dy}{y} = -\frac{b}{a}dx,$$

whose integration is immediate:

$$\int \frac{dy}{y} = -\int \frac{b}{a}dx$$

Supposing $y > 0$,

$$\ln y = -\int \frac{b}{a}dx + \ln C_1$$

where $\ln C_1$ is an arbitrary constant, or

$$y = C_1 e^{-\int \frac{b}{a}dx}. \tag{A3}$$

Let us now consider one particular solution of (A2); we can choose such a solution by setting $C_1 = 1$ in (A3). Let us call this solution $v(x)$. Thus

$$v(x) = e^{-\int \frac{b}{a}dx}. \tag{A4}$$

Our final step is to look for the solution of (A1) in the form of the product $u(x)v(x)$, where $u(x)$ is a yet unknown function of x. Thus, if our solution is $y = u(x)v(x)$, $u(x)$ must be such that

$$a(uv)' + buv = g \tag{A5}$$

or

$$au'v + auv' + buv = g \tag{A6}$$

which can also be written as

$$au'v + u(av' + bv) = g. \tag{A7}$$

But we know that $v(x)$ is a solution of (A2), and therefore $av' + bv = 0$. So $u(x)$ is just the solution of equation

$$au'v = g \tag{A8}$$

or

$$u' = \frac{g}{av}. \tag{A9}$$

The solution of (A9) turns out to be

$$u = \int \frac{g}{av}dx + C. \tag{A10}$$

Therefore the general solution of (A1) is

$$y = Cv + v\int \frac{g}{av}dx \tag{A11}$$

where C is an arbitrary constant, and $v = e^{-\int (b/a)dx}$.

2.2 Solution in definite form

The solution (A11) is said to be in indefinite form because it carries the arbitrary constant C. It is often useful to have a solution in definite form, where the constant of integration C is identified by the knowledge of one point of the trajectory, $[x_0, f(x_0)] = (x^0, y^0)$; such a condition imposed upon the solution is often called an "initial condition".

Notice that when we chose a particular solution of (A2), we set $C_1 = 1$ and wrote that solution as $v(x) = \exp[-\int [b(x)/a(x)]dx]$ (eq. A4). But we could equivalently have written that particular solution as

$$v(x) = e^{-\int_{x_0}^x \frac{b(z)}{a(z)}dz}. \tag{A12}$$

In the same vein, the most general solution of (A10) can be written

$$u(x) = \int_{x_0}^x \frac{g(\xi)}{a(\xi)v(\xi)}d\xi + C \tag{A13}$$

where $v(\xi)$ is now $e^{-\int_{x_0}^\xi \frac{b(z)}{a(z)}dz}$.

Our general solution now reads:

$$y(x) = u(x)v(x) = e^{-\int_{x_0}^x \frac{b(z)}{a(z)}dz}\left(C + \int_{x_0}^x \frac{g(\xi)}{a(\xi)}e^{\int_{x_0}^\xi \frac{b(z)}{a(z)}dz}d\xi\right). \tag{A14}$$

We can finally identify the constant of integration C in (A14); we know that if $x = x_0, y = y_0$. Replacing in (A14) x by x_0 and y by y_0 yields $C = y_0$. Therefore, the solution of (1) in definite form is

$$y(x) = e^{-\int_{x_0}^x \frac{b(z)}{a(z)}dz}\left(y_0 + \int_{x_0}^x \frac{g(\xi)}{a(\xi)}e^{\int_{x_0}^\xi \frac{b(z)}{a(z)}dz}d\xi\right). \tag{A15}$$

Both forms of solutions will be used in this text.

Exercises

2.1 One of the most important properties of homogeneous functions of degree m is given by Euler's theorem which states that if

$$\lambda^m f(x_1,\ldots,x_n) = f(\lambda x_1,\ldots,\lambda x_n) \tag{56}$$

then

$$mf(x_1,\ldots,x_n) = \sum_{i=1}^n \frac{\partial f}{\partial x_i}(x_1,\ldots,x_n)x_i.$$

Demonstrate Euler's theorem. (Hint: denote $\lambda x_i = u_i$, $i = 1,\ldots,n$, take the derivative of the definitional equation (56) with respect to λ, and finally consider the limit of this derivative when λ tends to one).

2.2 Demonstrate another important property of homogeneous functions of order m: the partial derivatives of such functions are homogeneous of degree $m - 1$. What is the generalization of this property?

2.3 In this text we will make extensive use of production functions which are homogeneous of degree one. Show that in such case if there are n factors the average productivity of one factor (production divided by that factor) depends upon $n - 1$ variables only.

2.4 The following exercise will show you that you have to be very careful when drawing a production function $y = f(r)$ in (r, y) space, because the function may be increasing and concave, and yet imply a *negative* marginal productivity of labour. Can you depict a function $y = f(r)$ such that $f(r)$ is increasing and concave throughout but such that its marginal productivity of labour is negative on an interval of r? (Even) more challenging: can you construct an increasing and not necessarily concave function $y = f(r)$ such that its marginal productivity is negative over a given interval (r_A, r_B)?

2.5 The following two exercises are designed to show how the Cobb–Douglas function can be derived from any of its sections. In this exercise, you are given the vertical section $Y = Y_0(L/L_0)^{1-\alpha}$ of a homogeneous of degree one function that goes through point (Y_0, K_0, L_0) and you are asked to determine the function $Y = F(K, L)$. Hint: it is extremely useful to draw in 3-D space this section as a power function that goes through points $(Y, K, L) = (0, K_0, 0)$ and $(Y, K, L) = (Y_0, K_0, L_0)$, In the horizontal plane, choose any point (K, L). Draw the ray from the origin to point (K, L), and its intersection with the horizontal line K_0; this intersection has an abscissa L_1. You can then determine the production level corresponding to (K_0, L_1); finally, you know that being at (K, L) instead of at (K_0, L_1) scales the level of production by K/K_0. Finally, express L_1 in terms of K_0, K and L; you will get
$$Y = Y_0 \left(\frac{K}{K_0}\right)^\alpha \left(\frac{L}{L_0}\right)^{1-\alpha}.$$

2.6 Suppose that you are given the isoquant of a Cobb–Douglas function as a power function $K = aL^b (a > 0; b < 0)$ such that it goes through point (K_0, L_0). At such a point, the production level is Y_0. Derive the Cobb–Douglas from this information. (Hint: proceed in a similar way; this time draw in 3-D space the level curve corresponding to the isoquant; choose any point (K, L) in the horizontal plane; determine the intersection point with the isoquant.)

2.7 Make sure that you can derive the asymptotic properties of the neo-classical model by solving the equation of motion for $r(t) = K(t)/L(t)$ when the production function is Cobb–Douglas with labour augmenting technological progress (you can take g_L as a constant, and denote for simplicity $(1 - \alpha)g_L = g$; also set $A = 1$). Hint: you will get a non-autonomous Bernoulli-type differential equation which can be solved easily by making the change in variable $x = r^{1-\alpha}$, as we have done in section 2.2.2., when we dealt with an autonomous equation.

Answers

2.1 In the identity

$$\lambda^m f(x_1, \ldots, x_i, \ldots, x_n) = f(\lambda x_1, \ldots, \lambda x_i, \ldots, \lambda x_n)$$

replace λx_i by u_i, and differentiate each side with respect to λ. We get

$$m\lambda^{m-1} f(x_1, \ldots, x_i, \ldots, x_n) = \sum_{i=1}^{n} \frac{\partial f}{\partial u_i}(\lambda x_1, \ldots, \lambda x_i, \ldots, \lambda x_n)x_i$$

Set $\lambda = 1$; the above equality becomes Euler's identity

$$mf(x_1, \ldots, x_n) = \sum_{i=1}^{n} \frac{\partial f}{\partial u_i}(x_1, \ldots, x_n)x_i.$$

2.2 Differentiate both sides of equation

$$\lambda^m f(x_1, \ldots, x_i, \ldots, x_n) = f(\lambda x_1, \ldots, \lambda x_i, \ldots, \lambda x_n)$$

with respect to x_i; we get

$$\lambda^m \frac{\partial f}{\partial x_i} = \frac{\partial f}{\partial u_i}(\lambda x_1, \ldots, \lambda x_i, \ldots, \lambda x_n)\lambda$$

and

$$\lambda^{m-1} \frac{\partial f}{\partial x_i} = \frac{\partial f}{\partial u_i}(\lambda x_1, \ldots, \lambda x_i, \ldots, \lambda x_n)$$

which shows that the partial derivative is homogeneous of degree $m - 1$. Any second derivative is homogeneous of degree $m - 2$; any nth-order derivative is homogeneous of degree $m - n$.

In the case of a homogeneous of degree one production function, the marginal productivities (the partial derivatives of the function) are homogeneous of degree zero. From a geometric point of view, it means that the marginal productivities are constant along a ray from the origin.

2.3 Suppose $y = f(x_1, \ldots, x_i, \ldots, x_n)$ is homogeneous of degree one. Multiplying every variable $x_1, \ldots, x_i, \ldots, x_n$ by $1/x_i$ multiplies the function by the same amount $1/x_i$. We get the average productivity

$$\frac{y}{x_i} = f\left(\frac{x_1}{x_i}, \ldots, 1, \ldots, \frac{x_n}{x_i}\right)$$

which depends upon the $n - 1$ variables $x_1/x_i, \dots, x_n/x_i$ only.

As an example, consider

$$Y = F(K, L)$$

homogeneous of degree one. Then

$$\frac{Y}{L} = F\left(\frac{K}{L}, 1\right) = g(r); \ r = K/L$$

and

$$\frac{Y}{K} = F\left(1, \frac{L}{K}\right) = h(v); \ v = L/K.$$

We can verify that the marginal productivities are homogeneous of degree zero by writing

$$y = x_i f\left(\frac{x_1}{x_i}, \dots, 1, \dots, \frac{x_n}{x_i}\right).$$

Denote $x_j/x_i = r_j$ $(j = 1, \dots, n; j \neq i)$; the derivative of y with respect to x_i is

$$\frac{\partial y}{\partial x_i} = f\left(\frac{x_1}{x_2}, \dots, 1, \dots, \frac{x_n}{x_i}\right) + x_i \sum_{j=1}^{n} \frac{\partial f}{\partial r_j}\left(-\frac{x_j}{x_i^2}\right)$$

$$= f\left(\frac{x_1}{x_2}, \dots, 1, \dots, \frac{x_n}{x_i}\right) - \sum_{j=1}^{n} \frac{\partial f}{\partial r_j} \cdot \frac{x_j}{x_i}.$$

This derivative is indeed homogeneous of degree zero and depends upon $n - 1$ variables only. As an example, consider $Y = F(K, L)$ homogeneous of degree one. From $Y/L = F(K/L, 1)$ write

$$Y = LF(K/L, 1) = Lg(r), \ r = K/L.$$

The marginal productivities are

$$\frac{\partial Y}{\partial L} = g(r) + Lg'(r) \cdot \left(-\frac{K}{L^2}\right) = g(r) - rg'(r)$$

and

$$\frac{\partial Y}{\partial K} = Lg'(r) \cdot \frac{1}{L} = g'(r).$$

They are homogeneous of degree zero and depend solely on one variable, the capital-labour ratio r.

2.4 For the first part of this exercise, draw in (r, y) space a concave line with positive slope crossing the r axis (figure 2A.2). Draw also the ray from the origin tangent to $f(r)$. Draw also the tangent to $f(r)$ at a point whose abscissa

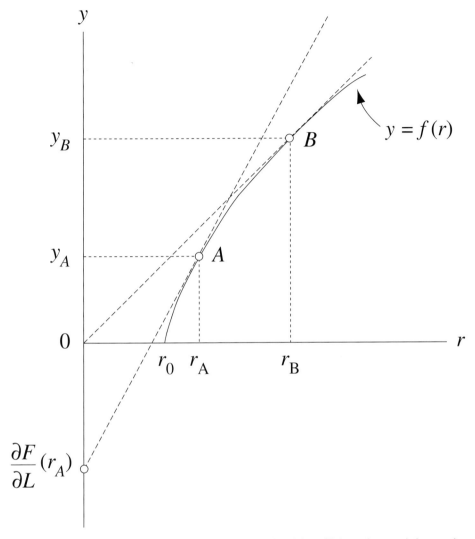

**Figure 2A.2 At point (r_B, y_B) the marginal productivity of labour is zero; it is negative
in the interval $[r_0, r_B)$.**

r_A is lower than r_B. At point (r_B, y_B) the marginal productivity of labour is
zero, and in the interval $[r_0, r_B)$ $\partial F / \partial L$ is negative. Any curve of the type
$y = A r^\alpha - \beta$, $A > 0$, $0 < \alpha < 1$, $\beta > 0$ will have those properties.

Consider now a given interval (r_1, r_2), $r_1 < r_2$ (figure 2A.3). You can
always construct a function $y = f(r)$, not necessarily concave, such that
$\partial F / \partial L$ is negative over a given interval. From the origin draw the rays to
points $T_1(r_1, y_1)$ and $T_2(r_1, y_2)$, supposing that their slopes are such that
$y_2 / r_2 > y_1 / r_1$.

The growth process

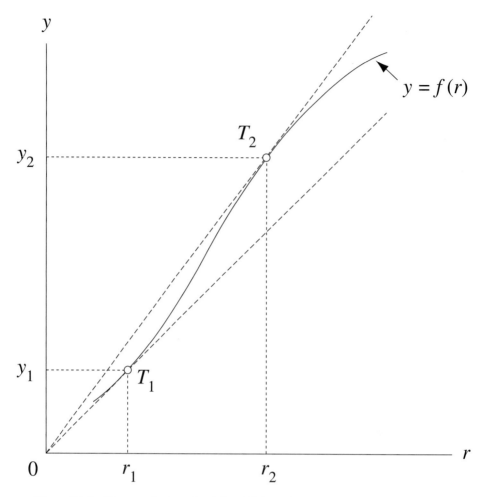

Figure 2A.3 The marginal productivity of labour is zero at r_1 and r_2, and negative in between.

Between points T_1 and T_2 draw a curve such that it is tangent to the rays at those points, such as the one indicated on figure 2A.3. At points T_1 and T_2 the marginal productivity of labour is zero; in between, it is negative.

2.5 Let (K, L) be any point in the horizontal plane (see figure 2A.4). The ray from the origin to that point meets the horizontal line K_0 at a point denoted (K_0, L_1), which corresponds to a production level $Y_0(L_1/L_0)^{1-\alpha}$. Being at (K, L) instead of at (K_0, L_1) scales the level of production by a factor K/K_0. So the production level at (K, L) is $\frac{K}{K_0}Y_0(L_1/L_0)^{1-\alpha}$. But we know also that $L_1/L = K_0/K$. So we have finally

$$Y = \frac{K}{K_0}Y_0\left(L\frac{K_0}{K}\frac{1}{L_0}\right)^{1-\alpha} = Y_0\left(\frac{K}{K_0}\right)^{\alpha}\left(\frac{L}{L_0}\right)^{1-\alpha}.$$

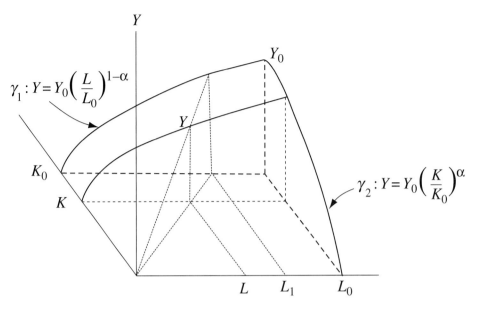

Figure 2A.4 A geometric construction of the Cobb–Douglas Function $Y = Y_0 \left(\frac{K}{K_0}\right)^\alpha \left(\frac{L}{L_0}\right)^{1-\alpha}$ **from one of its vertical sections (γ_1).**

2.6 Let us first determine the function $K(L)$ representing the isoquant (see figure 2A.5). Since it goes through point (K_0, L_0), a must be such that $K_0 = a L_0^b$; so $a = K_0 L_0^{-b}$ and $K = K_0 (L/L_0)^b$. Now choose any point (K, L) in the horizontal plane. The ray from the origin to (K, L) intersects the isoquant at point (K_1, L_1), to which corresponds a production level Y_0. The value K_1 can be determined as a function of L_1, using the isoquant function. We have $K_1 = K_0 (L_1/L_0)^b$. Let Y designate $F(K, L)$ (our unknown). We have $Y/Y_0 = L/L_1$, and $K/K_1 = L/L_1$. Thus we have the system

$$K_1 = K_0 \left(\frac{L_1}{L_0}\right)^b$$

$$\frac{Y}{Y_0} = \frac{K}{K_1}$$

$$\frac{K}{K_1} = \frac{L}{L_1}$$

a system of 3 equations in 5 unknowns (Y, K, L, K_1, L_1) from which we can get one equation in three unknowns (Y, K, L). We can write, using the first two equations

$$\frac{Y}{Y_0} = \frac{K}{K_1} = \frac{K}{K_0} \left(\frac{L_1}{L_0}\right)^{-b}.$$

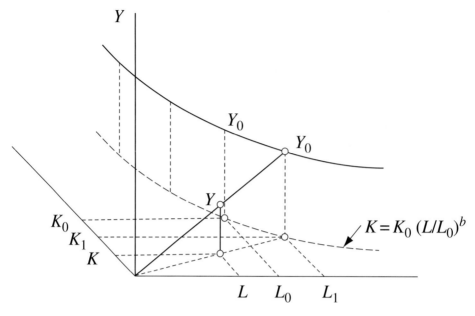

Figure 2A.5 Determination of the Cobb–Douglas production function from one of its isoquants.

L_1 can be determined from $Y/Y_0 = L/L_1$ as $L_1 = Y_0 L/Y$. Replacing in the above expression gives

$$\frac{Y}{Y_0} = \frac{K}{K_0} \left(\frac{Y_0 L}{Y L_0} \right)^{-b}$$

from which Y can be determined:

$$Y = Y_0 \left(\frac{K}{K_0} \right)^{\frac{1}{1-b}} \left(\frac{L}{L_0} \right)^{-\frac{b}{1-b}}.$$

Observe that since b is negative, the power of L/L_0 is positive, and that the powers of K/K_0 and L/L_0 add up to one, which corresponds to homogeneity of degree one, as it should.

2.7 The production function will be:

$$Y = F(K, L, t) = K^{\alpha} (L e^{g_L t})^{1-\alpha}$$
$$= K^{\alpha} \left(L_0 e^{nt} \right)^{1-\alpha} e^{g_L (1-\alpha) t}.$$

As before, the rate of increase of r is

$$\dot{r}(t) = \frac{\dot{K} L - K \dot{L}}{L^2} = \frac{\dot{K}}{L} - nr = \frac{sY}{L} - nr.$$

Now the ratio $Y/L = Y/(L_0 e^{nt})$ is

$$\frac{Y}{L} = K^\alpha L^{-\alpha} e^{g_L(1-\alpha)t}.$$

To simplify notation, set $g_L(1-\alpha) \equiv g$. The equation of motion of $r(t)$ is then

$$\dot{r} = sr^\alpha e^{gt} - nr$$

or, dividing through by r^α:

$$r^{-\alpha}\dot{r} = se^{gt} - nr^{1-\alpha}.$$

Using the change in variable $x = r^{1-\alpha}$, we have $\dot{x} = (1-\alpha)r^{-\alpha}\dot{r}$ and thus the Bernoulli differential equation becomes linear in x:

$$\frac{\dot{x}}{1-\alpha} + nx = se^{gt}.$$

Its solution is

$$x_t = \left(x_0 - \frac{s}{\frac{g}{1-\alpha}+n} \right) e^{-n(1-\alpha)t} + \frac{s}{\frac{g}{1-\alpha}+n} e^{gt}$$

and, coming back to $r(t) = [x(t)]^{1/(1-\alpha)}$, we have finally

$$r(t) = \left[\left(r_0^{1-\alpha} - \frac{s}{g_L+n} \right) e^{-n(1-\alpha)t} + \frac{s}{g_L+n} e^{(1-\alpha)g_L t} \right]^{\frac{1}{1-\alpha}}$$

since $x_0 = r_0^{1-\alpha}$.

The asymptotic behaviour of $r(t)$ when $t \to \infty$ is

$$\lim_{t \to \infty} r(t) = \frac{s}{g_L+n} e^{g_L t}$$

from which the limiting growth rates of $r(t)$, $K(t)$, $Y(t)$ and $y(t)$ can be immediately inferred. The limiting growth rate of r is the coefficient of labour augmenting technical progress g_L. The growth rate of $K(t)$ will tend toward that of $r(t)L(t)$, i.e. $g_L + n$; that of Y will be $\lim_{t\to\infty}(e_{Y,K}\dot{K}/K + e_{Y,L}\dot{L}/L + (1/y)\partial Y/\partial t)$, i.e. $\alpha(g_L+n) + (1-\alpha)n + (1-\alpha)g_L = n + g_L$. Note that this result could have been reached equivalently by observing that, $Y = F(K, Le^{g_L t})$ being homogeneous of degree one in the variables $K, Le^{g_L t}$, and $K(t)$ growing asymptotically at rate $n + g_L$, the growth rate of $Le^{g_L t}$, then Y will grow at the same rate. Finally, income per person will grow at rate g_L.

CHAPTER 3

A production function of central importance

In 1961, Kenneth Arrow, Hollis Chenery, Bagicha Minhas and Robert Solow made a major discovery. Not only did it modify forever the way economists looked at production functions, but it also had a considerable influence on another field of research, namely utility theory. We will explain here how the so-called constant elasticity of substitution (CES) production function was found. We will start with the concept of the elasticity of substitution, and then turn to the derivation of the CES function itself and its main properties.

I Motivation

Throughout history, the rental price of capital has decreased while the wage rate has increased. At the same time the capital–labour ratio has increased. For any given, fixed level of production there is also a positive relationship between the wage–rental ratio and the capital–labour ratio. The elasticity of substitution is the elasticity of the latter relationship.

We then need to recall first the concept of factor demand because the capital–labour ratio is precisely the ratio of the demand functions of capital and labour. Suppose that to the use of capital during a given time span corresponds a price that we will call the rental rate, denoted q; the measurement units of this rental rate is $ per unit of capital, per unit of time. So in units we have:

$$q = \frac{\text{``dollars''}}{\text{``unit of capital'' . ``unit of time''}}.$$

The use of labour costs the wage rate w, expressed in $ per unit of labour, per unit of time. Also in units we have:

$$w = \frac{\text{``dollars''}}{\text{``unit of labour'' . ``unit of time''}}.$$

The cost of using both factors in quantities K and L is thus

$$C = qK + wL.$$

Suppose now that the firm, or society, wants to use those rare resources in the most efficient way. An efficient way may have different meanings. For instance, it could be minimizing the cost of production subject to a given production level; or it could mean the "dual problem" of maximizing output subject to a cost constraint. Let us see what the implications of the first of these cases are. Minimizing the cost of production with respect to a production level Y_0 leads to writing a Lagrangian

$$\mathcal{L} = qK + wL + \lambda[Y_0 - F(K, L)]$$

where $F(K, L)$ is a concave function in (K, L). Setting to zero the gradient of $\mathcal{L}$, we have:

$$\frac{\partial \mathcal{L}}{\partial K} = q - \lambda \frac{\partial F}{\partial K}(K, L) = 0 \tag{1}$$

$$\frac{\partial \mathcal{L}}{\partial L} = w - \lambda \frac{\partial F}{\partial L}(K, L) = 0 \tag{2}$$

$$Y_0 = F(K, L) \tag{3}$$

The above system of three equations in the three unknowns K, L and λ can generally be solved in K, L and λ to yield the factor demand functions K and L, which depend on the parameters Y_0, w and q.[1] So we can derive the functions

$$K = K(Y_0; w, q)$$
$$L = L(Y_0; w, q).$$

An example may be helpful. Suppose that $Y = K^\alpha L^{1-\alpha}$. With $\partial F/\partial K = \alpha K^{\alpha-1} L^{1-\alpha}$ and $\partial F/\partial L = (1-\alpha)K^\alpha L^{-\alpha}$, equations (1), (2) and (3) are:

$$q - \lambda \alpha K^{\alpha-1} L^{1-\alpha} = 0 \tag{4}$$

$$w - \lambda(1-\alpha)K^\alpha L^{-\alpha} = 0 \tag{5}$$

$$Y_0 = K^\alpha L^{1-\alpha} \tag{6}$$

Eliminating λ between (4) and (5), and using (6), we get the demand functions

$$K = Y_0 \left(\frac{\alpha}{1-\alpha} \frac{w}{q} \right)^{1-\alpha} \equiv K(Y_0; w, q) \tag{7}$$

---

[1] Note that the set of equations (1)–(3) plus the convexity of the Lagrangian ensures that we have a global minimum. On this see for example K. Sydsaeter and P. J. Hammond, *Mathematics for Economic Analysis*, Prentice Hall, Englewood Cliffs, N.J., 1995, p. 667.

and

$$L = Y_0 \left(\frac{\alpha}{1-\alpha} \frac{w}{q} \right)^{-\alpha} \equiv L(Y_0; w, q). \tag{8}$$

We note that both K and L are linear (positive) functions of Y_0 – therefore their ratio will be independent from Y_0. Also, the demand for K is a decreasing function of the rental price q and an increasing function of the wage rate w. The converse is true for L.

As to the capital–labour ratio, it is given by

$$\frac{K}{L} = \frac{\alpha}{1-\alpha} \frac{w}{q}, \tag{9}$$

a linear function of w/q.

1.1 Definition of the elasticity of substitution

The elasticity of substitution is the elasticity of the capital/labour ratio r with respect to the wage/capital rental ratio m.

The elasticity of substitution is denoted σ. It is then equal to:

$$\sigma = \frac{dr/r}{dm/m} = \frac{d \log r}{d \log m} \tag{10}$$

where $r \equiv K/L$ and $m \equiv w/q$.

Example: in the Cobb–Douglas case seen above, the relationship between r and m is linear (equation (9)). Hence $\sigma = 1$. Note that the Cobb–Douglas function has a unit elasticity of substitution even if it is not homogeneous of degree one: indeed, for the production function $Y = A K^\alpha L^\beta$ where $\alpha + \beta \neq 1$, the ratio of the factor demands would be

$$\frac{K}{L} = \frac{\alpha}{\beta} \frac{w}{q}, \tag{11}$$

also a linear function of $w/q = m$; as a consequence, the elasticity of substitution would also be equal to one in this more general case.

1.2 Geometrical representation

The elasticity of substitution has been defined as the following limit:

$$\sigma = \lim_{\Delta m \to 0} (\Delta r/r)/(\Delta m/m).$$

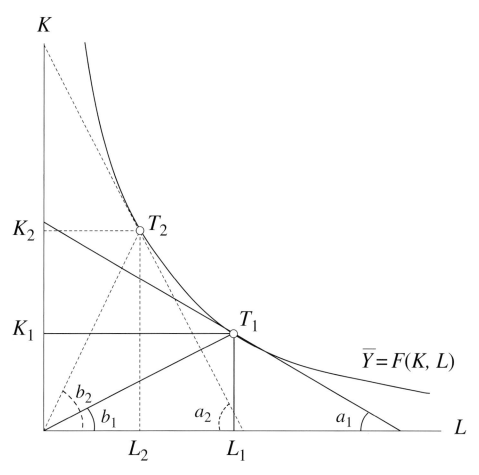

Figure 3.1 A geometrical interpretation of the elasticity of substitution. With $|dK/dL|_{Y=Y_0} = (\partial F/\partial L)/(\partial F/\partial K) = w/q = m = |\operatorname{tg} a|$ and $K/L = r = \operatorname{tg} b$, the elasticity of substitution σ is given by the limit:

$$\sigma = \lim_{\Delta m \to 0} \frac{\Delta r/r}{\Delta m/m} = \lim_{\Delta \operatorname{tg} a \to 0} \frac{\Delta \operatorname{tg} b/\operatorname{tg} b}{\Delta \operatorname{tg} a/\operatorname{tg} a}.$$

If the production function is Cobb–Douglas ($\sigma = 1$), then not only $dr/r = dm/m$, but $\Delta r/r = \Delta m/m$ in exact value.

From a geometrical point of view, we may consider the ratio $m = w/q$ as minus the slope[2] of the isoquant $\overline{Y} = F(K, L)$ (figure 3.1). We have:

$$\left. \frac{dK}{dL} \right|_{\overline{Y}=F(K,L)} = -\frac{\frac{\partial F}{\partial L}(K, L)}{\frac{\partial F}{\partial K}(K, L)} \tag{12}$$

---

[2] This slope in absolute value is often called the "marginal rate of substitution" between K and L.

and

$$-\frac{dK}{dL}\bigg|_{\overline{Y}=F(K,L)} = \frac{\frac{\partial F}{\partial L}(K,L)}{\frac{\partial F}{\partial K}(K,L)} = \frac{w}{q} \equiv m \qquad (13)$$

(by the minimization of cost process described earlier: from equations (1) and (2), eliminating λ). Geometrically, $m = \text{tg } a$ in figure 3.1. Also, $r = \text{tg } b$. Therefore, the ratio $(\Delta r/r)/(\Delta m/m)$ is the relative change of tg$b$ divided by the relative change in tg$a$, and the elasticity of substitution σ is the limit of this ratio when $\Delta m \to 0$. Notice that if the production function is Cobb–Douglas, the linear relationship between r and m as given by (9) or (11) implies that $\Delta r/\Delta m$ is independent of the size of Δm. Therefore, in that case σ is always exactly equal to $(\Delta r/r)/(\Delta m/m) = 1$, and $\Delta r/r = \Delta m/m$. This means that in the Cobb–Douglas case the relative increase of tg b is *exactly* equal to the relative increase in tg a, whatever the size of Δm.

It is important not to confuse the elasticity of substitution with the curvature of an isoquant. Both concepts are fundamentally different. Curvature of a curve in a plane is measured as follows: consider two points, A and B of the curve $h(x)$. The slope of the tangent line at A, θ, becomes $\theta + \Delta\theta$ at B, and the length of arc AB is Δs. The *average curvature* of arc AB is defined as the ratio $\Delta\theta/\Delta s$, and the *curvature at point A* is the limit of this ratio, it if exists, when $\Delta s \to 0$. So the curvature at A is $k = \lim_{\Delta s \to 0} \Delta\theta/\Delta s = d\theta/ds$, which can be determined as the ratio of the differentials $d\theta$ and ds, considering both θ and s as functions of x. We have $\theta = \arctan h'(x)$; thus $d\theta = [h''/(1+h'^2)]dx$; and $ds = (1+h'^2)^{1/2}dx$. So $k = d\theta/ds = h''/(1+h'^2)^{3/2}$. On the other hand, $\sigma = e_{h/x,h'} = \frac{d(h/x)}{dh'} \cdot \frac{h'}{h/x} = \frac{h'x-h}{h''x^2} \cdot \frac{h'}{h/x} = h'(xh'-h)/xhh''$, a completely different formula. It is not possible to compare one concept to the other because curvature is measured in radians per length unit, while σ is unitless. Two examples may illustrate how remote the two concepts are from each other: first, in the Cobb-Douglas case, the elasticity of substitution is constant at any point of any isoquant; but curvature tends to zero on any of those isoquants when $K \to \infty$ or $L \to \infty$. Secondly, an arc of circle exhibits constant curvature at all its points, whilst its elasticity of substitution is variable everywhere.[3]

1.3 Properties

We will now demonstrate three fundamental properties of the elasticity of substitution in the case where the production function is homogeneous of degree one:

---

[3] Sometimes curvature is defined not in the classical sense, but simply as the second derivative of the function, $h''(x)$. But this last concept, measured in h units/(x units)^2, cannot be compared to σ either, for the same reasons explained above. On this subject see La Grandville, "Curvature and the Elasticity of Substitution: Straightening it Out", *Journal of Economics*, Vol. 66, no. 1 (1997), pp. 23–34.

- the elasticity of substitution σ is positive if and only if the marginal product of capital is a decreasing function of capital;
- σ depends only on the capital-labour ratio r;
- σ is identically equal to the elasticity of income per person with respect to the wage rate; it is also equal to the elasticity of the average productivity of capital with respect to the rental price of capital.

1.3.1 If the production function is homogeneous of degree 1, the elasticity of substitution is positive if and only if the marginal product of capital is a decreasing function of capital

This property is so important that we will prove it in two different ways.

FIRST PROOF From Figure 1 note that $\sigma > 0$ if and only if the isoquant is strictly convex, implying $d^2K/dL^2 > 0$. Let us then determine this second derivative in the case of homogeneous of degree one production functions.

If $Y = F(K, L)$ is homogeneous of degree 1, we have

$$tY = F(tK, tL) \tag{14}$$

and we can replace t by $1/L$, yielding

$$\frac{Y}{L} \equiv y = F\left(\frac{K}{L}, 1\right) = f(r) \tag{15}$$

and

$$Y = Lf(r). \tag{16}$$

From (16) we determine the marginal productivities as functions of the sole variable r:

$$\boxed{\frac{\partial Y}{\partial L} = f(r) - rf'(r) = y - ry'} \tag{17}$$

$$\boxed{\frac{\partial Y}{\partial K} = f'(r) = y'} \tag{18}$$

So the slope of the isoquant is

$$\frac{dK}{dL} = -\frac{y - ry'}{y'} = r - \frac{y}{y'} = r - \frac{f(r)}{f'(r)} \tag{19}$$

and the second derivative is, after simplifications:

$$\frac{d^2K}{dL^2} = -\frac{K}{L^2}\left\{\frac{f(r)f''(r)}{[f'(r)]^2}\right\} \tag{20}$$

which is positive if and only if $f''(r)$ is negative. Now consider the second derivative $\partial^2 Y/\partial K^2$; from (18) we have:

$$\frac{\partial^2 Y}{\partial K^2} = f''(r) \left(\frac{1}{L} \right). \tag{21}$$

$f''(r)$ will be negative if and only if $\partial^2 Y/\partial K^2 < 0$, hence our result: σ is positive if and only if $d^2 K/dL^2$ is positive, implying $\partial^2 Y/\partial K^2 < 0$.

For homogeneous of degree one production functions, decreasing returns to capital thus constitute a necessary and sufficient condition to ensure that an increase in the wage-rental ratio will lead to an increase in the capital-labour ratio, or, equivalently, that there exists a function

$$r = r(m) \tag{22}$$

such that its derivative is positive.

SECOND PROOF   An alternative approach would be to say that there is an increasing function between m and r if and only if the derivative $m'(r)$ is strictly positive. We have, from (13), (17) and (18):

$$m = \frac{f(r) - rf'(r)}{f'(r)} = \frac{y - ry'}{y'} \tag{23}$$

and

$$m'(r) = -\frac{f(r)f''(r)}{[f'(r)]^2} = -\frac{yy''}{(y')^2} \tag{24}$$

which is positive if and only if $f''(r) < 0$, and $\partial^2 Y/\partial K^2 < 0$ as before.

1.3.2 If the production function is homogeneous of degree one, the elasticity of substitution depends solely upon the capital–labour ratio

PROOF   The value of the elasticity of substitution can be determined as the following function of the sole variable r. From (24), if $y'' < 0$, m is a (positive) monotonic function of r; it can therefore be inverted, and the derivative $r'(m)$ is just the inverse of $m'(r)$. We then have, using (24):

$$\sigma = \frac{dr/r}{dm/m} = \frac{dr}{dm} \cdot \frac{m}{r} = -\frac{(y')^2}{yy''} \cdot \frac{y - ry'}{ry'} = -\frac{y'(y - ry')}{ryy''}. \tag{25}$$

Note that property 1.3.2 is even more general, because it applies to any homogeneous function, irrespective of its degree of homogeneity (indeed, m is the ratio of marginal productivities; if the function is homogeneous of degree m, this ratio is homogeneous of degree zero; it depends solely on r).

1.3.3 If the production function is homogeneous of degree one, the elasticity of substitution is equal to the elasticity of income per person with respect to the wage rate

This property is known as "Allen's theorem", from R. G. D. Allen, a British mathematician and economist who discovered it in the thirties.

PROOF We have:

$$e_{y,w} \equiv \frac{dy}{dw} \cdot \frac{w}{y} = \frac{y'dr}{d(y-ry')} \cdot \frac{y-ry'}{y}. \tag{26}$$

The differential in the denominator is

$$d(y-ry') = [y'-(y'+ry'')]dr = -ry''dr \tag{27}$$

and therefore

$$e_{y,w} = -\frac{y'(y-ry')}{ryy''} = \sigma \tag{28}$$

(by (25)) and the theorem is proved.

Observe also that a corollary is intuitively motivated by the symmetrical roles played by L and w, on the one hand, and K and q on the other.

COROLLARY *If the production function is homogeneous of degree one, the elasticity of substitution is equal to the elasticity of income per unit of capital with respect to the rental rate.*

PROOF We have, by definition:

$$e_{Y/K,\,q} = \frac{\dfrac{d(Y/K)}{Y/K}}{\dfrac{dq}{q}}. \tag{29}$$

Y/K can be written as

$$\frac{Y}{K} = \frac{Y}{L}\frac{L}{K} = \frac{f(r)}{r} = \frac{y}{r};$$

so, with $q = \partial F/\partial K = y'$,

$$e_{Y/K,\,q} = \frac{\dfrac{d(y/r)}{y/r}}{\dfrac{dy'}{y'}} = \left(\frac{y'r-y}{r^2}\right)dr \cdot \frac{r}{y}\frac{y'}{y''dr}$$

$$= -\frac{(y-ry')y'}{ryy''} = \sigma \tag{30}$$

as before. Note that an alternative proof of this corollary would have been the following. Both variables K and L play symmetrical roles in the production function. Therefore what is true for the elasticity of the average product of one variable with respect to its marginal product must be true for the average product of the other variable with respect to its marginal product.

This corollary of Allen's theorem will turn out to be as important as the theorem itself, although it will play a very different role. It implies that if the elasticity of substitution is constant (by which we mean that it is constant at any point (K, L)), then there must be a power relationship between the average product of capital Y/K and the rental rate q of the form $Y/K = hq^\sigma$ where h is a constant. We will identify this constant in chapter 4 and apply this property in optimal growth theory, in chapter 13.

2   The links between the elasticity of substitution and income distribution

Suppose that we are interested in comparing the evolution of the capital's share in total income to that of labour. Consider the ratio

$$\frac{\text{share of capital}}{\text{share of labour}} = \frac{\text{capital's income}}{\text{labour's income}} = \frac{qK}{wL} = \frac{K/L}{w/q} = \frac{r}{m}, \tag{31}$$

which just turns out to be the capital/labour ratio divided by the marginal rate of substitution. We can see that the share of capital increases (relatively to that of labour) if and only if $dr/r > dm/m$, or equivalently if and only if $\sigma = (dr/r)/(dm/m) > 1$. It decreases if and only if $\sigma < 1$, and it remains constant if and only if $\sigma = 1$. We can note here that, historically, the prime motive of introducing the concept of elasticity of substitution was precisely the direct relationship between that concept and the evolution of income distribution.

There are two other ways of proving this fundamental property. They rest upon Allen's theorem and its corollary. Let us first use Allen's theorem. Call θ the share of labour's income in total income:

$$\theta = \frac{wL}{Y} = \frac{w}{Y/L} = \frac{w}{y}.$$

Suppose that w increases. The share of labour's income in total income will increase if and only if $dw/w > dy/y$, or, equivalently, if and only if $(dy/y)/(dw/w) = \sigma < 1$. It is also clear that it will stay constant, or decrease, if and only if $\sigma = 1$, or $\sigma > 1$, respectively. The same reasoning applies using the corollary to Allen's theorem (see exercise 2.2).

We had observed earlier that the Cobb–Douglas function implied constant shares for each factor, each equal to $(\partial Y/\partial K)K/Y = \alpha$ and $(\partial Y/\partial L)(L/Y) = 1 - \alpha$ respectively. This is of course confirmed by the observation that $\sigma = 1$ for the Cobb–Douglas. Now the following question arises: is this true in reality? Do we observe that the labour share is constant? If that were the case, we should have

$$\frac{wL}{Y} = \frac{w}{y} = 1 - \alpha = \frac{1}{a} \tag{32}$$

where a is a constant, or equivalently a *linear* relationship between y and w

$$y = aw. \tag{33}$$

In 1961, K. Arrow, H. Chenery, B. Minhas and R. Solow asked this very question. They observed that such a linear relationship between w and y was rejected empirically. Instead of scattering around a straight line through the origin in (y, w) space, observations tended to delineate a concave function. The authors tested a logarithmic relationship, and a power function. The power function

$$y = aw^b, \tag{34}$$

with $a > 0$ and $0 < b < 1$ turned out to give the best regression results and was therefore retained. The coefficient b equal to $(dy/y)/(dw/w)$, and therefore to the elasticity of substitution, was *observed* to be positive and *smaller* than one.

   This empirical observation was of considerable importance. It implied that there was a contradiction between production theory and the data on income distribution. One could not postulate the existence of a Cobb–Douglas production function – entailing constant factor shares in income – while observing an increase in labour's share. To reconcile production theory and empirical observation, one had to ask: what is the production function corresponding to the observed power relationship (34)? The answer is in our next section.

3 Determining the constant elasticity of substitution production function

The question that now arises is to determine the production function which is implied by the concave power function (34) between the wage rate and income per person. This is tantamount to asking what is the production function whose elasticity of substitution (the elasticity of income per person with respect to the wage rate) is constant and equal to b, with $b < 1$.

   We owe to Arrow, Chenery, Minhas and Solow (1961) the remarkable idea of replacing in (34) the wage rate by the marginal productivity of a production function homogeneous of degree one, equal as we know to $y - ry'$. The authors thus transformed (34) into the differential equation

$$y = a(y - ry')^b \tag{35}$$

which, if integrated, yields the production function with constant elasticity of substitution b.[4] To integrate (35), first write

$$a^{-\frac{1}{b}} y^{\frac{1}{b}} = y - ry';$$ (36)

then

$$r\frac{dy}{dr} = y(1 - a^{-\frac{1}{b}} y^{\frac{1}{b}-1}).$$ (37)

Before separating the variables, let us make a simplification in the notation. We will denote

$$a^{-\frac{1}{b}} \equiv \alpha$$ (38)

and

$$\frac{1}{b} - 1 \equiv \rho.$$ (39)

It is important to remark that *both* α and ρ are functions of b, the elasticity of substitution.

Equation (37) now reads:

$$r\frac{dy}{dr} = y(1 - \alpha y^{\rho}).$$ (40)

Separating the variables, we have

$$\frac{dr}{r} = \frac{dy}{y(1 - \alpha y^{\rho})}.$$ (41)

The right-hand side of (41) has the form of a fraction that can be expanded in the following way; denoting $dy \equiv A$, $y \equiv B$ and $1 - \alpha y^{\rho} \equiv C$, we have:

$$\frac{dy}{y(1 - \alpha y^{\rho})} \equiv \frac{A}{BC} = \frac{A}{B} + \frac{A(1 - C)}{BC} = \frac{dy}{y} + \frac{\alpha y^{\rho}}{y(1 - \alpha y^{\rho})} dy$$

$$= \frac{dy}{y} + \frac{\alpha y^{\rho-1}}{1 - \alpha y^{\rho}} dy.$$ (42)

---

[4] Note that an alternative method to find the constant elasticity of substitution production function would have been to integrate the differential equation

$$\sigma = -\frac{y'(y - ry')}{ryy''} = b.$$

This method, however, is more cumbersome because it implies solving a non-linear second-order differential equation. Each method, it may be noted, involves the identification of two integration constants, as we will see.

We can now integrate (41) as follows:

$$\int \frac{dr}{r} = \int \frac{dy}{y} + \int \frac{\alpha y^{\rho-1}}{1 - \alpha y^{\rho}} dy \qquad (43)$$

which yields

$$\ln r = \ln y - \frac{1}{\rho} \ln(1 - \alpha y^{\rho}) + \frac{1}{\rho} \ln \beta \qquad (44)$$

where we have chosen $\frac{1}{\rho} \ln \beta$ as our integration constant, for convenience – it will indeed simplify the final leg of the demonstration. Exponentiating (44) gives

$$r = y(1 - \alpha y^{\rho})^{-\frac{1}{\rho}} \beta^{\frac{1}{\rho}} \qquad (45)$$

or

$$\beta r^{-\rho} = y^{-\rho}(1 - \alpha y^{\rho}) = y^{-\rho} - \alpha. \qquad (46)$$

Finally we obtain income (or output) per person as a function of r:

$$y = (\beta r^{-\rho} + \alpha)^{-\frac{1}{\rho}} \qquad (47)$$

from which the production function can be derived. Equation (47) corresponds to

$$\frac{Y}{L} = \left[\beta \left(\frac{K}{L} \right)^{-\rho} + \alpha \right]^{-\frac{1}{\rho}}, \qquad (48)$$

and this leads to

$$Y = \left[\beta K^{-\rho} + \alpha L^{-\rho} \right]^{-\frac{1}{\rho}} \qquad (49)$$

which is the celebrated "constant elasticity of substitution" – or CES – production function.

Before going further, it is important to identify the constants α and β in (49).

3.1 Identifying constant α

First, recall that α has been set equal to $a^{-1/b}$ (equation (38)). We know what b is (it is the elasticity of substitution σ). But what is a? It is a constant in the regression equation $y = aw^b$, which in turn is the most general solution of the differential equation

$$\frac{dy}{y} \bigg/ \frac{dw}{w} = b. \qquad (50)$$

So a is in fact an integration constant that may be identified as follows.

Suppose that at a given point of time (denoted $t = 0$ for instance), we can measure the capital stock K_0, the quantity of labour L_0, the level of output or income Y_0, and the factor rental prices of capital and labour, q_0 and w_0 respectively. Then we have, using (34):

$$y_0 = a w_0^b \tag{51}$$

and

$$a = y_0 w_0^{-b}. \tag{52}$$

Equation (34) now becomes

$$y = y_0 \left(\frac{w}{w_0} \right)^b. \tag{53}$$

We are now in a position to identify α. We have, from (38) and (52):

$$\alpha = a^{-1/\sigma} = (y_0 w_0^{-\sigma})^{-1/\sigma} = y_0^{-1/\sigma} w_0$$

$$= \left(\frac{Y_0}{L_0} \right)^{-\rho-1} w_0 = \left(\frac{Y_0}{L_0} \right)^{-\rho} \frac{w_0 L_0}{Y_0}. \tag{54}$$

where we used the fact that $\rho = 1/\sigma - 1$.

3.2 Identifying constant β

There only remains to identify the constant of integration β. With $Y_0 = F(K_0, L_0)$, we have:

$$Y_0 = \left[\beta K_0^{-\rho} + \alpha L_0^{-\rho} \right]^{-1/\rho} = \left[\beta K_0^{-\rho} + Y_0^{-\rho} \frac{w_0 L_0}{Y_0} \right]^{-1/\rho}.$$

Raising both sides to the power $-\rho$ and simplifying yields

$$\beta = \left(\frac{Y_0}{K_0} \right)^{-\rho} \left(1 - \frac{w_0 L_0}{Y_0} \right) = \left(\frac{Y_0}{K_0} \right)^{-\rho} \pi_0 \tag{55}$$

where π_0 denotes the capital share in total income at time 0. Plugging (54) and (55) into (49) yields

$$\boxed{Y = Y_0 \left[\pi_0 \left(\frac{K}{K_0} \right)^{-\rho} + (1 - \pi_0) \left(\frac{L}{L_0} \right)^{-\rho} \right]^{-1/\rho}.} \tag{56}$$

which is the constant elasticity of substitution (CES) production function. We will turn to the properties of this important function in our next chapter.

Exercises

3.1 Suppose that you observe a linear relationship between the wage rate and income per person. What would be the corresponding production function?

(Hint: in the linear relationship $y = aw$, replace the wage rate by the marginal productivity of labour $w = y - ry'$, and integrate the corresponding differential equation; also, identify the constant of integration by setting $y(r_0) = y_0$.)

3.2 Can you find another way of demonstrating the corollary of Allen's theorem? (Hint: you know that $w = y - ry' = f(r) - rf'(r)$. If $f''(r) < 0$, w is an increasing function of r and you can determine its reciprocal $r = r(w)$ in the CES case. Replace this value into $y = f(r)$ to determine $y(w)$, and take the elasticity of y with respect to w.

3.3 Can you find another way of proving Allen's theorem?

3.4 Using Allen's corollary, show that capital's share increases (decreases, stays constant) with r if and only if the elasticity of substitution is larger than one (smaller than one, equal to one respectively).

Answers

3.1 First, observe from $y = aw$ that $a = y/w > 1$; note also that $1/a = w/y = wL/Y$ is the labour's share in total income). Then integrate the differential equation

$$y = a(y - ry')$$

by separating the variables:

$$y(1 - a) = -ar\frac{dy}{y}.$$

This leads to

$$\int \frac{dy}{y} = \frac{a - 1}{a} \int \frac{dr}{r},$$

which gives

$$\ln y = \frac{a - 1}{a} \ln r + \ln C$$

(where C is a constant of integration) and therefore

$$y = Cr^{\frac{a-1}{a}}.$$

Identifying the constant of integration, we may write $y(r_0) = y_0$; then

$$y_0 = Cr_0^{\frac{a-1}{a}}$$

or

$$C = y_0 r_0^{\frac{1-a}{a}}.$$

Hence

$$y = y_0 \left(\frac{r}{r_0} \right)^{1-\frac{1}{a}}.$$

Replacing y, r and r_0 by Y/L, K/L and K_0/L_0 respectively, we finally find the Cobb–Douglas function

$$Y = Y_0 \left(\frac{K}{K_0} \right)^{1-\frac{1}{a}} \left(\frac{L}{L_0} \right)^{\frac{1}{a}},$$

which is consistent with what we have seen in chapter 1; it is homogeneous of degree 1 (the powers of K and L add up to one), and each of those powers are the shares of the factors in total income ($1/a$ for L, $1 - 1/a$ for K).

3.2 Using the CES function, there is another way of proving that the elasticity of substitution is equal to the elasticity of income per unit of capital, with respect to the rental rate of capital. Consider output (or income) per person

$$y = f(r) = [\delta r^p + (1 - \delta)]^{1/p}. \tag{1}$$

We know that the marginal productivity of capital, $\partial F/\partial K$, is equal to $y'(r)$ and that $q = y'(r)$ is a decreasing function of r; so we can determine its reciprocal function $r = r(q)$, insert it into the above expression, divide it by r to obtain $y/r = Y/K$, and determine the elasticity of Y/K (or y/r) with respect to q.

We have

$$y'(r) = [\delta r^p + (1 - \delta)]^{\frac{1}{p}-1} \delta r^{p-1}$$

$$= [\delta r^p + (1 - \delta)]^{\frac{1-p}{p}} \delta r^{\frac{1-p}{p} \cdot (-p)}$$

$$= [\delta + (1 - \delta)r^{-p}]^{\frac{1-p}{p}} \delta = q, \tag{2}$$

from which we determine r as a function of q:

$$r = \left[\frac{1 - \delta}{\left(\frac{q}{\delta} \right)^{\frac{p}{1-p}} - \delta} \right]^{1/p}. \tag{3}$$

Replacing the value of r as a function of q into $y = f(r)$ gives

$$y = \left\{ \delta \left[\frac{1-\delta}{\left(\frac{q}{\delta}\right)^{\frac{p}{1-p}} - \delta} \right] + 1 - \delta \right\}^{1/p}. \tag{4}$$

Dividing by r leads, after simplifications, to:

$$\frac{Y}{K} = \frac{Y/L}{K/L} = \frac{y}{r} = \left(\frac{q}{\delta}\right)^{\frac{1}{1-p}} = \left(\frac{q}{\delta}\right)^{\sigma} \tag{5}$$

and we can see immediately from this expression that the elasticity of Y/K with respect to q is σ.

3.3 A similar argument may have been carried out by determining r as a function of σ from $w = y - ry'$. Symmetry shows that we would have obtained

$$\frac{Y}{L} = y = \left(\frac{w}{1-\delta}\right)^{\sigma} \tag{6}$$

from which Allen's theorem can be deduced. Note finally that those last two equations (5) and (6), are consistent with the very definition of the elasticity of substitution. Indeed, eliminating y between (5) and (6) yields

$$r\left(\frac{q}{\delta}\right)^{\sigma} = \left(\frac{w}{1-\delta}\right)^{\sigma}, \tag{7}$$

from which we deduce

$$r = \left(\frac{\delta}{1-\delta}\right)^{\sigma} \left(\frac{w}{q}\right)^{\sigma}. \tag{8}$$

This corresponds to equation (10); σ is indeed the elasticity of r with respect to w/q.

3.4 The share of capital is

$$1 - \theta = \frac{qK}{Y} = \frac{\partial F}{\partial K} \frac{K}{Y} = y' \frac{K/L}{Y/L} = \frac{y'r}{y}.$$

This share increases with r if and only if $d(1-\theta)/\partial r > 0$; we have:

$$\frac{d(1-\theta)}{dr} = \frac{ryy'' + y'(y - ry')}{y^2}, \text{ which is positive}$$

if and only if $y'(y - ry') > -ryy''$; since $y'' < 0$, this is equivalent to

$$\sigma = -\frac{y'(y - ry')}{ryy''} > 1,$$

which was to be shown.

CHAPTER 4

The CES production function as a general mean

The discoverers of the CES production function, K. Arrow, H. Chenery, B. Minhas and R. Solow had observed that it was a linear transformation of a general mean of order $-\rho$. It turns out that income per person, the central variable of economic growth theory, is also a general mean. Its properties will prove to be of great importance. In this chapter, we will first recall the definition of a general mean and its main properties. We will then examine how they apply directly to the CES function and the resulting income per person.

From chapter 3, we know that $-\rho = 1 - 1/\sigma$. To simplify notation, we will denote $-\rho = p$. We thus have

$$p = 1 - \frac{1}{\sigma} \tag{1}$$

where p, the order of the general mean, is an increasing function of σ. We thus have between σ and p a positive correspondence to which we will often refer. It is also very useful to visualize this relationship (see figure 4.1). Notice that in the vicinity of $\sigma = 1$, the linear approximation of p is $\sigma - 1$ i.e. a straight line with slope equal to $+1$. We will use this observation later. Table 4.1 gives the correspondence between σ and p for some important values of σ.

Total income, expressed as the index number Y/Y_0, is a general mean of order $p = 1 - 1/\sigma$ of the indices K/K_0 and L/L_0:

$$\frac{Y}{Y_0} = \left[\pi_0 \left(\frac{K}{K_0} \right)^p + (1 - \pi_0) \left(\frac{L}{L_0} \right)^p \right]^{\frac{1}{p}}. \tag{2}$$

Consider now income per person expressed as the index y/y_0; it is also a general mean. Indeed, it is the mean of order p of the index r/r_0 and 1:

$$\frac{Y/L}{Y_0/L_0} = \frac{y}{y_0} = \left[\pi_0 \left(\frac{r}{r_0} \right)^p + (1 - \pi_0) \right]^{\frac{1}{p}} \tag{3}$$

where $r = K/L$ and $r_0 = K_0/L_0$.

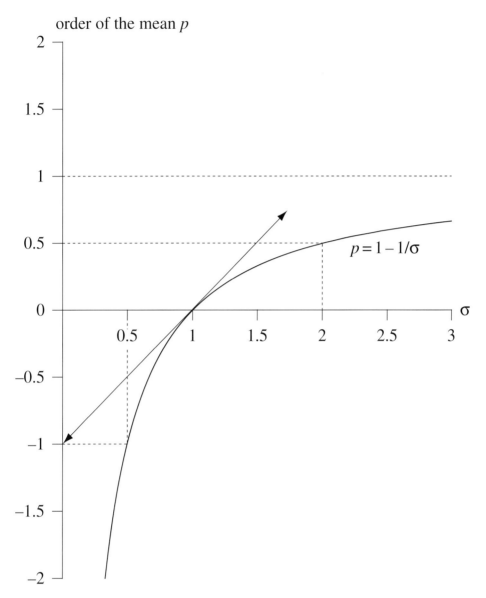

Figure 4.1 **The relationship between the order of the mean** p **and the elasticity of substitution** σ. **In the neighbourhood of** $\sigma = 1$, p **behaves in linear approximation like** σ. **At** $\sigma = 1$, **the order of the mean is zero; the mean of order zero is the geometric mean and the production function becomes Cobb–Douglas. When** $\sigma \to 0$, $p \to -\infty$; **the mean tends toward** $\min(K/K_0, L/L_0)$ – **the Walras–Leontieff production function. If** $\sigma \to \infty$, $p \to 1$ **and the mean becomes the arithmetic average of** K/K_0 **and** L/L_0; **the production function becomes linear.**

Table 4.1   Relationship between the elasticity of substitution σ and the order of the mean $p = 1 - 1/\sigma$

Elasticity of substitution σ	Order of the mean p
0	$-\infty$
1	0
∞	1

I   The concept of the general mean of order p, and its fundamental properties

The familiar arithmetic, geometric and harmonic means are just particular cases of the "general mean of order p", defined as follows.

1.1   Definition

Let $x_1, \ldots, x_n$ be positive numbers; let $f_1, \ldots, f_n$ be positive numbers adding up to 1. We call f_i "weights". The mean of order p of $x_1, \ldots, x_n$ is defined by

$$M(p) = \left[\sum_{i=1}^{n} f_i x_i^{p} \right]^{1/p}. \tag{4}$$

1.2   Important particular cases

It can be easily seen that the means of order 1 and -1 are the arithmetic and the harmonic means, respectively. We have

$$M(1) = \sum_{i=1}^{n} f_i x_i, \tag{5}$$

the arithmetic mean of the x_i's, and

$$M(-1) = \left[\sum_{i=1}^{n} f_i x_i^{-1} \right]^{-1}, \tag{6}$$

the harmonic mean of the x_i's.

In order to show that the mean of order 0 is the geometric mean, first take the logarithm of (4):

$$\log M(p) = \frac{1}{p} \log \left(\sum_{i=1}^{n} f_i x_i^{p} \right). \tag{7}$$

When $p \to 0$, the ratio $(0/0)$ can be determined by applying L'Hospital's rule. We get:

$$\lim_{p \to 0} \log M(p) = \lim_{p \to 0} \frac{\sum\limits_{i=1}^{n} f_i x_i^p \log x_i}{\sum\limits_{i=1}^{n} f_i x_i^p} = \sum_{i=1}^{n} f_i \log x_i \qquad (8)$$

so that

$$\log M(0) = \sum_{i=1}^{n} f_i \log x_i \qquad (9)$$

and thus

$$M(0) = \prod_{i=1}^{n} x_i^{f_i}, \qquad (10)$$

the geometric mean of the x_i's, with f_i as weights.

Other limits are of interest. First, the mean of order $-\infty$ is the minimum (the smallest number) of $(x_1, \ldots, x_n)$. This can be seen as follows: let x_1 be the smallest of numbers $x_1, \ldots, x_n$. We can write, factoring x_1^p in (4):

$$M(p) = x_1 \left[f_1 + f_2 \left(\frac{x_2}{x_1} \right)^p + \cdots + f_n \left(\frac{x_n}{x_1} \right)^p \right]^{1/p}$$

$$= x_1 \left[f_1 + f_2 \left(\frac{x_1}{x_2} \right)^{-p} + \cdots + f_n \left(\frac{x_1}{x_n} \right)^{-p} \right]^{1/p}. \qquad (11)$$

When p tends to $-\infty$, $-p$ tends to $+\infty$ and $1/p$ tends to zero. Each term $(x_1/x_i)^{-p}$ tends to zero, and the bracketed term to the power $1/p$ tends to one. Thus the mean of order $-\infty$ is

$$M(-\infty) = x_1 = \min(x_1, \ldots, x_n). \qquad (12)$$

Using a similar method (factoring x_n^p if x_n is the largest of the numbers $x_1, \ldots, x_n$) it can be shown that the mean of order $+\infty$ is the maximum, or the largest number among $x_1, \ldots, x_n$.

Suppose that

$$x_n = \max(x_1, \ldots, x_n).$$

Then, factoring x_n^p in (4):

$$M(p) = x_n \left[f_1 \left(\frac{x_1}{x_n} \right)^p + \cdots + f_n \right]^{1/p}.$$

When $p \to +\infty$, the bracketed term to the power $1/p$ tends to one, so we have

$$M(+\infty) = x_n = \max(x_1, \ldots, x_n).$$

1.3   The fundamental property of general means

The reader may remember from his high-school days that the harmonic, geometric and arithmetic means are in increasing order. In fact, this results from the following fundamental property: the general mean is an increasing function of its order p. The classical demonstration of this property is quite involved (see Hardy, Little, and Polya (1952)); it builds upon successive discoveries that go back to Halley, Newton and Cauchy. I owe to Robert Solow a simple, analytic proof; it can be found in the appendix of this chapter.

The importance of this property for our subject is that in the CES production function the order of the mean (p) is an increasing function of the elasticity of substitution ($p = 1 - 1/\sigma$). Therefore it can be immediately seen that, for any K, L and any given value of the parameters of the production function, income as well as income per person are increasing functions of the elasticity of substitution.

The importance of this property is compounded by the following observation: the slope of the mean of order p when $n = 2$ goes through one and only one maximum. In other words, the general mean of any two numbers, considered as a function $M(p)$, has one and only one point of inflection. We have not been able to prove this property due to the extreme complexity of the second derivative of (4). However, we have relied on numerical calculations to come to this conclusion.[1]

The importance of the fact that the $M(p)$ curve has one and only one inflection point is the following: the inflection point of $M(p)$ is very close to the origin for weights such as 0.3 and 0.7, values that are typical of a CES production function. Now $p = 0$ corresponds to $\sigma = 1$ (because $p = 1 - 1/\sigma$); this implies that a change in σ (which may be in the vicinity of $\sigma = 1$) has a considerable impact upon income and income per person.

Figure 4.2 illustrates the general mean of 1 and 4 with equal weights (the harmonic, geometric and arithmetic means are 1.6; 2 and 2.5 respectively; these correspond to points H, G and A in figure 4.2).

2   Applications to the CES production function

We can now derive easily the particular cases of the CES production function when σ takes the values 0, 1 and $+\infty$.

---

[1] On this see O. de La Grandville and R. Solow, "A Conjecture on General Means", *Journal of Inequalities in Pure and Applied Mathematics*, Vol. 7, no. 1, 2006.

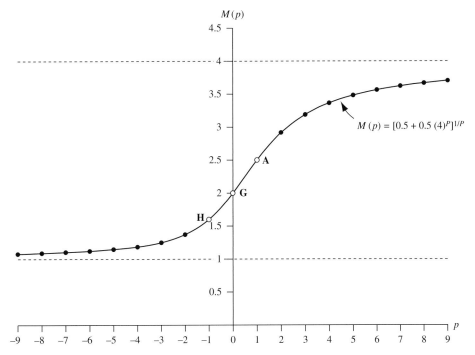

Figure 4.2 **The general mean of 1 and 4 with weights $1/2$ and $1/2$ as a function of its order. Special cases are the following: the harmonic mean is the mean of order -1; $M(-1) = [0.5(1)^{-1} + 0.5(4)^{-1}]^{-1} = 8/5 = 1.6$ (point H); the geometric is $M(0) = 1^{1/2} \cdot 4^{1/2} = 2$ (point G); the arithmetic is $(1 + 4)/2 = 2.5$ (point A). The mean of order $-\infty$ is $\min(1, 4) = 1$; the mean of order $+\infty$ is $\max(1, 4) = 4$.**

First, if $\sigma = 0$, $p \to -\infty$. From the properties of the general mean we just saw, we know that Y/Y_0 is then $\min\left(K/K_0, L/L_0\right)$, which is represented by the corner of a pyramid made by the minimum of the two planes K/K_0 and L/L_0 (figure 4.3). The planes intersect along an edge whose projection on the horizontal plane is given by

$$\frac{K}{K_0} = \frac{L}{L_0} \tag{13}$$

or the ray through the origin

$$K = \frac{K_0}{L_0} L. \tag{14}$$

If $\sigma = 1$, $p = 0$. Then Y/Y_0 becomes the geometric mean, and we get

$$\frac{Y}{Y_0} = \left(\frac{K}{K_0}\right)^{\delta} \left(\frac{L}{L_0}\right)^{1-\delta}, \tag{15}$$

the Cobb–Douglas function, where δ denotes $\pi_0 = 1 - w_0 L_0/Y_0$, i.e. the capital share at time 0.

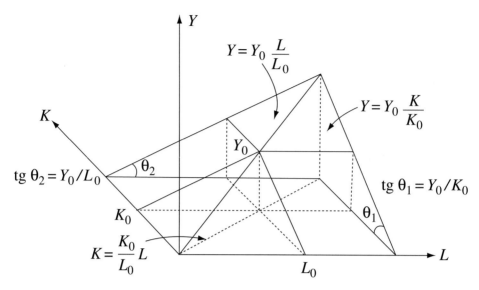

Figure 4.3   The Walras–Leontief production function

$$Y = Y_0 \min \left(\frac{K}{K_0}, \frac{L}{L_0} \right).$$

If $\sigma \to +\infty$, $p \to 1$ and the production function becomes the arithmetic mean, or the linear function

$$\frac{Y}{Y_0} = \delta \frac{K}{K_0} + (1 - \delta) \frac{L}{L_0}. \tag{16}$$

The following table summarizes these special cases.

Table 4.2   *The special cases of the CES production function*
$$Y = Y_0 [\delta(K/K_0)^p + (1 - \delta)(L/L_0)^p]^{1/p}$$

σ	$p = 1 - \dfrac{1}{\sigma}$	Production function	Type
0	$-\infty$	$Y = Y_0 \min \left(\dfrac{K}{K_0}, \dfrac{L}{L_0} \right)$	Walras-Leontief
1	0	$Y = Y_0 \left(\dfrac{K}{K_0} \right)^{\delta} \left(\dfrac{L}{L_0} \right)^{1-\delta}$	Cobb-Douglas
∞	1	$Y = Y_0 \left[\delta \dfrac{K}{K_0} + (1 - \delta) \dfrac{L}{L_0} \right]$	Linear function

3 The qualitative behaviour of the CES function as σ changes

We have seen in the preceding section that both the CES production function Y and the corresponding income per person function y were general means of order $p = 1 - 1/\sigma$, and therefore increasing functions of σ for any given (K, L). It is now useful to see how the function behaves when σ changes. In order to show that the whole surface opens up around a ray from the origin when σ increases from 0 to ∞, we first concentrate on the isoquants[2]

$$\overline{Y} = F_\sigma(K, L) = [\delta K^p + (1 - \delta)L^p]^{1/p}.$$

3.1 The opening up of the surface $F_\sigma(K, L)$ when σ increases

Suppose we study the family of isoquants such that $\overline{Y} = 1$. Their equation in implicit form is

$$1 = [\delta K^p + (1 - \delta)L^p]^{1/p}; \tag{17}$$

in explicit form, it is:

$$K = \left[\frac{1 - (1 - \delta)L^p}{\delta}\right]^{1/p}. \tag{18}$$

All those isoquants pass through the fixed point $(K, L) = (1, 1)$. At that point, they have a common tangent. Indeed, the slope of any isoquant at point (K, L) is given by

$$\frac{dK}{dL} = -\frac{1 - \delta}{\delta}\left(\frac{K}{L}\right)^{1-p} = -\frac{1 - \delta}{\delta}\left(\frac{K}{L}\right)^{\frac{1}{\sigma}}, \tag{19}$$

(for $\sigma > 0$) and at point $(K, L) = (1, 1)$ – or, more generally, along the ray $K = L$ – they have a common slope equal to $-(1 - \delta)/\delta$. In the example that follows, we choose $\delta = 1/3$, so the common slope is -2 (figure 4.4).

Let us first take up the three limiting cases $\sigma = +\infty$, $\sigma = 0$ and $\sigma = 1$.

- if $\sigma = +\infty$ (and $p = 1$), the CES function is the linear function

$$Y = \delta K + (1 - \delta)L \tag{20}$$

and with $Y = 1$ the isoquant is the affine function

$$K = \frac{1}{\delta}[1 - (1 - \delta)L] \tag{21}$$

---

[2] In what follows, Y, K and L always designate the indices Y/Y_0, K/K_0 and L/L_0 respectively. We will always take $Y_0 = 1$, $K_0 = 1$ and $L_0 = 1$.

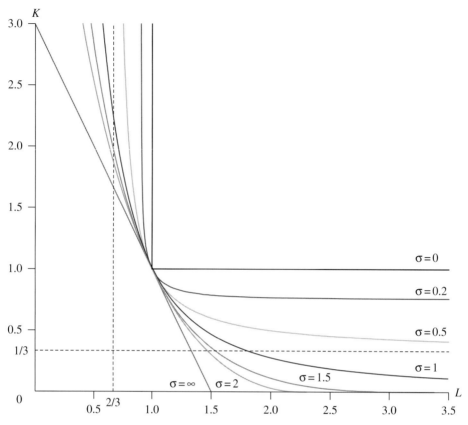

Figure 4.4 **Isoquants of the CES production function. For $0 < \sigma \le 1$, the isoquants are asymptotical to positive, finite values. For $\sigma = 1$, the asymptotes become the (K, L) axes. For $\sigma > 1$, the isoquants cut the axes. For $\sigma \to +\infty$, the isoquants tend to the straight line $K = \left(\frac{\delta - 1}{\delta}\right) L + \frac{1}{\delta}$ ($K = -2L + 3$ in this case).**

which is represented in figure 4.3 as the straight line with slope $-(1 - \delta)/\delta = -2$ and an ordinate at the origin $1/\delta = +3$.

- if $\sigma = 0$, we know from the previous section that the production function is

$$Y = \min(K, L),$$

represented in (Y, K, L) space by the corner of a pyramid. The isoquant corresponding to $Y = 1$ is L-shaped: this is the projection on the (K, L) place of a horizontal section of the corner of the pyramid at height $Y = 1$. It is therefore the right-angled corner represented in figure 4.4.

- if $\sigma = 1$, the production function becomes the Cobb–Douglas $Y = K^{\delta}L^{1-\delta}$. The isoquant for $Y = 1$ is therefore

$$1 = K^{\delta}L^{1-\delta} \tag{22}$$

or, in explicit form:

$$K = L^{\frac{\delta - 1}{\delta}}. \tag{23}$$

In our case (where $\delta = 1/3$), the isoquant is the power function $K = L^{-2}$ (see figure 4.4).

Let us now show that all isoquants are strictly convex (for $\sigma \in (0, \infty)$) and are located in decreasing order between the right-angled isoquant ($\sigma = 0$) and the straight line ($\sigma \to +\infty$).

The strict convexity is immediate: from (19), the second derivative is[3]

$$\frac{d^2 K}{dL^2} = -\frac{1}{\sigma} \left(\frac{1 - \delta}{\delta} \right) \left(\frac{K}{L} \right)^{\frac{1}{\sigma} - 1} \cdot \left(-\frac{K}{L^2} \right) > 0.$$

The fact that all isoquants are located in reverse order between the straight line and the right-angled isoquant rests on the fundamental property of general means, according to which the mean is an increasing function of its order. Consider any given value of L different from 1, for instance the value L_1. To L_1 is associated a given K_1 on an isoquant corresponding to an elasticity of substitution σ_1. Consider now another isoquant with a *higher* elasticity of substitution, $\sigma_2 (\sigma_2 > \sigma_1)$, and let us determine the amount K_2 that would correspond to that isoquant. We know that our mean has to remain equal to one. We know also that the order of the mean, p_1, has increased (because $p = 1 - 1/\sigma$ is an increasing function of σ); so the new value of K, K_2, must be *lower* than K_1. Hence the isoquant corresponding to σ_2 will be lower than the initial isoquant.

We can now easily picture how the whole surface $F_\sigma(K, L)$ opens up around the ray from the origin in space (Y, K, L) when σ increases from 0 to infinity.

---

[3] An alternative proof would have been the following. We know from chapter 3 that the isoquants of a homogeneous of degree one production function (our case) are convex if and only if $\partial^2 F / \partial K^2 < 0$ or, equivalently, if and only if $f''(r) < 0$ (because $\partial^2 F / \partial K^2 = (1/L) f''(r)$ – see equation (21) in chapter 3). Let us then determine $f''(r)$ in the case of the CES production function. We have

$$\frac{Y}{L} = f(r) = [\delta r^p + (1 - \delta)]^{1/p}$$

and, after simplifications,

$$f'(r) = \delta [\delta + (1 - \delta) r^{-p}]^{\frac{1}{p} - 1}.$$

Therefore, the second derivative is

$$f''(r) = \delta (1 - \delta)(p - 1)[\delta + (1 - \delta) r^{-p}]^{\frac{1}{p} - 2} r^{-p - 1}.$$

The term $p - 1$ is equal to $-1/\sigma$ and is always negative; therefore we have everywhere $f''(r) < 0$ and $d^2 K / dL^2 < 0$.

It is interesting to show at this point a property which is far from obvious, and which does not seem to be well known: for an elasticity of substitution between 0 and 1 the isoquant becomes asymptotical to a horizontal line $\bar{K} = \delta^{-1/p} = \delta^{\sigma/(1-\sigma)}$, and to a vertical of abscissa $\bar{L} = (1 - \delta)^{-1/p} = (1 - \delta)^{\sigma/(1-\sigma)}$.

Consider the equation of the isoquant (18). If $0 < \sigma < 1$, then $p < 0$. Let us evaluate the limit of K when $L \to \infty$. It is equal to $\lim_{L \to \infty} K \equiv \bar{K} = \delta^{-1/p}$. For instance, if $\sigma = 1/2$ ($p = -1$) and $\delta = 1/3$, this limit is $\bar{K} = \delta = 1/3$.

Since K and L play identical roles, we can also express the limit of L when $K \to \infty$ as $\bar{L}$, equal to $\lim_{K \to \infty} L = \bar{L} = (1 - \delta)^{-1/p}$. In the example just considered, this limit is $\bar{L} = 1 - \delta = 2/3$: figure 4.4 presents these asymptotes, as well as the isoquant in this case.

More generally, let us consider all possible values of $\bar{K}$ and $\bar{L}$ for $0 < \sigma < 1$ and the various values of δ (we will choose $\delta = 0.25; 0.3; 1/3$ and 0.4). The results are in diagrams 4.5a and 4.5b. Notice that as σ approaches 1, the $\bar{K}$ asymptote approaches 0 much quicker than $\bar{L}$ does. For instance, for $\delta = 1/3$ as before and for $\sigma = 0.8$, $\bar{K} = 0.012$, but $\bar{L}$ is still very much a positive value (0.2).

The isoquant is thus asymptotical to perpendicular axes intersecting at point $(\bar{K}, \bar{L})$ depending parametrically upon (σ, δ) through the system

$$\bar{K} = \bar{K}(\sigma, \delta) = \delta^{\sigma/(1-\sigma)}$$
$$\bar{L} = \bar{L}(\sigma, \delta) = (1 - \delta)^{\sigma/(1-\sigma)}$$

In space (K, L), for any given value δ, that point describes a curve $\varphi_\delta(\bar{L})$, which can be expressed explicitly as

$$\bar{K} = \varphi_\delta(\bar{L}) = \bar{L}^{\log \delta / \log(1-\delta)},$$

a strictly convex curve if and only if $\delta < 1/2$ (the usual case); it becomes the straight line $\bar{K} = \bar{L}$ if and only if $\delta = 1/2$.

This curve has been drawn in figure 4.5c for $\delta = 1/3$ and for values of σ ranging from 1 (lower point of the curve) to 0 (higher point), by steps of 0.1; the curve is $\bar{K} = \bar{L}^{\log 0.3 / \log 0.7} \approx \bar{L}^{3.38}$. All curves of the family $\varphi_\delta(\bar{L})$ increase from the origin $(0, 0)$ (the Cobb–Douglas case, with $\sigma = 1$) to $(1, 1)$ (the Walras–Leontief case, $\sigma = 0$).

If the production function is written in the normalized form $Y = Y_0 [\delta (K/K_0)^P + (1 - \delta) (L/L_0)^P]^{1/P}$, and if we consider the family of isoquants leading to output Y_0, the curve $\varphi_\delta(\bar{L})$ giving the minimum amounts of K and L necessary to produce Y_0 is expressed by the system

$$\bar{K} = K_0 \delta^{\sigma/(1-\sigma)}$$
$$\bar{L} = L_0(1 - \delta)^{\sigma/(1-\sigma)}$$

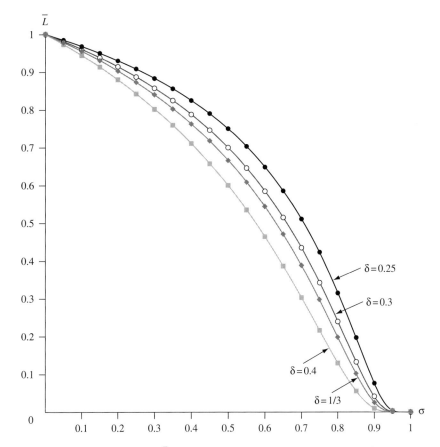

Figure 4.5a   The asymptote $\bar{L}$ as a function of σ, for various values of δ.

and, explicitly, by

$$\bar{K} = \frac{K_0}{L_0} \bar{L}^{\log \delta / \log(1-\delta)}.$$

This curve $\bar{K} = \varphi_\delta(\bar{L})$ of all points $(\bar{K}, \bar{L})$ is a linear rescaling of the former one, with point (K_0, L_0) now replacing point $(1, 1)$.

Notice the behaviour of the point $(\bar{K}, \bar{L})$ as σ tends toward one: both minimal amounts of capital and labour necessary to produce any given amount of output decrease and tend toward zero. This confirms the efficiency character of the elasticity of substitution. Observe also that the convexity of the curve φ_δ implies the property we noted before: the component $\bar{K}$ decreases toward zero much faster than $\bar{L}$. It means that, as long as $\delta < 1/2$ (the usual case) an economy governed by a CES function with $0 < \sigma < 1$ is definitely less demanding in the minimum amount of capital (relative to what it would be if $\sigma = 0$) than it is in terms of the minimum requirements of labour – which makes a lot of sense.

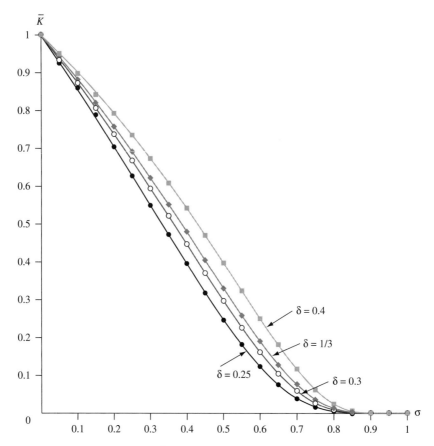

Figure 4.5b The asymptote $\bar{K}$ as a function of σ, for various values of δ.

One conclusion emerges: the fact that whenever σ is smaller than one the isoquants are asymptotic to positive numbers reveals that the elasticity of substitution is an efficiency parameter: the lower its value, the higher the minimal values of K and L requested to produce anything.

We conclude from this analysis of the isoquants that when σ increases from 0 to $+\infty$ (when p increases from $-\infty$ to $+1$), the surface – denoted $F_\sigma(K, L)$ – opens up from the corner of the pyramid $\min(K, L)$ to the plane $Y = \delta K + (1 - \delta)L$. It does so around a ray from the origin whose projection on the horizontal plane is $K = L$. For any point (K, L) not belonging to that ray, the height of the surface increases. This is just the geometric interpretation of the fundamental property of a general mean: the general mean of K and L increases with its order; and the mean is not sensitive to its order if and only if the numbers are the same (if and only if we are on the ray $K = L$).

The fact that the surface $F_\sigma(K, L)$ opens up when σ increases gives an inkling of a property that will turn out to be of central importance in growth theory: any *vertical* section of the surface will also open up; from a kinked line it will become

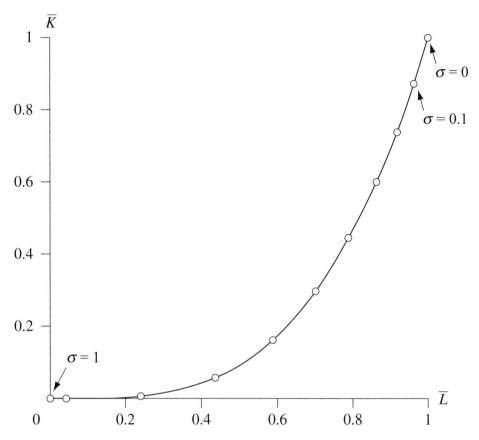

Figure 4.5c **Origins of asymptote axes systems for values of sigma between 1 and 0, by decreasing steps of 0.1 (delta = 0.3).**

a concave curve, and finally a straight line. For instance, at $L = 1$, the vertical section of the surface is given by $F(K, 1)$; it goes from the kinked line $\min(K, 1)$ to the straight line $\delta K + 1 - \delta$. Why is this significant? Because we know from chapter 2 that if $F(K, L)$ is homogeneous of degree one, the section $F(K, 1)$ is nothing else than $F(K/L, 1) = f(r)$, income per person. We are then prompted to have a close look at the section $y = F(K, 1)$.

3.2 Income per person as a function of r

Income per person, denoted $f_\sigma(r)$, is

$$y = f_\sigma(r) = [\delta r^p + (1 - \delta)]^{1/p} = [\delta r^{1-1/\sigma} + (1 - \delta)]^{\sigma/(\sigma-1)}. \quad (24)$$

We recognize here a general mean of r and 1, of order p. This formulation implies that σ is different from 1 and 0. Consider first those particular cases:

- If $\sigma = 1$ (if $p = 0$), we have the geometric mean between r and 1: $y = r^\delta$, which is the per capita Cobb–Douglas function.
- If $\sigma = 0$ (if $p \to -\infty$), we have the minimum between r and 1: $y = \min(r, 1)$ (the per capita Walras–Leontief function).

If σ is different from 0 and 1 two general cases must be distinguished, as in the preceding section: $0 < \sigma < 1$ ($-\infty < p < 0$) and $\sigma > 1$ ($p > 0$).

3.2.1   The case $0 < \sigma < 1$

When $r \to 0$, $\lim_{r \to 0} f_\sigma(r) = 0$. What is important, however, is to realize that when $r \to \infty$ income per person is *bound by an upper limit* whenever σ is lower than one ($p < 0$). Indeed, in such a case we have

$$\lim_{r \to \infty} y = (1 - \delta)^{1/p} = (1 - \delta)^{\frac{\sigma}{\sigma - 1}} \tag{25}$$

and this limit is surprisingly low for a value of σ such 0.8, for instance. If $\delta = 1/3$, we then have, with $1/p = \sigma/(\sigma - 1) = -4$, $\lim_{r \to \infty} y = 5.06$. This means that if the capital–labour ratio increases from 1 to 1000, income per person increases from 1 to 5 only (figure 4.6a).

3.2.2   The case $\sigma > 1$

The behaviour of $f_\sigma(r)$ is entirely different when $\sigma > 1$. First, at the origin its value is not zero any more. It is equal to $(1 - \delta)^{1/p} = (1 - \delta)^{\sigma/(\sigma - 1)}$; if $\delta = 1/3$ and $\sigma = 1.5$, this ordinate is ≈ 0.3; if $\sigma = 2$, it becomes $0.\bar{4}$. Secondly, $f_\sigma(r)$ tends to infinity when $r \to \infty$. Figure 4.6b shows how quickly income per person tends toward an affine function of r (a straight line) with positive slope when σ takes a value as low as 1.5.

Consider now the slope of $f_\sigma(r)$ when $r \to 0$. The derivative of (24) is

$$y'(r) = [\delta r^p + (1 - \delta)]^{\frac{1-p}{p}} \delta r^{p-1}$$

$$= \delta[\delta r^p + (1 - \delta)]^{\frac{1-p}{p}} r^{-p\left(\frac{1-p}{p}\right)}$$

$$= \delta[\delta + (1 - \delta)r^{-p}]^{\frac{1-p}{p}} = \delta[\delta + (1 - \delta)r^{\frac{1}{\sigma} - 1}]^{\frac{1}{\sigma - 1}}. \tag{26}$$

When $r \to \infty$, the slope of $f_\sigma(r)$ tends to the limit

$$\lim_{r \to \infty} f'_\sigma(r) = \delta^{\frac{\sigma}{\sigma - 1}}. \tag{27}$$

Notice that the limit of this slope is an increasing function of σ. This limit will play a central role in the determination of the threshold value of σ above which we can have permanent growth of income per person, even in the absence of technological progress. Indeed, since $f_\sigma(r)$ behaves more and more like a

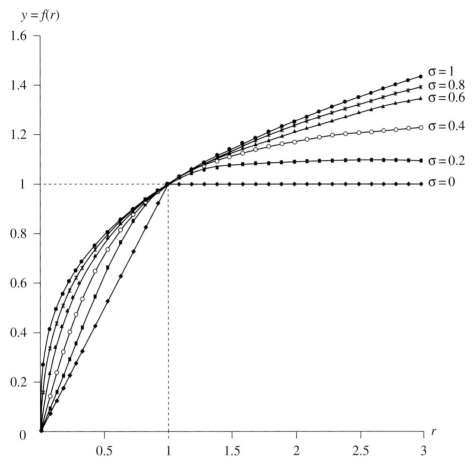

Figure 4.6a   Production and income per person when the elasticity of substitution σ is between 0 (the Walras–Leontief case) and 1 (the Cobb–Douglas case).

$$y = f(r) = [\delta r^{1-1/\sigma} + 1 - \delta]^{\sigma/(\sigma-1)}$$

If $\sigma < 1$, income per person will always tend toward a finite limit, equal to $(1 - \delta)^{\sigma/(\sigma-1)}$ when $r \to \infty$. This limit is surprisingly low; for instance, when $\sigma = 0.8$ and $\delta = 1/3$, $\lim_{r \to \infty} y = 5.06$ only.

straight line when $r \to \infty$ with an increasing slope, we may well figure out that for sufficiently high σ, $s f_\sigma(r)$ will always remain above the ray nr. This implies that $\dot{r} = s f_\sigma(r) - nr$ will always be positive. Such a threshold value for σ exists, indeed, and is given by the value of σ, denoted $\hat{\sigma}$, such that the slope of $s f_\sigma(r)$ is always higher than or equal to the slope of the ray nr. Since the *minimum* value of $f'_\sigma(r)$ is $\delta^{\sigma/(\sigma-1)}$, our condition becomes

$$s \delta^{\sigma/(\sigma-1)} \geq n \qquad\qquad (28)$$

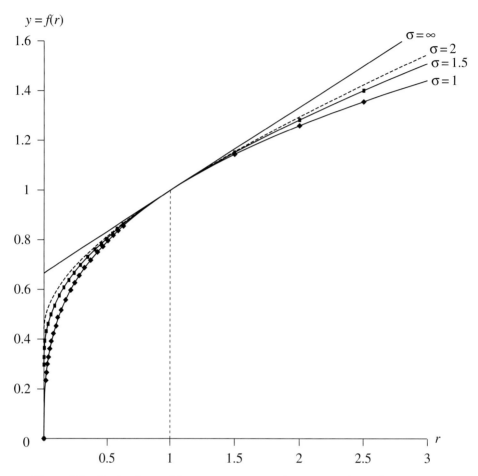

Figure 4.6b Production and income per person when the elasticity of substitution σ is between 1 (the Cobb–Douglas case) and $+\infty$ (the linear case).

$$y = f(r) = [\delta r^{1-1/\sigma} + 1 - \delta]^{\sigma/(\sigma-1)}$$

For $\sigma \geq 1$, income per person tends to infinity when $r \to \infty$. Notice how quickly $y = f(r)$ becomes an affine function of r when σ and r increase.

which leads to

$$\sigma \geq \hat{\sigma} = \frac{1}{1 + (\log \delta)/(\log s/n)}. \tag{29}$$

We will deal with this threshold value of σ in more detail in chapter 5.

3.3 An economic interpretation of the coefficient δ

The expression of income per person as a function of r, expressed in (24) allows an economic interpretation of the δ coefficient. The coefficient δ is usually known as a "distribution parameter". We can be more precise, and show that δ is the geometric mean between the capital share and the real rate of interest (times one year), the weights being $1 - p$ and p, respectively.

We will show that

$$\delta = \pi^{1-p} i^{p} \tag{30}$$

where π denotes the capital share $F'(K)K/Y$ and i, the real interest, is equal in competitive equilibrium to the marginal product of capital (this will be justified later, in chapter 11).

Consider the system of two equations in two unknowns r and δ:

$$\frac{\partial F}{\partial K}\frac{K}{Y} = f'(r)\frac{r}{f(r)} = \frac{\delta r^{p}}{\delta r^{p} + (1-\delta)} = \pi \tag{31}$$

$$\frac{\partial F}{\partial K} = f'(r) = \delta[\delta + (1-\delta)r^{-p}]^{\frac{1}{p}-1} = i \tag{32}$$

From (31) we can determine r as

$$r = \left[\frac{\pi(1-\delta)}{\delta(1-\pi)}\right]^{1/p} \tag{33}$$

($p \neq 0$) and replace this value in (32) to obtain (30). Note that, in the particular case where F is Cobb–Douglas, $\sigma = 1$, $p = 0$ and, from (31) we get $\delta = \pi$ as we should. Also, $\delta = \pi$ is just the particular case where $r = 1$.

A corollary of this property is that the capital's share π is the geometric average between δ and i, the weights being σ and $1 - \sigma$ respectively. From (30),

$$\pi = \delta^{\frac{1}{1-p}} i^{-\frac{p}{1-p}}. \tag{34}$$

From $p = 1 - 1/\sigma$, $1/(1 - p) = \sigma$ and $-p/(1 - p) = 1 - \sigma$. Therefore

$$\pi = \delta^{\sigma} i^{1-\sigma}. \tag{35}$$

We will make ample use of this result in chapter 13.

In chapter 3, we demonstrated the corollary of Allen's theorem: the elasticity of substitution is equal to the elasticity of the average product of capital (Y/K) with respect to the real rental rate. We mentioned that if the elasticity of substitution is constant, then Y/K must be a power function of the real rental, of the type $Y/K = hq^{\sigma}$, where h is a constant to be identified. We can now proceed to do so.

Let us write the real rental rate as $q = i = \partial F/\partial K = f'(r)$; from equation (31), we have $Y/K = i/\pi$; from (30), $\pi = (\delta/i^{p})^{\frac{1}{1-p}}$; replacing this value in

i/π yields

$$\frac{Y}{K} = \left(\frac{i}{\delta}\right)^{\sigma}, \tag{31a}$$

a result we will also use in chapter 13.

3.4   Income per person as a function of σ

We have analysed in the previous section the properties of income per person $y = f(r, \sigma)$ as a function of the capital–labour ratio r, for various values of σ. We will now take one step further, and consider σ not just as one parameter, but as a full-fledged production factor.

We will thus discuss the evolution of income per person when σ becomes the variable, considering r as a parameter. We have made the conjecture that mean y, considered in space (y, p), has one and only one point of inflection. We will now ask the question whether this holds true in (y, σ) space. As we mentioned previously, the conjecture in (y, p) space seems impossible to prove analytically because of the extreme complexity of the second derivative $f''(p)$. Now the second derivative of $f[p(\sigma)]$ with respect to σ is

$$f''(\sigma) = f''(p)[p'(\sigma)]^2 + f'(p)p''(\sigma); \tag{36}$$

since $f''(p)$ is untractable, $f''(\sigma)$ is even less so. Therefore, we will have to proceed, as before, with calculations and care. We will be led to extend the conjecture to (y, σ) space. Why is it important? Because we will show that economies, at present, may very well be located precisely in the range of the σ values where there *is* an inflection point. It means that if σ increases, it imparts maximal effects on income per person.

Figure 4.7a depicts the evolution of y as a function of σ for various values of r, ranging between $r = 4$ and $r = 30$ by steps of 4. What is striking is that, for any given value of r, $f(\sigma, \bar{r})$ behaves exactly as a production function of the variable σ, with a first phase of increasing returns, followed by decreasing returns.[4] For each of those curves $y = f(\sigma, \bar{r})$, we observe one and only one inflection point. The abscissa σ^* of this point of inflection is itself an increasing, concave, function of the capital–labour ratio r. We have plotted in figure 4.7b this relationship between

---

[4] The very fact that $f(\sigma, \bar{r})$ behaves like a production function where σ is the independent variable prompted Hing-Man Leung to try to locate, in (f, σ) space, an optimal point maximizing the difference between output and cost, as a function of σ (see H. M. Leung, 2006). Indeed, if benefits are to be gained from an increasing elasticity of substitution, they may have their costs. This echoes an observation made by Edmond Malinvaud (in a personal communication): it seems important to be able to compare the costs of increasing the rate of technological progress to those corresponding to an enhancement of the elasticity of substitution.

income per person $y = f_\sigma(\bar{r})$

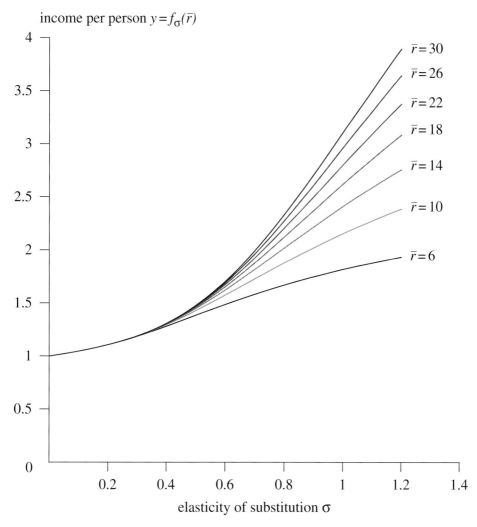

elasticity of substitution σ

Figure 4.7a Income per person $y = f(\bar{r}, \sigma)$ as a function of σ for values of $\bar{r}$ ranging from 6 (lower curve) to 30 (upper curve) by steps of 4.

r and the inflection value of σ^*, denoted $\sigma^*(r)$. It is important to note here that $\sigma^*(r)$ does *not* have an analytical form but a *numerical* form only, since we cannot find the analytical solution of $f''(\sigma) = 0$. Nevertheless, it is always possible to compute $\sigma^*(r)$ and its reciprocal $r(\sigma^*)$.

The question we now want to ask is the following; are OECD economies in a range close to this inflection point? One way of answering the question is to consider the relationship between the capital–output ratio $v = K/Y$ and the point of inflexion of the elasticity of substitution σ^*. Since we have a (numeric) increasing relationship between σ^* and r and an (analytical) increasing relationship between

value of elasticity of substitution σ^*
leading to inflection point

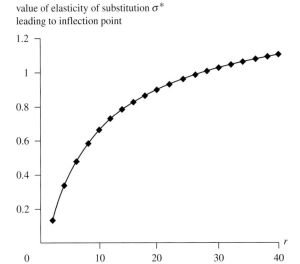

Figure 4.7b   Relationship between a given capital–labour ratio $\bar{r}$ and the elasticity of substitution σ^* corresponding to the inflection point (σ^*, y^*) of the curve $y = f(\bar{r}, \sigma)$.

r and K/Y, given by

$$v = \frac{K}{Y} = \frac{K/L}{Y/L} = \frac{r}{f(r)} = [\delta + (1 - \delta)r^{-P}]^{-1/P},$$

we can determine numerically the relationship between σ^* and the capital–output ratio v corresponding to that σ^*. We just have to calculate

$$v^* = [\delta + (1 - \delta)r^{*-P^*}]^{-1/P^*}$$

where p^* denotes $1 - 1/\sigma^*$. This relationship is given in figure 4.7c. On the other hand, the capital–output ratio is equal, in competitive equilibrium, to

$$v = \frac{K}{Y} = \frac{K}{Y}\frac{\partial F/\partial K}{i} = \frac{\pi}{i}$$

(because $\partial F/\partial K = i$). We now can put numbers on π and i to obtain an estimate of the capital–output ratio. Suppose that we set $\pi = 0.30$ and $i = 4\%$ (that could include a risk premium – more will be said on this in chapters 9 and following). We would then get a capital–output ratio whose order of magnitude is 7.5; reading from figure 4.7c, the corresponding point of inflexion σ^* is in the neighbourhood of 0.8. Many estimates of the elasticity of substitution fall in this vicinity. From this we conclude that OECD economies may very well be in a range close to their inflection point in (y, σ^*) space, and that any increase in the elasticity of substitution will have a strong impact on income per person.

The importance of this impact will be confirmed in chapter 13 when we measure the effect of an increase in the elasticity of substitution on the maximum sum of

value of elasticity of substitution
leading to inflection point

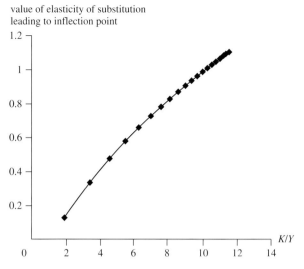

Figure 4.7c   Relationship between a given capital–output ratio and the elasticity of substitution σ^* corresponding to the inflection point (σ^*, y^*) of the curve $y = f(\bar{r}, \sigma)$.

future discounted consumption that society can acquire. We will show this effect to be considerably more important than the result of a similar increase in the rate of technical progress.

Appendix: On general means: an alternative proof of a famous theorem and a conjecture

by
Olivier de La Grandville and Robert M. Solow

Let $x_1, \ldots, x_n$ be n positive numbers and $M(p) = \left(\sum_{i=1}^{n} f_i x_i^p \right)^{1/p}$ the mean of order p of the x_i's; $0 < f_i < 1$ and $\sum_{i=1}^{n} f_i = 1$. One of the most important theorems about a general mean is that it is an increasing function of its order. A proof can be found in G. Hardy, J. E. Littlewood and G. Polya (1952; theorem 16, pp. 26–7). The proof rests in part on Hölder's inequality and on successive contributions to the theory of inequalities that go back to Halley and Newton. In this note, we first offer a direct, analytical proof.

Furthermore, we make a conjecture about the curve $M(p)$ in (M, p) space. If it is well known that $M(p)$ is increasing with p, it seems that the exact properties of the curve $M(p)$ have not yet been uncovered. We offer here the conjecture that for $n = 2$, it has one and only one inflection point, irrespective of the size of the x_i's and the f_i's. Because of the extreme complexity of $M''(p)$, a proof for the time being seems intractable, and we could only rely on calculations. In section 2 of this note we explain the importance of this property.

I   An alternative proof of a famous theorem

For simplicity, we consider $n = 2$; the extension to any number of variables is only notational.

Let the mean of order p, $M(p) = \left(f_1 x_1^p + f_2 x_2^p\right)^{1/p}$ be defined for $p \in (-\infty, 0)$ and $p \in (0, +\infty)$. For $p = 0$, we have $M(0) \equiv G = x_1^{f_1} x_2^{f_2}$, the geometric mean (by L'Hospital's rule).

Consider first the case where $p \neq 0$. Differentiating $\log M$ with respect to p:

$$
\begin{aligned}
\frac{\partial \log M}{\partial p} &= \frac{-1}{p^2} \log\left[f_1 x_1^p + f_2 x_2^p\right] + \frac{1}{p} \frac{f_1 x_1^p \log x_1 + f_2 x_2^p \log x_2}{\left[f_1 x_1^p + f_2 x_2^p\right]} \\
&= \frac{-1}{p^2} \log\left[f_1 x_1^p + f_2 x_2^p\right] + \frac{1}{p^2} \frac{f_1 x_1^p \log x_1^p + f_2 x_2^p \log x_2^p}{\left[f_1 x_1^p + f_2 x_2^p\right]} \\
&= \frac{1}{p^2 \left[f_1 x_1^p + f_2 x_2^p\right]} \left\{ -\left[f_1 x_1^p + f_2 x_2^p\right] \log\left[f_1 x_1^p + f_2 x_2^p\right] \right. \\
&\qquad\qquad\qquad\qquad \left. + f_1 x_1^p \log x_1^p + f_2 x_2^p \log x_2^p \right\}.
\end{aligned}
$$

Denote for simplicity $x_1^p \equiv a_1$ and $x_2^p \equiv a_2$. Then

$$
\begin{aligned}
\operatorname{sgn} \frac{\partial \log M}{\partial p} = \operatorname{sgn}\{ &-[f_1 a_1 + f_2 a_2] \log[f_1 a_1 + f_2 a_2] \\
&+ f_1 a_1 \log a_1 + f_2 a_2 \log a_2 \}
\end{aligned}
\tag{1}
$$

Let $H(z) = z \log z$. $H(z)$ is convex since $H''(z) = \frac{1}{z} > 0$. We have

$$
\operatorname{sgn} \frac{\partial \log M}{\partial p} = \operatorname{sgn}\{ -H(f_1 a_1 + f_2 a_2) + f_1 H(a_1) + f_2 H(a_2) \}.
\tag{2}
$$

The RHS is positive by convexity of H. This completes the proof for $p \neq 0$.

Consider now the special case corresponding to $p = 0$ (the geometric mean $G = x_1^{f_1} x_2^{f_2}$). We first want to show that for $p > 0$ the general mean $M(p)$ is larger than $M(0) = G$. We must show that

$$
[f_1 x_1^p + f_2 x_2^p]^{1/p} \geqq x_1^{f_1} x_2^{1-f_1}
\tag{3}
$$

with the equality sign if and only if $x_1 = x_2$. Divide both sides by x_2 and set $x_1/x_2 = r$:

$$
[f_1 r^p + f_2]^{1/p} \geqq r^{f_1}.
\tag{4}
$$

Raising both sides to power p:

$$f_1 r^p + f_2 \geqq r^{p f_1} \tag{5}$$

because a, b, $p > 0$ imply that $a > b$ if and only if $a^p > b^p$. This inequality says that the arithmetic mean of r^p and 1 with weights f_1, $1 - f_1$ exceeds the geometric mean of r^p and 1 with the same weights. Call D the difference between the arithmetic mean and the geometric mean, and denote $r^p \equiv v$:

$$D(v) = f_1 v + f_2 - v^{f_1}. \tag{6}$$

At $v = 1$, $D = 0$. At that point $D'(1) = 0$; but the second derivative of $D(v)$ is $D''(v) = f_1^2 v^{f_1 - 2} > 0$ for any value of v; so the point $(1, 0)$ is a global minimum of $D(v)$. Hence $D(v) > 0$ with $v \neq 1$.

The proof $M(p) < M(0) = G$ for $p < 0$ is immediate: writing (3) and (4) with the reverse sign, we want to show that

$$[f_1 r^p + f_2]^{1/p} \leqq r^{f_1}. \tag{7}$$

Raising both sides of (7) to power p implies, with $p < 0$, a reversal of the inequality sign, which leads back to (4) and to the remaining part of the above demonstration.

2 A conjecture

On the basis of numerical calculations, we offer the following conjecture. In (M, p) space the curve $M(p)$ has one and only one inflection point for $n = 2$. Between its limiting values $(\lim_{p \to -\infty} M(p) = \min(x_1, x_2)$ and $\lim_{p \to \infty} M(p) = \max(x_1, x_2))$, $M(p)$ is in a first phase convex and then turns concave.

The importance of this property stems from the following reason. We know that if the production function is a CES function, both income $(Y = [\delta K^p + (1 - \delta)L]^{1/p}$ and income per person $(y = [\delta r^p + (1 - \delta)]^{1/p})$ are general means of order p, and that p is an increasing function of $\sigma (p = 1 - 1/\sigma)$. If the conjecture about the relationship between the general means and its order is true – and we have very strong reasons to believe it is – it may well extend to the relationship between σ and y, i.e. $y = f[p(\sigma)]$; we have confirmed in section 3.4 of this chapter that there exists indeed, for all usual values of σ, one and only one point of inflection of the curve $y = y(\sigma)$, and that our economies may very well be in the neighbourhood of this point. This is the reason why any change in σ imparts a lot of change in income per person, and why σ will play such an important role in optimal growth, as we will see in chapter 13.

CHAPTER 5

Capital–labour substitution and economic growth

(in collaboration with Robert M. Solow)

Ever since its emergence in John Hicks's *Theory of Wages* (1932), the elasticity of substitution has figured primarily in the theory of distribution. The standard proposition states that, with two factors, constant returns to scale and cost minimization, the faster-growing factor increases or decreases its share in income accordingly as this parameter is larger or smaller than one.

However, the elasticity of substitution is by definition a technological fact, a characteristic of a production function which would turn out to play an important role. Indeed, as shown in La Grandville (1989) and extended in this chapter, a higher value of the elasticity of substitution *ceteris paribus* does more than merely alter production possibilities, it expands them. Naturally, then, the elasticity of substitution should have significance in all branches of economics where technology matters. And it does. The purpose of this chapter is to explore the role of the elasticity of substitution in the aggregative theory of economic growth.

There are historical overtones to this technical theme. Broadly speaking, the capital–labour ratio has probably been rising since the beginning of sedentary agriculture made large-scale accumulation of capital possible. The ratio of the wage to the rental rate of capital has presumably also increased through history, though less regularly than the factor ratio. In the tradition of economics, accounting for these characteristics of the long-term growth path involves an interplay between technical progress and the evolution of capital–labour substitution possibilities (along with possible non-market forces that are not our concern here). In practice, growth theory has placed more emphasis on the analysis of technical change. We propose to focus our attention on the significance of a changing elasticity of substitution.

It is understood that in any one-composite-good representation of a many-good economy, substitution on the consumption side between goods of different capital intensity will function much like direct input substitution. An early reference on this is R. Jones (1965); see also the more recent work by Klump and Preissler (2000) and E. Malinvaud ((2002) and (2003).

It has been known since the beginning of "neoclassical" growth theory that permanently sustained growth *is* possible even without technological progress, provided that diminishing returns to capital-intensity operates very weakly. We underline the verb "is" only because this fact is sometimes casually denied in the literature. In section 1 of this chapter we show precisely under what conditions this kind of substitution-driven growth can occur. The key parameters are the saving-investment rate, population increase, a measure of capital's productivity, and σ itself; we can calculate the asymptotic rate of growth when it does occur, in terms of those parameters. (This is *not* steady-state growth in the usual sense, because the capital–labour ratio is not constant, but increasing.)

We will have a lot to say about the many cases where σ does not reach that threshold value. In particular, we will show how any change in σ impacts upon an economy at any stage of its development, on its growth rate, on its equilibrium income per person and on production costs. We discuss these relationships in section 1 by relying on a central property of generalized means, and illustrate them in section 2. In section 3 we extend those results to an economy exhibiting both capital and labour-augmenting technical progress.

Section 4 reverts to the estimating equation used by Arrow *et al.* (1961), and we use it in the same way to provide some new estimates of σ based on data from 16 countries for the interval 1966–97. These are econometrically unsophisticated ordinary least square calculations. Our main intention here is to exhibit the usual outcome that cross-section estimates tend to be smaller than time-series estimates, and then to interpret this regularity in terms of theory developed earlier. In the concluding section 5, we return to the broader significance of the macroeconomic elasticity of substitution and discuss whether it offers any opening for deliberate policy.

I Further analytics of the CES function in a growth model

A first inkling of the property that the elasticity of substitution is an efficiency indicator in any productive system among other things is the following. Consider the picture of a family of isoquants with a common tangency point, corresponding to a given wage/rental rate (figure 4.4, chapter 4); to each isoquant is attached a given elasticity of substitution ranging from zero (the Walras–Leontief case, entailing a right angle isoquant) to infinity (the isoquant becomes a straight line, the tangent common to all isoquants). For all levels of the factor–price ratio except that corresponding to the common tangency point the cost of producing a given level of output is a decreasing function of the elasticity of substitution. Equivalently, the unfolding of the production surface (around a ray from the origin) resulting from an increasing elasticity of substitution implies a higher level of output everywhere except on the said ray. Therefore the elasticity of substitution acts exactly like technical progress, displacing the production function in the right way.

In the (1989) paper mentioned above, the following questions were asked: suppose that at some point of time, an economy is characterized by its capital stock, its labour force, the resulting total income, the rental rates of capital and labour, and its elasticity of substitution. What would be the consequences of various levels of the elasticity of substitution σ on later growth? In particular, does a threshold value of σ exist for which there could be no steady equilibrium? In other words, is there a minimal value of σ which would lead to a permanent increase of income per person even in the absence of technological progress? And if that threshold is not attained, is there a positive relationship between the growth rate of income per person and the elasticity of substitution? To answer these questions, the author relied on a geometrical argument based upon the unfolding of the surface $F_\sigma(K, L)$ implied by an increasing σ, coupled with the equation of motion of the economy. The threshold was determined, albeit in implicit form. (In fact, this formulation can be simplified, yielding the explicit form we will give in this paper.)

This led to the natural, converse question of determining a threshold value of the savings rate s that would, for a given level of σ, lead to permanent growth even without technological progress. That minimum value of savings was obtained and checked with the particular case that had been considered by R. Solow (1956) with $\sigma = 2$.

It was also shown that even if the economy did not attain those threshold values for σ (or for s), the temporary growth rate of income per person at any time was an increasing function of the elasticity of substitution and that the steady-state value of income per person was also an increasing function of σ. This led the author to conjecture that part of the explanation of miracle growth in Japan or South Asian countries lay not only in a high savings rate but also in a high elasticity of substitution between factors in their industrial sectors. That conjecture was tested by Ky-Hyang Yuhn (1991) in the case of South Korea and, seemingly, was proved right.

A decade later, Klump and La Grandville (2000) demonstrated algebraically the two following theorems:

THEOREM 1 *If two economies are described by CES production functions differing only by their elasticity of substitution, and share initially a common capital/labour ratio, population growth rate and savings-investment rate, then at any stage of its development the economy with the higher elasticity of substitution will have a higher level of per capita income.*

THEOREM 2 (With the same premises as in theorem 1). *If the levels of the elasticities of substitution guarantee the existence of steady states, then the economy with the higher elasticity of substitution will have a higher capital intensity and a higher level of per capita income in the steady state.*

The demonstrations of both theorems required quite lengthy calculations. We will first show in this section how, using the fundamental property of general means (as described in G. Hardy, J. E. Littlewood and G. Polya, *Inequalities*, chapter 2), those theorems become extremely simple to prove; we will add another theorem, pertaining to the cost of producing one unit of national output. The threshold value of the elasticity of substitution will then be determined in *explicit* form, and not in implicit form only. We will also give some numerical illustrations.

Recall that the CES was written in chapter 3 as

$$Y = [\delta K^p + (1 - \delta)L^p]^{1/p}, \tag{1}$$

with $p = 1 - 1/\sigma$, where σ is the elasticity of substitution. Y, K and L are understood to be indices, and the per capita function is

$$y = [\delta r^p + (1 - \delta)]^{1/p}. \tag{2}$$

Written explicitly, these index numbers appear in the following form:

$$Y = Y_0 \left[\pi_0 \left(\frac{K}{K_0} \right)^p + (1 - \pi_0) \left(\frac{L}{L_0} \right)^p \right]^{1/p} \tag{3}$$

where K_0, L_0, Y_0 and π_0, equal to $(\partial Y/\partial K)(K/L)$ at (K_0, L_0), are benchmark values. This form had been obtained in chapter 3 by identifying the integration constants introduced in the derivation of the CES function. Today empiricists use that formulation (see, for instance, Thomas Rutherford (2003)). The per capita version of (3) is

$$\frac{Y/L}{Y_0/L_0} = \frac{y}{y_0} = \left[\pi_0 \left(\frac{r}{r_0} \right)^p + (1 - \pi_0) \right]^{1/p} \tag{4}$$

1.1 Simple proofs of theorems 1 and 2, and additional results

We are now in a position to give simple proofs of theorems 1 and 2, applying the theory of general means. We will then show how the relationship between the production function and σ extends to its dual, and that the cost of producing one unit of national output is general mean of the input prices, its order being a decreasing function of the elasticity of substitution.

1.1.1 Proof of Theorem 1

Theorem 1 is a direct consequence of one of the fundamental properties of general means: income per person, as given by equation (10), is a mean (of order p) of r and 1, and therefore an increasing function of its order ($r \neq 1$). Since p, the order of the mean, is itself increasing with σ ($p = 1 - 1/\sigma$), theorem 1 is proved.

1.1.2 Proof of Theorem 2

Using (2), the equation of motion of a CES economy with no technological progress (and no depreciation) is

$$\dot{r} = s[\delta r^p + (1 - \delta)]^{1/p} - nr \tag{5}$$

Consider two values of the elasticity of substitution σ_1, σ_2 such that $\sigma_2 > \sigma_1$. Suppose that for σ_1 there exists an equilibrium capital/labour ratio, denoted ($r^* \neq 1$). We know from Theorem 1 or from the general property of means that $f_{\sigma_2}(r_1^*) > f_{\sigma_1}(r_1^*)$. Since r_1^* is such that $sf_{\sigma_1}(r_1^*) = nr_1^*$, $sf_{\sigma_2}(r_1^*) > nr_1^*$; then, if an equilibrium value r_2^* corresponding to σ_2 exists, it must be larger than r_1^*. Therefore $r_2^* > r_1^*$ and $f_{\sigma_2}(r_2^*) > f_{\sigma_1}(r_1^*)$. Theorem 2 is thus proved. Additional theorems now follow:

1.1.3 Theorem 3

At any stage of an economy's development, the cost of producing one unit of national product is a decreasing function of the elasticity of substitution.

PROOF   Consider minimizing the cost of production $C = qK + wL$ subject to (3). The unit cost index turns out to be

$$c = \left[\delta \left(\frac{q}{q_0} \right)^{1-\sigma} + (1 - \delta) \left(\frac{w}{w_0} \right)^{1-\sigma} \right]^{\frac{1}{1-\sigma}} \tag{6}$$

(a derivation under general conditions is given in the appendix; this formulation corresponds to Thomas Rutherford (2003)).

We recognize here a general mean of order $1 - \sigma$ of the price indices of capital and labour. The theory of general means again applies: c/c_0 is an increasing function of $1 - \sigma$, and therefore a decreasing function of σ.

1.2 Equilibrium and disequilibrium, and the cases of ever-increasing or decreasing income per person

The very fact that the marginal productivity of capital, $\partial F/\partial K$, equal to $f'(r)$, has a positive, finite limit when $r \to \infty$ and $\sigma > 1$ ($\lim f'(r)_{r\to\infty} = \delta^{1/p} = \delta^{\sigma/(\sigma-1)}$), spells excellent news. On the other hand the existence of the same expression for $\lim_{r\to 0} f'(r)$ when $\sigma < 1$ (also equal to $\delta^{1/p} = \delta^{\sigma/(\sigma-1)}$) may

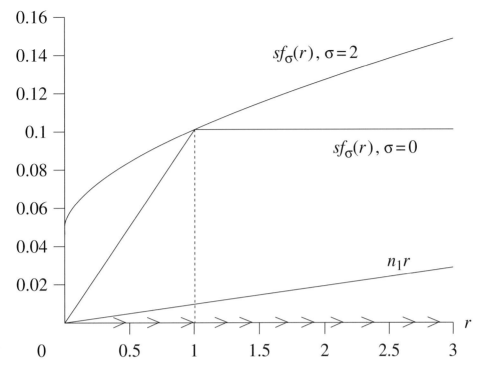

Figure 5.1a With $\sigma = 2$, s and n_1 are such that income per person will grow forever.

have disastrous consequences. Indeed, in the first case it means that for sufficiently high σ and s/n, income per person will increase forever. In the second case however, if σ and s/n are extremely low, income per person is *bound to decrease to zero*. Once more, the phase diagram will be most helpful to understand these issues. In figure 5.1a and 5.1b we have sketched $sf_\sigma(r)$ for $\sigma = 2$ and $\sigma = 0.5$, respectively. We can now picture rays nr with values n_1 and n_2 such that $n_1 < sf_2'(\infty)$ and $n_2 > sf_{0.5}'(0)$. Clearly, in the first case, income per person will grow forever whatever the initial position of the economy because we will have $\dot{r} = sf_2(r) - nr > 0$ for any r. On the other hand, in the second case disaster is looming since $\dot{r} < 0$ for any r.

Our purpose now is to investigate each of these situations. We will define in a precise way the values of the parameters δ, σ, s and n for which equilibrium is warranted or not. Our first step will be to introduce a constant linking parameters σ and δ of the CES function. We propose to call it the Pitchford constant for reasons that will be explained shortly.

1.2.1 Introducing the Pitchford constant

This constant will play a central role for three reasons. First, it will be used to determine the threshold value of the elasticity of substitution above which permanent

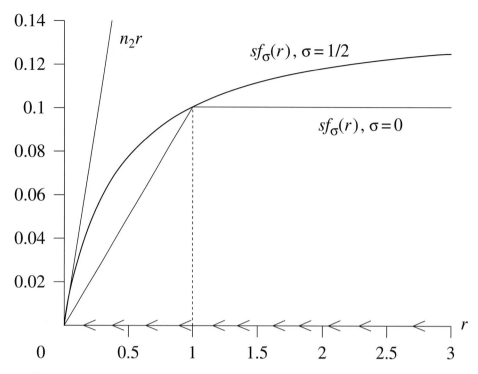

Figure 5.1b   With $\sigma = 0.5$, s and n_2 are such that income per person will decrease to zero.

growth of income per person is guaranteed even in the absence of technological progress. Secondly, it will prove essential to determine another threshold of σ: that under which income would start falling toward zero. Thirdly, the constant will turn out to be proportional to the limiting growth rate of income when the economy is either so efficient or so inefficient that it will not converge to a steady state,[1] with or without labour-augmenting technical progress.

Consider income per person as given by equation 24 of chapter 4, and its derivative (equation 26). We have:

$$ y = f_\sigma(r) = [\delta r^p + (1-\delta)]^{1/p} = [\delta r^{1-1/\sigma} + (1-\delta)]^{\sigma/(\sigma-1)}, \quad \sigma \neq 1 $$

and

$$ \frac{\partial F}{\partial K} = y'(r) = \delta[\delta + (1-\delta)r^{-p}]^{\frac{1-p}{p}} = \delta[\delta + (1-\delta)r^{\frac{1}{\sigma}-1}]^{\frac{1}{\sigma-1}}, \quad \sigma \neq 1 $$

Careful examination of $\partial F/\partial K = y'(r)$ shows that the two following limits, defined as $\lim_{r \to \infty} f'(r)$, with $\sigma > 1$ (or $0 < p < 1$) and $\lim_{r \to 0} f'(r)$, with

---

[1] A "steady state" is defined by an equilibrium situation where K, L and Y grow at the same rate.

$\sigma < 1$ (or $0 < p < 1$), are equal to the same constant, $\delta^{1/p} = \delta^{(\sigma/(\sigma-1))}$, which we denote $m_\delta(\sigma)$. The reason for doing so is that $m_\delta(\sigma)$ is at the same time the *minimum* value of $f'(r)$ when $\sigma > 1$, and the *maximum* value of $f'(r)$ when $\sigma < 1$. We thus have

$$m_\delta(\sigma) = \delta^{1/p} = \delta^{\sigma/(\sigma-1)} = \lim_{r \to \infty} f'(r) = \inf f'(r), \quad \sigma > 1$$
$$= \lim_{r \to 0} f'(r) = \sup f'(r), \quad \sigma < 1.$$

This constant was introduced by John Pitchford in 1960,[2] and we find most appropriate that it bears the name of its discoverer. Pitchford was investigating the possibility of permanent disequilibrium in a growth model based on a CES function. He introduced this constant as the upper limit of Y/K when $r \to \infty$ and $\sigma > 1$, and the lower limit of Y/K when $\sigma < 1$. Applying L'Hospital's rule, it is immediate that these limits are the same as those defined just above. In his innovative essay, which has been overlooked for too many years, Pitchford had clearly seen the two possibilities of disequilibria in the CES framework. Pitchford was working in $(\dot{r}/r, Y/K)$ space because the fundamental differential equation (14) of chapter 2 was written $\dot{r}/r = sy/r - n$); this space had been elected by Trevor Swan in his path-breaking essay.[3] We think however that it may be easier to work in the usual phase diagram space, i.e. in $(\dot{r}, r)$ space, because possibilities of equilibrium or disequilibrium can be easily inferred geometrically.[4]

This value of $m_\delta(\sigma)$ is represented in figure 5.2 as a function of σ, for values of δ ranging from 0.2 to 0.35. Except at $\sigma = 1$ where it has a discontinuity, it is always an increasing function of σ. For $0 \le \sigma < 1$, the function starts at 1, is strictly convex and tends to infinity when $\sigma \to 1$; for $\sigma > 1$, the function starts at 0 and is first strictly convex; it goes through an inflection point at $\sigma = 1 - (1/2)\log\delta$ (larger than 1 since $0 < \delta < 1$); it then becomes concave, tending asymptotically toward δ.

All these properties of $m_\delta(\sigma)$ will play a particularly important role, with and without technological progress. Indeed, we will show that m is proportional to the ultimate growth rate of income when the economy does not converge toward a steady state, the coefficient of proportionality being the net savings (or net investment) rate s.

---

[2] In his essay "Growth and the Elasticity of Substitution", *Economic Record*, 36, 491–504, 1960. We have taken the liberty of adapting Pitchford's notation to ours.

[3] Trevor Swan, "Economic Growth and Capital Accumulation", *Economic Record*, 32, 340–61, 1956.

[4] Another reason is that one of us had already used the limit of $f'(r)$ when $r \to \infty$ and $\sigma > 1$ (La Grandville, 1989).

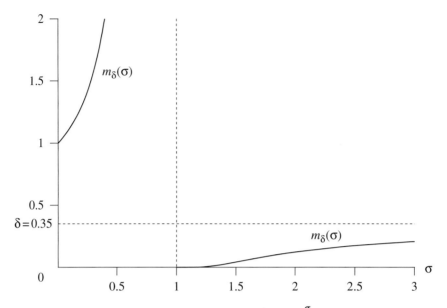

Figure 5.2a The structural constant $m_\delta(\sigma) = \delta^{1/p} = \delta^{\frac{\sigma}{\sigma-1}}$. The general outlook for $\delta = 0.35$. *Note:* The remarkable discontinuity of $m_\delta(\sigma)$ at $p = 0$ (or $\sigma = 1$) is entirely akin to that of $e^{-1/x}$ at $x = 0$ (see Courant (1953, p. 197)). Indeed, since $0 < \delta < 1$, $m_\delta(\sigma)$ can always be written as $e^{-|\log \delta|(1/p)}$.

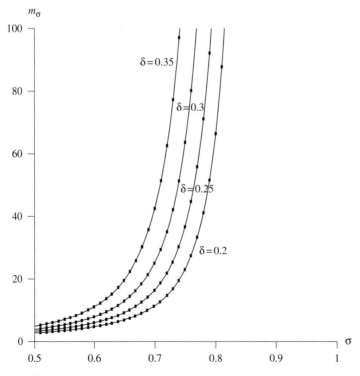

Figure 5.2b $m_\delta(\sigma)$ for $\sigma \in [0.5, 1)$.

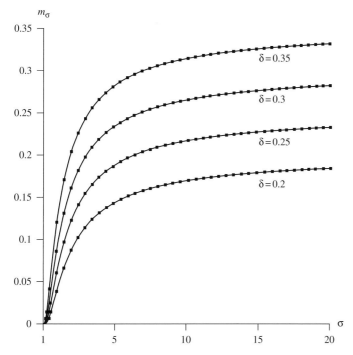

Figure 5.2c $m_\delta(\sigma)$ for $\sigma \in [1, 20]$.

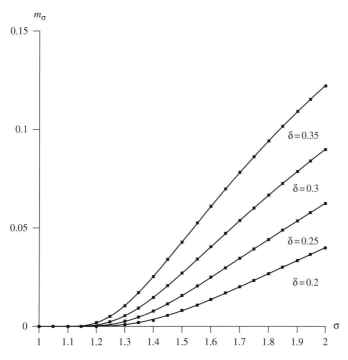

Figure 5.2d $m_\delta(\sigma)$ for $\sigma \in (1, 2]$. Detailed representations for $\delta = 0.2, 0.25, 0.3$ and 0.35 (Note that on each diagram the scales differ.).

1.2.2   The threshold value of the elasticity of substitution generating permanent growth

We will now determine the threshold value of the elasticity of substitution, denoted $\hat{\sigma}$, that, together with a net investment rate s and population growth rate n, would guarantee permanent growth of income per person. We will look for a value of σ such that $\lim_{r\to\infty} sf'_\sigma(r) \geq n$.

Observe first that parameters σ, s and n must be within some bounds for the problem to have a solution. First, $\sigma > 1$ (or $0 < p < 1$) since we know from first principles that $\lim_{r\to\infty} sf'_\sigma(r) = 0$ if $\sigma \leq 1$, entailing necessarily an equilibrium value r^*_σ if $n > 0$. Second, we must have $n \leq s\delta$, or $s/n \geq 1/\delta$; indeed, investment per person in the case of $\sigma \to \infty$ is $s[\delta r + (1 - \delta)]$, a straight line in the phase diagram, with slope $s\delta$. A value of n larger than that slope would lead to an equilibrium value r^*. So our parameters must necessarily meet the conditions:

$$\sigma > 1; \; p = 1 - 1/\sigma > 0 \tag{7}$$

and

$$n \leq s\delta. \tag{8}$$

(this last condition implying $s/n \geq 1/\delta$). The condition for the threshold value of σ is $\lim_{r\to\infty} sf'_\sigma(r) \geq n$ or

$$\lim_{r\to\infty} f'_\sigma(r) \geq \frac{n}{s}. \tag{9}$$

We know from section 2.1.2 that $\lim_{r\to\infty} f'(r)$ is equal to the Pitchford constant $m_\delta(\sigma)$. So our condition (9) implies

$$\lim_{r\to\infty} f'_\sigma(r) = m_\delta(\sigma) = \delta^{\frac{\sigma}{\sigma-1}} \geq \frac{n}{s}. \tag{10}$$

Taking into account the above restrictions on σ, n, s and δ, this inequality translates into

$$\sigma \geq \hat{\sigma} = \frac{1}{1 + (\log \delta)/\log(s/n)}, \quad \sigma > 1 \text{ and } s/n > 1/\delta. \tag{11}$$

The expression of the threshold value $\hat{\sigma}$ makes good economic sense: first, it is a decreasing function of the partial elasticity of production with respect to capital at the base year $\pi_0 = \delta$. Furthermore, keeping in mind that $\log \delta < 0$, we notice that $\hat{\sigma}$ is also a decreasing function of s, and an increasing function of n. In space $(s/n, \sigma)$, we can delineate the area corresponding to permanent growth of income per person as the hatched area in the right-hand side of figure 5.3a.

Table 5.1   The threshold value $\hat{\sigma}$ of the elasticity of substitution leading to permanent growth without any technical progress

(Population growth rate: $n = 1\%/\text{year}$)

savings-investment rate s	Calibrated capital's share in total income δ		
	0.25	0.3	0.33
0.08	3	2.38	2.12
0.09	2.71	2.21	2
0.1	2.51	2.1	1.91
0.11	2.37	2.01	1.85
0.12	2.26	1.94	1.79
0.13	2.18	1.88	1.75
0.14	2.11	1.84	1.71
0.15	2.05	1.80	1.68
0.16	2	1.77	1.66
0.17	1.96	1.74	1.63
0.18	1.92	1.71	1.61
0.19	1.89	1.69	1.60
0.2	1.86	1.67	1.58
0.21	1.84	1.65	1.56
0.22	1.81	1.64	1.55
0.23	1.79	1.62	1.54
0.24	1.77	1.61	1.53
0.25	1.76	1.60	1.52
0.26	1.74	1.59	1.51
0.27	1.73	1.58	1.50
0.28	1.71	1.57	1.49
0.29	1.70	1.56	1.48
0.30	1.69	1.55	1.48

Some illustrations   Suppose that in a given economy, the growth rate of population and employment is $n = 1\%$ per year; the savings/investment rate is $s = 20\%$ and the initial share of capital in national income is $\delta = 1/3$. Applying (11), the threshold value of σ that will guarantee permanent growth is $\hat{\sigma} = 1.58$. Table 5.1 gives the values of $\hat{\sigma}$ for various levels of the savings/investment rate and various levels of δ.

Corollary: the threshold value of the savings and the population growth rates entailing permanent growth   Consider now a converse problem: suppose that the elasticity of substitution σ is given. Then there exists a threshold value for the savings/investment rate s that will keep income per person growing; this

Table 5.2 *The threshold value ŝ of the savings-investment rate leading to permanent growth without any technical progress*

(Population growth rate: $n = 1\%/year$)

elasticity of substitution σ	Calibrated capital's share in total income δ		
	0.25	0.3	0.33
1.5	0.64	0.37	0.27
1.6	0.403	0.247	0.187
1.7	0.290	0.186	0.144
1.8	0.226	0.150	0.118
1.9	0.187	0.127	0.102
2	0.16	0.111	0.09
2.1	0.141	0.10	0.081
2.2	0.127	0.091	0.075
2.3	0.116	0.084	0.07
2.4	0.108	0.079	0.066
2.5	0.101	0.074	0.062
2.6	0.095	0.071	0.06
2.7	0.09	0.068	0.057
2.8	0.086	0.065	0.055
2.9	0.083	0.063	0.053
3	0.08	0.061	0.052

value, determined by inverting (10), is equal to

$$\hat{s} = \frac{n}{m_\delta(\sigma)} = \frac{n}{\delta^{\frac{\sigma}{\sigma-1}}} \quad (12)$$

The threshold value of the savings/investment ratio is of course an increasing function of n, and a decreasing function of δ and σ. As an example, consider for instance the case studied by Solow (1956) with $\sigma = 2$. With the same values as above, the threshold of s is $\hat{s} = 9\%$.

Table 5.2 indicates the threshold value $\hat{s}$ of the savings-investment rate leading to permanent growth without any technical progress, for various values of σ and δ, the population growth rate being $n = 1\%/year$.

A similar threshold value for n can be obtained by inverting (10). We get the maximum value of the population growth rate (denoted $\hat{n}$) leading to permanent growth of income per person:

$$\hat{n} = s\delta^{\sigma/(\sigma-1)} = sm_\delta(\sigma) \quad (13)$$

For instance, if $\delta = 0.33$, $s = 0.2$ and $\sigma = 1.4$, then $\hat{n} = 0.43\%$. Note finally that the maximum value $\hat{n}$ is an increasing function of s, δ and σ – which makes good economic sense.

Limiting values of the share of capital and the growth rate of income per person Suppose now that in a given economy the level of σ is equal or higher than its threshold value $\hat{\sigma}$. The fact that r and y increase indefinitely has some surprising consequences.

First, the capital share $\pi(r)$ tends to 1: this is seen by letting $r \to \infty$ in $\pi(r) = \frac{K}{Y}\frac{\partial F}{\partial K} = \frac{r}{f_\sigma(r)}f'_\sigma(r) = \delta[\delta + (1-\delta)r^{-P}]^{-1}$, and the growth rate of y,

$$\frac{\dot{y}}{y} = \pi_\sigma(r)\left\{s[\delta r^P + (1-\delta)]^{1/P}/r - n\right\}, \tag{14}$$

tends by decreasing values toward

$$\lim_{r\to\infty}\dot{y}/y = s\delta^{1/P} - n = sm_\delta(\sigma) - n. \tag{15}$$

This limit itself tends toward zero if the elasticity of substitution tends through diminishing values toward its threshold $\hat{\sigma}$ (because, as we have seen, $\hat{\sigma}$ is determined by $m_\delta(\sigma) = n/s$. In the example above (where $\sigma = 2$), $\lim_{r\to\infty}\dot{y}/y = 1.\bar{2}\%$. Notice that, from (15), the limiting growth rate of Y is

$$\lim_{r\to\infty}\dot{Y}/Y = sm_\delta(\sigma). \tag{16}$$

Why should it be so? The reason is as follows. We have seen that $\lim_{r\to\infty}\pi_\sigma(r) = 1$. This implies, in the limit, $\frac{\partial F}{\partial K}\frac{K}{Y} = 1$ and $\dot{K}/K = \dot{Y}/Y$; $\dot{K}$ being sY, we get in the limit $\dot{Y}/Y = \dot{K}/K = sY/K = sf'(r) = sm_\delta(\sigma)$.

A number of properties of this limit growth rate should be noted:

- it is equal to or higher than n (since it corresponds to $sm_\delta(\sigma) \geq n$)
- it depends positively on s, δ and σ (because of the properties of the Pitchford constant $m_\delta(\sigma)$ mentioned before).

1.2.3 The case of disequilibrium with ever decreasing income per person

This case corresponds to $\sigma < 1$ *and* $sf'(0) \leq n$, or $sm_\delta(\sigma) \leq n$, with $s/n < 1$. Solving this inequality similarly to what we did before, we are led to the condition

$$\sigma \leq \bar{\sigma} = \frac{1}{1 + (\log\delta)/\log(s/n)}, \quad \sigma < 1 \text{ and } s/n < 1.$$

This disequilibrium area is pictured in figures 5.3a and 5.3b (hatched area on the left-hand side).

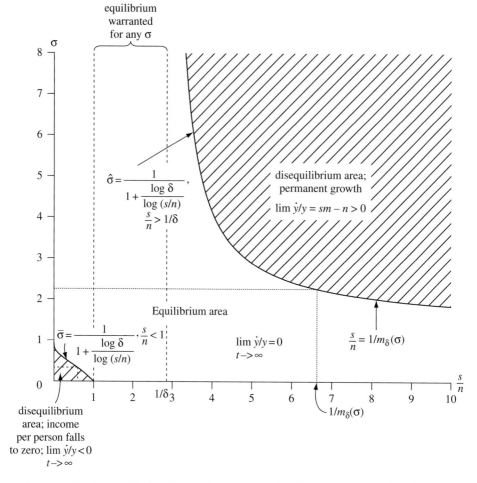

Figure 5.3a Areas of $(s/n, \sigma)$ space leading to equilibrium or disequilibrium ($\delta = 0.35$). For any value of σ, the curves $\hat{\sigma}$ and $\bar{\sigma}$ give the crucial value of s/n, equal to $1/m_\delta(\sigma)$.

In turn, we can find a threshold value for the savings rate, $\bar{s}$, under which income per person would decrease forever. From $sm_\delta(\sigma) \leq n$, we get

$$s \leq \bar{s} = \frac{n}{m_\delta(\sigma)} = \frac{n}{\delta(\sigma/(\sigma-1))}, \quad \sigma < 1.$$

This threshold value is just the population growth rate divided by the Pitchford constant. Putting some numbers on this inequality, consider for instance the case $n = 2\%$, $\sigma = 0.5$ and $\delta = 0.3$. The inverse of the Pitchford constant is then 0.3, entailing a savings rate equal to or less than 0.6%. Such small savings rates might be observed in very poor countries and hence cannot, unfortunately, be dismissed.

For exactly the same reasons as before, the limiting growth rate of Y will also be $sm_\delta(\sigma)$; indeed, $\lim_{r \to 0} \pi(r) = 1$ when $0 < \sigma < 1$ (when $p < 0$), and from

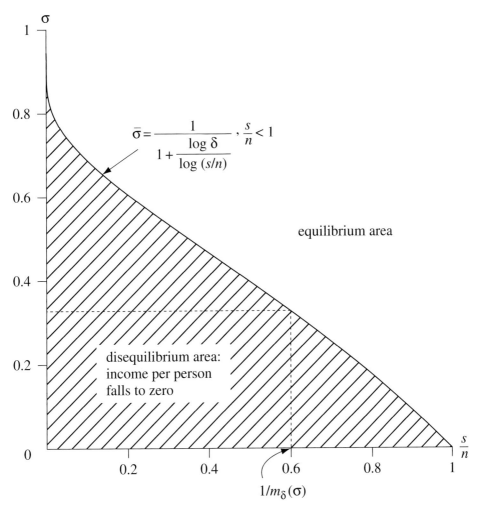

Figure 5.3b Enlargement of area $0 \leq \frac{s}{n} \leq 1$, $0 \leq \sigma < 1$; $\delta = 0.35$.

(14) $\lim_{r \to 0} \dot{y}/y = s m_\delta(\sigma) - n$, which will be *negative*. In the above example, if $s = 0.5\%$, the limiting growth rate of y will be *minus* 0.3%.

2   The elasticity of substitution at work

We now have all the tools to examine the benefits an economy can derive from a higher elasticity of substitution, putting some numbers on the preceding theorems 1 and 2. These tests are necessary, because the theorems could be perfectly correct but of little import if changes in the elasticity of substitution entailed only marginal changes in income per person at the various stages of development of an economy.

Table 5.3   *The elasticity of income per person with respect to the elasticity of substitution as a function of the capital/labour ratio r and the elasticity of substitution σ*

$$e_{y,\sigma} = \frac{\partial y}{\partial \sigma}\frac{\sigma}{y}(\sigma, r; \delta) \text{ (Initial value of capital share: } \delta = 33\%)$$

Capital/labour	Value of the elasticity of substitution σ				
ratio r	0.8	0.9	1	1.1	1.2
1	0	0	0	0	0
2	0.06	0.055	0.050	0.047	0.043
3	0.15	0.136	0.127	0.118	0.111
4	0.23	0.215	0.202	0.189	0.178
5	0.30	0.287	0.272	0.256	0.242
6	0.37	0.354	0.337	0.319	0.301
7	0.43	0.415	0.398	0.378	0.357
8	0.48	0.472	0.454	0.432	0.410
9	0.53	0.524	0.507	0.484	0.459
10	0.58	0.574	0.557	0.533	0.506
20	0.92	0.948	0.942	0.914	0.873
30	1.14	1.204	1.214	1.187	1.137
40	1.30	1.401	1.429	1.404	1.346
50	1.43	1.562	1.607	1.585	1.520
60	1.54	1.700	1.760	1.741	1.671
70	1.63	1.819	1.895	1.880	1.805
80	1.71	1.925	2.016	2.004	1.924
90	1.78	2.021	2.126	2.117	2.033
100	1.84	2.108	2.227	2.221	2.132
1000	3.59	4.70	5.30	5.29	4.88

2.1   *How σ can boost an economy at various stages of its development*

Let us illustrate theorem 1 by determining the elasticity of income per person with respect to the elasticity of substitution for any value of the capital–labor ratio. From (2) we have

$$e_{y,\sigma}(r, \sigma; \delta) = \frac{\partial y}{\partial \sigma} \cdot \frac{\sigma}{y} = \frac{\partial \log y}{\partial p}\frac{dp}{d\sigma}\sigma$$

$$= \frac{1}{\sigma p}\left\{-\frac{1}{p}\log\left[\delta r^p + (1-\delta)\right]\right\} + \frac{\delta r^p \log r}{\delta r^p + (1-\delta)} \qquad (17)$$

Theorem 1 ensures that this elasticity is positive, and table 5.3 displays its values for various values of σ at several stages of the economy's development (i.e. for various values of the capital–labor ratio r).

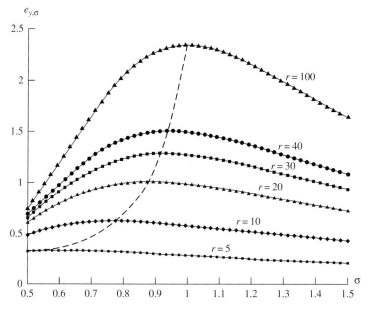

Figure 5.4 Elasticity of income per person with respect to the elasticity of substitution at various stages of an economy's development $e_{y,\sigma}(\sigma;r,\bar{\delta})$ **for** $\bar{\delta} = 0.33$ **and** $r = 5, 10, 20, 30, 40, 100$.

This elasticity increases significantly with r; for instance, with $\delta = 1/3$ and $\sigma = 0.8$, a 1% increase in the elasticity of substitution will increase income per person by 0.3% if $r = 5$ and by 0.92% if $r = 20$.

Notice that while $e_{y,\sigma}(r, \sigma; \delta)$ is an increasing function of r and δ, it is not a monotonic function of σ, as can be seen in table 5.3 and on figure 5.2: when σ is relatively small, $e_{y,\sigma}(r, \sigma; \delta)$ is an increasing function of σ for a given r; it then becomes a slowly decreasing function of σ.

The sensitivity of income per person to changes in the elasticity of substitution goes through a maximum which is located, in $(e_{y,\sigma}, \sigma)$ space, on a line which is always increasing; this is the dashed line in figure 5.4. This means that for very large values of r there is an extremely high sensitivity of income per person to a change in σ if the production function is Cobb–Douglas or *nearly* Cobb–Douglas. This is a direct consequence of the observation we made about the inflection point of the general mean in chapter 4.

2.2 The consequences of an increasing elasticity of substitution on equilibrium income per person

The force exerted by the elasticity of substitution on the growth process can also be thrown in full light by measuring the sensitivity of the steady state income per person y^* to a change in σ. We thus illustrate theorem 2 by determining the elasticity of y^* with respect to σ, denoted $e_{y^*,\sigma}$.

Denote the steady state values of y and r as r^* and y^* respectively; they are such that $sy^* = nr^*$, or $y^* = (n/s)r^*$. This linear relationship between r^* and y^* implies that the elasticity of y^* with respect to σ is equal to the elasticity of r^* with respect to σ. We will make use of this property to determine $e_{y^*,\sigma}$ as follows:

$$e_{y^*,\sigma} \equiv \frac{\partial y^*}{\partial \sigma}\frac{\sigma}{y^*} = \frac{\partial r^*}{\partial \sigma}\frac{\sigma}{r^*} = \frac{\partial r^*}{\partial p}\frac{dp}{d\sigma}\frac{\sigma}{r^*} = \frac{\partial \log r^*}{\partial p}\frac{dp}{d\sigma}\sigma \qquad (18)$$

The solution of $sy = s[\delta r^p + 1 - \delta]^{1/p} = nr$ is

$$r^* = \left[\frac{1-\delta}{(n/s)^p - \delta}\right]^{1/p}.$$

Taking the log of r^*, and calculating (18), we get:

$$e_{y^*,\sigma} = \frac{-1}{p\sigma}\left\{\frac{1}{p}\log\left[\frac{1-\delta}{(n/s)^p - \delta}\right] + \frac{(n/s)^p \log(n/s)}{(n/s)^p - \delta}\right\} \qquad (19)$$

How do we know that the right-hand side of (19) is always positive? Through theorem 2 or, equivalently, noting that (18) is equal to the derivative of a general mean (y^*) with respect to its order (p), a positive number, multiplied by $(dp/d\sigma)(\sigma/y^*) = (\sigma y^*)^{-1}$, also a positive number.

Not only is the RHS of (19) positive, but it is a surprisingly fast increasing function of σ. Indeed, it becomes asymptotical to a vertical at the threshold value $\hat{\sigma}$, where it is not defined any more. In figure 5.5, $e_{y^*,\sigma}$ is represented for $n = 0.01$, $s = 0.2$, and for four values of δ (0.2; 0.25; 0.3; 0.33). The striking feature is the strong convexity of the elasticity of y^* with respect to σ in the interval of $\sigma(\sim 0.7, \sim 1.2)$ where we believe most economies are presently located.

We conclude this section by observing that illustrations of theorems 1 and 2 testify to the tremendous impact even a small change in the elasticity of substitution can have on an economy at *any* stage of its development. Precise as these numbers may be, however, they are only static measures of the sensitivity of the economy to changes in σ: they should be complemented by a complete, dynamic analysis of any stepwise change of σ on the economy. We thus should know how such a change would impact upon the sum of the infinite stream of discounted benefits society could enjoy in the future. Furthermore, this should be done in a model exhibiting a measure of technical progress, so that the total benefits of a change in σ can be compared to those generated by a change in technological progress. This however will have to wait until we have covered the subject of optimal growth (Part II); we will address this important issue in Part III, chapter 13.

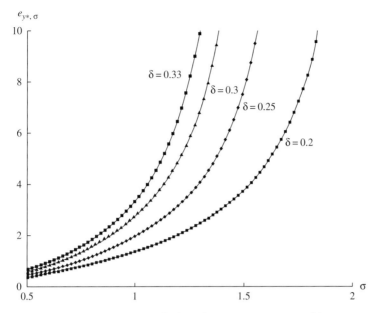

Figure 5.5 Elasticity of equilibrium income per person with respect to the elasticity of substitution for various values of $\pi_0 = \delta \ e_{y*,\sigma}(\sigma; \delta, \bar{s}, \bar{n})$ for $\bar{s} = 0.2$; $\bar{n} = 0.01$ and $\delta = 0.2, 0.25, 0.3, 0.33$.

3 Introducing technical progress

As mentioned earlier, the standard neoclassical model is capable of sustained growth without technical progress, but only provided that there are very weakly diminishing returns to capital. In equation (11) and table 5.1, we have made that statement precise in terms of the minimal elasticity of substitution compatible with sustained growth under unchanging technology, with given population growth and saving-investment rate. In that case of substitution-based growth, the growth rate rises to a limiting value of $s\delta^{\sigma/(\sigma-1)} = sm_\delta(\sigma)$. This theoretical possibility evidently requires a larger value of σ than conventionally appears in calibrations of growth models. The main source of modern growth is pretty clearly technological progress. But it seems important to be able to measure how a change in the elasticity compares to a change in technological progress in terms of its impact upon the whole future of an economy.

This is a good place to emphasize a point made in section 1. In the language of the one-sector growth model, the elasticity of substitution between labour and capital appears as a parameter of the production function, a given technological fact. But the model itself is intended to "represent" an economy with many goods and many industries. In that context, substitution between labour and capital can also take the form of induced substitution *on the demand side* between goods with different characteristic capital-intensities. Thus a reduction in the rental rate on capital can induce direct substitution of capital for labour within each industry. In a competitive environment, it will also reduce the price of capital-intensive goods relative to labour-intensive goods. If the sales and output of capital-intensive goods rise and those of labour-intensive goods fall, capital will be substituted for labor indirectly as well. Both channels affect the measured "aggregative" elasticity of substitution. Only long-run mobility of capital is required. We will return to this mechanism in a little more detail in section 4.

So far we have made use of the CES production function without technological progress, as represented in (1). The natural next step is to introduce technical progress in order to analyze its interaction with the elasticity of substitution in the generation of sustainable growth.

3.1 General specifications of technical progress and results

Consider capital-augmenting progress depicted by a function of time $h(t)$ (with $h'(t) > 0$) multiplying K and a labour-augmenting progress $g(t)$ ($g'(t) > 0$) function multiplying $L(t)$. If the production function is CES, equation (3) is now replaced by

$$\frac{Y}{Y_0} = \left\{ \delta \left[h(t) \frac{K}{K_0} \right]^p + (1 - \delta) \left[g(t) \frac{L}{L_0} \right]^p \right\}^{1/p} \tag{20}$$

The main results of section 2 now can be extended in the form of the following theorems:

3.1.1 Theorem 4

If an economy is driven by a CES production function exhibiting either capital- or labour-augmenting technical progress, or both, then at any stage of its development income per person is an increasing function of its elasticity of substitution.

PROOF   Factoring out $\dfrac{L}{L_0}$ in (20) yields the income per person index:

$$y = \frac{Y/Y_0}{L/L_0} = \left\{ \delta \left[h(t) \frac{K}{K_0} \right]^p + (1 - \delta) g(t)^p \right\}^{1/p}. \tag{21}$$

The RHS of (21) is a general mean of $h(t) K / K_0$ and $g(t)$ of order p, and therefore an increasing function of σ.

3.1.2 Theorem 5

If an economy is driven by a CES production function with either capital- or labour-augmenting progress, or both, then at any stage of its development the cost of producing one unit of national product is a decreasing function of the elasticity of substitution.

PROOF   Minimize the cost function $qK + wL$, or alternatively, for simpler calculations, the cost index

$$\frac{C}{C_0} = \delta\left(\frac{q}{q_0}\right)\left(\frac{K}{K_0}\right) + (1-\delta)\left(\frac{w}{w_0}\right)\left(\frac{L}{L_0}\right) \tag{22}$$

subject to the production constraint (20). The unit cost index, $(C/C_0)/(Y/Y_0) \equiv c$, is then equal to

$$c = \left\{\delta\left[\frac{q}{q_0}h_t^{-1}\right]^{1-\sigma} + (1-\delta)\left[\frac{w}{w_0}g_t^{-1}\right]^{1-\sigma}\right\}^{\frac{1}{1-\sigma}} \tag{23}$$

(see appendix).

We recognize in (23) a general mean of $(q/q_0)h_t^{-1}$ and $(w/w_0)g_t^{-1}$ of order $1-\sigma$, and therefore a decreasing function of σ.

3.2 *Asymptotic growth with labour-augmenting technical progress*

For simplicity we will mainly consider the purely labour-augmenting case. More general formulations would lead to qualitatively similar conclusions, but do not lend themselves to compact descriptions. To simplify notation, we set the base values Y_0, K_0 and L_0 to unit. Y, K and L are then to be viewed as indexes. In this section, we also specify $g(t)$ as $e^{\lambda t}$. Normalizing Y_0, K_0 and L_0 to 1, the production function has the form

$$Y = \left[\delta K^p + (1-\delta)(e^{\lambda t}L)^p\right]^{1/p}.$$

At this point it is extremely useful to make a change of variables in order to transform the differential equation governing the economy into an autonomous one. The reason is not that it necessarily simplifies its solution, because in any case the equation does not allow an analytical solution – numerical methods will have to be used. The reason is that in the new space of variables we will define, a phase diagram will be available, which will be quite handy to understand the issues related to the long-term evolution of the economy. If $L = e^{nt}$ represents the evolution of labour, we define *efficient* labour units as $e^{(n+\lambda)t}$; income per unit of efficient labour, denoted y_γ, will be equal to

$$y_\gamma = \frac{Y}{e^{(n+\lambda)t}}.$$

With this notation, income per person, our variable of central importance, becomes

$$y = \frac{Y}{L} = \frac{Y}{e^{nt}} = y_\gamma e^{\lambda t};$$

the growth rate of income per person is then

$$\frac{\dot{y}}{y} = \frac{\dot{y}_\gamma}{y_\gamma} + \lambda;$$

(this will prove very useful later). We can now write

$$y_\gamma = \frac{Y}{e^{(n+\lambda)t}} = \left[\delta K^p + (1-\delta)e^{p(n+\lambda)t}\right]^{1/p} e^{-(n+\lambda)t\frac{p}{p}}$$

$$= \left[\delta K^p e^{-p(n+\lambda)t} + 1 - \delta\right]^{1/p}.$$

Denoting in a similar way capital per efficient labour unit as r_γ, we have

$$r_\gamma = \frac{K}{Le^{\lambda t}} = \frac{K}{e^{(n+\lambda)t}}.$$

We can then write y_γ as

$$y_\gamma = \left[\delta r_\gamma^p + 1 - \delta\right]^{1/p}.$$

Let us now derive the differential equation governing r_γ. The growth rate of r_γ is, from the definition of r_γ

$$\frac{\dot{r}_\gamma}{r_\gamma} = \frac{\dot{K}}{K} - (n+\lambda).$$

As before, $\dot{K} = sY$; therefore,

$$\frac{\dot{K}}{K} = \frac{sY}{K} = s\frac{y_\gamma}{r_\gamma}$$

and the equation of motion governing r_γ is

$$\dot{r}_\gamma = sy_\gamma - (n+\lambda)r_\gamma.$$

We have thus what we wanted: an autonomous equation which can be depicted in $(r_\gamma, \dot{r}_\gamma)$ space. It has all the same qualitative properties as those of the corresponding equation in $(r, \dot{r})$ space; the only difference is that ray nr is now replaced by $(n+\lambda)r_\gamma$.

In the preceding section, we had shown that, without any technological progress, there was a threshold $\hat{\sigma}$ above which income per person would grow permanently, and another threshold $\bar{\sigma}$ under which income per person would decrease toward zero. Let us now examine what can be the ultimate convergence of income per person in the presence of labour-augmenting technological progress. We should distinguish two principal cases : $\sigma > 1$ and $\sigma > 1$, each with important subcases.

Before we do this, note two properties that will prove essential: first, the Pitchford constant will remain the same as before: $m_\delta(\sigma) = \delta^{1/p}$ will be equal to $\lim_{r_\gamma \to \infty} y'_\gamma(r_\gamma) = \lim_{r_\gamma \to \infty} y_\gamma / r$ with $\sigma > 1$ and to $\lim_{r_\gamma \to 0} y'_\gamma(r_\gamma) = \lim_{r_\gamma \to 0} y_\gamma / r$ with $\sigma < 1$. Secondly, the elasticity of y_γ with respect to r_γ, $\pi(r_\gamma) = r_\gamma y'_\gamma / y_\gamma$ will tend toward 1 in the *two* following cases: first when $r_\gamma \to \infty$ and $\sigma > 1$, *and also* when $r_\gamma \to 0$ and $\sigma < 1$.

3.2.1 Asymptotic growth when $\sigma \geq 1$

The growth rate of income per efficient unit of labour is

$$\frac{\dot{y}_\gamma}{y_\gamma} = y'_\gamma \frac{r_\gamma}{y_\gamma} \frac{\dot{r}_\gamma}{r_\gamma} = \pi(r_\gamma) \frac{\dot{r}_\gamma}{r_\gamma} = \pi(r_\gamma) \left[s \frac{y_\gamma}{r_\gamma} - (n+\lambda) \right] \tag{24}$$

and the growth rate of income per person is

$$\frac{\dot{y}}{y} = \frac{\dot{y}_\gamma}{y_\gamma} + \lambda = \pi(r_\gamma) \left[s \frac{y_\gamma}{r_\gamma} - (n+\lambda) \right] + \lambda \tag{25}$$

We are now able to discuss the various cases of equilibrium and disequilibrium.

The case $\sigma \geq 1$ and $n + \lambda > sm_\delta(\sigma)$.

In this case an equilibrium (denoted r_γ^*) exists[5] (see figure 5.6a; in this diagram we have chosen $n = 0.01$; $\lambda = 0.005$; $s = 0.1$; $\delta = 0.35$; $\sigma = 1.1$). This means $\lim_{r_\gamma \to r_\gamma^*} \dot{r}_\gamma^*/r_\gamma = 0$; since $\lim_{r_\gamma \to r_\gamma^*} \pi(r_\gamma)$ is finite, $\lim_{r_\gamma \to r_\gamma^*} \dot{y}_\gamma / y_\gamma = 0$; also, $\lim_{r_\gamma \to r_\gamma^*} y_\gamma = y(r_\gamma^*) = y_\gamma^*$. We have then, for the ultimate evolution of y:

$$\text{if } n + \lambda > sm_\delta(\sigma), \ \lim_{t \to \infty} y(t) = \lim_{t \to \infty} y_\gamma e^{\lambda t} = y_\gamma^* e^{\lambda t}.$$

Therefore, equilibrium means that income per person will increase asymptotically at rate λ; total income's asymptotical growth rate will be $n + \lambda$.

The case $\sigma \geq 1$ and $n + \lambda \leq sm_\delta(\sigma)$.

This case corresponds to figure 5.6b (here $\sigma = 2.25$). Since the limit of $\pi(r_\gamma)$ when $r_\gamma \to \infty$ is one, we can see from the last expression on the right-hand side of (24) that

$$\text{if } n + \lambda \leq sm_\delta(\sigma), \ \lim_{r_\gamma \to \infty} \frac{\dot{y}_\gamma}{y_\gamma} = sm_\delta(\sigma) - (n+\lambda);$$

y_γ will therefore increase asymptotically at rate $sm_\delta(\sigma) - (n + \lambda)$; y and Y will do so at rates $sm_\delta(\sigma) - n$ and $sm_\delta(\sigma)$ respectively. Note that the ultimate growth rate of y will be *higher* than λ if $sm_\delta(\sigma) - n > \lambda$. We will call σ^{**} the threshold value of σ corresponding to inequality $n + \lambda \leq sm_\delta(\sigma)$. It will be of course given

---

[5] It is given by $sy_\gamma = nr_\gamma$, i.e. by $r_\gamma^* = \left[\frac{1-\delta}{(n+\lambda)/s - \delta} \right]^{1/p}$.

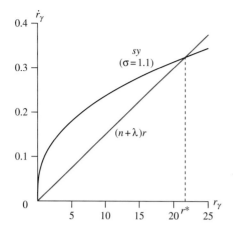

Figure 5.6a   The case $\sigma \geq 1$ and $n + \lambda > sm_\delta(\sigma)$; $\lim_{t\to\infty} \dot{y}/y = \lambda$.

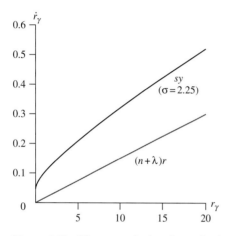

Figure 5.6b   The case $\sigma \geq 1$ and $n + \lambda \leq sm_\delta(\sigma)$; $\lim_{t\to\infty} \dot{y}/y = sm_\delta(\sigma) - n \geq \lambda$.

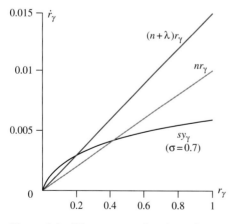

Figure 5.6c   The case $\sigma < 1$ and $n + \lambda < sm_\delta(\sigma)$; $\lim_{t\to\infty} \dot{y}/y = \lambda$.

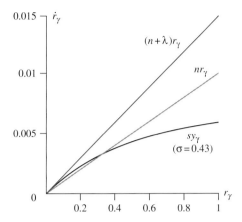

Figure 5.6d The case $\sigma < 1$ and $n < \mathrm{sm}_\delta(\sigma) < n + \lambda; 0 < \lim \dot{y}/y < \lambda.$

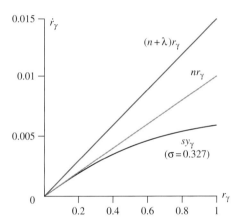

Figure 5.6e The case $\sigma < 1$ and $n = \mathrm{sm}_\delta(\sigma); \lim_{t \to \infty} \dot{y}/y = 0.$

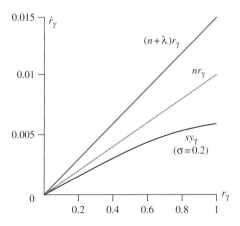

Figure 5.6f The case $\sigma < 1$ and $n > \mathrm{sm}_\delta(\sigma); \lim_{t \to \infty} \dot{y}/y < 0.$

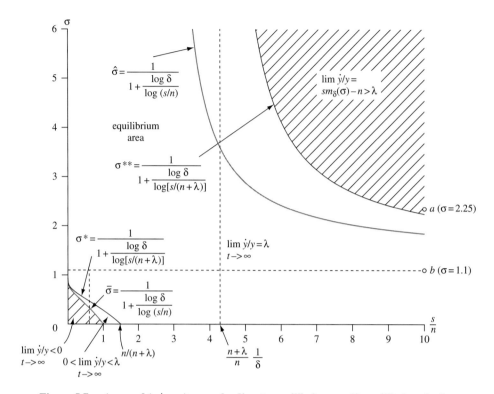

Figure 5.7a   Areas of $(s/n, \sigma)$ space leading to equilibrium or disequilibrium in the case of labour-augmenting technical progress at rate $\lambda(\lambda = 0.005)$; points a and b correspond to figures 5.6a and 5.6b.

by equation (11) where n is replaced by $n + \lambda$, i.e. by

$$\sigma \geq \sigma^{**} = \frac{1}{1 + (\log \delta)/ \log(s/(n + \lambda)}. \tag{26}$$

The corresponding threshold value for s is

$$s^{**} = \frac{n + \lambda}{m_\delta(\sigma)} = (n + \lambda)\delta^{-(1/p)}. \tag{27}$$

Figure 5.7a depicts the equilibrium and disequilibrium areas in space $(s/n, \sigma)$. The cases just discussed above correspond to points above the horizontal $\sigma = 1$, in areas respectively below and above the curve $\sigma^{**}(s/n)$. For instance, point a in the diagram corresponds to $s = 0.1$, $n = 0.01$ (therefore $s/n = 10$) and $\sigma = 2.25$; it lies just above the threshold $\sigma^{**}(10) = 2.24$. It will then lead to a limiting growth rate of y, $sm_\delta(\sigma) - n$, higher than λ. Another diagram describes the ultimate growth rate of *total* income as a function of σ (figure 5.8a), where $m_\delta(\sigma)$ has been drawn for $\delta = 0.35$ and various values of s. It fixes all the parameters except σ, and shows the asymptotic growth rate of Y as a function of σ. When σ is less than the critical value σ^{**}, Y eventually grows at its "natural" rate $\lambda + n$; we are in the standard neoclassical steady state. For values of the elasticity of substitution

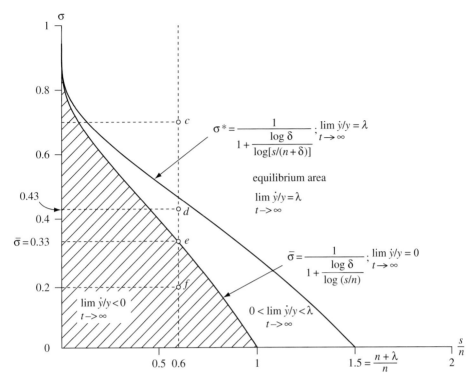

Figure 5.7b Enlargement of area $(0 \leq s/n) \leq 2, 0 \leq \sigma \leq 1)$ of figure 5.7a. Points c, d, e and f correspond to figures 5.6c, 5.6d, 5.6e and 5.6f.

larger than σ^{**}, the asymptotic growth rate of Y is sm_σ which is now larger than $\lambda + n$, the difference being the contribution of substitution-driven growth. Points a and b in figure 5.7a are also represented in figure 5.8a.

The diagram shows that a higher elasticity of substitution implies a higher asymptotic growth rate, other things equal. It is now easy to see what happens if other parameters change. A higher λ or n simply lifts the initial horizontal part of the growth-rate curve, and extends it to the right until it intersects the rising curve $m_\delta(\sigma)$. A higher value of δ or s does several things: it raises the upper limit of the growth rate; it lifts the whole rising portion of the growth-rate curve, and it moves σ^{**} to the left, to the point where the higher growth-rate curve intersects the $(\lambda + n)$-horizontal. Thus the critical value of σ is lower for higher δ or s, or lower n and λ.

3.2.2 Asymptotic growth when $\sigma < 1$

The case $n + \lambda < sm_\delta(\sigma); \sigma^* < \sigma < 1$.

Let us call σ^* the threshold value corresponding to equality $n + \lambda = sm_\delta(\sigma)$ *and to* $\sigma < 1$. If an equilibrium is warranted for r_γ (if $n + \lambda \leq sm_\delta(\sigma)$, or

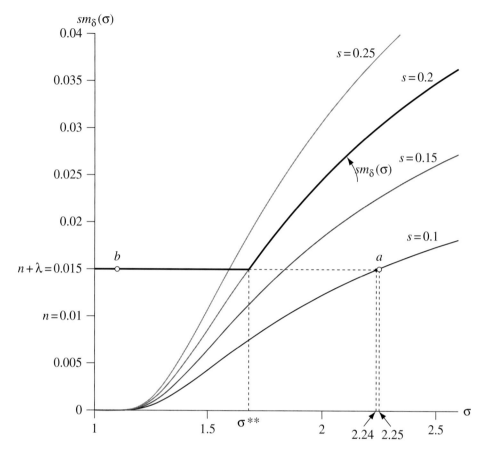

Figure 5.8a **The asymptotic growth rate of *total income* γ as a function of σ; the case $\sigma > 1$; $\delta = 0.35$; $\lim_{t \to \infty} \dot{y}/y = \max(sm_\delta(\sigma), n + \lambda)$; the asymptotic growth rate of y is $\lim_{t \to \infty} \dot{y}/y = \max(sm_\delta(\sigma) - n, \lambda)$.**

equivalently if $\sigma^* < \sigma < 1$) then as before r_γ and y_γ will tend toward finite limits; the asymptotic growth rate of y and Y will be λ and $\lambda + n$ respectively (see figure 5.6c).

The case $n + \lambda \geq sm_\delta(\sigma)$; $\sigma \leq \sigma^*$.

Now suppose that $n + \lambda > sm_\delta(\sigma)$. We consider here the case of a poor economy where the rate of *net* savings is extremely small (but as we have stressed before, we cannot, unfortunately, dismiss that possibility). It can be seen from the corresponding phase diagram (figure 5.1b, adapted to the new notation) that r_γ will decrease toward zero, whatever the initial value r_γ^0 may be. The ultimate (asymptotic) growth rate of y_γ will be $sm_\delta(\sigma) - (n + \lambda)$; that of y will be $sm_\delta(\sigma) - n$. This is where we have to be careful: *three* cases must be considered. Define $\bar{\sigma}$ such that $sm_\delta(\sigma) = n$.

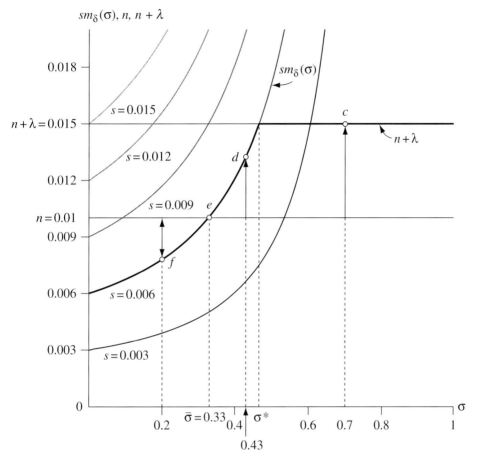

Figure 5.8b The asymptotic growth rate of total income Y as a function of σ; the case $\sigma \leq 1$.

$$\lim_{t \to \infty} \dot{Y}/Y = \min(sm_\delta(\sigma), n + \lambda).$$

The asymptotic growth rate of income per person, $\lim_{t \to \infty} \dot{y}/y$, is $\lim_{t \to \infty} \dot{y}/y - n = \min(sm_\delta(\sigma) - n, \lambda)$; it is indicated by the vertical arrows. In the case of point f, it is the *negative* of the double arrow.
- Case $\sigma \geq \sigma^*$: income per person ultimately grows at rate $n + \lambda$
- Case $\bar{\sigma} < \sigma < \sigma^*$: $\lim_{t \to \infty} \dot{y}/y = sm_\delta(\sigma) - n < \lambda$ a constant
- Case $\sigma = \bar{\sigma}$: income per person ultimately tends toward a constant
- Case $\sigma < \bar{\sigma}$: income per person ultimately declines to zero. For $\sigma = 0.2$, the asymptotic growth rate of income per person is *minus 0.0022*.

i) $n < sm_\delta(\sigma) < n + \lambda$; equivalently, $\bar{\sigma} < \sigma < \sigma^*$ (see figure 5.6d); income per person will ultimately grow at the *positive* rate $sm_\delta(\sigma) - n < \lambda$ (although y_γ is always decreasing).

ii) $sm_\delta(\sigma) = n$; $\sigma = \bar{\sigma}$ (figure 5.6e); the growth rate of income per person will converge toward zero; therefore y will converge toward a constant value.

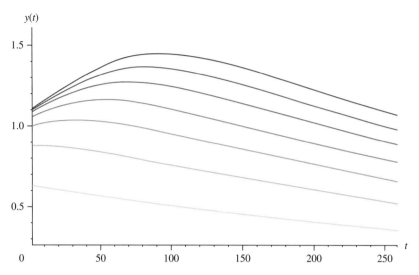

Figure 5.9   Time paths of income per person $y(t)$ **corresponding to** $\sigma = 0.2$ **(case c of figure 5.6b). All trajectories will tend toward zero, with an asymptotical growth rate of y equal to *minus* 0.0022.**

iii) $sm_\delta(\sigma) < n$; $\sigma < \bar{\sigma}$ (figure 5.6f); the growth rate $\dot{y}/y$ will converge toward a *negative* value, $sm_\delta(\sigma) - n$; it implies that *income per person* will eventually *decrease forever* toward zero even though we are in a model with labour augmenting progress. This of course is a first surprise. The second surprise is that it is quite possible, according to the initial conditions and the parameters $s, \delta, \sigma, \lambda$ and n, that income per person will *increase* in a first phase (although y_γ always decreases), before falling toward its doom. We have illustrated this situation in the following case ($s = 0.006$; $\sigma = 0.2$), marked by the double arrow on diagram 5.8b. The long-term growth rate of income per person, $\lim_{t \to \infty} \dot{y}/y$, is equal to $sm_\delta(\sigma) - n = 0.006(0.35)^{-1/4} - 0.01 = -0.0022$ in this case (on figure 5.8b, it is the *negative* of the distance marked with the double arrow). Figure 5.9 depicts the trajectories that our colleague Ernst Hairer has solved for us with his program Dopri 5 for seven initial values of r_γ^0 ($= r^0$) between 0.5 and 2, by steps of 0.25. The corresponding trajectories of y have been calculated from those of r_γ and y_γ. Note that the quick accumulation of the initial points y^0 corresponding to the initial r_γ^0 values is due to the strong concavity of $y_\gamma(r_\gamma)$ when σ is low (our case).

The increasing property of some trajectories $y(t)$ can clearly be seen. The indeterminacy of their slope in the general case can be explained as follows. Recall that the growth rate $\dot{y}/y$ is given by expression

$$\frac{\dot{y}}{y} = \frac{\dot{y}_\gamma}{y_\gamma} + \lambda = \pi(r_\gamma)\frac{\dot{r}_\gamma}{r_\gamma} + \lambda = \pi(r_\gamma)\left[s\frac{y_\gamma}{r_\gamma} - (n + \lambda) \right] + \lambda. \qquad (28)$$

The bracketed expression above is equal to $\dot{r}_\gamma / r_\gamma$, and we know that it is negative for any r_γ. The sign of $\dot{y}/y$ is determined by the relative sizes of the parameters combined to those of the variables r_γ and y_γ. However, the qualitative behaviour of y can be inferred analytically at least at the initial point defined by $t = 0$ and $r_\gamma(0) = r(0) = 1$; $y_\gamma[(r_\gamma(0)] = y[(r(0)] = 1$. Indeed, at that point $\pi(1) = y'(1) = \delta$; therefore, we have

$$\dot{y}(0)/y(0) = \delta\,[s - (n + \lambda)] + \lambda = \delta s + (1 - \delta)\lambda - \delta n. \qquad (29)$$

Whether the economy will experience a first phase of growth (an increase in income per person) will depend solely on the respective sizes of parameters σ, δ, s and n, according to a rule that makes a lot of economic sense. Indeed a necessary and sufficient condition for an economy to go through such a first phase of growth in the iii) scenario (when $s/n < 1/m_\delta(\sigma)$), is that the average of s and λ is higher than δn.

We cannot emphasize too much the importance of the role played by the elasticity of substitution. A high σ can bring excellent news: if it is high enough, there is a possibility that the ultimate growth rate of income per person will exceed the rate of technological progress. But it gives also a strenuous warning: if both σ and the savings rate are very small, not only income per person may decrease toward a constant value, but it can even collapse to zero.

3.3 How does a change in the elasticity of substitution compare to a change in technological progress?

The natural question now is to compare impacts for society of changes in the elasticity of substitution σ and in the technical progress rate λ. We cannot simply rely on measures like elasticities of income per person at some point with respect to each of those parameters; indeed, we need to consider the whole time picture represented by the infinite stream of income per person generated by the possible values of those parameters.

The answer to this important question will have to wait until we have introduced optimal growth theory. Indeed, we will then show how to determine an optimality criterion for society over a long period of time, and the resulting optimal savings rate. It is with that optimality reference that we will carry out our comparative analysis. This will be done in chapter 13.

4 Time-series and cross-section estimates

In this section we present some new estimates of the elasticity of substitution. They are derived from time-series and cross-section analysis of data of OECD countries (see tables 5.4 and 5.5), and we interpret them using the theory already developed.

Table 5.4 *The increase of the elasticity of substitution from period 1966–81 to period 1982–97; σ is estimated from $y = aw^{\sigma}$*

Country	1966–81			1982–1997		
	σ	st. dev.	R^2	σ	st. dev.	R^2
Austria	0.951	0.007	0.997	1.031	0.016	0.997
Belgium	0.914	0.005	0.999	1.129	0.028	0.992
Denmark	0.984	0.009	0.999	1.173	0.022	0.995
Finland	1.010	0.012	0.998	1.025	0.038	0.980
France	0.948	0.007	0.999	1.243	0.016	0.998
Germany	0.932	0.007	0.999	1.138	0.020	0.996
Great Britain	0.997	0.007	0.999	0.984	0.018	0.995
Greece	0.965	0.014	0.997	1.058	0.012	0.998
Ireland	0.994	0.010	0.998	1.271	0.025	0.995
Italy	1.015	0.006	0.999	1.129	0.028	0.992
Luxembourg	0.801	0.057	0.983	1.006	0.022	0.993
Netherlands	0.947	0.008	0.999	1.097	0.049	0.972
Portugal	0.886	0.030	0.984	0.997	0.008	0.999
Spain	0.955	0.005	0.999	1.048	0.015	0.997
Sweden	0.969	0.011	0.998	0.985	0.02	0.991
United States	0.981	0.01	0.999	1.041	0.01	0.998

Source: OECD data

Table 5.5 *Cross-section estimates of the elasticity of substitution σ. Regression: $y = aw^{\sigma}$*

year	σ	st.dev.	R^2	year	σ	st. dev.	R^2
1966	0.815	0.060	0.935	1982	0.938	0.043	0.974
1967	0.835	0.061	0.934	1983	0.972	0.044	0.973
1968	0.819	0.062	0.931	1984	0.984	0.043	0.976
1969	0.822	0.069	0.917	1985	0.986	0.040	0.979
1970	0.821	0.071	0.938	1986	0.962	0.045	0.973
1971	0.823	0.065	0.925	1987	0.946	0.047	0.969
1972	0.826	0.057	0.941	1988	0.934	0.047	0.968
1973	0.773	0.070	0.902	1989	0.952	0.048	0.968
1974	0.841	0.083	0.888	1990	0.950	0.052	0.962
1975	0.896	0.091	0.881	1991	0.917	0.062	0.944
1976	0.917	0.083	0.903	1992	0.922	0.060	0.947
1977	0.879	0.058	0.947	1993	0.898	0.052	0.958
1978	0.853	0.049	0.960	1994	0.917	0.051	0.961
1979	0.870	0.053	0.955	1995	0.927	0.049	0.964
1980	0.836	0.070	0.916	1996	0.934	0.058	0.952
1981	0.866	0.059	0.943	1997	0.953	0.066	0.941

Source: OECD data.

Table 5.4 exhibits time-series estimates of σ for 16 OECD countries, derived from equation $y = aw^b$ without a time term.[6] In each case there are separate regressions for the intervals 1966–81 and 1982–97. Every correlation is very high, but of course y and w have strong trends.

The interesting regularity is that nearly all of the estimated elasticities of substitution are slightly below one in the first period and slightly above one in the second period (notice that the highest elasticity of substitution in the second period is observed in Ireland, where it is as high as 1.27). In only one case (Great Britain) does the earlier estimate exceed the later one. The empirical meaning is straightforward: w/y is just the labour share of output. In the first period, the labour share is generally rising in these countries, so y is increasing proportionately less than w. The implication is that $\sigma < 1$. In the second period, the wage share is generally falling, so y is increasing more than proportionately with w, and the estimated σ is above one.

Underlying these facts must be a mixture of short-run and long-run forces. If capital-intensity continues to increase in these countries, and if the elasticity of substitution indeed exceeds unity, then there could be a continuing tendency for the wage share to fall. Alternatively there could be social and political pressure for change in the institutions governing income distribution and the demand for labour.

Table 5.5 reproduces estimates of σ from a series of annual cross-country regressions parallel to the time-series equations. (For reasons of data availability, only 15 countries can be included.) Here two more striking regularities are visible, and require interpretation in terms of the theory. First of all, every cross-section estimate is less than one. (The same was true of the international cross-section estimates found by Arrow, Chenery, Minhas and Solow in 1961.) Secondly, the later ones are systematically larger than the earlier ones. The drift is not smooth, and may have business-cycle components. But the 1966 estimate is 0.815 and the 1997 estimate is 0.953, so the average drift is half a per cent per year.

In Arrow, Chenery, Minhas and Solow (1961) the elasticity of substitution was estimated from equation $y = aw^\sigma (= y_0(w/w_0)^\sigma)$, valid for any CES function, applied to an international cross-section. That formulation omitted technological progress. Our first step here is to reconstruct the analogous equation with technological progress. An easy way makes use of equation (20). Setting $h(t) = 1$

[6] We are grateful to Claudio Sfredo who provided us with the OECD data, which he had made comparable in his PhD thesis "Trade, Technology, and Factor Prices: A GDP Function Approach for the European Union", Geneva 2001, and which we used in these regressions.

and keeping in mind that $g(0) = g_0 = 1$, we have:

$$Y = Y_0 \left[\delta \left(\frac{K}{K_0} \right)^p + (1 - \delta) \left(g_t \frac{L}{L_0} \right)^p \right]^{1/p}. \tag{30}$$

The first step is to verify that $1 - \delta$ remains the labour share at the base year $t = 0$, i.e. $1 - \delta = w_0 L_0 / Y_0$. The marginal productivity of labour, equal to the wage rate w, is:

$$w = \frac{\partial Y}{\partial L} = Y_0 \left[\delta \left(\frac{K}{K_0} \right)^p + (1 - \delta) \left(g_t \frac{L}{L_0} \right)^p \right]^{\frac{1-p}{p}}$$
$$\cdot (1 - \delta) \left(g_t \frac{L}{L_0} \right)^{p-1} g_t \frac{1}{L_0}. \tag{31}$$

Setting $t = 0$, $K = K_0$ and $L = L_0$ in (31) gives $w_0 = Y_0 (1 - \delta) \frac{1}{L_0}$ and therefore $1 - \delta = w_0 L_0 / Y_0$.

Observe now that the bracketed term in (31) is equal, from (30), to $(Y / Y_0)^{1-p}$. Using this value as well as that of $1 - \delta$, we can write (31) as:

$$w = \frac{Y_0}{L_0} \frac{w_0 L_0}{Y_0} \left(\frac{Y}{Y_0} \right)^{1-p} g_t^p \left(\frac{L}{L_0} \right)^{p-1}$$
$$= w_0 \left(\frac{Y/L}{Y_0/L_0} \right)^{1-p} g_t^p \equiv w_0 \left(\frac{y}{y_0} \right)^{1-p} g_t^p. \tag{32}$$

Hence we have:

$$\frac{y}{y_0} = g_t^{\frac{p}{p-1}} \left(\frac{w}{w_0} \right)^{\frac{1}{1-p}} \tag{33}$$

or, using $p = 1 - 1/\sigma$,

$$y = y_0 g_t^{1-\sigma} \left(\frac{w}{w_0} \right)^\sigma, \tag{34}$$

which reduces to the standard form referred to above if we set $g(t) = 1$. Notice also that income per person, as an index number (y/y_0) is a geometric mean of the wage rate index (w/w_0) and the technical progress coefficient g_t, the elasticity of substitution acting as the weight; equivalently, the growth rate of income per person is the arithmetic average of the growth rates of w and g_t. We have

$$\dot{y}/y = (1 - \sigma)\dot{g}/g + \sigma \dot{w}/w. \tag{35}$$

(This squares well also with the particular case of the Cobb–Douglas, where $\sigma = 1$, entailing $\dot{y}/y = \dot{w}/w$ and $y = aw$).

Suppose $g(t) = e^{\lambda t}$. Then a time-series-based estimate of σ is the coefficient of $\ln(w/w_0)$ in a regression of $\ln y$ on $\ln(w/w_0)$ and t, and the coefficient of t is an estimate of $\lambda(1 - \sigma)$. In practice, $\ln(w/w_0)$ and t are likely to be collinear, and the regression estimates will be imprecise for that reason.[7] One possible recourse is simply to omit the term in λt. Then the OLS regression coefficient of $\ln w$ will be a biased estimate[8] of σ. The bias may be substantial: suppose that the wage index follows approximatively an exponential $e^{\omega t}$, where $\omega = \dot{w}/w$; equivalently, it implies that $\ln(w/w_0)$ behaves roughly like ωt, so $t \approx \omega^{-1} \ln(w/w_0)$. We then have:

$$\ln y = \text{constant} + (1 - \sigma)\lambda t + \sigma \ln(w/w_0)$$

$$= \text{constant} + (1 - \sigma)\frac{1}{\omega} \ln(w/w_0) + \sigma \ln(w/w_0) \tag{36}$$

$$= \text{constant} + \left[\left(1 - \frac{\lambda}{\omega}\right)\sigma + \frac{\lambda}{\omega} \right] \ln(w/w_0). \tag{37}$$

The innocuous-looking equation (37) bears important, far-reaching implications regarding the values of the rate of technical progress λ and the wage growth rate ω and their consequences on the estimate of σ. Before dealing with those implications, notice first that there are three cases where there is no bias between τ, the (bracketed) coefficient of $\ln(w/w_0)$, and σ. The first case corresponds to $\lambda = 0$, entailing $\tau = \sigma$. The two other cases each imply $\sigma = 1$: the second case corresponds to an estimate of τ equal to one: whatever λ and ω may be, it implies $\sigma = 1$. The third no-bias case corresponds to $\lambda = \omega$, and $\sigma = 1$ also.

Hence, for $\tau \neq 1$, $\lambda \neq 0$ and $\lambda \neq \omega$, there will always be a bias which needs to be carefully studied. Whether the estimate of τ will be above or below 1 will have important consequences, because the implied estimate of σ will behave entirely differently as a function of the ratio λ/ω. First, observe from (38) that the implied valued of σ is

$$\sigma\left(\frac{\lambda}{\omega}, \tau\right) = \frac{\frac{\lambda}{\omega} - \tau}{\frac{\lambda}{\omega} - 1} \tag{38}$$

with a derivative $\partial\sigma/\partial(\lambda/\omega) = (\tau - 1)/[(\lambda/\omega) - 1]^2$, which is positive or negative according to $\tau > 1$ or $\tau < 1$. Let us first consider the more usual case $\tau < 1$.

---

[7] A result confirmed by our own regressions.

[8] This possibility of bias if technological change is ignored has been mentioned in the literature. An excellent and detailed recent discussion in the case of the United States is in a paper by Pol Antràs: "Is The U.S. Aggregate Production Function Cobb–Douglas? New Estimates of the Elasticity of Substitution," September 2003. This paper contains other references. It also considers the symmetric analogue to $y = aw^b$ based on capital productivity and the rental rate, as well as estimates based upon the very definition of σ, and the inverses of all these relations; and it goes deeply into matters of econometric technique that are not the focus of attention for us.

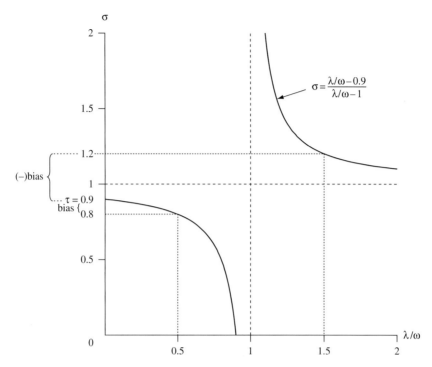

Figure 5.10 **The estimate of the elasticity of substitution σ as a function of λ/ω, assuming an estimate of τ lower than one (in this case: $\tau = 0.9$).**

Figure 5.10 depicts σ as a function of λ/ω for $\tau = 0.9$. The ordinate of the curve at the origin is $\tau = 0.9$; the bias $\tau - \sigma$ can be read off the diagram for any value of λ/ω. (As examples, we have shown those biases for $\lambda/\omega = 0.5$ and $\lambda/\omega = 1.5$.) Note that the estimate of σ will be lower than 1 (higher than 1) if and only if λ/ω is lower (higher) than 1. Some surprising outcomes now emerge: it can be seen that

(a) for the estimate of the elasticity of substitution to be higher than 0.5 if $\tau = 0.9$, λ/ω must be lower that 0.8; more generally, with $\tau < 1$, for $0.5 < \sigma < \tau$ we must have $\lambda/\omega < 2\tau - 1$.
(b) for σ to remain positive we must have $\lambda/\omega < \tau$.
(c) whenever $\lambda/\omega > 1$, the estimate of σ is larger than 1.
(d) whenever λ is very close to ω, our estimate of σ is likely to be either much too low or much too high.

Consider now the case $\tau > 1$. All conclusions are different. This time a value of λ/ω lower than one implies $\sigma > 1$, and vice-versa. Figure 5.11 depicts the case $\tau = 1.1$.

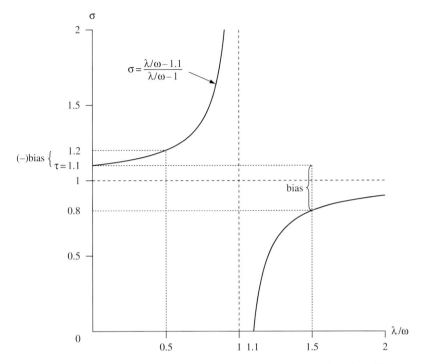

Figure 5.11 **The estimate of the elasticity of substitution σ as a function of λ/ω, assuming an estimate of τ above one (in this case: $\tau = 1.1$).**

(a) for the estimate to be between 1.1. and 1.2, λ/ω must be lower than 0.5.
(b) for σ to be positive, λ/ω must be larger than 1.1; more generally, for $\sigma > 0$, λ/ω must be larger than $2\tau - 1$.
(c) whenever $\lambda/\omega < 1$, the estimate of σ is lower than 1.
(d) values of λ/ω between 1 and τ leads to negative values of σ; values of λ/ω a little lower than 1 lead to unreliably high values of σ.

We conclude this analysis by observing that the direction of the bias $\tau - \sigma$ will depend crucially on the size of τ: if $\tau < 1$, the bias is positive for $\lambda/\omega < 1$ and negative for $\lambda/\omega > 1$; if $\tau > 1$, the contrary is true. Whatever the magnitude of τ, the absolute value of the bias gets huge whenever λ/ω gets close to one.

Let us now tentatively interpret table 5.4, using figures 5.10 and 5.11, as well as the preceding observations. A safe bet is to assume that in the last 40 years ω has remained larger than λ, but that the gap has been narrowing between the period when the labour share was growing and the period when that share was decreasing. So we could assume that λ/ω has been smaller than 1 throughout, but that it has been increasing. Consider now the first period: it corresponds to $\tau < 1$, with $\lambda/\omega < 1$ (figure 5.10). In the second period, $\tau > 1$ with $\lambda/\omega < 1$ but somewhat larger (figure 5.11). We can safely infer from this that the elasticity of substitution, from numbers smaller than 1, may have significantly increased over the τ estimate (itself above 1) in the second period, the more so since λ/ω has probably increased from the first to the second period.

5 The broader significance of the elasticity of substitution in the context of economic growth

We have shown that the elasticity of substitution is in part an efficiency parameter. An increase in it has permanent effects on the economy which are akin to those generated by a higher rate of technical progress. This is one reason why the size of σ is socially important. We want to suggest others.

As we stated earlier, the elasticity of substitution is in principle a property of a production function, and therefore a purely technological parameter. That is how we have treated it so far, in a one-good economy. But the one-good economy is intended as a prototype-model for an economy with many goods and many industries.

In that context, "the" elasticity of substitution performs much the same function that it does in the one-good economy. It provides an answer to the question: how big a change in the capital–labour ratio is induced by a (small) percentage change in the wage–rental ratio? But now the correct answer is a general-equilibrium matter, involving in principle the whole economy. (We understand, for example, though we do not dwell on it, that the correct answer will depend on how the initiating change in the wage–rental ratio is brought about.)

John Hicks understood this from the very beginning in his 1932 *Theory of Wages*. He asks what determines the magnitude of the elasticity of substitution, and mentions three categories of factors: the degree of capital–labour substitutability within the various industries, the extent to which the character of technological innovations is influenced by relative factor prices, and finally the range of capital–labour ratios to be found in the collection of industries and the degree to which the goods that they produce are substitutable for one another in the purchases of ultimate consumers.

We have already mentioned the mechanism by which general-equilibrium effects could be expected to amplify the within-industry response of the aggregate capital–labour ratio to differences in the wage–rental ratio: a higher wage–rental ratio increases the cost (and eventually the price) of labour-intensive goods relative to capital-intensive goods, the overall capital–labour ratio would tend to rise (even if there were very little technical substitution of capital for labour within industries). This process was analysed with great clarity and force by Ronald Jones (1965). Edmond Malinvaud (2003), using a slightly different model, uncovers a complication: the end result depends also on income-elasticities of demand because the change in factor prices redistributes income. This could in principle upset the "natural" conclusion that substitution on the demand side augments the elasticity of substitution; but Malinvaud thinks that this perverse outcome is empirically unlikely.

Looked at from the other direction, a high value of σ means that the economy can adapt to large changes in K/L while experiencing relatively small changes in w/q. On the whole, this strikes us as a good thing. In principle, what matters for social welfare is that w and q should be large and growing, or even more fundamentally that y should be large and growing. That is more a matter of efficiency than anything else. Nevertheless, efficiency aside, it is probably easier for an economy to adapt to – possibly erratic – shifts in K/L if it can be done without large changes in relative factor prices. We have already observed that the imputed *share* of capital rises toward unity as K/L increases so long as $\sigma > 1$. This raises questions about political and economic equity, and about the distribution of property ownership, that are far beyond the scope of this chapter. It is probably a desirable outcome of economic evolution that the contribution of capital to production should come to dwarf that of labour, so long as the output is equitably distributed. We are a long way from that possible nirvana.

It seems clear to us that growth theory and associated empirical analysis have given less attention to the elasticity of substitution than it deserves as an important parameter of the growth process. (One obvious reason for this is the unique convenience of the Cobb–Douglas function in both theoretical and econometric work.) We have shown that small differences in σ can have noticeable effects on the path traced out by the standard model economy. Pure and applied growth theory have become fixated almost exclusively on the growth rate of total factor productivity. That is certainly important research. But we think it would be worthwhile to divert some of that effort to attempts to understand the origin and effects of the differences in σ from country to country and from time to time that are illustrated in tables 5.4 and 5.5 above.

Another possibility, not yet mentioned, is that some economies have strong customary or regulatory barriers to large changes in capital–labour ratios, and other economies do not. Aggregative observations will characterize the first group as having a lower σ than the second group. Long run behaviour will bear out this characterization, though it originates neither in supply-side nor demand-side "substitution" as normally understood.

A further potential research path has to do with the direction of endogenous technical change. The usual approach is to focus on the role of factor intensity: will new technology tend to be labour-augmenting or capital-augmenting, or otherwise biased? One might also wonder if there are forces leading new technology toward higher or lower σ. The analogy that comes to mind is George

Stigler's argument that uncertainty about expected output should lead a firm to prefer a fairly flat unit cost curve to one with a lower but more sharply defined minimum.

There may well be other interesting approaches to this question. From the growth-theoretic angle, the key characteristic is the whole economy's ability to absorb large increases in capital intensity (measured by K/L) without sharply diminishing returns, that is to say without a sharp fall in the rental rate for capital goods. Looking at the matter this way underlines the parallel between a high elasticity of substitution and a substantial rate of technological progress: both forces keep the return on capital from falling rapidly as capital intensity rises in the course of economic development. This parallel helps to make the empirical disentangling of the two effects so difficult. (One difference is that high σ makes the share of capital rise, even as the real wage rises.)

One may be led by these considerations to wonder about the welfare significance of a high elasticity of substitution in the extended sense, and whether this can be an object of policy. Those are questions that go to the heart of the role played by capital accumulation at any time or place, with its costs and rewards. They underline the importance of the distribution of ownership of human and physical capital. Answering them may help understand and shape our future.

Appendix: Derivation of the cost function with capital and labour-augmenting progress

Minimize the cost index[9]

$$\frac{C}{C_0} = \delta \left(\frac{q}{q_0}\right)\left(\frac{K}{K_0}\right) + (1-\delta)\left(\frac{w}{w_0}\right)\left(\frac{L}{L_0}\right) \tag{A1}$$

subject to the production constraint (22). The following Hicksian demand functions result:

$$\frac{K}{K_0} = \frac{Y}{Y_0}\left[\delta\left(\frac{q}{q_0}\right)^{\frac{p}{p-1}} h_t^{\frac{p}{1-p}} + (1-\delta)\left(\frac{w}{w_0}\right)^{\frac{p}{p-1}} g_t^{\frac{p}{1-p}}\right]^{-1/p} \left(\frac{q}{q_0}\right)^{\frac{1}{1-p}} h_t^{\frac{p}{1-p}} \tag{A2}$$

$$\frac{L}{L_0} = \frac{Y}{Y_0}\left[\delta\left(\frac{q}{q_0}\right)^{\frac{p}{p-1}} h_t^{\frac{p}{1-p}} + (1-\delta)\left(\frac{w}{w_0}\right)^{\frac{p}{p-1}} g_t^{\frac{p}{1-p}}\right]^{-1/p} \left(\frac{w}{w_0}\right)^{\frac{1}{1-p}} g_t^{\frac{p}{1-p}} \tag{A3}$$

---

[9] This cost index arises from $\frac{C}{C_0} = \frac{qK+wL}{q_0 K_0 + w_0 L_0} = \frac{(q_0 K_0)(q/q_0)(K/K_0)+(w_0 L_0)(w/w_0)(L/L_0)}{C_0} = \delta(q/q_0)(K/K_0) + (1-\delta)(w/w_0)(L/L_0)$, since $q_0 K_0/C_0 = \delta$ and $w_0 L_0/C_0 = 1-\delta$.

from which the cost index can be determined, after simplifications, as

$$\frac{C}{C_0} = \frac{Y}{Y_0} \left\{ \delta \left[\frac{q}{q_0} h_t^{-1} \right]^{\frac{p}{p-1}} + (1 - \delta) \left[\frac{w}{w_0} g_t^{-1} \right]^{\frac{p}{p-1}} \right\}^{\frac{p-1}{p}}. \qquad \text{(A4)}$$

Expressed in terms of σ, the unit cost index becomes

$$c = \frac{C/C_0}{Y/Y_0} = \left\{ \delta \left[\frac{q}{q_0} h_t^{-1} \right]^{1-\sigma} + (1 - \delta) \left[\frac{w}{w_0} g_t^{-1} \right]^{1-\sigma} \right\}^{\frac{1}{1-\sigma}}. \qquad \text{(A5)}$$

a general mean of order $1 - \sigma$ of the price indices q/q_0 and w/w_0 (respectively divided by $h(t)$ and $g(t)$), and therefore a decreasing function of σ.

CHAPTER 6

The long-term growth rate as a random variable, with an application to the US economy

A growth process is far from linear. The economy is submitted to random shocks and undergoes cycles, their length and amplitude hardly predictable. In this chapter, we will ask the following specific question: suppose that we make an estimate about the future yearly growth rates of an economy; each of these growth rates is considered as a random variable, with given mean and variance. What can we infer from those estimates about the n-year horizon expected growth rate and its variance? The answer is far from intuitive. Indeed, we might be tempted to say that the expected long-term growth rate is the expected yearly growth rate over that horizon. That this is not so will be illustrated in the following example.

We should first realize that the long-term growth rate, in the case of any variable annual growth rate, *cannot* be the average of the annual growth rates for the simple reason that such an average would be devoid of any meaning. Consider for instance the value of an asset growing from 100 to 300 in one year, falling then from 300 to zero in the second year. The first growth rate is $R_{0,1} = (300 - 100)/100 = +2 = +200\%$; the second one is $R_{1,2} = (0 - 300)/300 = -100\%$. The average of both growth rates is $+50\%$, but no one would ever use that number to assess the profitability of that asset, which has in fact lost all its value. The correct long-term growth rate is the rate which transforms the initial value ($S_0 = 100$) into the future value ($S_2 = 0$) after two years. It is therefore $R_{0,2}$ such that $S_0(1 + R_{0,2})^2 = S_2$, or $R_{0,2} = (S_2/S_1)^{1/2} - 1$; in this case, we would have $R_{0,2} = (0/100)^{1/2} - 1 = -100\%$. More generally, for successive values $S_1, \ldots S_t, \ldots S_n$ spanning n years, the n-year horizon growth rate $R_{0,n}$ is given by $R_{0,n} = (S_n/S_0)^{1/n} - 1$. Let us now determine how $R_{0,n}$ is related to the yearly growth rates: $R_{0,n}$ is such that

$$S_0(1 + R_{0,n})^n = S_n.$$

Table 6.1 *Expected yearly growth rates and their standard deviations*

	Sector A	Sector B
Expected yearly growth rate	10%	9%
Standard deviation	20%	10%

Now S_n/S_0 can be written

$$\frac{S_n}{S_0} = \left(\frac{S_1}{S_0} \cdot \frac{S_2}{S_1} \cdots \frac{S_t}{S_{t-1}} \cdots \frac{S_n}{S_{n-1}}\right)^{1/n} - 1$$

and therefore

$$R_{0,n} = [(1 + R_{0,1})(1 + R_{1,2}) \ldots (1 + R_{t-1,t}) \ldots (1 + R_{n-1,n})]^{1/n} - 1.$$

We can see the precise relation between the long-term growth rate and the annual growth rates: if we call *one plus* the annual growth rate $R_{t-1,t}$ the annual *growth factor* of S (i.e. $1 + R_{t-1,t} = S_t/S_{t-1}$), the long-term growth rate $R_{0,n}$ is the (simple) *geometric mean* of the growth factors, minus one. From chapter 4, we know that the geometric mean (the general mean of order zero) is smaller than the arithmetic average (the mean of order one); therefore we should not be surprised that the long-term growth rate will always be *smaller* than the average of the yearly growth rates. How much smaller is what we are going to discover in this chapter. We will find that this difference depends positively upon two factors: the variance of the yearly growth rates, and the length of the horizon.

Let us now illustrate the importance of this issue. Consider two countries (or two sectors of an economy, or two assets), A and B. In sector A, the expected yearly growth rate is 10% per year, with a standard deviation of 20%. In sector B the expected yearly growth rate is 9% with a standard deviation of 10%. We suppose that in each sector the yearly growth rates are independent and identically distributed, although at this stage we do not make any particular hypothesis about the probability distribution of each growth rate. Table 6.1 summarizes these estimates for each sector.

What then is the 10-year expected yearly growth rate in each sector? The surprise is that sector B fares better: its expected 10-year growth rate is 8.57% per year, while sector A's expected 10-year growth rate is 8.31% only.

The aim of this chapter is to explain how to determine such results. We will also show how we can estimate the probability distribution of the long-term growth rate even if we do not know the probability law governing the yearly growth rates.

We will first explain what can be deduced from hypotheses about daily growth rates if we want to infer anything about yearly growth rates. We will then turn to the estimate of the first moments of the long-term growth rate and its probability distribution. Those results will finally be applied to the long-term evolution of the US economy.

I   From daily to yearly growth rates

We will use the following notation; j always refers to a day; t refers to a year.

- $S_0 \equiv$ value at the beginning of a year
- $S_j \equiv$ value at the end of day j ($j = 1, \ldots, 365$).
- $S_j/S_{j-1} \equiv$ daily growth factor
- $\dfrac{S_j - S_{j-1}}{S_{j-1}} = R_{j-1,j} \equiv$ daily growth rate (compounded once a day)
- $\log(S_j/S_{j-1}) = r_{j-1,j} \equiv$ continuously compounded daily growth rate
- $S_{365}/S_0 = X_{t-1,t} =$ yearly growth factor
- $\dfrac{S_t - S_{t-1}}{S_{t-1}} = X_{t-1,t} - 1 = R_{t-1,t} \equiv$ yearly growth rate (compounded once a year)
- $\log X_{t-1,t} = r_{t-1,t} \equiv$ continuously compounded yearly growth rate

Let S_0 be an observed value at the beginning of a year and S_{365} the value at the end of the year. We can write:

$$S_{365} \equiv S_0 \cdot \frac{S_1}{S_0} \cdots \frac{S_{365}}{S_{364}} \equiv S_0 e^{\log(S_1/S_0)} \ldots e^{\log(S_{365}/S_{364})}$$

$$\equiv S_0 e^{r_{0,1}} \ldots e^{r_{364,365}} \equiv S_0 e^{\sum_{j=1}^{365} r_{j-1,j}} \tag{1}$$

then

$$\sum_{j=1}^{365} r_{j-1,j} = \log(S_{365}/S_0) = \log X_{t-1,t} = r_{t-1,t}. \tag{2}$$

Each of the 365 continuously compounded daily growth rates $r_{j-1,j}$ is a random variable. Suppose its mean and variance are estimated at m and s^2 respectively. We have thus $E(r_{j-1,j}) = m$ and $VAR(r_{j-1,j}) = s^2$. Suppose also that those rates are independent and identically distributed. Then the central limit theorem applies to the sum of those 365 variables, which is none other than $r_{t-1,t}$, the continuously compounded yearly growth rate.

The central limit theorem tells us that $r_{t-1,t}$ will converge in law toward a normal distribution[1] with mean $\mu = 365m$ and variance $\sigma^2 = 365s^2$. We can thus

---

[1] For spectacular illustrations of the power of the central limit theorem, see the diagrams in J. Pitman, *Probability*, Springer Verlag, New York, 1993.

write:

$$r_{t-1,t} \underset{law}{\to} N(365m, 365s^2) \equiv N(\mu, \sigma^2) \tag{3}$$

and, equivalently

$$\log X_{t-1,t} = r_{t-1,t} = \mu + \sigma Z, \ Z \sim N(0, 1) \tag{4}$$

where Z is the unit normal distribution.

From the fact that $r_{t-1,t}$ is normally distributed, we conclude that the yearly growth factor $X_{t-1,t}$ is the exponential of a normal variable; indeed, if $\log X_{t-1,t} = r_{t-1,t} = \mu + \sigma Z, Z \sim N(0, 1)$ we can conclude that

$$\boxed{X_{t-1,t} = e^{\mu+\sigma Z}, \ Z \sim N(0, 1)} \tag{5}$$

i.e. $X_{t-1,t}$ is a "lognormal variable" as it is always called. (Notice how unfortunate this expression is: it would have been much more clear to call a variable such as $X_{t-1,t}$, the exponential of a normal variable, an "exponormal variable". A "lognormal variable" is intended to mean a variable *whose logarithm* is normal, leaving the reader with the exercise of figuring out that it is a variable such as described in equation (5), i.e. the *exponential* transformation of a normal variable.)

A lognormal variable has extremely important properties. These have immediate intuitive appeal if we have in mind the geometric interpretation of this exponential transformation of a normal random variable – see the example in figure 6.1. Furthermore, the moments of a lognormal variable are very easy to determine because they turn out to be just linear transformations of the moment generating function of a unit normal variable.[2]

Consider first the expected value of the yearly growth rate $R_{t-1,t}$. It is the expected value of the growth factor $X_{t-1,t}$ minus one:

$$E(R_{t-1,t}) = E(X_{t-1,t} - 1) = E(X_{t-1,t}) - 1. \tag{6}$$

In turn, we have, from (5):

$$E(X_{t-1,t}) = E(e^{\mu+\sigma Z}) = e^{\mu} E(e^{\sigma Z}), \ Z \sim N(0, 1). \tag{7}$$

Thus $E(X_{t-1,t})$ is just a linear transformation of the moment generating function of $Z \sim N(0, 1)$, where σ plays the role of the parameter. Since $E(e^{\sigma Z}) = e^{\sigma^2/2}$ (see exercise 6.1), this yields

$$\boxed{E(X_{t-1,t}) = e^{\mu+\sigma^2/2}} \tag{8}$$

---

[2] The moment generating function of a continuous random variable W is $\varphi_W(\lambda) = E(e^{\lambda W})$, where λ is a parameter. For a reminder on moment generating functions, see appendix 1.

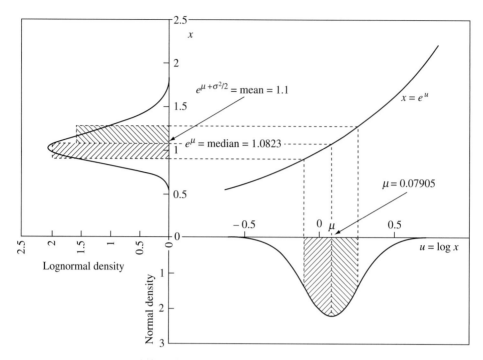

Figure 6.1 **A geometrical interpretation of three fundamental properties of the lognormal distribution: (a) the expected value of $X_{t-1,t} = e^{U} = e^{\mu+\sigma Z}(Z \sim N(0,1))$, $E(X) = e^{\mu+\sigma^2/2}$ is above the median e^{μ}; (b) the probability that $X_{t-1,t}$ is below its expected value is above 50%; and (c) the expected value of $X_{t-1,t}$ is an increasing function of the variance of U, σ^2. In this example, $E(\log X) = E(U) = 0.07905$; $\sigma(\log X) = \sigma_U = 0.18033$.**

and the expected value of the yearly growth rate is

$$E(R_{t-1,t}) = e^{\mu+\sigma^2/2} - 1. \tag{9}$$

From figure 6.1, it can be readily understood why the mean $E(X_{t-1,t})$ is somewhat *above* $e^{\mu} = e^{E(\log X_{t-1,t})}$. The value e^{μ} is just the median of the lognormal variable $X_{t-1,t}$. Indeed, the mean of the normal $\log X_{t-1,t}$, μ, is also the median of the normal. Therefore, this median transformed through the exponential becomes the median of $X_{t-1,t}$. Now observe that the exponential transformation is strictly convex. This implies that transforming any couple of equal mass probabilities, taken symmetrically on either side of μ, will translate into *asymmetric* mass probabilities on either side of e^{μ}. Because of the strict convexity of $e^{\log X_{t-1,t}}$, the base of the upper mass probability will always be wider than the base of the lower one, thus entailing a displacement of the centre of gravity of these masses *above* e^{μ}. It is not surprising therefore that the mean of $X_{t-1,t}$ is above its median.

How much above it? As can be seen from equation (8), this depends *positively* upon the sole parameter σ^2, the variance of the continuously compounded yearly growth rate. That the dependency is positive is clear from the geometric construction of the lognormal (figure 6.1). The higher the variance of $\log X_{t-1,t}$, the more asymmetry we obtain for the mass probabilities on the vertical axis and therefore the more the centre of gravity is displaced, up and away from the median e^{μ}. This is why the mean of the lognormal is an increasing function of the parameter σ^2.

Let us now turn to the variance of $R_{t-1,t}$. This is just the variance of $X_{t-1,t}$, and therefore we may write:

$$VAR(R_{t-1,t}) = VAR(X_{t-1,t}) = E(X^2_{t-1,t}) - E^2(X_{t-1,t}). \tag{10}$$

The second moment of $X_{t-1,t}$ is

$$E(X^2_{t-1,t}) = E\left[\left(e^{\mu+\sigma Z}\right)^2\right] = E(e^{2\mu+2\sigma Z})$$
$$= e^{2\mu} E(e^{2\sigma Z}) = e^{2\mu+2\sigma^2} \tag{11}$$

(the last step uses the fact that $E(e^{2\sigma Z})$ is just the moment generating function of Z, the unit normal variable, where 2σ plays the role of the parameter; it is therefore equal to $e^{2\sigma^2}$).

The variance of $R_{t-1,t}$ is then

$$VAR(R_{t-1,t}) = e^{2\mu+2\sigma^2} - e^{2\mu+\sigma^2} = e^{2\mu+\sigma^2}(e^{\sigma^2} - 1). \tag{12}$$

In summary, it implies that when the continuously compounded yearly growth rate is normally distributed $N(\mu, \sigma^2)$, the expected value of $X_{t-1,t} = 1 + R_{t-1,t}$ and the variance of $R_{t-1,t}$ are given by the pair of formulas

$$E_{X_{t-1,t}} = e^{\mu+\sigma^2/2} \tag{13}$$

$$V_{X_{t-1,t}} = e^{2\mu+\sigma^2}(e^{\sigma^2} - 1). \tag{14}$$

Consider now the converse problem. Suppose that we are given estimates of $E_{X_{t-1,t}}$ and $V_{X_{t-1,t}}$, and that we want to know what are the implied values for the mean μ and variance σ^2 of the continuously compounded yearly growth rate. The answer to this question, crucial in the problem of estimating the first moment of the long-term growth rate, is simply obtained by determining μ and σ^2 as functions of $E_{X_{t-1,t}}$ and $V_{X_{t-1,t}}$ from system (13), (14).

Denoting $X_{t-1,t} \equiv X$ for short, observe from (14) that V_X can be written as

$$V_X = E^2_X(e^{\sigma^2} - 1) \tag{15}$$

from which σ^2 can be deduced as

$$\sigma^2 = \log\left(1 + \frac{V_X}{E_X^2}\right). \tag{16}$$

The expression for μ can be determined by replacing (16) into (13). We obtain finally

$$\mu = \log E_X - \frac{1}{2}\log\left(1 + \frac{V_X}{E_X^2}\right). \tag{17}$$

This is exactly the procedure we have followed to construct the curves in figure 6.1. Consider a random variable with annual expected growth rate equal to $E(R_{t-1,t}) = 10\%$ and standard deviation s.d.$(R_{t-1,t}) = 20\%$.[3] This implied that $E(X_{t-1,t}) = E(1 + R_{t-1,t}) = 1 + E(R_{t-1,t}) = 1.1$, and $VAR(R_{t-1,t}) = $ [s.d.$(R_{t-1,t})]^2 = 0.04$. Our starting point thus is:

$$E(X_{t-1,t}) \equiv E_X = 1.1$$
$$VAR(X_{t-1,t}) \equiv V_X = 0.04$$

We can now apply equations (17) and (16) to determine the mean μ and variance σ^2 of $\log X_{t-1,t}$, the continuously compounded yearly growth rate, which is supposedly normally distributed, because of the central limit theorem. We thus obtain:

$$\mu = \log E_X - \frac{1}{2}\log\left(1 + \frac{V_X}{E_X^2}\right) = 0.07905$$

$$\sigma^2 = \log\left(1 + \frac{V_X}{E_X^2}\right) = 0.03252$$

and

$$\sigma = 0.18034.$$

Such are the parameters μ, σ of the normal variable $\log X_{t-1,t} \sim N(\mu, \sigma^2)$ which is represented under the horizontal axis $u = \log x$ in figure 6.1.

Our last task is to represent the lognormal distribution $X = e^U = e^{\log X}$, where the realization variable x is on the vertical axis of figure 6.1. This also is easy to

---

[3] Equivalently, this variable could be considered as a financial asset with expected annual return equal to 10% and standard deviation equal to 20%.

do: denote $f(u)$ the probability density function of the normal $U = \log X_{t-1,t}$ $\sim N(\mu, \sigma^2)$. We have

$$f(u) = \frac{1}{\sigma\sqrt{2\pi}} e^{-\frac{1}{2}\left(\frac{u-\mu}{\sigma}\right)^2},$$

and let $g(x)$ be the density of the lognormal $X = e^U$ we want to determine. We just have to note that any differential element $f(u)du$ under the normal curve must be equal to a corresponding element $g(x)dx$ under the lognormal $g(x)$. So $g(x)$ must be such that[4]

$$g(x)dx = f(u)du$$

Since $x = e^u$ is an increasing function of u, it is invertible; with $u = \log x$, we may write:

$$g(x) = f(u)/(dx/du) = f[u(x)]/x,$$

which gives:

$$g(x) = \frac{1}{x\sigma\sqrt{2\pi}} e^{-\frac{1}{2}\left(\frac{\log x - \mu}{\sigma}\right)^2}$$

which is the lognormal density function of X with parameters μ and σ. This density, determined with the parameters μ and σ indicated above, is represented on the vertical axis of figure 6.1.

We are now ready to tackle the expected value and the variance of the long-term yearly growth rate.

2 The first moments of the long-term yearly growth rate

Let $S_1, \ldots, S_t, \ldots, S_n$ denote the values of S at the end of each year $1, \ldots, t, \ldots, n$. The n-year yearly growth rate, denoted as $R_{0,n}$, is such that it transforms S_0 into S_n after n years, each growth rate being compounded once a

---

[4] Note that this procedure is valid because the transformation of the variable u, $x = e^u$, is an increasing function of u. If we had wanted to determine the density function of a *decreasing* transformation of u, we would have had to make sure that the differential element $g(x)dx$ (the incremental area under the density curve) is positive. For that purpose, we would have written $g(x)|dx| = f(u)|du|$; therefore the general formula for $g(x)$ is $g(x) = f[u(x)]/|x'[u]|$.

year. $R_{0,n}$ is then defined by

$$S_0(1 + R_{0,n})^n = S_n \qquad (18)$$

and is equal to

$$R_{0,n} = \left(\frac{S_n}{S_0}\right)^{1/n} - 1. \qquad (19)$$

This n-year horizon yearly rate can be written using our variable $X_{t-1,t}$ in the following way. Denoting $Y_{0,n} = 1 + R_{0,n}$, we have

$$
\begin{aligned}
Y_{0,n} = 1 + R_{0,n} &= \left(\frac{S_n}{S_0}\right)^{1/n} = \left(\frac{S_1}{S_0}\cdot\frac{S_2}{S_1}\cdots\frac{S_n}{S_{n-1}}\right)^{1/n} \\
&= (X_{0,1}\ldots X_{t-1,t}\ldots X_{n-1,n})^{1/n} \\
&= (e^{\log X_{0,1}}\ldots e^{\log X_{t-1,t}}\ldots e^{\log X_{n-1,n}})^{1/n} \\
&= e^{\frac{1}{n}\Sigma_{t=1}^n \log X_{t-1,t}}. \qquad (20)
\end{aligned}
$$

There are now two methods of obtaining the first moments of $Y_{0,n}$. The first one uses the results of section 1 and supposes that the variables $\log X_{t-1,t}$ are normally distributed $N(\mu, \sigma^2)$ and independent. The second method assumes that the variables are independent and identically distributed with mean μ and variance σ^2 – without making any inference as to their probability distribution – and appeals to the central limit theorem.

2.1 First method: supposing that the $\log X_{t-1,t}$ variables are normal $N(\mu, \sigma^2)$ and independent

With that hypothesis, the sum $\Sigma_{t=1}^n \log X_{t-1,t}$ is normally distributed $N(n\mu, n\sigma^2)$. Then

$$\sum_{t=1}^n \log X_{t-1,t} \sim N(n\mu, n\sigma^2) = n\mu + \sqrt{n}\sigma Z, \ Z \sim N(0, 1), \qquad (21)$$

and

$$\frac{1}{n}\sum_{t=1}^n \log X_{t-1,t} = \mu + \frac{\sigma}{\sqrt{n}}Z \qquad (22)$$

entailing, from (20)

$$Y_{0,n} = e^{\mu + \frac{\sigma}{\sqrt{n}}Z}. \qquad (23)$$

Thus $Y_{0,n} = 1 + R_{0,n}$ turns out to be a lognormal variable. Its first moments are immediately determined as

$$E(1 + R_{0,n}) = E(Y_{0,n}) = e^{\mu} E\left(e^{\frac{\sigma}{\sqrt{n}} Z}\right) = e^{\mu + \frac{\sigma^2}{2n}} \qquad (24)$$

(again we have met in $\left(e^{\frac{\sigma}{\sqrt{n}} Z}\right)$ the moment generating function of Z, this time with $\sigma/\sqrt{n}$ playing the role of the parameter).

So finally

$$E(R_{0,n}) = e^{\mu + \frac{\sigma^2}{2n}} - 1. \qquad (25)$$

We can verify that (25) gives $E(R_{0,1}) = e^{\mu + \sigma^2/2}$ when $n = 1$, as it should.

Notice a fundamental property of the expected value of the geometric mean $Y_{0,n}$: it diminishes when n increases, and in the limit, when $n \to \infty$, tends toward $e^{\mu} = e^{E(\log X_{t-1,t})}$. We will come back to this property later.

The second moment of $Y_{0,n}$ is

$$E(Y_{0,n}^2) = E\left(e^{2\mu + \frac{2\sigma}{\sqrt{n}} Z}\right) = e^{2\mu + \frac{2\sigma^2}{n}} \qquad (26)$$

and the variance of $R_{0,n}$ and $Y_{0,n}$ is, using (26) and simplifying,

$$VAR(R_{0,n}) = e^{2\mu + \frac{\sigma^2}{n}} (e^{\frac{\sigma^2}{n}} - 1). \qquad (27)$$

Two observations are in order: we verify that the variance of $R_{0,n}$ is the variance of $R_{0,1}$ when $n = 1$ (as given by equation (14)); also, it is zero either if $\sigma = 0$ or if $n \to \infty$, as it should.

2.2 Second method: the variables $\log X_{t-1,t}$ are i.i.d. with mean μ and variance σ^2; no probability distribution is inferred about them

In such a case, we can apply the central limit theorem to the sum $\sum_{t=1}^{n} \log X_{t-1,t}$. It will converge in law toward a normal distribution $N(n\mu, n\sigma^2)$. We have

$$\sum_{t=1}^{n} \log X_{t-1,t} \xrightarrow{\text{law}} N(n\mu, n\sigma^2) = n\mu + n\sqrt{\sigma} Z, \ Z \sim N(0, 1) \qquad (28)$$

and the rest of the demonstration of section 2.1 follows.

Notice that in each method we have used the central limit theorem, if only at different stages. In the first method, we used it at the level of the sum of 365 continuously compounded *daily* returns, thus inferring a yearly continuously compounded return $\log X_{t-1,t}$ as a normal variable $N(\mu, \sigma^2)$. In the second method, we supposed that we did not know the probability distribution of $\log X_{t-1,t}$, and we applied the theorem when adding n of those i.i.d. variables. The reader may wonder now what kind of difference in the results we obtain for the expected long-term growth rate if, for some reason, the true probability distribution of $\log X_{t-1,t}$ is far from normal, being for instance a uniform distribution. We have done this test by supposing that $\log X_{t-1,t}$ had a uniform distribution instead of a normal one.[5] The surprise is how close the results are, even for very low n: for $n = 2$, the first four digits of $E(R_{0,2})$ are the same; for $n = 4$, the first six digits are the same. This illustrates of course the strength of the central limit theorem.

2.3 The expected value and variance of the long-term growth rate in terms of $E(X_{t-1,t})$ and $VAR(X_{t-1,t})$

Until now our results have been expressed in terms of $\mu = E(\log X_{t-1,t})$ and $\sigma^2 = VAR(\log X_{t-1,t})$. This is definitely cumbersome, because for all practical purposes it implies translating data usually available in terms of $E(R_{t-1,t})$ (or $E X_{t-1,t}$) into expressions depending on (μ, σ), and then applying (25) and (27). It would be much more expedient and clear to have formulas directly expressed in terms of $E X_{t-1,t}$ and $V X_{t-1,t}$. This is why we had made the conversion of (μ, σ^2) into (E_X, V_X) earlier (equations (16) and (17)). Using those equations enables us to write directly our final results:

$$E(R_{0,n}) = \frac{E_X}{\left(1 + \frac{V_X}{E_X^2}\right)^{\frac{1}{2}\left(1-\frac{1}{n}\right)}} - 1 \tag{29}$$

$$VAR(R_{0,n}) = E_X^2 \cdot \left(1 + \frac{V_X}{E_X^2}\right)^{\left(\frac{1}{n}-1\right)}\left[\left(1 + \frac{V_X}{E_X^2}\right)^{\frac{1}{n}} - 1\right] \tag{30}$$

We can verify that if $n = 1$, equations (29) and (30) yield $E(R_{0,1}) = E X_{t-1,t} - 1$ and $VAR(R_{0,1})$ as they should. When V_X is zero, $VAR(R_{0,n})$ is zero and $E(R_{0,n}) = E(R_{0,1})$. If $n \to \infty$, $VAR(R_{0,n}) \to 0$ and

$$\lim_{n\to\infty} E(R_{0,n}) = \frac{E_X}{\left(1 + \frac{V_X}{E_X^2}\right)^{1/2}} - 1, \tag{31}$$

which corresponds to the limit expressed before as $e^\mu - 1$.

[5] The interested reader is referred to our paper: "The Long-Term Expected Rate of Return: Setting it Right", *The Financial Analysts Journal*, 1998.

2.4   Determining probabilities for intervals of the n-horizon growth rate

The fact that $Y_{0,n} = 1 + R_{0,n}$ is given by

$$Y_{0,n} = 1 + R_{0,n} = e^{\mu + \frac{\sigma}{\sqrt{n}} Z}, \quad Z \sim N(0,1)$$

(equation (23)) means that $Y_{0,n}$ is a lognormal variable with parameters $\mu, \sigma/\sqrt{n}$. In turn it implies that determining the probabilities for the long-term growth rate to be within a given interval is easy to achieve. Suppose for instance, that we want to know the probability for $R_{0,n}$ to be between two numbers a, b. We can write:

$$p(a < R_{0,n} < b) = p(1 + a < 1 + R_{0,n} < 1 + b)$$

$$= p(1 + a < e^{\mu + \frac{\sigma}{\sqrt{n}} Z} < 1 + b)$$

$$= p\left[\log(1+a) < \mu + \frac{\sigma}{\sqrt{n}} Z < \log(1+b) \right]. \quad (32)$$

Finally, solving for Z, this probability is equal to:

$$p\left(\frac{\log(1+a) - \mu}{\sigma/\sqrt{n}} < Z < \frac{\log(1+b) - \mu}{\sigma/\sqrt{n}} \right)$$

$$= \Phi\left(\frac{\log(1+b) - \mu}{\sigma/\sqrt{n}} \right) - \Phi\left(\frac{\log(1+a) - \mu}{\sigma/\sqrt{n}} \right) \quad (33)$$

where $\Phi(z)$ is the cumulative probability distribution of the unit normal variable.

For instance, suppose we want to determine the probability that the long-run growth rate will be below its expected value, $e^{\mu + \sigma^2/2n} - 1$. This is

$$p\left(R_{0,n} < e^{\mu + \frac{\sigma^2}{2n}} - 1 \right) = p\left(1 + R_{0,n} < e^{\mu + \frac{\sigma^2}{2n}} \right)$$

$$= p\left(e^{\mu + \frac{\sigma}{\sqrt{n}} Z} < e^{\mu + \frac{\sigma^2}{2n}} \right) = p\left(Z < \frac{\sigma}{2\sqrt{n}} \right). \quad (34)$$

In the next section, we will understand why this probability converges toward $p(Z < 0) = 1/2$ when $n \to \infty$.

2.5   The convergence toward the geometric mean

We have shown that the expected value of $1 + R_{0,n} \equiv Y_{0,n}$ was, in terms of (μ, σ^2), $e^{\mu + \sigma^2/2n}$. It is clearly a decreasing function of the horizon n. Furthermore, its limit when $n \to \infty$ is

$$\lim_{n \to \infty} (1 + R_{0,n}) \equiv 1 + R_{0,\infty} \equiv Y_{0,\infty} = e^{\mu} = e^{E(\log X_{t-1,t})}. \quad (35)$$

We had observed before that e^{μ} was the median of the lognormal distribution. But there is something more to it that we will now discover.

Some means are quite familiar: the arithmetic mean of a discrete random variable is $\Sigma_{i=1}^{n} f_i x_i$; for a continuous variable it is $\int_D x f(x) dx$ where D is the domain of definition of the variable. The geometric mean of a discrete variable is $\prod_{i=1}^{n} x_i^{f_i}$ (all x_i's are positive); but what is the geometric mean of a continuous (positive) random variable? In order to define it, we have to think of the product of an infinite number of values which converges toward a fixed number. The way to do this is to consider a *continuous* product of the x values over the domain of X, each of those values being taken to the power $f(x)dx$.[6] So we could define the geometric mean of a continuous random variable X over a domain D, with probability density $f(x)$, as the continuous product

$$G_X = \mathcal{P}_D x^{f(x)dx}. \tag{36}$$

We can summarize those four means in table 6.2:

Table 6.2   *Arithmetic and geometric means for discrete and continuous random variables*

	Discrete random variable	Continuous random variable
Arithmetic mean	$\sum_{i=1}^{n} f_i x_i$, $\sum_{i=1}^{n} f_i = 1$	$\int_D x f(x)dx$, $\int_D f(x)dx = 1$
Geometric mean	$\prod_{i=1}^{n} x_i^{f_i}$, $x_i > 0$, $\sum_{i=1}^{n} f_i = 1$	$\mathcal{P}_D x^{f(x)dx}$, $x > 0$, $\int_D f(x)dx = 1$

Now we can write $x = e^{\log x}$, and the geometric mean of a continuous random variable becomes

$$\mathcal{P}_D e^{\log x f(x)dx} = e^{\int_D \log x f(x)dx} = e^{E(\log X)}. \tag{37}$$

In our case, $E(\log X_{t-1,t})$ was denoted μ. Remember that

$$Y_{0,n} = (X_{0,1} . X_{1,2} \ldots X_{n-1,n})^{1/n}, \tag{38}$$

i.e. $Y_{0,n}$ is the geometric mean of the $X_{t-1,t}$'s. We have just shown that when $n \to \infty$, $Y_{0,n}$ tends toward $e^{\mu} = e^{E(\log X)}$, and this is the *geometric mean* of the variable X. Thus the law of large numbers, which applies to the arithmetic mean, extends to the geometric mean as well.

It can now be seen why the probability of $R_{0,n}$ being smaller than $E(R_{0,n})$ converges to $1/2$ when $n \to \infty$ in the case where $X_{t-1,t}$ is lognormal : this is because the geometric mean of the lognormal is equal to its median.

---

[6] Intuitively, we can think of each power $f(x)dx$, being infinitely small, as exactly what we need in order for the continuous product not to converge toward one nor to tend toward infinity, but to coverage toward some (positive) finite value.

We conclude from this section that the expected long-term growth rate of a sector or of an economy may be significantly lower than its expected yearly growth rate. Also, what matters most is the first two moments of the yearly growth rate, rather than its probability distribution.

3 Application to the long-term growth rates of the US economy

Let us now consider the following problem. We want to know how much we can rely on the first two moments of the annual growth rate to make a prediction on the long-term growth rate. Suppose that in 1790 we try to predict, for the United States, the long-term growth rates of real GDP per person from 1790 to 2005, i.e. over 215 years. To do that, we rely on two statistics: the expected annual growth rate of GDP per person, denoted $E(R_{t-1,t})$, and the estimated standard deviation of this annual growth rate, $sd(R_{t-1,t})$. We know that the 215-year horizon expected growth rate is given by equation (29), where E_X designates $E(X_{t-1,t})$ and is equal to $E(1 + R_{t-1,t})$; V_X stands for the estimated variance of $X_{t-1,t}$ and $R_{t-1,t}$, and is therefore the square of $sd(R_{t-1,t})$. The expected 215-year horizon growth rate is then:

$$E(R_{0,215}) = \frac{1 + E(R_{t-1,t})}{\left[1 + \left(\frac{sd(R_{t-1,t})}{E(R_{t-1,t})} \right)^2 \right]^{\frac{1}{2}\left(1 - \frac{1}{215}\right)}} - 1. \tag{39}$$

Suppose that in 1790 our predictions about $E(R_{t-1,t})$ and $sd(R_{t-1,t})$ had been right in the sense that they did correspond to the observed data, which we owe to Louis D. Johnston and Samuel H. Williamson (2005).[7] From their series it is possible to determine the annual growth rates of GDP, $R_{t-1,t}$, as well as the mean $E(R_{t-1,t})$ and the standard deviation of the sampled $R_{t-1,t}$ variables, $sd(R_{t-1,t})$. The results are the following: over the 215-year period,

$$E(R_{t-1,t})|_{215 \text{ years}} = 1.8362\% \approx 1.84\%$$
$$sd(R_{t-1,t})|_{215 \text{ years}} = 4.4643\% \approx 4.46\%.$$

The 215-year growth rate would have been estimated at, using equation (39):

$$E(R_{0,215}) = 1.74\%$$

---

[7] Louis D. Johnston and Samuel H. Williamson, "*The Annual Real and Nominal GDP for the United States, 1790–Present*", Economic History Services, October 2005, URL: www.eh.net/hmit/gdp/. This table not only gives the nominal and real GDP, but indicates also yearly figures for the population, nominal GDP per person and real GDP per person.

Now compare this estimate to the *actual*, observed 215-year growth rate, calculated as $(\text{GDP}_{2005}/\text{GDP}_{1790})^{1/215} - 1$; from the Johnston-Williamson table this is equal to $(37232/916)^{1/215} - 1 = 1.74\%$ (!). The first four decimals of the long-term rate are the same. Observe that we have made no inference about the probability distribution of the $R_{t-1,t}$ variables. The fact that the estimate is so close to the actual outcome is of course a testimony of the strength of the central limit theorem, to which we had already called the reader's attention in section 2.

Suppose now that we want to do the same prediction of the long-term growth rate of real GDP per person, but from a later date, namely 1900, i.e. for a 105-year horizon. The estimates of $E(R_{t-1,t})$ and $sd(R_{t-1,t})$ would be the following: over the 105-year period,

$$E(R_{t-1,t})\big|_{105 \text{ years}} = 2.0752\% \approx 2.08\%$$

$$sd(R_{t-1,t})\big|_{105 \text{ years}} = 5.3413\% \approx 5.34\%.$$

The estimate of the 105-year growth rate, from (39) is

$$E(R_{0,105}) = 1.94\%$$

and the actual, observed growth rate is $(\text{GDP}_{2005}/\text{GDP}_{1900})^{1/105} - 1 = (37232/4943)^{1/105} - 1 = 1.94\%$ as well; here also the first four digits of the estimate and the actual result are the same.

We can conclude that whenever you are making estimates of the long-term growth rate, you can safely rely on the estimates of the first two moments of the yearly growth rate and apply formula (39). You do not need to worry about the probability distribution of the yearly rate; just let the central limit theorem work for you.

Appendix: A reminder on moment generating functions

Let X denote a continuous random variable. The moment generating function of X is defined as the expected value of the random variable $e^{\lambda X}$. It will be denoted $\varphi_X(\lambda)$.[8] We have by definition

$$\varphi_X(\lambda) = E(e^{\lambda X}). \tag{A1}$$

Thus the random variable X undergoes two transformations: first, a linear transformation (λX) and then an exponential one $(e^{\lambda X})$.

Let D designate the domain of definition of X and x the outcome values of X; let $f(x)$ denote the probability density of X. Then the moment generating function

---

[8] The usual notation for the variable of the moment generating function is t. We use here instead λ, in order to avoid any confusion with our variable t, designating years throughout this chapter.

is determined by the integral

$$\varphi_X(\lambda) = E(e^{\lambda X}) = \int_D e^{\lambda x} f(x) dx. \tag{A2}$$

A fundamental property of $\varphi_X(\lambda)$ is that its kth derivative at $\lambda = 0$ gives the kth moment of the random variable X. This is easily seen as follows. The derivative of $\varphi_X(\lambda)$ with respect to λ is:

$$\varphi_X'(\lambda) = \int_D x e^{\lambda x} f(x) dx; \tag{A3}$$

at point $\lambda = 0$, this is just the first moment of X:

$$\varphi_X'(0) = \int_D x f(x) dx = E(X). \tag{A4}$$

The second derivative of $\varphi_X(\lambda)$ at point $\lambda = 0$ can be shown to be equal to $\varphi_X''(0) = \int_D x^2 f(x) dx = E(X^2)$. More generally the kth derivative of $\varphi_X(\lambda)$ is

$$\varphi_X^{(k)}(\lambda) = \int_D x^k e^{\lambda x} f(x) dx \tag{A5}$$

and at point $\lambda = 0$ this is the kth moment of X:

$$\varphi_X^{(k)}(0) = \int_D x^k f(x) dx = E(X^k).$$

It is very useful now to consider, as an example, the moment generating function of a unit normal variable, $Z \sim N(0, 1)$. This is

$$\varphi_Z(\lambda) = \int_{-\infty}^{+\infty} e^{\lambda z} f(z) dz, \tag{A6}$$

where $f(z) = (2\pi)^{-1/2} e^{-z^2/2}$. It is easy to show (see exercise 6.1) that $\varphi_Z(\lambda) = e^{\lambda^2/2}$. We will often have recourse to this result in this chapter, as it will avoid any further calculations.

Exercises

6.1 This exercise is for the reader who is not familiar with the central result (for this chapter) that the moment generating function of the unit normal variable $Z \sim N(0, 1)$ is $\varphi_Z(\lambda) = e^{\lambda^2/2}$. To show this result, determine $E(e^{\lambda Z}) = \int_{-\infty}^{+\infty} e^{\lambda z} f(z) dz$ where $f(z)$ is the density of the unit normal.

6.2 Prove the results corresponding to the example we gave at the beginning of this chapter.

6.3 Suppose that the continuously compounded rate of growth over one year is normal $N(\mu, \sigma^2)$. What is the probability that the yearly growth rate $R_{t-1,t}$ will be lower than its expected value $E(R_{t-1,t})$?

6.4 With the same hypotheses as in exercise 6.3, determine the probability that the n-year growth rate $R_{0,n}$ will be lower than its expected value $E(R_{0,n})$. What is the limit of this probability when $n \to \infty$?

Answers

6.1 Since the density of the unit normal variable $Z \sim N(0, 1)$ is $(2\pi)^{-1/2}e^{-z^2/2}$, the moment generating function is

$$\varphi_Z(\lambda) = E(e^{\lambda Z}) = \int_{-\infty}^{+\infty} e^{\lambda z} \frac{1}{(2\pi)^{1/2}} e^{-z^2/2} dz.$$

In the right-hand side, the exponent of e is $-\frac{z^2}{2} + \lambda z$, which can be written $-\frac{1}{2}(z^2 - 2\lambda z + \lambda^2) + \frac{\lambda^2}{2}$ (by "completing the square"). We can now make the change of variable $w = z - \lambda$, with $dw = dz$. The moment generating function thus becomes

$$\varphi_Z(\lambda) = \int_{-\infty}^{+\infty} \frac{1}{(2\pi)^{1/2}} e^{-\frac{1}{2}w^2 + \frac{\lambda^2}{2}} dw$$

$$= e^{\lambda^2/2} \int_{-\infty}^{+\infty} \frac{1}{(2\pi)^{1/2}} e^{-\frac{1}{2}w^2} dw = e^{\lambda^2/2}.$$

6.2 This is a straight application of the formulas in the text. You have to be careful that $E_{X_{t-1,t}}$ is equal to $E(1 + R_{t-1,t})$ – it is one plus the expected value of the yearly growth rate.

6.3 We should determine

$$\mathrm{Prob}(R_{t-1,t} < E(R_{t-1,t}))$$

which amounts to

$$\mathrm{Prob}(1 + R_{t-1,t} < 1 + E(R_{t-1,t}))$$

or

$$\mathrm{Prob}(X_{t-1,t} < e^{\mu + \sigma^2/2}) = \mathrm{Prob}(e^{\mu + \sigma Z} < e^{\mu + \sigma^2/2})$$

(because $X_{t-1,t}$ is the lognormal variable $e^{\mu + \sigma Z}$).
So the probability is simply

$$\mathrm{Prob}(\mu + \sigma Z < \mu + \sigma^2/2) = \mathrm{Prob}(Z < \sigma/2) = \Phi(\sigma/2)$$

where $\Phi(.)$ is the cumulative normal distribution function.

6.4 In a similar way, let us determine

$$\text{Prob}(R_{0,n} < E(R_{0,n})).$$

The random variable $R_{0,n}$ is equal to $Y_{0,n} - 1$, with

$$Y_{0,n} = (X_{0,1} \ldots X_{n-1,n})^{1/n} = (e^{\log X_1} \ldots e^{\log X_n})^{1/n}$$

$$= e^{\frac{1}{n} \sum_{t=1}^{n} \log X_{t-1,t}} = e^{\frac{1}{n}(n\mu + \sqrt{n}\sigma Z)} = e^{\mu + \frac{\sigma}{\sqrt{n}} Z}.$$

Here $E(R_{0,n}) = e^{\mu + \frac{\sigma}{2n}} - 1$. So we can write

$$\text{Prob}(R_{0,n} < E(R_{0,n})) = \text{Prob}(1 + R_{0,n} < 1 + E(R_{0,n}))$$

$$= \text{Prob}(e^{\mu + \frac{\sigma}{\sqrt{n}} Z}) < e^{\mu + \frac{\sigma^2}{2n}})$$

which yields

$$\text{Prob } Z < \sigma/2n = \Phi(\sigma/2n).$$

We can verify that we obtain from this result $\Phi(\sigma/2)$ if $n = 1$ (the answer to question 6.3).

PART II

Optimal growth theory

In Part I of this book we have shown how the motion of an economy is described by a differential equation whose solution depends in an essential way on three kinds of hypotheses: the structure of the production process, which includes some form of technical progress, the saving and investment decisions made by society, and the growth of the labour force. In particular, to any savings-investment hypothesis corresponds a particular trajectory of income per person.

The natural question to ask now is the following: among all possible growth paths that would result from society's savings-investment decisions, is there one that would be optimal? The answer to this question requires that we first define an optimality criterion. Once this is done, we need to develop the tools necessary to solve such problems. This is the object of the second part of this book. We will provide an introduction to the calculus of variations and the Pontryagin maximum principle. Care will be taken to give economic interpretations of each, i.e. intuitive ways of obtaining their fundamental equations.

CHAPTER 7

Optimal growth theory: an introduction to the calculus of variations

We know how an economy might behave under a number of hypotheses regarding the way factors of production are linked to output, and the way each of those factors are modified over time: labour through population growth; capital through investment. Also, technical progress can enter the picture in a number of different ways. Finally, the structure of the production function itself may be modified through time due to changes in the elasticity of substitution between capital and labour.

The question we now want to ask is the following: among all possible time paths that we might want to choose by setting a given investment policy, is one of those optimal in a sense to be defined? This question is at the heart of optimal growth theory, and has given rise to a huge volume of literature, sometimes controversial. We first have to determine the objective function, and for historical reasons which go back to Ramsey (1928), the objective supposedly defined by society is to maximize the sum, over a time span which may be finite or infinite, of discounted utility flows pertaining to consumption, given a production function constraint.

We will first give an example of such an objective; the example is voluntarily simplified in order for the reader to grasp easily the nature of the problem at stake.

Suppose that the production function is given by $Y_t = F(K_t, L_t, t)$, where, as before, Y is the net domestic product (net of capital depreciation); so investment is $I_t = dK_t/dt \equiv \dot{K}_t$, and consumption is $C_t = Y_t - I_t = Y_t - \dot{K}_t$. Let $U(C)$ be a strictly concave utility function; we thus have $U'(C) > 0$ and $U''(C) < 0$. The objective of society may be to choose the investment time path $\dot{K}_t$ or, equivalently, taking account an initial condition $K(0) = K_0$, the capital time path K_t that maximizes the integral

$$\int_0^\infty U[C_t] e^{-it} dt \tag{1}$$

177

where i is a discount rate, subject to the constraint

$$C_t = Y_t - \dot{K}_t = F(K_t, L_t, t) - \dot{K}_t, \qquad (2)$$

assuming that the trajectory L_t is known. Replacing the constraint into the objective function, our task is to determine the entire time path $\vec{K}$ such that

$$\max_{K} \int_0^\infty U\,[F(K_t, L_t, t) - \dot{K}_t]\,e^{-it}dt. \qquad (3)$$

This integral defines a relationship between an entire time path $(\vec{K})$ and a number, the definite integral. Such a relationship is a *functional*. Traditional differential calculus deals with optimization of functions, relationships between a number (or several numbers) and a number. In this case we have a relationship between a *function* and a number, which will require a new methodology.

In traditional calculus, the basic idea of finding a point that is a candidate to maximize a function $f(x)$ is to give an increase to the independent variable, determine the limit of the resulting rate of increase of the function, and examine whether there are any values of the variable where that limit is equal to zero. Geometrically, this implies looking for points of the function where its tangent line might be horizontal. Analytically, we look for possible roots of the equation $f'(x) = 0$. In the case of a functional, we cannot give an increase to the function in the same way as we do to a variable in differential calculus. However, we will be able to impart a *variation* to the function (which will amount to giving an increase to a variable, yet to be defined) – hence the name "calculus of variations" given to this extension of the differential calculus. This chapter is a short introduction to this beautiful area of mathematics.

I   The Euler equation

In 1696, Johan Bernouilli asked, in the form of a competition, the following problem: determine the curve between A and B such that a bead, starting at A and gliding without friction along the curve, would join B in minimum time. Suppose that A is at the origin of axes, and B is point (3, -1), as in figure 7.1. Consider three possible curves: the straight line (a), and curves (b) and (c). Intuitively, some people might choose the shortest path (the straight line; many, however would rather choose (b) as a better solution than either (a) or (c). In reality, with its *increasing* segment, (c) is the correct answer (a demonstration is provided in Appendix 2 of this Chapter).

This problem admirably exemplifies the nature of the calculus of variations, as well as its difficulty. Bernouilli had to extend the deadline of his competition before he received (correct) answers from the best mathematicians of his time: his brother Jacob, Leibniz, the Marquis de L'Hospital, Newton and Tschirnhaus. Each of them

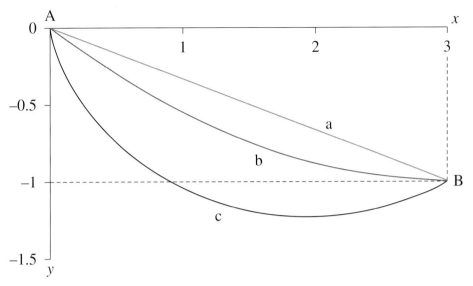

Figure 7.1 A fundamental problem of the calculus of variations (Bernouilli, 1696): if a bead is released from A, which curve will lead it to B in minimum time?

used subtle geometrical arguments combined with physical considerations. None of them, however, provided a general method of optimising functionals. It is only nearly half a century later that the first major result of the calculus of variations was found by Leonhard Euler. Euler discovered in 1744 the differential equation defining the function $y(x)$ that would be the solution of the problem

$$\max_{y(x)} \int_a^b F\,[x,\,y(x),\,y'(x)]\,dx \qquad (4)$$

of which (3) is a particular case. To do this, he resorted to geometrical arguments and to finite differences methods, very much akin to methods used today in numerical analysis. Ten years later, in 1754, he received from a young Italian living in Torino, Ludovico de La Grange Tournier[1] (he was 19 years old) a letter containing a purely analytic method leading to this differential equation[2]. This method, introducing the concept of the variation of a function, was enthusiastically embraced by Euler, giving full credit to its author and calling this new branch of mathematics "calculus of variations". Lagrange's beautiful argument will now be presented, albeit with the simpler notation that came into use at the end of the eighteenth century.

---

[1] His name was changed to Lagrange during the french revolution.

[2] See Hector J. Sussmann and Jan C. Willems, 300 Years of Optimal Control: From the Brachistochrone to the Maximum Principle, *IEEE Contol Systems,* June 1997, pp. 33–44. See also Herman Goldstine, A *History of the Calculus of variations, Springer-verlag, New York, 1981.*

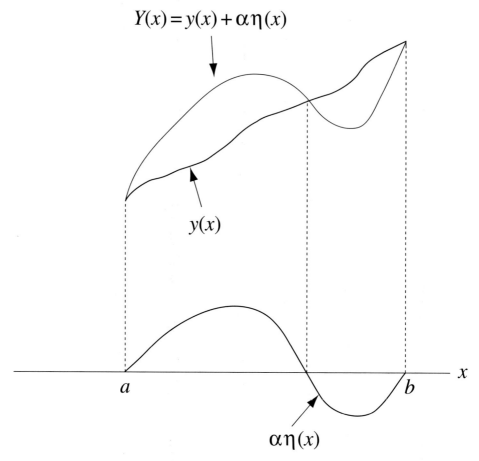

Figure 7.2 **Giving a variation to the solution** $y(x)$**.** $\alpha\eta(x)$ **is a variation of** $y(x)$**;** $\eta(x)$ **is a fixed function and** α **is a real number.**

Suppose that $y(x)$ is the solution to the problem defined by (4). Let us examine what kind of condition $y(x)$ must then meet. Consider a new function defined by

$$Y(x) = y(x) + \alpha\eta(x)$$

where $\eta(x)$ is a fixed, differentiable function such that $\eta(a) = \eta(b) = 0$, and α is any real number. We call $\alpha\eta(x)$ a *variation* of $y(x)$ – see figure 7.2.

If $Y(x)$ is inserted into the integral

$$I[y] = \int_a^b F[x, y(x), y'(x)]\, dx \tag{5}$$

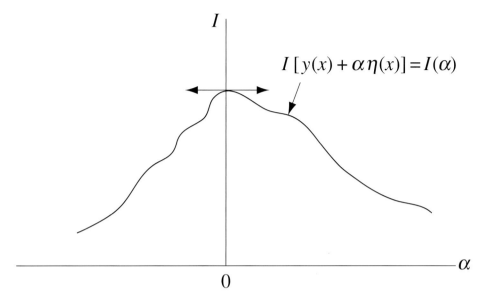

$$I[y(x) + \alpha\eta(x)] = I(\alpha)$$

Figure 7.3 The functional $I[y(x) + \alpha\eta(x)] = I(\alpha)$. If $y(x)$ is the solution that maximizes the functional $I[y(x) + \alpha\eta(x)]$ and if $\eta(x)$ is a fixed function, then I becomes a function of the sole variable α that has a maximum at $\alpha = 0$. Hence $I'(\alpha)|_{\alpha=0} = 0$.

we get

$$I[y + \alpha\eta] = \int_a^b F[x, Y(x), Y'(x)]\,dx$$

$$= \int_a^b F[x, y(x) + \alpha\eta(x), y'(x) + \alpha\eta'(x)]\,dx. \qquad (6)$$

Since $y(x)$ and $\eta(x)$ are fixed, I becomes a function of the sole variable α, and can thus be denoted $I(\alpha)$. If $y(x)$ is the unique solution to the problem, it means that $I(\alpha)$ must have a maximum when $Y(x)$ is $y(x)$, that is when $\alpha = 0$ (figure 7.3). This implies that $I'(\alpha)|_{\alpha=0} = 0$, or $I'(0) = 0$. Let us then determine $I'(0)$.

We have:

$$I'(\alpha) = \int_a^b \left[\frac{\partial F}{\partial Y}\eta(x) + \frac{\partial F}{\partial Y'}\eta'(x) \right] dx. \qquad (7)$$

When $\alpha = 0$, $Y = y$; (7) then becomes

$$I'(0) = \int_a^b \left[\frac{\partial F}{\partial y}\eta(x) + \frac{\partial F}{\partial y'}\eta'(x) \right] dx. \qquad (8)$$

Integrate the second part of the integral, $\int_a^b \frac{\partial F}{\partial y'}\eta'(x)dx$, by setting

$$u = \frac{\partial F}{\partial y'}; \quad dv = \eta'(x)\,dx$$

which implies

$$du = \frac{d}{dx}\left[\frac{\partial F}{\partial y'}\right]dx; \; v = \eta(x);$$

we then get:

$$\int_a^b \frac{\partial F}{\partial y'}\eta'(x)\,dx = \frac{\partial F}{\partial y'}\eta(x)\bigg|_a^b - \int_a^b \eta(x)\frac{d}{dx}\left[\frac{\partial F}{\partial y'}\right]dx. \tag{9}$$

In (9), the term $\frac{\partial F}{\partial y'}\eta(x)\big|_a^b$ vanishes because of the way $\eta(x)$ has been defined: $\eta(a) = \eta(b) = 0$. Inserting (9) into (8) and factoring $\eta(x)$ then gives:

$$I'(0) = \int_a^b \eta(x)\left[\frac{\partial F}{\partial y} - \frac{d}{dx}\frac{\partial F}{\partial y'}\right]dx. \tag{10}$$

The bracketed term in the integrand of (10) can be written as a function of x, denoted $g(x)$. So our maximizing condition $I'(0) = 0$ is

$$I'(0) = \int_a^b \eta(x)g(x)dx = 0. \tag{11}$$

We now have to determine a condition on $g(x)$ for $I'(0) = 0$. We can do this by resorting to the so-called fundamental lemma of the calculus of variations, which states that if an integral such as (11), where $g(x)$ is a continuous function, has to be equal to zero, then $g(x)$ must be identically equal to zero at each point of the interval $[a, b]$. This is easily proved as follows.

Suppose that at any given point of $[a, b]$, for example at c, $g(c) > 0$. By continuity of $g(x)$, there exists an interval around c, $[c_1, c_2]$, where $g(x) > 0$. Since the function $\eta(x)$ can be chosen in an entirely arbitrary manner, we can choose it as depicted in figure 7.4. It is then obvious that

$$\int_a^b \eta(x)g(x)dx = \int_{c_1}^{c_2} \eta(x)g(x)dx > 0,$$

thus entailing a contradiction.

We then have the following result: if $y(x)$ is to maximize I, it must meet the condition $g(x) = 0$, or, written in full:

$$\boxed{\frac{\partial F}{\partial y}(x, y, y') - \frac{d}{dx}\frac{\partial F}{\partial y'}(x, y, y') = 0} \tag{12}$$

which is the celebrated Euler equation (1744).

The fact that a necessary condition for $y(x)$ to maximize I is expressed in the form of a differential equation is perfectly natural. If, as in the case of the calculus of variations, we want to determine a whole function, it can be surmised that we will not be led to solve an equation – as in the case of ordinary differential calculus when we want to maximize $f(x)$, for instance – but a differential equation.

$g(x), \eta(x)$

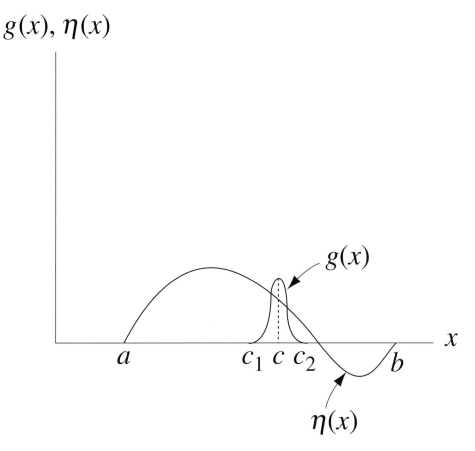

Figure 7.4 The fundamental lemma of the calculus of variations. If $g(x)$, a continuous function, is non-zero for one value (c for example) of the interval $[a, b]$, then it is non-zero over an interval (c_1, c_2) around c. Since the variation $\eta(x)$ can be chosen at will, it can be chosen as on the diagram; the definite integral $\int_a^b \eta(x)g(x)dx$ will be equal to $\int_{c_1}^{c_2} \eta(x)g(x)dx$, and therefore non-zero. Hence $g(x)$ must be zero over the whole interval $[a, b]$ for $\int_a^b \eta(x)g(x)dx$ to be identically equal to zero.

2 Fundamental properties of the Euler equation

It is important to write in full equation (12) in order to understand the nature of this second-order, non-linear differential equation. Taking the total derivative of $\frac{\partial F}{\partial y'}$ yields:

$$\frac{\partial F}{\partial y}(x, y, y') - \frac{\partial^2 F}{\partial y' \partial x}(x, y, y') - \frac{\partial^2 F}{\partial y' \partial y}(x, y, y')y' - \frac{\partial^2 F}{\partial y'^2}(x, y, y')y'' = 0.$$

(13)

Generally, the first two terms of (13) are functions of x, y and y'; and so are, in the next two terms, the coefficients of y' and y''. So this second-order equation is such that its coefficients depend not only upon x, but upon y and y' as well.

The consequence is that very rarely does the equation have an analytic solution, which forces us therefore to rely on numerical methods. The brachistochrone problem mentioned in section 1 is one of the rare cases of practical problems which leads to an analytical solution, as presented in appendix 1. In growth theory, we will definitely need to resort to numerical analysis, which is fortunately readily available in a number of softwares (for instance MAPLE 9).

3 An important particular case

Suppose that the integrand of the functional (4) has the particular form of an affine function of $y'(x)$. This means that $F(x, y, y')$ has the following form:

$$F(x, y, y') = M(y, x) + N(y, x)y' \tag{14}$$

and therefore the variational problem is to determine $y(x)$ such that

$$\max_{y(x)} \int_a^b \left[M(y, x) + N(y, x)y' \right] dx. \tag{15}$$

The Euler-Lagrange equation in this case is

$$
\begin{aligned}
\frac{\partial F}{\partial y} - \frac{d}{dx}\frac{\partial F}{\partial y'} &= \frac{\partial M}{\partial y}(y, x) + \frac{\partial N}{\partial y}(y, x)y' - \frac{d}{dx}N(y, x) \\
&= \frac{\partial M}{\partial y}(y, x) + \frac{\partial N}{\partial y}(y, x)y' - \frac{\partial N}{\partial y}(y, x)y' - \frac{\partial N}{\partial x}(y, x) \\
&= \frac{\partial M}{\partial y}(y, x) - \frac{\partial N}{\partial x}(y, x) = 0
\end{aligned}
\tag{16}
$$

Equation (16) is not a differential equation any more but an ordinary equation between y and x. This case will receive an important application in chapter 13.

4 A necessary and sufficient condition for $y(x)$ to maximize the functional $\int_a^b F(x, y, y')dx$

The calculus of variations was invented in the 18th century and further developed in the next centuries mainly to solve problems of a geometrical or physical nature. As we have seen, Euler had established a necessary condition for $y(x)$ to optimize the functional $I[y(x)]$. It turns out that sufficient conditions are difficult to define. Some of the most renowned mathematicians of the 19th century have contributed to define *sets* of conditions which, taken together with the Euler equation, constitute *sufficient* conditions for $I[y(x)]$ to be optimized. The names of Legendre, Weierstrass or Jacobi are associated with some of those sets. The reason for this difficulty comes from the fact that mathematicians had to deal with the general problem where $F(x, y, y')$ could not be assessed to be concave or convex over all the domain of y and y'. Fortunately, in economics and particularly in economic growth theory, we are blessed by the fact that our integrand $F(x, y, y')$ is often concave in (y, y'). This led Akira Takayama (1964) to provide an extremely useful theorem. It gives a necessary *and* sufficient condition for $y(x)$ to yield a maximum.

We will now indicate and demonstrate Takayama's theorem (his original theorem considers functionals defined on vectors of functions $(y_1, \ldots, y_n)$, i.e. $\int_a^b F(x, y_1, \ldots, y_n, y'_1, \ldots, y'_n)dx$; here we just need functionals defined on the single function y; also, we have adapted his notation to ours).

THEOREM (Takayama, 1964). *Let $F(x, y(x), y'(x))$ be differentiable with respect to $y(x)$ and $y'(x)$, where $y(x)$ is twice differentiable on the closed interval $[a, b]$, with $y(a) = y_a$ and $y(b) = y_b$. Suppose that F is a concave function in y and y'. Then a necessary and sufficient condition for y to maximize the integral $I[y] = \int_a^b F(x, y, y')dx$ is that it satisfies the Euler condition $\frac{\partial F}{\partial y} - \frac{d}{dx}\frac{\partial F}{\partial y'} = 0$.*

PROOF As before, let $Y(x) = y(x) + \alpha\eta(x)$; $y(x)$ is supposed to be the solution of the problem and $\alpha\eta(x)$ is the variation of $y(x)$ such that $\eta(a) = \eta(b) = 0$. $y(x)$ maximizes the functional if and only if $I[Y(x)] \leqq I[y(x)]$. Consider now the difference

$$I[Y(x)] - I[y(x)] = \int_a^b [F(x, Y, Y') - F(x, y, y')]\,dx. \qquad (17)$$

From the concavity of F with respect to y and y', we know that for any value of x the differential of F will be larger than or equal to the increase of F in exact value. So we have the inequality

$$F(x, Y, Y') - F(x, y, y') \leqq \frac{\partial F}{\partial y}(x, y, y') \cdot (Y - y) + \frac{\partial F}{\partial y'}(x, y, y')(Y' - y')$$

$$= \frac{\partial F}{\partial y}\alpha\eta(x) + \frac{\partial F}{\partial y'}\alpha\eta'(x), \qquad (18)$$

using our preceding notation $Y - y = \alpha\eta(x)$, $Y' - y' = \alpha\eta'(x)$. Since this is true for any value x, it is also true for the definite integral of each member of inequality (18):

$$\int_a^b [F(x, Y, Y') - F(x, y, y')]dx \leqq \alpha \int_a^b \left[\frac{\partial F}{\partial y} \cdot \eta(x) + \frac{\partial F}{\partial y'} \cdot \eta'(x)\right]dx. \quad (19)$$

In section 2 of this chapter, we had integrated by parts the second term of the integral on the right-hand side of (19), and had obtained

$$\int_a^b \frac{\partial F}{\partial y'} \cdot \eta'(x)dx = -\int_a^b \eta(x) \cdot \frac{d}{dx}\frac{\partial F}{\partial y'}\,dx. \qquad (20)$$

Table 7.1   *Set of sufficient conditions for y to yield a global maximum of* $\int_a^b F(x, y, y') dx$.

---

1) y solves the Euler equation

$$\frac{\partial F}{\partial y}(x, y, y') - \frac{d}{dx}\frac{\partial F}{\partial y'}(x, y, y') = 0$$

2) F is concave in $y, y,'$; this is true if and only if, for any x

a) $\dfrac{\partial^2 F}{\partial y^2} \leqq 0$

b) $\dfrac{\partial^2 F}{\partial y'^2} \leqq 0$

c) $\dfrac{\partial^2 F}{\partial y^2} \cdot \dfrac{\partial^2 F}{\partial y'^2} - \left(\dfrac{\partial^2 F}{\partial y \partial y'}\right)^2 \geqq 0$

Note: if F is concave in (y, y'), then 1) is both a necessary and sufficient condition for $\int_a^b F(x, y, y') dx$ to be maximized; that is Takayama's theorem. The second part of these conditions (a, b and c) is proven in Appendix 3 of this chapter.

The right-hand side of (19) is then equal to

$$\int_a^b \eta(x) \left[\frac{\partial F}{\partial y'} - \frac{d}{dx}\frac{\partial F}{\partial y'}\right] dx.$$

Since y solves the Euler equation, this expression is equal to zero, and the inequality $I[Y(t)] - I[y(t)] \leq 0$ holds; the theorem is thus proved.

Concavity of F with respect to y and y' implies a global maximum of the functional; strict concavity implies a unique global maximum. The reverse is true: the convexity of F leads to a global minimum of the functional; strict convexity will give a unique global minimum.

It will prove very useful to have necessary and sufficient conditions for the integrand $F(x, y, y')$ to be concave in y, y'. These conditions are given in the second part of table 7.1.

Suppose finally that the integrand of the functional has the special, following form : it is an *increasing,* concave function of a function $F(x, y, y')$ which is itself concave in y, y'. (That case will be repeatedly found in optimal growth theory.) So, if $B(\cdot)$ is such that $B' > 0$ and $B'' < 0$, our functional is $\int_a^b B[F(x, y, y')]dx$, with $F(\cdot)$ concave in y and y'.) Then, by theorem 17.6 in K. Sydsaeter and J. Hammond (1995), $B[F(x, y, y')$ is concave in y and y'. The proof can be found in the above reference, p. 628.

*

*   *

Before we take up applications of the calculus of variations to optimal growth theory, it may be useful to get some familiarity with another major tool used in optimal dynamic systems, the Pontryagin maximum principle, which generalizes somewhat the calculus of variations. We will deal with this topic in our next chapter.

Appendix 1: Differentiating an integral with respect to a parameter – the Leibniz formula; a geometrical interpretation

Often in this book we will have recourse to definite integrals that depend upon a parameter. We know that, generally, a definite integral is a functional which depends upon three elements: the function to be integrated, the lower bound of integration and its upper bound. It may often be the case, however, that some of these elements – or all – depend upon a parameter. We have just encountered such an example in the calculus of variations when the function to be integrated was given a variation, defined as the product of a fixed function and a variable parameter. But many other examples arise: the value of capital depends parametrically upon the times of reference used to measure the generated cashflows; and in the field of statistics, a moment generating function of a continuous random variable is defined analytically as an integral depending upon a parameter.

Let $I(\alpha)$ be such an integral. We can write it as

$$I(\alpha) = \int_{a(\alpha)}^{b(\alpha)} f(x, \alpha)\,dx. \tag{A1}$$

The Leibniz formula states that its derivative with respect to α is

$$I'(\alpha) = \int_{a(\alpha)}^{b(\alpha)} \frac{\partial f}{\partial \alpha}(x, \alpha)\,dx + \frac{db}{d\alpha}(\alpha)f[b(\alpha), \alpha] - \frac{da}{d\alpha}(\alpha)f[a(\alpha), \alpha]. \tag{A2}$$

A rigorous proof of the formula – especially the first part of it – requires some advanced analysis and can be found in specialized texts. However the formula has a straightforward geometrical interpretation. It is just an extension of the classic interpretation of the derivative of an integral with respect to its upper bound, which is the value of the function to be integrated at its upper bound (the derivative of $\int_a^x f(u)du$ is just $f(x)$).

Consider in figure 7.5 the area under the curve $f(x, \alpha)$ for a given value of α. Suppose that we give a small increment to α, denoted $\Delta\alpha$. Suppose that the effects of this are the following: the bounds of integration move to the right, and the function to be integrated receives a variation such as the one indicated on figure 7.5. If $\Delta\alpha$ is sufficiently small, we could feel justified to consider that a

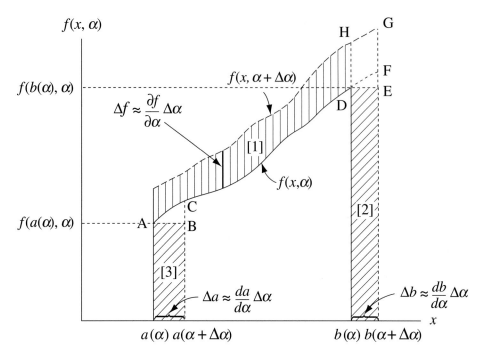

Figure 7.5   A geometrical interpretation of the Leibniz formula.

first order approximation of the net increase received by the area is the sum of the hatched areas, [1] plus [2], minus area [3].[3]

Consider first area [1]. It is the integral sum, from $a(\alpha)$ to $b(\alpha)$, of infinitely numerous vertical elements whose width is dx; their height is, in linear approximation, the differential of the function $f(x, \alpha)$ at point (x, α) in the direction of α, which is $\frac{\partial f}{\partial \alpha}(x, \alpha)\Delta\alpha$. So the area of such an element is simply $\frac{\partial f}{\partial \alpha}(x, \alpha)\Delta\alpha dx$, and as an approximation we then have

$$area\ [1] \approx \int_{a(\alpha)}^{b(\alpha)} \frac{\partial f}{\partial \alpha}(x, \alpha)\Delta\alpha\, dx = \Delta\alpha \int_{a(\alpha)}^{b(\alpha)} \frac{\partial f}{\partial \alpha}(x, \alpha)\, dx. \qquad (A3)$$

Area [2] is a rectangle whose width is, in linear approximation, the differential of $b(\alpha)$ i.e. $\frac{db}{d\alpha}(\alpha)\Delta\alpha$. Its height is $f[b(\alpha), \alpha]$, so we have approximatively

$$area\ [2] \approx \frac{db}{d\alpha}(\alpha)\Delta\alpha\ f[b(\alpha), \alpha]. \qquad (A4)$$

---

[3] Why should we feel justified to neglect the small, blank areas ABC, DEF, GHDF? The reason is the following. These areas are of a higher order of smallness than areas [1], [2] and [3]. Indeed, when $\Delta\alpha$ goes to zero, each of those areas is reduced by the shrinking of 2 dimensions. For instance, area GHDF is reduced by two combining effects: a decrease in the variation of the function *and* a smaller increase in the upper bound of integration. As to areas [1], [2] and [3], only *one* factor makes them become smaller. Each of these areas has one element which is not affected by a smaller $\Delta\alpha$. For instance, in area [1] the curve AD is invariant to a change in $\Delta\alpha$.

Similarly, area [3] is in linear approximation

$$area\ [3] \approx \frac{da}{d\alpha}(\alpha)\Delta\alpha\ f[a(\alpha), \alpha].\tag{A5}$$

As a result, an approximation of the increase ΔI is given by

$$\Delta I \approx \Delta\alpha \int_{a(\alpha)}^{b(\alpha)} \frac{\partial f}{\partial \alpha}(x, \alpha)dx + \frac{db}{d\alpha}(\alpha)\Delta\alpha\ f[b(\alpha), \alpha)] - \frac{da}{d\alpha}(\alpha)\Delta\alpha\ f[a(\alpha), \alpha)].$$
$$\tag{A6}$$

Dividing through (A6) by $\Delta\alpha$ leads to the Leibniz formula (A2). Notice how the classic formula $\frac{d}{dx}\int_a^x f(u)du = f(x)$ is just a particular case of (A2): here x plays the role of α, with $x = \alpha$ and $b(\alpha) = \alpha$; $\frac{db}{d\alpha}(\alpha) = 1$. The integral depends parametrically upon α only because the upper bound of integration does. So the first and the third term of (A2) vanish, and the derivative of the integral is just the value of the function at the upper bound, i.e. $f(x)$.

Appendix 2: Solution of the brachistochrone problem

Each of the great mathematicians of the 18th century whom we mentioned in this chapter (Johan and Jacob Bernouilli, Newton, the Marquis de L'Hospital, Tschirn-haus) had come up with a solution to the problem posed by Johan Bernouilli, discovering in his own way that the optimal curve joining point A to B was an arc of cycloid, i.e. a curve generated by the point of a circle rolling along a given, straight direction. We will give here one of the classical solutions to the problem. This one follows L. Elsgolc.[4] We will then apply it to the example given at the beginning of this chapter.

Let (x_0, y_0)be the initial point A of the curve $y(x)$ we are looking for, and (x_1, y_1) its terminal point B. The initial time t_0 is 0; the time when the bead reaches B is t_1.We need to determine $y = f(x)$ such that t_1 is minimized.

Let m designate the mass of the bead, v its speed and g the acceleration constant. At any point (x, y) of the curve we are looking for, the potential energy of the bead transforms itself into kinetic energy; the latter $((1/2)mv^2)$ is equal to the difference between the initial potential energy mgy_0 and the potential energy at point (x, y), equal to mgy. So we have:

$$\frac{1}{2}mv^2 = mgy_0 - mgy = mg(y_0 - y).\tag{A7}$$

The problem is thus independent of the mass of the bead, whose speed is just

$$v = [2g(y_0 - y)]^{1/2}.\tag{A8}$$

[4] L. Elsgolc, *Calculus of Variations*, Pergamon Press, London, 1964. We will however keep the ordinate axis pointing upward; this will lead to a sign change in y and y'.

At point (x, y), the distance s travelled by the bead is such that

$$\frac{ds}{dt} = v, \tag{A9}$$

and, with obvious initial conditions, the time taken by the bead to reach (x, y) is given by integrating

$$dt = \frac{1}{v}ds, \tag{A10}$$

i.e. by

$$\int_0^t d\tau = \int_0^s \frac{1}{v}d\sigma. \tag{A11}$$

We can express the differential of the distance travelled, ds (denoted $d\sigma$ in (A11)), in terms of x and y. We have:

$$ds = \sqrt{dx^2 + dy^2} = \sqrt{1 + y'^2}dx. \tag{A12}$$

Taking into account (A8), the time t_1 taken by the bead to reach x_1 is given by

$$t_1 = \frac{1}{\sqrt{2g}} \int_{x_0}^{x_1} \sqrt{\frac{1 + y'^2}{y_0 - y}}dx. \tag{A13}$$

This duration t_1 is thus seen as a functional of the type $\int_a^b f(x, y, y')dx$ with one – fortunate – proviso: in this case our integrand does not depend explicitly upon the integration variable x. Therefore the term $\frac{\partial^2 F}{\partial x \partial y'}$ in the Euler equation vanishes; denoting $F = F(y, y')$, the Euler equation reduces to

$$F_y - F_{yy'}y' - F_{y'y'}y'' = 0, \tag{A14}$$

which can be shown to reduce to a first-order differential equation, as follows.

Let us multiply each side of (A14) by y'; the left-hand side of (A14) then becomes the derivative with respect to x of $F - y'F_y$, divided by y'. Indeed, we have:

$$\frac{d}{dx}(F - y'F_{y'}) = F_y y' + F_{y'}y'' - y''F_{y'} - y'F_{y'y}y' - y'F_{y'y'}y''$$
$$= y'(F_y - F_{yy'}y' - F_{y'y'}y''). \tag{A15}$$

Thus, when F does not depend explicitly upon x, the Euler equation is equivalent to

$$\frac{d}{dx}(F - y'F_{y'}) = 0, \tag{A16}$$

which turns into the first order equation

$$F(y, y') - y'F_{y'}(y, y') = C, \tag{A17}$$

the highly useful Beltrami equation,[5] where C is a constant of integration.

We will now simplify the notation of (A13) by considering that the ordinate points downwards, and that point A is at the origin of the axes; thus $x_0 = y_0 = 0$. We then have to find $y(x)$ such that

$$\min_{y(x)} t_1 = \frac{1}{\sqrt{2g}} \int_0^{x_2} \sqrt{\frac{1 + y'^2}{-y}} \, dx, \tag{A18}$$

membering that y is negative.

We can apply the Beltrami equation (A17) to (A18) to get:

$$\left(\frac{1 + y'^2}{-y} \right)^{\frac{1}{2}} - \frac{y'^2}{[-y(1 + y'^2)]^{1/2}} = C, \tag{A19}$$

which reduces to

$$-y(1 + y'^2) = C_1, \tag{A20}$$

where C_1 is a new constant. Equation (A20) is then the first order equation whose solution will yield the optimal path we are looking for. Notice that it will imply two integration constants, to be identified thanks to the location of points A and B.

Equation (A20) can be solved in a number of ways; one of the simplest is to look for the solution in parametric form by making the change of variable $y' = -\cot \beta$. We then get:

$$y = \frac{-C_1}{1 + \cot^2 \beta} = -C_1 \sin^2 \beta = \frac{C_1}{2}(\cos 2\beta - 1). \tag{A21}$$

We also have:

$$dx = \frac{dy}{y'} = \frac{-C_1 \sin 2\beta \, d\beta}{-\cot \beta} = \frac{2 C_1 \sin \beta \, \cos \beta \, d\beta}{\cot \beta} = 2 C_1 \sin^2 \beta$$
$$= C_1(1 - \cos 2\beta) \, d\beta \tag{A22}$$

which can be integrated to yield

$$x = C_1 \left(\beta - \frac{\sin 2\beta}{2} \right) + C_2 = \frac{C_1}{2}(2\beta - \sin 2\beta) + C_2. \tag{A23}$$

The optimal curve joining A to B is then given parametrically by the system:

$$y = \frac{C_1}{2}(\cos 2\beta - 1) \tag{A24}$$

$$x = \frac{C_1}{2}(2\beta - \sin 2\beta) + C_2. \tag{A25}$$

---

[5] This equation was discovered in 1868 by the Italian mathematician Eugenio Beltrami.

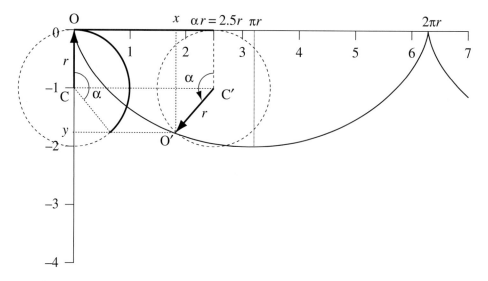

Figure 7.6   The cyloid is generated by the point (O) of a circle rolling on a horizontal axis. If the circle rolls by an angle α, the ray CO becomes $C'O'$. The coordinates of O' are $x = r(\alpha - \sin\alpha)$ and $y = r(\cos\alpha - 1)$. In our example, $r = 1$ and $\alpha = 2.5$.

We can make a further simplification by denoting $C_1/2 = r$, a constant to be identified, and $2\beta = \alpha$, a parameter whose interpretation will soon be given. System (A24), (A25) then becomes

$$y = r(\cos\alpha - 1) \tag{A26}$$

$$x = r(\alpha - \sin\alpha) + C_2. \tag{A27}$$

Let us first identify C_2, using the fact that the point of departure of the curve is $x = 0$, $y = 0$. Obviously, since $r \neq 0$, the first equation $0 = r(1 - \cos\alpha)$ leads to $\cos\alpha = 1$ and $\alpha = 0$; then, with $x = 0$ and $\alpha = 0$, (A27) gives $C_2 = 0$. Our system becomes

$$y = r(\cos\alpha - 1) \tag{A28}$$

$$x = r(\alpha - \sin\alpha), \tag{A29}$$

which is the equation of a cycloid, i.e. the curve generated by a point of a circle with ray r, rolling along a horizontal axis, and having accomplished a rotational angle α. We will now show why this is so.

Consider the origin of the axes as a point O on a circle of radius r (figure 5.6). Let this circle roll to the right with a rotational angle α. The abscissa of the new position of the center (C') is $r\alpha$. The position of the radius OC changes to $O'C'$. The coordinates of the initial point O on the circle move from (0,0) to (x, y). Now the coordinate x is equal to the difference $x = r\alpha - (r\alpha - x) = r\alpha - r\sin\alpha$ (since $\sin\alpha = (r\alpha - x)/r$); on the other hand $y = -r - (-r - y)$; since $\cos\alpha = -(-r - y)/r$, $y = -r + r\cos\alpha = r(\cos\alpha - 1)$. The coordinates of the cycloid thus are exactly given by system (A28, A29) above. Hence the constant $r (= C_1/2)$ is nothing else than the radius of the rolling circle, and C_1 is its diameter; the variable $\beta (= \alpha/2)$ is half its rotation angle.

To determine the cycloid passing through point (x_1, y_1), it suffices to determine the radius r_1 and the rotation angle α_1 of its generating circle. This is done by solving the system

$$y_1 = r(\cos\alpha - 1) \tag{A30}$$

$$x_1 = r(\alpha - \sin\alpha). \tag{A31}$$

This leads to the sole equation in α

$$\frac{\cos\alpha - 1}{\alpha - \sin\alpha} = \frac{y_1}{x_1} \tag{A32}$$

which can be solved numerically for α. Then r is given equivalently by

$$r_1 = \frac{y_1}{\cos\alpha - 1} = \frac{x_1}{\alpha - \sin\alpha}. \tag{A33}$$

In the problem at the beginning of this chapter, the coordinates of the terminal point B were $x_1 = 3$; $y_1 = -1$. So $y_1/x_1 = -1/3$. Solving (A32) for $y_1/x_1 = -1/3$ yields $\alpha \simeq 4.05$ $(0 < \alpha < 2\pi)$, and (A33) gives $r_1 \simeq 0.62$. So the equation of curve (c) in figure 1 is

$$y_1 = 0.62(\cos\alpha - 1) \tag{A34}$$

$$x_1 = 0.62(\alpha - \sin\alpha). \tag{A35}$$

Coming back to system (A28, A29), important properties of the brachystochrone (the cycloid) can be immediately noticed. From its first and second derivatives $y' = -\cot\beta = -\cot(\alpha/2)$ and $y'' = 1/\left[2\sin^2(\alpha/2)\right]$, the brachystochrone appears to be convex everywhere; it becomes vertical at $\alpha = 0$ and $\alpha = 2\pi$, and it goes through a minimum at $\alpha = \pi$ (i.e. at point $x = \pi r$, $y = -2r$).

You may wonder under which circumstances the brachystochrone is increasing on an interval, as in our example. From the minimum property shown above, everything hinges upon the ratio y_1/x_1 only, corresponding to point B: it suffices that $y_1/x_1 > -2r/\pi r = -2/\pi \simeq -0.64$ for the brachystochrone to have an increasing segment. In our example, $y_1/x_1 = -1/3$, so this condition is fulfilled.

The brachystochrone has another remarkable, nonintuitive property. Being a cycloid, it is a tautochrone: whatever the initial position at which beads are released along a cycloid, they will reach the minimum of the curve at the same time! This result was proved by Huygens in 1673 (the proof, a bit long, is omitted here; it can be found in specialized treaties, and also on the web).

There exist two wonderful web sites displaying spectacular animations of the brachystochrone. If you visit the site http://home.ural.ru/~iagsoft/BrachJ2.html, conceived and constructed by Alexei Ivanov, you can choose point (x_1, y_1) and compare the performance of the cycloid to that of the straight line and other curves. You can even choose the initial speed of the bead. The second site, http://www.sm.luth.se/~johanb/applmath/chap.en/part7.htm is due to Johan Byström, Lars-Erik Persson and Fredrik Strömberg. On this site you should go to "chapter III. Introduction to the calculus of variations." An animation of the cycloid is accompanied by an impressive illustration of its tautochrone property.

Appendix 3: Necessary and sufficient conditions for the integrand of the functional $\int_a^b F(x, y, y')dx$ to be concave in y, y'

Takayama's theorem, demonstrated in this chapter, states that if $F(x, y, y')$ is concave in (y, y'), y yields a global maximum of the functional $\int_a^b F(x, y, y')dx$ if and only if y solves the Euler equation $\frac{\partial F}{\partial y} - \frac{d}{dx}\frac{\partial F}{\partial y'} = 0$. We must now determine necessary and sufficient conditions for $F(x, y, y')$ to be concave in y, y'. This last condition rests upon the second differential of F being negative or zero. Using our notation, the first differential of $F(x, y, y')$ is

$$dF = \frac{\partial F}{\partial y}\alpha\eta(x) + \frac{\partial F}{\partial y'}\alpha\eta'(x) \tag{A36}$$

where $\eta(x)$ and $\eta'(x)$ are arbitrary, fixed variations of y and y', and α is any number different from 0. The second differential of F is

$$d^2F = \frac{\partial}{\partial y}\left[\frac{\partial F}{\partial y}\alpha\eta(x) + \frac{\partial F}{\partial y'}\alpha\eta'(x)\right]\alpha\eta(x)$$

$$+ \frac{\partial}{\partial y'}\left[\frac{\partial F}{\partial y}\alpha\eta(x) + \frac{\partial F}{\partial y'}\alpha\eta'(x)\right]\alpha\eta'(x)$$

$$= \alpha^2\left\{\frac{\partial^2 F}{\partial y^2}\eta^2(x) + 2\frac{\partial^2 F}{\partial y\partial y'}\eta(x)\eta'(x) + \frac{\partial^2 F}{\partial y'^2}\eta'^2(x)\right\} \tag{A37}$$

We thus have to discuss under which conditions the quadratic form in the brackets is negative or zero. In order to simplify the notation, we set $\frac{\partial^2 F}{\partial y^2} \equiv A$, $\frac{\partial^2 F}{\partial y\partial y'} \equiv B$, $\frac{\partial^2 F}{\partial y'^2} \equiv C$; on the other hand, the variables are denoted $\eta(x) \equiv u$ and $\eta'(x) \equiv v$, and the bracketed term is $f(u, v)$. We now have to prove that $f(u, v) = Au^2 + 2Buv + Cv^2 \leq 0$ if and only if $A \leq 0$, $C \leq 0$ and $AC - B^2 \geq 0$.

This is just a particular case of general negative semi-definite quadratic forms. We will repeatedly need this necessary and sufficient condition, and we borrow a demonstration from Kurt Sydsaeter and Peter J. Hammond's excellent text (1995, pp. 528–529).[6]

First suppose that $f(u, v)$ is negative semi-definite ($f(u, v) = Au^2 + 2Buv + Cv^2 \leq 0$). Then $f(1, 0) = A \leq 0$ and $f(0, 1) = C \leq 0$. If $A = 0$, $f(u, 1) = 2Bu + C$, an affine function of u which is negative or zero for any value of u only if $B = 0$. Thus $AC - B^2 = 0$. Consider now the case where $A < 0$; then $f(-B, A) = AB^2 - 2AB^2 + CA^2 = A(AC - B^2)$ is ≤ 0, so $AC - B^2 \geq 0$.

Conversely, suppose that $A \leq 0$, $C \leq 0$ and $AC - B^2 \geq 0$. If $A = 0$, $AC - B^2 \geq 0$ implies $B = 0$ and $f(u, v) = Cv^2 \leq 0$. If $A > 0$, the quadratic form can be written

$$f(u, v) = A \left(u + \frac{B}{A} v \right)^2 + \left(C - \frac{B^2}{A} \right) v^2,$$

which is always positive or zero since $AC - B^2 \geq 0$.

Exercises

7.1 Determine the Euler equation in the following cases:

   a) the integrand F of the functional does not depend on y'; $F = F(y, x)$
   b) F does not depend explicitly either on x or y; it depends solely on y'
   c) F depends on x and y' only
   d) F depends on y and y' only.

7.2 The cycloid, or brachistochrone, has surprisingly simple properties. One of them was discovered by Gilles de Roberval in 1634: the area under an arch of the cycloid is three times the area of its generating circle. Somewhat later, in 1658, Christopher Wren proved that the length of that arch was four times the diameter of the circle. Verify those properties; it is not difficult if you keep the cycloid in the form of system $x = f(\alpha)$, $y = g(\alpha)$; it is simplest also to consider the arch in the positive quadrant, writing $x = r(\alpha - \sin \alpha)$ and $y = r(1 - \cos \alpha)$. For the Roberval property, at some point, use $\cos^2 \alpha = 1/2 + (1/2) \cos \alpha$; for the Wren property, use $1 - \cos \alpha = 2 \sin^2(\alpha/2)$.

7.3 The calculus of variations as presented in this introduction can be extended in several directions. For instance, we may want to find a functional whose integrand depends upon x, y, and the first n derivatives of $f(x)$, $y', \ldots, y^{(n)}$.

---

[6] K. Sydsaeter and P. J. Hammond, *Mathematics for Economic Analysis*, Prentice Hall, Englewood Cliffs, N.J., 1995, pp. 528–529.

Other classical problems are to find a vector of m functions $y_1(x), \ldots, y_m(x)$ that maximizes a functional whose integrand depends on x, the vector $y_1, \ldots, y_m$, as well as on the vectors of derivatives $y'_1, \ldots, y'_m; y''_1, \ldots, y''_m;$ $\ldots; y_1^{(n)}, \ldots, y_m^{(n)}$. Also, we could look for a surface $z = f(x, y)$ maximizing a double integral $\int \int_D F(x, y, z, \frac{\partial z}{\partial x}, \frac{\partial z}{\partial y}) dx$, and so on.

In this exercise, you are asked to derive the so-called Euler–Poisson equation corresponding to the maximization of

$$\int_a^b F(x, y, y', y'') dx.$$

Hint: in order to do so, you need to define additional conditions on the admissible curves $y(x) + \alpha \eta(x)$, and more precisely on the admissible variation. We already have set, in the original problem, $\eta(a) = \eta(b) = 0$ so that, for any α, $y(a) = y_a$ and $y(b) = y_b$. Now we add the conditions $y'(a) = y'_a$ and $y'(b) = y'_b$. In other words, at points $x = a$ and $x = b$, not only has the function $f(x)$ specified values, but $f'(x)$ is uniquely defined as well. This implies that $y'_a + \alpha \eta'(a) = y'_a$ for any value of α, therefore $\eta'(a) = 0$. Similarly, if $y'_b + \alpha \eta'(b) = y'_b$, then $\eta'(b) = 0$. You should now give y a variation as we have done in this chapter; when you take the derivative of the functional with respect to α, integrate once by parts the second term of the definite integral, and twice by parts the third term.

Answers

7.1 a) If $F = F(x, y)$, the Euler equation reduces to $\frac{\partial F}{\partial y}(x, y) = 0$, an algebraic equation in (x, y) and not a differential equation. For a solution to exist, the solution must contain the boundary conditions, so these conditions cannot be set arbitrarily as we have done in this chapter. This case is similar to what we have seen in section 3 of this chapter, when the functional was an affine function of y'.

b) If F depends on y' only, the Euler equation is $\frac{d}{dt} \frac{\partial F}{\partial y'}(y') = 0$, or $\frac{\partial^2 F}{\partial y'^2}(y') y'' = 0$. Either $y'' = 0$ or $\partial^2 F / \partial y'^2 = 0$. The first case leads to $y' = C_1$ and $y = C_1 x + C_2$. In the second case, we have an equation in the sole variable y', which may or may not have solutions. Suppose it has a solution s. So $y' = s$, and the linear solution is $y = sx$, a particular solution of $y = C_1 x + C_2$ when $C_1 = s$ and $C_2 = 0$.

c) If F depends upon x and y' only, the first term of the Euler equation cancels, and we have

$$\frac{d}{dt}\frac{\partial F}{\partial y'}(x, y') = 0.$$

The Euler equation therefore reduces to the first-order differential equation $\frac{\partial F}{\partial y'}(x, y') = 0$.

d) In appendix 3, we have given Elsgolc's solution of the brachistochrone. You will notice that this problem corresponds precisely to such a case where the integrand depends solely on y and on y' and we were led to the Beltrami equation. We meet here one of those rare variational problems in physics that is amenable to an analytic solution, thanks to the reduced order of the underlying differential equation. (We will later benefit from such an analytic simplification – see chapter 10.)

7.2 For Roberval's property: calculate the area $A = \int_0^{2\pi r} y\,dx$ by changing the variable of integration, using the system $x = r(\alpha - \sin\alpha)$ and $y = r(1 - \cos\alpha)$. You finally get $A = 3\pi r^2$. The Wren property can be obtained by calculating the length $l = \int_D ds$ where $ds = [(dx)^2 + (dy)^2]^{1/2}$, which gives $l = 8r$.

7.3 The problem may be written

$$\text{Max } I = \int_a^b F(x, y, y', y'')dx.$$

Let us suppose that y is the solution, such that $y(a) = y_a$; $y(b) = y_b$; $y'(a) = y_a$; $y'(b) = y_b$. Let $\alpha\eta(x)$ be a variation given to the solution $y(x)$. The comparison function is $y(x) + \alpha\eta(x)$. Since for any α we must have $y'(\alpha) + \alpha\eta'(a) = y_a' + \alpha\eta'(a) = y_a'$, $\eta(\alpha)$ must be equal to 0. Similarly, $\eta'(b) = 0$. Since y is fixed as the solution, and $\eta(x)$ is arbitrarily fixed, the functional I reduces to a function of α :

$$I = I(\alpha) = \int_a^b F(x, y + \alpha\eta,\ y' + \alpha\eta',\ y'' + \alpha\eta'')dx.$$

Denote $Y = y + \alpha\eta$; $Y' = y' + \alpha\eta'$; $Y'' = y'' + \alpha\eta''$. Then

$$I'(\alpha) = \int_a^b \left[\frac{\partial F}{\partial Y}\eta(x) + \frac{\partial F}{\partial Y'}\eta'(x) + \frac{\partial F}{\partial Y''}\eta''(x)\right]dx$$

and

$$I'(0) = \int_a^b \left[\frac{\partial F}{\partial y}\eta(x) + \frac{\partial F}{\partial y'}\eta'(x) + \frac{\partial F}{\partial y''}\eta''(x)\right]dx.$$

As we have seen in this chapter, integrating by parts the second term yields $-\int_a^b \eta(x)\frac{d}{dx}\frac{\partial F}{\partial y'}dx$. Integrate now twice by parts the third term. We have:

$$\int_a^b \frac{\partial F}{\partial y''}\eta''(x)dx = \frac{\partial F}{\partial y''}\eta'(x)\Big|_a^b - \int_a^b \eta'(x)\frac{d}{dx}\frac{\partial F}{\partial y''}dx$$

$$= \frac{\partial F}{\partial y''}\eta'(x)\Big|_a^b - \eta(x)\frac{d}{dx}\frac{\partial F}{\partial y''}\Big|_a^b + \int_a^b \eta(x)\frac{d^2}{dx^2}\frac{\partial F}{\partial y''}dx.$$

Since $\eta(a) = \eta(b) = \eta'(a) = \eta'(b) = 0$, this integral reduces to $\int_a^b \eta(x)\frac{d^2}{dx^2}\frac{\partial F}{\partial y''}dx$. We can factor out $\eta(x)$ in the integrand of $I(0)$ to obtain

$$I(0) = \int_a^b \eta(x)\left[\frac{\partial F}{\partial y} - \frac{d}{dx}\frac{\partial F}{\partial y'} + \frac{d^2}{dx^2}\frac{\partial F}{\partial y''}\right]dx.$$

In order to get a condition on y leading to $I(0) = 0$, we can now apply the fundamental lemma of the calculus of variations we have seen in this chapter: the bracketed term in the integrand of the above equation should be zero, which leads to the Euler–Poisson equation

$$\frac{\partial F}{\partial y} - \frac{d}{dx}\frac{\partial F}{\partial y'} + \frac{d^2}{dx^2}\frac{\partial F}{\partial y''} = 0.$$

Note that this is, generally, a fourth-order differential equation. Indeed, if we write explicitly this Euler–Poisson equation – quite a tedious task – at a point we have to take the second derivative of $\frac{\partial F}{\partial y''}(x, y, y', y'')$ (the third term of the above equation). The first derivative is

$$\frac{d}{dx}\frac{\partial F}{\partial y''} = \frac{\partial^2 F}{\partial y''^2} + \frac{\partial^2 F}{\partial y\partial y''}y' + \frac{\partial^2 F}{\partial y'\partial y''}y'' + \frac{\partial^2 F}{\partial y''^2}y'''.$$

In turn, when taking the derivative of this expression with respect to x, the fourth derivative $y^{(iv)}$ will appear. Needless to say, we cannot hope, generally, to solve analytically the Euler equation of this type, and only numerical methods may be applied. Fortunately, however, we will be blessed with an economic application where it is possible to have an analytic solution (chapter 11); this is due to the fact that the integrand of our functional will depend solely upon y'', and not on any of the arguments x, y or y'.

The real surprise will come when we discover that there are much quicker ways to obtain the Euler–Poisson, which rest upon extensions of the Dorfmanian, to be introduced in our next chapter (8).

Other major tools for optimal growth theory: the Pontryagin maximum principle and the Dorfmanian

Complex dynamic systems, in particular those with inequality constraints, have made it necessary to extend the classical calculus of variations. This work has been carried after the Second World War by Richard Bellman in the United States, in the form of dynamic programming, and by Lev Pontryagin and his associates in Russia. This latter contribution is also called "optimal control theory"; its central result is known as the Pontryagin maximum principle.

The full-fledged maximum principle requires some very advanced mathematics and its proof extends over some 50 pages.[1] We will indicate here only the result in its simplest form, using the beautiful economic interpretation of this principle that was given by Robert Dorfman[2] (1969). The power of Robert Dorfman's analysis will be obvious: not only does it permit us to solve dynamic optimization problems, but it will also enable us to obtain the classical results of the calculus of variations (the Euler–Lagrange equation and its extensions) through economic reasoning.

But the reason why Dorfman's contribution is so important is that it goes well beyond a very clever, intuitive, explanation of the Pontryagin maximum principle. Robert Dorfman introduced a new Hamiltonian, which has profound economic significance. To honour Professor Dorfman's memory, we call this "modified

---

[1] The original contribution by Pontryagin and his associate is: L. S. Pontryagin, V. G. Boltyanskii, R. V. Gamkrelidze and E. F. Mishchenko, *The Mathematical Theory of Optimal Processes* (translated by K. N. Trirogoff). Interscience, New York, 1962.

    Very precise and complete results of optimal control theory can be found in K. J. Arrow, "Applications of Control Theory to Economic Growth", American Mathematical Society, *Mathematics of the Decision Sciences, Part 2*. Providence 1968, pp. 85–119; K. J. Arrow and M. Kurz, *Public Investment, the Rate of Return, and Optimal Fiscal Policy*. Stanford University Institute for Mathematical Studies in the Social Sciences, 1968.

[2] Professor Robert Dorfman (1917–2002) taught at Berkeley and at Harvard University. His article "An Economic Interpretation of Optimal Control Theory" (1969) is a masterpiece.

Hamiltonian" a Dorfmanian. In turn this Dorfmanian can be extended to obtain all high-order equations of the calculus of variations (the Euler–Poisson and the Ostrogradski equations).

The reader will notice in this chapter and those that follow that many tools are at his disposal to solve the simple variational problems of optimal economic growth: he can use the classical calculus of variations, the Pontryagin maximum principle and the Dorfmanian. He may then ask two questions: is one of the methods to be preferred? And if the choice between methods is completely open, would some be redundant? For simple problems like the ones we will deal with, there is indeed complete equivalency in the methods. But there is certainly no redundancy: the Dorfmanian offers remarkable insights which are not present in the calculus of variations, and we would never have been able to prove the second part of Adam Smith's theorem, as enunciated in our introduction, without the Dorfmanian. We hope that this will be evident to the reader in chapter 15.

I   The maximum principle in its simplest form

Let k_t be a state variable (for instance the stock of capital of a nation, or that of a firm); this is a variable which is inherited at time t from past conditions and decisions. Let x_t be a control variable; for instance, it may be the consumption of a nation at time t, or some kind of expenditure made by a firm at time t. The trajectory of k_t will be determined by an initial condition at time $t = 0$ and by the time derivative of k_t, denoted $\dot{k}_t$. This derivative is supposed to depend upon three variables: the value of the state variable itself at time t, k_t; the control variable x_t; and time t. This last hypothesis means that the relationship between $\dot{k}_t$ on the one hand, and k_t and x_t on the other, is time dependent. So we have the constraint

$$\dot{k}_t = f(k_t, x_t, t). \tag{1}$$

On the other hand, we have an objective function in the form of the definite integral of a so-called profit function. Denoted u, the profit function depends, at any time t, upon the state variable k_t, the control variable x_t and time. We have

$$u = u(k_t, x_t, t) \tag{2}$$

and the optimal control problem is to find the whole trajectory of x such that it maximizes

$$\int_t^T u(k_\tau, x_\tau, \tau)d\tau \tag{3}$$

under the constraint

$$\dot{k}_\tau = f(k_\tau, x_\tau, \tau). \tag{1}$$

This problem can be solved by setting a Hamiltonian[3] defined as

$$H = u(k_t, x_t, t) + \lambda(t) f(k_t, x_t, t)$$

where $\lambda(t)$ is a function of time to be determined. The optimal trajectory x_t, as well as k_t and $\lambda(t)$ are determined by the following system of three equations:

$$\frac{\partial H}{\partial x_t} = \frac{\partial u}{\partial x_t} + \lambda(t) \frac{\partial f}{\partial x_t} = 0 \tag{4}$$

$$\frac{\partial H}{\partial k_t} = \frac{\partial u}{\partial k_t} + \lambda(t) \frac{\partial f}{\partial k_t} = -\dot{\lambda}(t) \tag{5}$$

$$\frac{\partial H}{\partial \lambda_t} = \dot{k}_t = f(k_t, x_t, t). \tag{6}$$

Among these three equations, number (6) just comes from the definition of $\dot{k}_t$, as $f(k_t, x_t, t)$. Our task will be to give an intuitive explanation of equations (4) and (5). Before we do so, let us check that this principle does generalize the calculus of variations.

2   The relationship between the Pontryagin maximum principle and the calculus of variations

It is important to see how the Pontryagin principle can be used to obtain the Euler equation. Remember that the basic variational problem is to find $y(x)$ such as to maximize

$$\int_a^b F[y(x), y'(x), x]dx.$$

Compare this to the problem of finding x_t such that

$$\max_{x_t} \int_a^b u(k_t, x_t, t)dt$$

subject to

$$\dot{k}_t = f(k_t, x_t, t).$$

We can make the second problem equivalent to the first by considering that the three-variable function $\dot{k}_t = f(k_t, x_t, t)$ reduces to x_t, so that $\dot{k}_t = f(k_t, x_t, t) = x_t$. The Hamiltonian is then:

$$H = u(k_t, \dot{k}_t, t) + \lambda(t)\dot{k}_t. \tag{7}$$

---

[3] This name is given in honour of the Irish mathematician and physicist William Rowan Hamilton (1805–65). At age 22, Hamilton was named Royal Astronomer and full professor of mathematics at Trinity College, Dublin.

Applying the Pontryagin maximum principle, equations (4) and (5) lead to

$$\frac{\partial H}{\partial x_t} = \frac{\partial u}{\partial \dot{k}_t} + \lambda(t) = 0 \tag{8}$$

and

$$\frac{\partial H}{\partial k_t} = \frac{\partial u}{\partial k_t} = -\dot{\lambda}(t) \tag{9}$$

respectively.

In order to eliminate $\lambda(t)$ between these two equations, let us take the derivative of (8) with respect to t. We get $\dot{\lambda}(t) = -\dfrac{d}{dt}\dfrac{\partial u}{\partial \dot{k}_t}$; replacing $\dot{\lambda}(t)$ into (9) yields

$$\frac{\partial u}{\partial k_t} - \frac{d}{dt}\frac{\partial u}{\partial \dot{k}_t} = 0, \tag{10}$$

which is the Euler equation.

3 An economic derivation of the maximum principle

Robert Dorfman gave two methods of deriving the fundamental equations of the maximum principle from an economic point of view. Each is highly interesting in its own right.

3.1 First derivation

The reader may remember the way Lagrange solved the fundamental problem of the calculus of variations: he managed to transform the problem of optimizing a functional, $I[y(x)]$, into the familiar problem of optimizing a function $I[y(x) + \alpha\eta(x)] = I(\alpha)$, where both $y(x)$ and $\eta(x)$ are fixed; $y(x)$ is fixed because it is supposed to be the solution of the problem; as to $\eta(x)$, it is an arbitrary, fixed, variation of $y(x)$.

The same kind of reasoning can be applied here. Instead of trying to determine the whole trajectory of x maximizing the functional $\int_t^T u(k_\tau, x_\tau, \tau)d\tau$ subject to $\dot{k}_\tau = f(k_\tau, x_\tau, \tau)$, let us suppose that we know the optimal time path of x from $t + \Delta t$ onwards (where Δt is extremely small), and that we are to determine the single value of x at time t, x_t. So we write

$$\int_t^T u(k_\tau, x_\tau, \tau)d\tau = u(k_t, x_t, t)\Delta t + \int_{t+\Delta t}^T u(k_\tau, x_\tau, \tau)d\tau. \tag{11}$$

The integral on the right-hand side of (11) does not depend any more on the trajectory of x, since the latter is fixed as the optimal time path of x from time $t + \Delta t$ to time T. From $t + \Delta t$ onward, the whole trajectory of k is determined by the differential equation $\dot{k}_\tau = f(k_\tau, x_\tau, \tau)$, and, since x_τ is known from $\tau = t + \Delta t$

to $\tau = T$, it hinges solely upon the initial value of k at time $t + \Delta t$, $k_{t+\Delta t}$. Therefore, for a fixed value T, the integral on the right-hand side of (11) depends solely upon $k_{t+\Delta t}$ and $t + \Delta t$.[4] This function of $k_{t+\Delta t}$ and $t + \Delta t$ can be denoted $V(k_{t+\Delta t}, t + \Delta t)$; we have

$$V(k_{t+\Delta t}, t + \Delta t) = \int_{t+\Delta t}^{T} u(k_\tau, x_\tau, \tau)d\tau. \tag{12}$$

Our task is to determine the optimal value x_t that will maximize

$$u(k_t, x_t, t)\Delta t + \int_{t}^{T} u(k_\tau, x_\tau, \tau)d\tau = u(k_t, x_t, t)\Delta t + V(k_{t+\Delta t}, t + \Delta t). \tag{13}$$

It is important to underline at this point the dependency that exists between the first argument of V (which is $k_{t+\Delta t}$) and x_t. Indeed, we have in linear approximation

$$k_{t+\Delta t} \approx k_t + \dot{k}_t \Delta t = k_t + f(k_t, x_t, t)\Delta t.$$

Hence, if we maximize (13) with respect to x_t, we are led to the first-order condition

$$\frac{\partial u}{\partial x_t}\Delta t + \frac{\partial V}{\partial x_t}(k_{t+\Delta t}, t + \Delta t) = \frac{\partial u}{\partial x_t}\Delta t + \frac{\partial V(k_{t+\Delta t}, t + \Delta t)}{\partial k_{t+\Delta t}} \cdot \frac{\partial f}{\partial x_t}\Delta t = 0. \tag{14}$$

The rate of increase of the optimal value V with respect to one unit of the state variable at time $t + \Delta t$ may be interpreted as the *price* of the state variable at time $t + \Delta t$ and denoted $\lambda(t + \Delta t)$. Therefore (14) becomes

$$\frac{\partial u}{\partial x_t}\Delta t + \lambda(t + \Delta t)\frac{\partial f}{\partial x_t}\Delta t = 0. \tag{15}$$

Dividing both sides of (15) by Δt and taking $\Delta t \to 0$ leads to equation (4).

In order to derive equation (5), suppose that equation (4) has enabled us to determine x_t. Therefore the functional in the left-hand side of (11) can be written as the optimal value $V(k_t, t)$, and (11) becomes the identity

$$V(k_t, t) = u(k_t, x_t, t)\Delta t + V(k_{t+\Delta t}, t + \Delta t). \tag{16}$$

Take the derivative of (16) with respect to k_t:

$$\frac{\partial V}{\partial k_t} = \frac{\partial u}{\partial k_t}\Delta t + \frac{\partial V}{\partial k_{t+\Delta t}} \cdot \frac{\partial k_{t+\Delta t}}{\partial k_t}. \tag{17}$$

---

[4] Basically, it implies that V depends on the point of time we start from $(t + \Delta t)$, and on the amount of the state variable that is available at that time $(K_{t+\Delta t})$.

In (17) we can consider, as before, the first-order approximation

$$k_{t+\Delta t} \approx k_t + f(k_t, x_t, t)\Delta t \qquad (18)$$

and hence

$$\frac{\partial k_{t+\Delta t}}{\partial k_t} \approx 1 + \frac{\partial f}{\partial k_t}\Delta t. \qquad (19)$$

On the other hand

$$\frac{\partial V}{\partial k_{t+\Delta t}} = \lambda(t + \Delta t) \approx \lambda(t) + \dot\lambda(t)\Delta t. \qquad (20)$$

Finally, we can use our notation $\lambda(t) \equiv \partial V/\partial k_t$ to write (17) as follows:

$$\lambda(t) = \frac{\partial u}{\partial k_t}\Delta t + \left(\lambda(t) + \dot\lambda(t)\Delta t\right)\left(1 + \frac{\partial f}{\partial k_t}\Delta t\right) \qquad (21)$$

which becomes

$$\lambda(t) = \frac{\partial u}{\partial k_t}\Delta t + \lambda(t) + \lambda(t)\frac{\partial f}{\partial k_t}\Delta t + \dot\lambda(t)\Delta t + \dot\lambda(t)\frac{\partial f}{\partial k_t}(\Delta t)^2. \qquad (22)$$

Cancelling $\lambda(t)$ on both sides of (22), neglecting the second-order term in $(\Delta t)^2$, and dividing through by Δt, we finally get

$$0 = \frac{\partial u}{\partial k_t} + \lambda(t)\frac{\partial f}{\partial k_t} + \dot\lambda(t) \qquad (23)$$

which is just equation (5).

This fine reasoning proposed by Dorfman to get the fundamental equations of the Pontryagin maximum principle is wonderfully matched by the alternative derivation proposed by Dorfman himself. The careful reader of page 822 of Dorfman's essay will certainly be impressed by the fact that his second demonstration came as a remarkable afterthought, when the author had completed his first demonstration.

3.2 A beautiful idea

Robert Dorfman proposed to consider a *modified* Hamiltonian H^* defined as follows:

$$
\begin{aligned}
H^* &= u(k_t, x_t, t) + \frac{d}{dt}[\lambda(t)k_t] \\
&= u(k_t, x_t, t) + \lambda(t)\dot k_t + \dot\lambda(t)k_t \\
&= H + \dot\lambda(t)k_t.
\end{aligned} \qquad (24)
$$

Its economic interpretation is the following. At any time t, H^* constitutes the total benefits generated both *directly* through the profit function $u(k_t, x_t, t)$, and *indirectly* through the rate of increase of the *value* of the state variable k_t. The value of the state variable is equal to the amount of the variable, k_t, times its price $\lambda(t)$. This value can change for two reasons: a change in quantity, giving $\lambda(t)\dot{k}_t$ – in linear approximation – and a change in price, whose outcome is measured by $\dot{\lambda}(t)k_t$. Robert Dorfman called H^* a "modified Hamiltonian". As a tribute to the memory of Professor Robert Dorfman, we will call H^* a *Dorfmanian*.

The Dorfmanian H^* is equal to the ordinary Hamiltonian H plus the rate of increase of the state variable's value due to the sole change of its price, $\dot{\lambda}k_t$. A first-order condition for H^* to be maximized at any time t is to take both partial derivatives of H^* (with respect to x_t and k_t) and equate them to zero:

$$\frac{\partial H^*}{\partial x_t} = \frac{\partial u}{\partial x_t} + \lambda(t)\frac{\partial f}{\partial x_t} = 0 \tag{25}$$

$$\frac{\partial H^*}{\partial k_t} = \frac{\partial u}{\partial k_t} + \lambda(t)\frac{\partial f}{\partial k_t} + \dot{\lambda}(t) = 0. \tag{26}$$

Equations (25) and (26) are just equations (4) and (5) of the maximum principle, obtained with no calculations at all.

4   First application: deriving the Euler equation from economic reasoning

The power of the Dorfmanian is best illustrated by the fact that this economic construct enables us to derive the Euler equation in two lines.[5] To show this, revert to the initial problem of the calculus of variations, with the initial notation where x designates the variable of integration:

$$\underset{y(x)}{\text{Max}} \int_a^b F(y, y', x)\, dx.$$

Let $\lambda(x)$ be the price of the variable y, and $\lambda(x)y(x)$ the total value of the variable. The Dorfmanian is then

$$H^* = F(y, y', x) + \frac{d}{dx}[\lambda(x)y(x)]$$
$$= F(y, y', x) + \lambda'y + \lambda y'. \tag{27}$$

---

[5] Contrast this to the early developments of the calculus of variations. It took nearly half of a century to find the solution of general variational problems. Indeed, the brachistochrone problem was posed by Johan Bernouilli in 1698 and Leonhard Euler found in 1744, through finite difference methods, the second-order differential equation corresponding to the general problem. An analytic derivation (due to Lagrange) had to wait ten more years.

Set both $\dfrac{\partial H^*}{\partial y}$ and $\dfrac{\partial H^*}{\partial y'}$ equal to zero. We get:

$$\frac{\partial H^*}{\partial y} = \frac{\partial F}{\partial y} + \lambda' = 0 \tag{28}$$

and

$$\frac{\partial H^*}{\partial y'} = \frac{\partial F}{\partial y'} + \lambda = 0. \tag{29}$$

Take now the derivative of (29) with respect to x; we then get $\lambda' = -\dfrac{d}{dx}\dfrac{\partial F}{\partial y'}$; replacing λ' into (28) yields

$$\frac{\partial F}{\partial y}(x, y, y') - \frac{d}{dx}\frac{\partial F}{\partial y'}(x, y, y') = 0,$$

the Euler equation.

We will apply those methods to optimal growth theory in the chapters that follow.

5 Further applications: deriving high-order equations of the calculus of variations

The Dorfmanian can itself be generalized to tackle higher-order equations of the calculus of variations, i.e. those corresponding to functionals depending not only on $y(x)$ and its first derivative $y'(x)$, but on higher derivatives as well. Consider for instance the problem of finding the extremal of the functional $\int_a^b F(x, y, y', y'')dx$. Analytical methods enable us to show that the extremal must satisfy the fourth-order differential equation

$$\frac{\partial F}{\partial y}(x, y, y', y'') - \frac{d}{dx}\frac{\partial F}{\partial y'}(x, y, y', y'') + \frac{d^2}{dx^2}\frac{\partial^2 F}{\partial y''}(x, y, y', y'') = 0 \tag{30}$$

i.e. the Euler–Poisson equation. This equation enables us to show, for instance, that the polynomial minimizing the curvature or the deformation energy of a continuous term structure curve – more on this in chapter 11 – must be of the third order.

We will now show that the Euler–Poisson equation can be derived by extending the Dorfmanian in either of two directions.

5.1 First extension

Consider a modified Dorfmanian defined as the original Dorfmanian, to which we add the rate of change of the *value* of the first derivative of y. Let $\lambda_0(x)$ denote the *price* of $y(x)$, and define now as $\lambda_1(x)$ the price of $y'(x)$. The *value* of $y'(x)$ is then $\lambda_1(x)y'(x)$. Define a modified Dorfmanian D^* as

$$D^* = D + \frac{d}{dx}[\lambda_1(x)y'(x)]$$

$$= F(x, y, y', y'') + \frac{d}{dx}[\lambda_0(x)y(x)] + \frac{d}{dx}[\lambda_1(x)y'(x)] \qquad (31)$$

$$= F(x, y, y', y'') + \lambda_0'y + (\lambda_0 + \lambda_1')y' + \lambda_1 y''. \qquad (32)$$

Consider now the derivatives of D^* with respect to y, y' and y'', respectively, and equate each to zero. We have:

$$\frac{\partial D^*}{\partial y} = \frac{\partial F}{\partial y} + \lambda_0' = 0 \qquad (33)$$

$$\frac{\partial D^*}{\partial y'} = \frac{\partial F}{\partial y'} + \lambda_0 + \lambda_1' = 0 \qquad (34)$$

$$\frac{\partial D^*}{\partial y''} = \frac{\partial F}{\partial y''} + \lambda_1 = 0. \qquad (35)$$

Differentiating (35) twice leads to $\lambda_1'' = -\frac{d^2}{dx^2}\frac{\partial F}{\partial y''}$; differentiating (34) once gives

$$\frac{d}{dx}\frac{\partial F}{\partial y'} + \lambda_0' + \lambda_1'' = 0. \qquad (36)$$

Replacing in (36) λ_1'' by its value enables us to determine λ_0', which finally can be replaced into (33) to yield the Euler–Poisson equation

$$\frac{\partial F}{\partial y} - \frac{d}{dx}\frac{\partial F}{\partial y'} + \frac{d^2}{dx^2}\frac{\partial F}{\partial y''} = 0.$$

5.2 Second extension

Consider now a new Dorfmanian D_C defined as the original Dorfmanian D to which we add the *convexity of the value* of the extremal we are looking for, $\lambda_0(x)y(x)$; this convexity is just the second derivative

$$\frac{d^2}{dx^2}[\lambda_0(x)y(x)] = \lambda_0''(x)y(x) + 2\lambda_0'(x)y'(x) + \lambda_0(x)y''(x).$$

The Dorfmanian with convexity is then

$$D_C = D + \frac{d^2}{dx^2}[\lambda_0(x)y(x)]$$

$$= F(x, y, y', y'') + \lambda_0'y + \lambda_0 y' + \lambda_0''y + 2\lambda_0'y' + \lambda_0 y''$$

$$= F(x, y, y', y'') + (\lambda_0' + \lambda_0'')y + (\lambda_0 + 2\lambda_0')y' + \lambda_0 y''. \qquad (37)$$

Taking the partial derivatives of (37) and equating them to zero leads to:

$$\frac{\partial H_C}{\partial y} = \frac{\partial F}{\partial y} + \lambda_0' + \lambda_0'' = 0 \tag{38}$$

$$\frac{\partial H_C}{\partial y'} = \frac{\partial F}{\partial y'} + \lambda_0 + 2\lambda_0' = 0 \tag{39}$$

$$\frac{\partial H_C}{\partial y''} = \frac{\partial F}{\partial y''} + \lambda_0 = 0. \tag{40}$$

Differentiating (40) with respect to x twice gives λ_0'' as $-\dfrac{d^2}{dx^2}\dfrac{\partial F}{\partial y''}$; differentiating (39) once enables to obtain λ_0'' and yields λ_0' as $-\dfrac{d}{dx}\dfrac{\partial F}{\partial y'} + 2\dfrac{d^2}{dx^2}\dfrac{\partial F}{\partial y''}$. Replacing λ_0' and λ_0'' into (38) leads to the Euler–Poisson equation.

5.3 *Further extensions*

These modified Dorfmanians D^* and D_C can both be extended to cover functionals of the type $\int_a^b F(x, y, y', \ldots, y^{(n)})dx$, leading to the Euler–Poisson equation of order $2n$

$$\frac{\partial F}{\partial y} - \frac{d}{dx}\frac{\partial F}{\partial y'} + \frac{d^2}{dx^2}\frac{\partial F}{\partial y''} + \cdots + (-1)^n \frac{d^n}{dx^n}\frac{\partial F}{\partial y^{(n)}} = 0, \tag{41}$$

and also functionals defined by multiple integrals. For instance, consider the problem of finding the function of two variables $z(x, y)$ maximizing the integral

$$\iint_D F\left(x, y, z, \frac{\partial z}{\partial x}, \frac{\partial z}{\partial y}\right) dxdy. \tag{42}$$

Denote $p \equiv \partial z/\partial x$ and $q \equiv \partial z/\partial y$; the integrand in (42) is a function of the arguments x, y, z, p, q where each of the arguments z, p and q are functions of x and y.

Let F_p and F_q denote the partial derivatives of F with respect to p and q respectively. Each in turn depends upon the five arguments x, y, z, p, q. We thus have:

$$\frac{\partial F}{\partial p} = F_p(x, y, z, p, q) \tag{43}$$

$$\frac{\partial F}{\partial q} = F_q(x, y, z, p, q). \tag{44}$$

Maximizing (42) leads to the Ostrogradski[6] second-order partial differential equation

$$\frac{\partial F}{\partial z} - \frac{\partial}{\partial x}\frac{\partial F}{\partial p} - \frac{\partial}{\partial y}\frac{\partial F}{\partial q} = 0. \tag{45}$$

Care must be exercised when reading (45), because the second and third terms on the left-hand side are *total* derivatives of the partials F_p and F_q. We have first, recalling that $p = \partial z/\partial x$ and $q = \partial z/\partial y$:

$$
\begin{aligned}
\frac{\partial}{\partial x}\frac{\partial F}{\partial p} &= \frac{\partial F_p}{\partial x} + \frac{\partial F_p}{\partial z}\frac{\partial z}{\partial x} + \frac{\partial^2 F}{\partial p^2}\frac{\partial p}{\partial x} + \frac{\partial^2 F}{\partial p \partial q}\frac{\partial q}{\partial p} \\
&= \frac{\partial F_p}{\partial x} + \frac{\partial F_p}{\partial z}\frac{dz}{dx} + \frac{\partial^2 F}{\partial p^2}\frac{\partial^2 z}{\partial x^2} + \frac{\partial^2 F}{\partial p \partial q}\frac{\partial^2 z}{\partial y \partial x}.
\end{aligned} \tag{46}
$$

The fact that the last two terms on the right-hand side of (46) are second-order derivatives of $z(x, y)$ gives the second-order characteristic of the Ostrogradski partial differential equation. Similarly, the third term on the left-hand side of (45) is

$$\frac{\partial}{\partial y}\frac{\partial F}{\partial q} = \frac{\partial F_q}{\partial y} + \frac{\partial F_q}{\partial z}\frac{\partial z}{\partial y} + \frac{\partial^2 F}{\partial p \partial q}\frac{\partial^2 z}{\partial x \partial y} + \frac{\partial^2 F}{\partial q^2}\frac{\partial^2 z}{\partial y^2}. \tag{47}$$

All high-order equations of the calculus of variations can be obtained from suitable extensions of the Dorfmanian.[7] This is a testimony of the power of Robert Dorfman's remarkable discovery. We will now apply those tools, in particular the Dorfmanian, to optimal growth.

---

[6] Mikhail Ostrogradsky (1801–62) was a Professor of Mathematics at the University of Kiev. He made major contributions in mathematics, probability theory and mathematical physics.

[7] The interested reader can find them in our paper: "New Hamiltonians for High-Order Equations of the Calculus of Variations: a Generalization of the Dorfman Approach, *Archives des Sciences*, 45, 1, 51–8, 1992.

CHAPTER 9

First applications to optimal growth

Our aim is now to look for optimal growth paths, given initial conditions of the economy. The reader will see that for most problems the calculus of variations is quite sufficient; but we feel that we should present applications of the maximum principle as well because it is so widely used.

Most important however, is the following caveat: in this chapter we will present the *traditional* results of optimal growth theory as they have been expounded in the literature for more than four decades. This bulk of literature is an outgrowth of the seminal paper by Frank Ramsey (1928) in which the author was looking for optimal investment trajectories maximizing a sum of *utility* flows entailed by consumption.

We should stress that the great part of this literature remained very much theoretical in the sense that it just posited the existence of a concave utility function that would be accepted by society as a whole. Results were discussed from a qualitative point of view, on the basis of the phase diagram that gave the directions of the fundamental variables of the economy – in general, the capital–labour ratio, on the one hand, and consumption per person on the other. Whenever the differential equations were solved (through numerical methods) at the beginning of the sixties, the strangest of results appeared whatever the utility functions used: for instance, exceedingly high savings rates (in the order of 60–70%). The consequence of this dire situation is that optimal economic growth always remained in the realm of theory, and no serious attempt to compare optimal investment policies to actual time paths was ever carried out.

In the next chapter we will show that the culprit is the very utility function itself. We will analyse in a systematic way the consequences of using any member of the whole spectrum of utility functions, and we will show the damage done by them. We will then suggest another, much more direct, way of approaching optimal growth, leading to applicable results.

For the time being, however, we want to stick to the traditional approach because the reader should be familiar with the hypotheses, methods and results of this mainstream approach.

1   The mainstream problem of optimal growth: a simplified presentation

We will now present a problem of optimal growth with a single aim in mind: to illustrate the methods of economic dynamics that were presented in the last chapter. For that purpose, we shall deal with the simplest model we can imagine; it is stripped of any complication which might interfere with the exposition of the way methods work.[1]

Thus we will suppose that capital is the only factor of production; net income (net of depreciation) is given by $Y_t = F(K_t)$, where $F(.)$ is strictly concave $(F'(.) > 0; F''(.) < 0)$. The problem is to determine K_t such that

$$\underset{K_t}{\text{Max}} \int_0^\infty U(C_t)e^{-it}dt \tag{1}$$

subject to the constraint

$$\dot{K}_t \equiv I_t = Y_t - C_t \tag{2}$$

where i is a discount rate which applies to all utility flows $U(C_t)$. The utility function, $U(.)$, is supposed to be concave (thus $U'(.) > 0$ and $U''(.) < 0$). By far the most widely used family of utility functions is given by

$$\begin{cases} U = \dfrac{C^\alpha - 1}{\alpha}, & \text{for } \alpha < 1 \\ U = \log C, & \text{for } \alpha = 0.[2] \end{cases} \tag{3}$$

There are two initial conditions: at time 0, the capital stock is K_0 and the initial investment is I_0. Equivalently, this last condition, coupled with the first, amounts to an initial condition on C_0: indeed, at $t = 0$, consumption is $F(K_0) - I_0 = C_0$.

To solve this problem, we shall first use the calculus of variations, which will lead to a second-order non-linear differential equation in K_t, or equivalently to a system of first-order differential equations in either K_t and $\dot{K}_t$, on the one hand, or K_t and C_t, on the other. We will then turn to the Pontryagin maximum principle, using first the Hamiltonian, and then the Dorfmanian.

2   The calculus of variations approach

In ordinary differential calculus, we know that very often we can maximize a function of severable variables under a given constraint by replacing in the objective

---

[1] A more elaborate model, involving n capital goods and m non renewable resources, can be found in our paper "Capital Theory, Optimal Growth, and Efficiency Conditions with Exhaustible Resources", *Econometrica*, Vol. 48, No 7, November 1980, pp. 1763–76.

[2] This is the limit of $U(C)$ when $\alpha \to 0$, which can be determined by applying L'Hospital's rule. We have $\lim_{\alpha \to 0} U(C) = \lim_{\alpha \to 0} C^\alpha \log C = \log C$.

function one of the variables expressed as a function of the remaining variables, using the constraint to that effect. We thus obtain the simpler problem of maximizing a function free of any constraint. Here we will do something very similar: in the objective functional we can replace C_t by $F(K_t) - \dot{K}_t$. We get:

$$\text{Max}_{K(t)} \int_0^\infty U[F(K_t) - \dot{K}_t]e^{-it}dt. \tag{4}$$

2.1 Applying the Euler equation

This classical problem of the calculus of variations permits a direct application of the Euler equation. Call the integrand in (4) $G(K_t, \dot{K}_t, t)$. Then the Euler equation

$$\frac{\partial G}{\partial K} - \frac{d}{dt}\frac{\partial G}{\partial \dot{K}} = 0 \tag{5}$$

yields

$$U'_C F'_K e^{-it} - \frac{d}{dt}[U'_C(-1)e^{-it}] = U'_C F'_K e^{-it} + \dot{U}'_C e^{-it} + U'_C e^{-it}(-i) = 0. \tag{6}$$

Dividing (6) through by $U'_C e^{-it}$ leads to

$$\boxed{i = F'_K + \frac{\dot{U}'_C}{U'_C}.} \tag{7}$$

We now have to verify that this Euler equation (7) – which will turn out to be a second-order differential equation – does entail a maximum of the functional (4). Remember Takayama's theorem: if the integrand of the functional is concave in its arguments K and $\dot{K}$, then the Euler equation constitutes a necessary and sufficient condition to yield a global maximum of the function. We should therefore check the concavity of the integrand. This integrand can be written, for any t, $G(K, \dot{K}, t) = U[C(K, \dot{K}, t)]$. Theorem 17.6 on concave functions by K. Sydsaeter and P. J. Hammond (1995), p. 628, mentioned at the end of our chapter 7, states that a composite function $M(\mathbf{x}) = M(N(\mathbf{x}))$ is concave in $\mathbf{x}$ if the two following conditions are met: N is concave in $\mathbf{x}$, and M is increasing and concave in N. In our case we know that $U(C)$ is concave and increasing in C; let us now check whether $C(K, \dot{K})$ is concave in K and $\dot{K}$. We have

$$C(K, \dot{K}) = [F(K) - \dot{K}].$$

Therefore:

$$C_{KK} = F_{KK} < 0$$
$$C_{\dot{K}\dot{K}} = 0$$
$$C_{K\dot{K}} = 0.$$

The set of necessary and sufficient conditions for $C(K, \dot{K})$ to be concave in $K, \dot{K}$, i.e. $C_{KK} \leqq 0$, $C_{\dot{K}\dot{K}} \leqq 0$ and $C_{KK}C_{\dot{K}\dot{K}} - C_{K\dot{K}}^2 \geqq 0$ is met. Thus $G(K, \dot{K}, t)$ is indeed concave in K and $\dot{K}$, and the Euler equation will lead to a global maximum for whatever initial conditions on K and $\dot{K}$ we impose.

This equation, sometimes called the "Ramsey equation" (although the Ramsey model and its equations were very different from the above) makes so much sense that we can in fact derive it from economic reasoning, in at least two ways. The first method focuses on a limited time span; the second method considers an infinite time span.

2.2 Economic derivations of the Ramsey equation

Suppose we are at time t. We have to decide whether the splitting of income Y between investment I and consumption C is optimal or not, and whether, for instance, we should rather decrease consumption by an amount dC in order to invest it. We can say that the splitting of Y between I and C will be optimal if the sacrifice entailed by consuming dC less is exactly compensated by the rewards we will receive in the future if we invest that amount.

Why should it be so? The argument is subtle, because we might be tempted to reason, falsely, as follows: why not prefer a situation in which the marginal reward is *larger* than the marginal sacrifice? The answer to this apparent paradox is at the heart of the nineteenth-century marginal analysis, and in fact comforted by mathematical reasoning. Maximizing net gain of society will *not* imply a situation where *marginal* income is larger than marginal cost as long as society can change its situation precisely to reap that net benefit. From a mathematical point of view, it means that if profit (defined as revenue less cost) is to be at a maximum, the derivative of profit should be equal to zero, thus implying the derivative of revenue (economists call it marginal revenue) equals the derivative of cost (marginal cost). Consider total profit as $\pi = R(q) - C(q)$ where R and C are the revenue and cost of a firm, for instance; both are functions of the quantity produced q. A first-order condition for maximizing π is $\pi'(q) = 0$, entailing $R'(q) = C'(q)$, not $R'(q) > C'(q)$. This means that in an optimal situation marginal revenue should not be larger than marginal cost, except in the very special cases where the firm or the economy would be prevented by some constraints from reaping the marginal benefit that is offered to it – entailing so-called "corner solutions".

We will thus evaluate the sacrifice and the reward and equate both. It turns out that several methods are available. A solution based upon approximations is first presented. We then offer exact methods, using either an infinite or a finite horizon.

2.2.1 A first, intuitive, approach with a very short time interval

Consider a very short period Δt, and suppose that we can evaluate costs and rewards either at the beginning of the period or at the end of it. We will choose to make that evaluation at the end of Δt.

The sacrifice is measured in terms of utility; consuming dC less costs, at time t, $U'_C(t)dC$; that amount of utility at time $t + \Delta t$, taking the discount rate in consideration, is worth $U'_C(t)dC + iU'_C(t)dC\Delta t$ at the end of period Δt.

On the other hand, investing an amount equivalent to dC means that the stock of capital is increased by $\Delta K = dC\Delta t$; in turn, this additional capital enables to increase income by $\Delta Y = F'_K(t + \Delta t)dC\Delta t$, which can be evaluated in terms of utility as $U'_C(t + \Delta t)F'_K(t + \Delta t)dC\Delta t$. At time $t + \Delta t$, we still have the additional amount of capital $dC\Delta t$ at our disposal,[3] which can be consumed, thus yielding dC, evaluated as $U'_C(t + \Delta t)dC$. In total, the rewards are $U'_C(t + \Delta t)F'_K(t + \Delta t)dC\Delta t + U'_C(t + \Delta t)dC$.

Equating costs to rewards yields:

$$U'_C(t)dC + iU'_C(t)dC\Delta t = U'_C(t + \Delta t)F'_K(t + \Delta t)dC\Delta t + U'_C(t + \Delta t)dC. \tag{8}$$

In equation (8), carry $U'_C(t)dC$ to the right-hand side, and divide throughout by $U'_C(t)dC\Delta t$ to get:

$$i = \frac{U'_C(t + \Delta t)F'_K(t + \Delta t)}{U'_C(t)} + \frac{1}{U'_C(t)}\left[\frac{U'_C(t + \Delta t) - U'_C(t)}{\Delta t}\right]. \tag{9}$$

Taking the limit of (9) when $\Delta t \to 0$ gives

$$i = F'_K(t) + \frac{\dot{U}'_C}{U'_C}$$

which is (7).

2.2.2 Infinite horizon

We can now reason over a period of infinite length. Consider the sacrifice of investing one unit of consumption at time t, in terms of utility. It is $U'_C(t)$ times one unit of consumption, i.e. $U'_C(t)$ (note the dimension of U'_C: it is utility units).

On the other hand, let us evaluate the rewards of this investment. At any time τ between t and $+\infty$, and during an infinitesimal interval $d\tau$, it yields an income $F'_K(\tau)d\tau$ which can be evaluated in terms of utility as $U'_C(\tau)F'_K(\tau)d\tau$.

---

[3] Remember that throughout this book, $F(K)$ is *net* income, i.e. net of capital depreciation. So one unit of capital invested at time t is still available at any later time, because provisions are continuously made to replace its part that depreciates.

This utility flow, discounted to time t, is equal to $U'_C(\tau)F'_K(\tau)e^{-i(\tau-t)}d\tau$. The total rewards, taken from $\tau = t$ to infinity are then $\int_t^\infty U'_C(\tau)F'_K(\tau)e^{-i(\tau-t)}d\tau$.

Equating costs to rewards at any time t thus gives

$$U'_C(t) = \int_t^\infty U'_C(\tau)F'_K(\tau)e^{-i(\tau-t)}d\tau. \tag{10}$$

Using Leibniz's formula, take the derivative of (10) with respect to time t:

$$\dot{U}'_C(t) = i\int_t^\infty U'_C(\tau)F'_K(\tau)e^{-i(\tau-t)}d\tau - U'_C(t)F'_K(t). \tag{11}$$

In the right-hand side of (11), replace the integral by $U'_C(t)$, and divide throughout by $U'_C(t)$. We get the Ramsey equation (7) again.

2.2.3 Finite horizon

We could now suppose that the investment is not made during a period of time of infinite length, but during a finite time span, of length $T - t$. At some time T in the future, the unit of capital that was invested may then be sold or consumed. The analysis of costs and rewards may be carried out either in present value (at time t), or in future value (in terms of time T). We shall consider flows in present value.

The sacrifice of investing one unit of consumption, in terms of utility at time t, is just $U'_C(t)$. The rewards are made of two parts: first, we have the sum of the production flows generated by the investment, these flows being translated into utility flows and discounted to time t. One such flow, received at time τ during a very short period $d\tau$, as we had seen earlier, is equal to $U'_C(\tau)F'_K(\tau)e^{-i(\tau-t)}d\tau$, and the sum of these flows from t to T is then $\int_t^T U'_C(\tau)F'_K(\tau)e^{-i(\tau-t)}d\tau$. On the other hand, when the unit of capital is transformed into consumption at time T, it generates a utility flow $U'_C(T)$ whose present value is $U'_C(T)e^{-i(T-t)}$. Altogether the advantages of investing are $\int_t^T U'_C(\tau)F'_K(\tau)e^{-i(\tau-t)}d\tau + U'_C(T)e^{-i(T-t)}$.

In equilibrium, we must then have:

$$U'_C(t) = \int_t^T U'_C(\tau)F'_K(\tau)e^{-i(\tau-t)}d\tau + U'_C(T)e^{-i(T-t)}. \tag{12}$$

There are now two ways of deriving the Ramsey rule from this equilibrium condition. We can either differentiate this equality with respect to t or to T.

First derivation: differentiating with respect to t
Taking the derivative of (12) with respect to t yields:

$$\dot{U}'_C(t) = \int_t^T U'_C(\tau)F'_K(\tau)e^{-i(\tau-t)} \cdot i\, d\tau - U'_C(t)F'_K(t) + U'_C(T)e^{-i(T-t)} \cdot i. \tag{13}$$

There are in turn two ways of completing the demonstration. First, factor out i from the integral on the right-hand side of (13); then, using (12), this integral is found to be equal to $U'_C(t) - U'_C(T)e^{-i(T-t)}$, and (13) can be written as

$$\dot{U}'_C(t) = i\left[U'_C(t) - U'_C(T)e^{-i(T-t)}\right] - U'_C(t)F'_K(t) + i.U'_C(T)e^{-i(T-t)}.$$

(14)

Cancelling equal terms and dividing by $U'_C(t)$ yields the Ramsey rule

$$i = F'_K(t) + \frac{\dot{U}'_C(t)}{U'_C(t)}.$$

Alternatively, consider the limiting value of (13) when $T \to t$. The integral in the right-hand side of (13) goes to zero, and the last term tends to $U'_C(t) \cdot i$. Dividing then through by $U'_C(t)$ yields the Ramsey equation.

Second derivation: differentiating with respect to T
Consider now the derivative of (12) with respect to T. We have then:

$$0 = U'_C(T)F'_K(T)e^{-i(T-t)} + \dot{U}'_C(T)e^{-i(T-t)} + U'_C(T)e^{-i(T-t)}(-i). \quad (15)$$

Dividing through by $e^{-i(T-t)}$ yields

$$0 = U'_C(T)F'_K(T) + \dot{U}'_C(T) + U'_C(T)(-i),$$

which must be true also when $T \to t$, thus entailing (7) again.

2.2.4 Alternative derivations in future value

We should stress that the time of reference used to make our evaluations (which is time t, considered as "today") is perfectly arbitrary. We could have used any time in the future – for instance time T; we would have obtained the Ramsey equation as well. The reason is that valuing costs and rewards as expressed in equation (12) in terms of any other time T implies multiplying both sides of (12) by $e^{i(T-t)}$; taking the derivative of the resulting products with respect to t does not alter the results.

3   The Pontryagin maximum principle approach

As we have stressed in the introduction of this chapter, the calculus of variations and the Euler equation are sufficient tools to solve the simple variational problems we envision in optimal growth theory. Nevertheless, most economic texts and papers in this area have recourse to optimal control theory in the form of the Pontryagin maximum principle. It is therefore necessary to show how this methodology applies here. We first use the Hamiltonian. We then use the Dorfmanian, introduced in chapter 8.

3.1 The Hamiltonian approach

The problem is to find K_t, or $\dot{K}_t$, that maximizes

$$\int_0^\infty U(C_t)e^{-it}dt$$

subject to the constraint $C_t = F(K_t) - \dot{K}_t$. Optimal control principles leave us the choice of selecting either consumption C_t or investment $I_t = \dot{K}_t$ as the control variable. We will select $I_t = \dot{K}_t$ as the control variable (choosing C_t as the control variable is offered as an end-of-chapter exercise).

The problem can be written as

$$\text{Max} \int_0^\infty U\left[F(K_t) - \dot{K}_t\right]e^{-it}dt.$$

Let us form the Hamiltonian

$$H = U\left[F(K_t) - \dot{K}_t\right]e^{-it} + \lambda(t)\dot{K}_t.$$

Equation (4) of the maximum principle is $\partial H/\partial x_t = 0$; here the control variable x_t is investment, i.e. $\dot{K}_t$. We then have

$$\frac{\partial H}{\partial \dot{K}} = -U'_C e^{-it} + \lambda(t) = 0. \tag{I}$$

Equation (II) is $\partial H/\partial K = U'_C F'_K e^{-it} = -\dot{\lambda}(t)$; it leads to

$$\frac{\partial H}{\partial K} = U'_C F'_K e^{-it} = -\dot{\lambda}(t). \tag{II}$$

(I) and (II) constitute two equations in three unknowns, $\lambda(t)$, K_t and C_t. To eliminate $\lambda(t)$, differentiate (I) with respect to time. We get

$$\dot{\lambda}(t) = \dot{U}'_C e^{-it} + U'_C e^{-it}(-i).$$

We can replace $\dot{\lambda}(t)$ in (II). This leads to the Ramsey equation

$$i = F'_K + \frac{\dot{U}'_C}{U'_C},$$

which, together with the constraint $C_t = F(K_t) - \dot{K}_t$ can lead, as we will see in section 4 of this chapter, either to a system of two non-linear differential equations in C_t and K_t, or to a second-order differential equation in K_t.

3.2   The Dorfmanian approach

Let us form the Dorfmanian

$$H^* = U\left[F(K_t) - \dot{K}_t\right]e^{-it} + \lambda(t)\dot{K}_t + \dot{\lambda}(t)K_t$$

and equate to zero its partial derivatives $\partial H^*/\partial\dot{K}$ and $\partial H^*/\partial K$. We get:

$$\frac{\partial H^*}{\partial\dot{K}} = -U'_C e^{-it} + \lambda(t) = 0$$

and

$$\frac{\partial H^*}{\partial K} = U'_C F'_K e^{-it} + \dot{\lambda}(t) = 0$$

which correspond to equations (I) and (II) of the Hamiltonian approach, leading to the same result.

4   Optimal paths

Our task is now to derive the optimal time paths implied by the Ramsey rule. We will show that the Ramsey equation (7), together with the constraint $C_t = F(K_t) - \dot{K}_t$, can be treated either as a second-order, non-linear differential equation in K_t, or as a system of two first-order, non-linear differential equations in K_t and C_t.

There we have already made an assumption about the utility function (we have supposed that it was given by (3)). There remains to make an assumption about the production function $F(K)$. In the spirit of this methodological section, we will make the simple hypothesis that it is given by the power function $Y = K^\delta$; this corresponds to a Cobb–Douglas production function where labour is constant, and Y is normalized, so that a capital stock of one unit yields an income flow of one unit per unit of time.

4.1   The second-order differential equation in K_t

Consider now the term $\dot{U}'_C/U'_C$ in (7). It is equal to

$$\frac{\dot{U}'_C}{U'_C} = \frac{U''_C}{U'_C} \cdot \dot{C} = \frac{C}{U'_C} \cdot U''_C \cdot \frac{\dot{C}}{C}. \tag{16}$$

So it is equal to the elasticity of the marginal utility of consumption with respect to consumption, $(C/U'_C)U''_C$, times the growth rate of consumption. From (3) we can see that this elasticity is equal to $\alpha - 1$. So we get

$$\frac{\dot{U}'_C}{U'_C} = (\alpha - 1)\frac{\dot{C}}{C}. \tag{17}$$

On the other hand, $F'_K = \delta K^{\delta-1}$. The Ramsey equation in this simple case thus reads:

$$i = \delta K^{\delta-1} + (\alpha - 1)\frac{\dot{C}}{C}. \tag{18}$$

Since $C = F(K) - \dot{K} = K^\delta - \dot{K}$, we have

$$\dot{C} = \delta K^{\delta-1}\dot{K} - \ddot{K}. \tag{19}$$

Replacing C and $\dot{C}$ by their values into (18) yields

$$i = \delta K^{\delta-1} + (\alpha - 1)\frac{\delta K^{\delta-1}\dot{K} - \ddot{K}}{K^\delta - \dot{K}}, \tag{20}$$

the second-order, non-linear differential equation in K. Solving it, i.e. obtaining the optimal paths of K_t, and subsequently those of $\dot{K}_t$, Y_t and C_t, can be done through numerical methods only. Today there exist software that enables us to do this. We would just have to set two initial values: K_0, and $\dot{K}_0 = I_0$. Notice that once the value of K_0 is set, deciding upon an initial value for $\dot{K}_0$ or I_0 implies deciding upon an initial consumption value, because K_0 implies $Y_0 = F(K_0)$ ($= K_0^\delta$ in this case), and $C_0 = Y_0 - I_0 = K_0^\delta - \dot{K}_0$.

4.2 The system of first-order differential equations in K_t and C_t and its phase diagram

More insight, however, can be gained into the behaviour of these optimal trajectories of K_t and C_t (two of the fundamental variables of our economy) by considering the system of the pair of first-order, non-linear differential equations in C_t and K_t given by equations

$$i = \delta K^{\delta-1} + (\alpha - 1)\frac{\dot{C}}{C} \tag{18}$$

and

$$C_t = K_t^\delta - \dot{K}_t \tag{21}$$

which can be conveniently written as the system

$$\dot{C}_t = \frac{C_t}{1 - \alpha}(\delta K_t^{\delta-1} - i) \tag{22}$$

$$\dot{K}_t = K_t^\delta - C_t. \tag{23}$$

Indeed, since the system (22), (23) is autonomous, we can draw a phase diagram indicating the general direction taken by each variable K_t and C_t as a function of their initial or acquired position (K, C).

First we can draw the locus of points in (K, C) space where C will remain constant. This locus is obtained by setting $\dot{C}_t = 0$ in (22), and is therefore given by $\delta K^{\delta-1} - i = 0$, equivalent to

$$K^* = \left(\frac{\delta}{i}\right)^{\frac{1}{1-\delta}}. \tag{24}$$

This locus of points (K, C) is seen to be independent of C; on figure 9.1, it is the vertical line of abscissa $K^* = (\delta/i)^{1/(1-\delta)}$. Suppose that $\delta = 0.3$ and $i = 0.06$. This abscissa is therefore $5^{10/7} \approx 9.97$. It means that if ever K_t were equal to the value $K^* = 9.97$, consumption would not change.

Similarly, the locus of points (K, C) leading to a constant K is obtained by setting $\dot{K}_t = 0$ in (23), which yields

$$C = K^{\delta}. \tag{25}$$

From an economic point of view, it means that consumption is equal to total production and income; therefore investment is zero – and of course K does not move. In figure 9.1, the power function $C = K^{\delta}$ gives this locus corresponding to $\dot{K} = 0$.

The vertical line K^* crosses the curve $C = K^{\delta}$ at height

$$C^* = F(K^*) = (K^*)^{\delta} = \left(\frac{\delta}{i}\right)^{\frac{\delta}{1-\delta}}; \tag{26}$$

with the same parameter values for δ and i as above, $C^* \approx 2$.

At point (K^*, C^*), denoted E, we have an equilibrium in the sense that if ever the economy were located at that point, it would not move from there. We mentioned earlier that $\dot{K} = 0$ implied that there was no net investment. This means that at point E the entire output is consumed. This is confirmed by the value of C^* given by (25): it is equal to $F(K^*) (= (\delta/i)^{\delta/(1-\delta)} \approx 2$ in this case).

Both loci, $K = K^*$ and $C = K^{\delta}$, delineate four areas in (K, C) space, denoted I to IV. In area I, we have $K < K^*$ and $C < K^{\delta}$. Let us examine first what $K < K^*$ implies. The value K^* was determined as that value of K such that $\delta K^{\delta-1} - i = 0$, i.e. that value of K such that the marginal productivity of capital $(\delta K^{\delta-1})$ is equal to i. Now $0 < \delta < 1$; thus the marginal productivity of capital is a *decreasing* function of K (see figure 9.2); then, if $K < K^*$, it means that $\delta K^{\delta-1}$ is *larger* than i; therefore

$$\delta K^{\delta-1} - i > 0$$

and

$$\dot{C}_t = \frac{C_t}{1-\alpha}\left(\delta K_t^{\delta-1} - i\right)$$

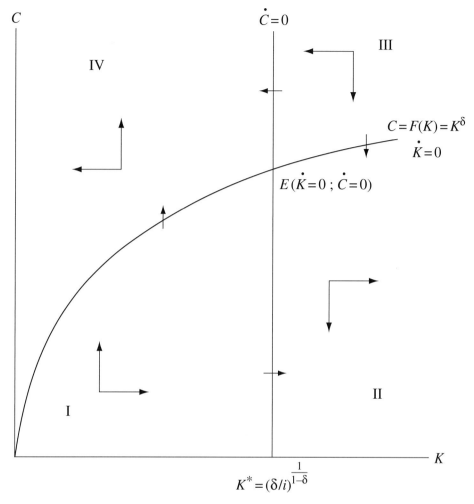

Figure 9.1 The phase diagram corresponding to the system of non-linear first-order differential equations

$$\begin{cases} \dot{C}_t = \frac{C_t}{1-\alpha}(F'_K - i) \\ \dot{K}_t = F(K) - C. \end{cases}$$

The locus of points (K, C) corresponding to $\dot{K} = 0$ is given by the curve $C = F(K)$. The locus (K, C) entailing $\dot{C} = 0$ is given by K^* such that $F'_{K^*} = i$; this is the vertical of abscissa K^*. To each quadrant corresponds a direction of displacement for each variable K and C. For instance, in quadrant I, $C < F(K)$, therefore $\dot{K} > 0$; also, $K < K^*$, implying $F'_K > F'_{K^*} = i$ (because F'_K is decreasing), and $\dot{C} > 0$.

together imply $\dot{C}_t > 0$. If the economy is in area I, it means that C will always increase. On the other hand, consider the behaviour of K_t in area I. By definition of this area, $C < K^\delta$ or $C < F(K) = Y$. We can conclude either from this inequality or directly from (23) that investment is positive, and thus that K increases in this area. This is the maximum qualitative information the phase diagram will give us.

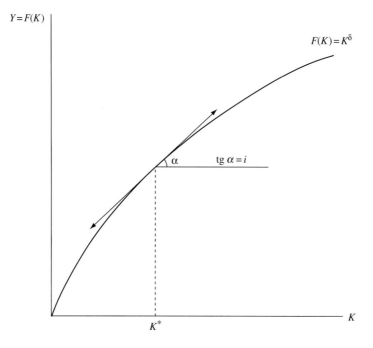

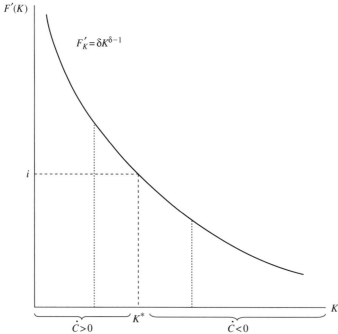

Figure 9.2 The concavity of the production function $F(K)$ and its consequences. The concavity of $F(K)$ implies that the marginal productivity $F'(K)$ is a decreasing function of K. As a consequence, any value of K smaller than K^* entails $F'_K > i$ and therefore $\dot{C} = \frac{C_t}{1-\alpha}(F'_K - i) > 0$; conversely, $K > K^*$ implies $\dot{C} < 0$.

It is conveyed by the pair of arrows depicted in areas I. The same type of analysis can be carried out for areas II, III and IV.[4]

Let us now consider what happens if, for some reason, the economy hits any point of the loci $\dot{K} = 0$ (the curve $C = F(K)$) or $\dot{C} = 0$ (the vertical of abscissa K^* corresponding to $F'_K = i$). Suppose first that the time path (K_t, C_t) hits a point of $C = F(K)$ at the border of areas I and IV. We know that if $C = F(K)$, $\dot{K}_t = 0$ and K does not change. Furthermore, since at such a point $K < K^*$, we know that $F'_K - i > 0$ and therefore $\dot{C} > 0$. We conclude that at such a point, K will not change, but C will continue to increase. We indicate this by a very small arrow crossing the border, pointing upwards. The reason the arrow is very small is that this holds over an interval of C infinitely small at the border point: below that point K increases, and above that point K decreases. The arrow at the border has the meaning of the *tangent* to the time path, with an indication of direction that holds over an interval of infinitely small length, for an infinitely small length of time. It is easy to figure out in a similar way what happens on the other borders of the various areas in the phase diagrams; the outcomes are represented by small arrows.

We must stress here that we do *not* know, from any initial point of area I, whether the time path (K_t, C_t) will eventually hit the vertical line $K = K^*$ – and as a consequence move into area II – or whether it will hit the curve $C = K^\delta$ – and therefore move into area IV; neither do we know whether it will move asymptotically toward the equilibrium point $E(K^*, C^*)$. To have an inkling of this, we *must* solve the system of equations (22), (23), and we must do this numerically.

It is therefore wrong to try to infer, from this sole information about the phase diagram, the position of a time path of the economy, given its initial location. We stress this point because all too many treatments of this question take the bold step of casually drawing those time paths, implying for instance properties about their convexity or concavity, or, worse, the position of the initial point (K_0, C_0) that will lead to the equilibrium point E.

To solve numerically system (22), (23), many software programs are available. Maple 9, for instance, enables us to carry out the following calculations. First, Maple 9 can solve numerically the second-order differential equation (20) once we give the program the initial conditions $K(0) = K_0$ and $\dot{K}(0) = \dot{K}_0 = I_0$. Second, Maple 9 can solve the system of first-order equations (22), (23), and draw the phase diagram corresponding to the time paths of K_t and C_t for any initial pair (K_0, C_0). Thus it is possible to determine, by trial and error, the initial value that leads asymptotically to the equilibrium point $E(K^*, C^*)$.

---

[4] Note that the *exact* direction of the economy at points not located on the areas' borders cannot be inferred solely by the system of arrows. Such a direction can be obtained analytically by the ratio $dC/dK = \dot{C}(K, C)/\dot{K}(K, C)$, i.e. by forming the ratio of the right-hand sides of equations (22) and (23).

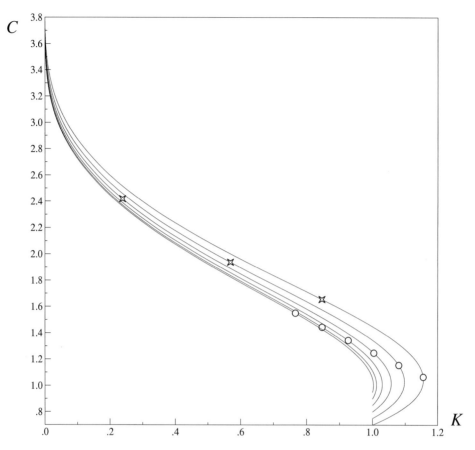

Figure 9.3a   The optimal trajectories of the economy in the case $\alpha = 0.5$, for six initial values of C_0 (0.7 to 0.95 by steps of 0.05).

The circles correspond to the location of the economy after one year (the stars: after two years). Notice that for C_0 equal to or above 0.85 the economy crashes within two years. Also, the economy accelerates toward its doom: along each curve the distance between the origin and the one-year point is smaller than the distance between the one-year point and the two-year point. This difference increases with C_0.

4.3   A first experiment with utility functions

It is natural to adopt, together with the parameters already chosen, a utility function with a parameter in the range of those commonly used in textbook treatments, that is $0 \leq \alpha < 1$. The case $\alpha = 0$ would correspond, as we mentioned earlier, to $U = \log C$. So we could start with a value $\alpha = 0.5$. Our system of differential equations thus becomes

$$\dot{C}_t = 2C_t\left(0.3K_t^{-0.7} - 0.06\right) \tag{27}$$

$$\dot{K}_t = K_t^{0.3} - C_t. \tag{28}$$

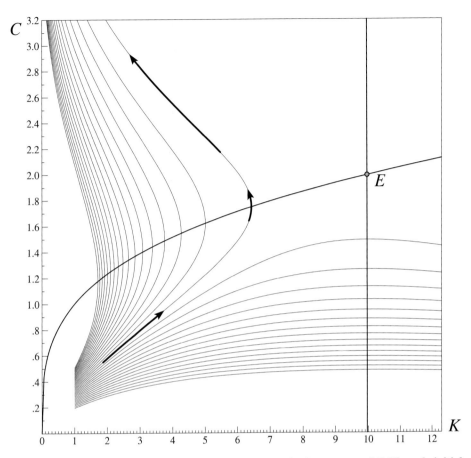

Figure 9.3b   The optimal trajectories of the economy in the case $\alpha = 0.5$. The only initial value C_0 leading asymptotically to the steady-state equilibrium E is in the vicinity of 0.34, implying a very high initial savings rate of 64%. The arrows correspond to a duration of exactly 3 years. The time path described with the arrows starts at $C_0 = 0.3449$; should the economy follow that trajectory, it would collapse within 22.5 years.

Let the initial value of K_t be $K_0 = 1$ (implying $Y_0 = 1$), and let us choose a range of C_0 values among commonly observed values (between 0.70 and 0.95).

The resulting optimal time paths are given in figure 9.3a.[5] The surprise is how far they are from anything that could be considered as optimal. Indeed, very quickly all time paths reach the point where all income is consumed, and net investment is nil – trajectories touch very quickly the locus $C = F(K)$ where $\dot{K} = 0$. Then the economy starts eating its own capital, until, in less than one

---

[5] I owe the construction of all phase diagrams in this book to the generosity of my colleague Ernst Hairer, who used his program Dopri 5 to that effect; see E. Hairer, S.P. Nørsett, G. Wanner, *Solving Ordinary Differential Equations*, Volume 1, Second Edition, Springer Verlag, New York, 2000.

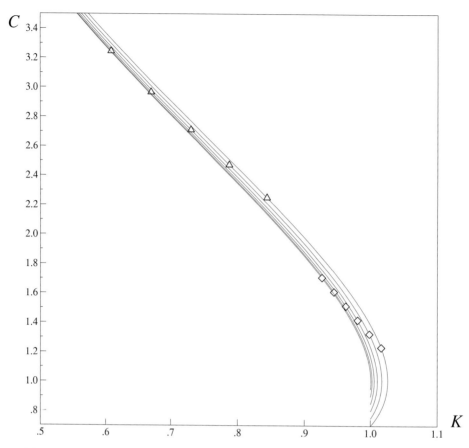

Figure 9.4a **The optimal trajectories of the economy in the case $\alpha = 0.9$, for six initial values of C_0 (0.7 to 0.95 by steps of 0.05). Increasing α from 0.5 to 0.9 spells bad news. The system becomes even more unstable than in the earlier case. Here the squases depict the location after 3 months only; the triangles, after 6 months.**

year, the economy collapses. Indeed, all those trajectories lead to $K = 0$ in finite (and short!) time, along curves that are first concave, and then turn convex. The exact time taken for the economy to crash is 0.77 years when C_0 is 0.70 and 0.62 years when C_0 is 0.95. As soon as K declines, production and income decline too; the fact that consumption rises is due solely to the fact that society is consuming its capital. When capital is equal to zero, production as well as consumption are nil.

We could try to remedy this situation by looking for the initial value of consumption that would place us on the stable trajectory leading to the equilibrium point E. The big surprise here is how low the initial consumption C_0 should be: using a software like Maple 9, the reader will quickly discover that C_0 is between 0.339901 and 0.339902, i.e. society should invest about 67% of its initial income. Figure 9.3b displays the optimal paths corresponding to a wide range of initial

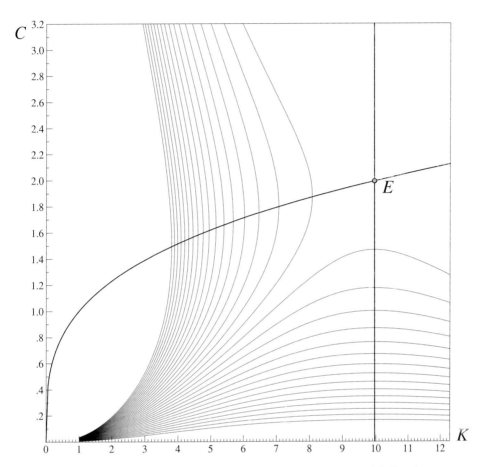

Figure 9.4b **The optimal trajectories of the economy in the case $\alpha = 0.9$. For the economy to be located on a stable arm leading to the equilibrium point E, an initial consumption level of slightly less than 0.02 is required, implying an initial savings rate of more than 98%.**

values C_0, including values of C_0 very close to the one that puts us on the stable trajectory leading asymptotically to the equilibrium point E.

On figure 9.3b, arrows are located on the trajectory starting at $C_0 = 0.3449$ (only 5 thousandths above the value of C_0 leading to E). The length of each arrow corresponds to a duration of exactly 3 years. The reader can see that the trajectory slows down in the vicinity of the point where $\dot{K} = 0$ (at the crossing of the $C = F(K) = K^{0.3}$ curve); this happens after about 13 years; it then abruptly veers away from the equilibrium point E and accelerates toward its doom; the economy crashes after 22.5 years.

Having come to this point, the experimenter will no doubt try another value of α in order to get a more acceptable optimal investment path. If he tries the seemingly more prudent $\alpha = 0.9$, he will face the big surprise that the economy becomes even

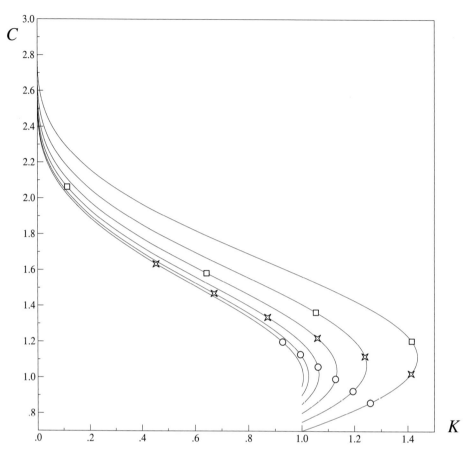

Figure 9.5a   Optimal trajectories of the economy in the case $\alpha = 0$ (or $U = \log C$) for six initial values C_0 (0.7 to 0.95 by steps of 0.05). The circles, stars and squares indicate the location of the economy after one, two and three years respectively. The stability of the system is slightly improved, but the economy still collapses within 5 years for an initial level C_0 equal to 0.7 (corresponding to a savings rate of 30%).

more unstable than in the case $\alpha = 0.5$. The system (22), (23) now becomes

$$\dot{C}_t = 10C_t(0.3K_t^{-0.7} - 0.06) \tag{29}$$

$$\dot{K}_t = K_t^{0.3} - C_t. \tag{30}$$

Two conclusions quickly emerge. First, for the same initial values as before ($C_0 = 0.7, \ldots, 0.95$), the economy crashes even quicker than in case $\alpha = 0.5$ (see figure 9.4a). Second, in order for the economy to converge toward the equilibrium E, the initial value of C_0 should be between 0.0191 and 0.0192, implying now that society should initially save and invest more than 98% of its income (see the family of trajectories of the economy in figure 9.4b).

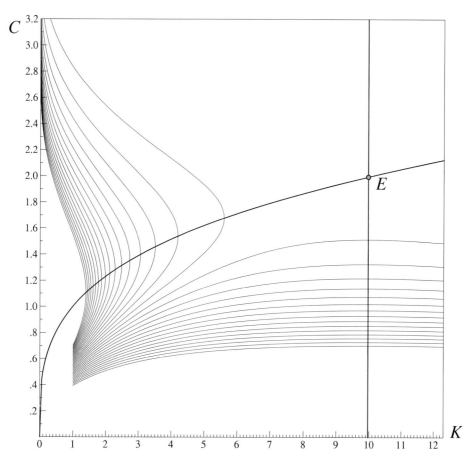

Figure 9.5b **Optimal trajectories of the economy in the case** $\alpha = 0$ **(or** $U = \log C$**). An initial savings rate of 45% is required for the economy to be set on the stable arm leading to** E**.**

Obviously, increasing α was not the right decision to take at this point; we could then think of reducing α to 0, and therefore use the utility function $U = \log C$.

The new system, corresponding to $U = \log C$, is

$$\dot{C}_t = C_t \left(0.3 K_t^{-0.7} - 0.06 \right) \tag{31}$$

$$\dot{K}_t = K_t^{0.3} - C_t \tag{32}$$

(the reader may verify that (31) can be obtained either by replacing α by 0 into (22), or by using $U = \log C$ in the Ramsey equation (7)).

The situation will hardly improve. As shown in figure 9.5a, the economy crashes after exactly 5 years for an initial consumption rate C_0 as low as 70%, and of course even sooner for all reasonable initial consumption values (see figure 9.5a); only a still exceedingly high initial investment ratio of about 55% puts the economy on the stable arm leading asymptotically to equilibrium E (see figure 9.5b).

At this juncture the reader or the experimenter may well conclude that our inability to obtain optimal growth paths that make sense is due to the oversimplification of the model. This is why we will now analyse, in the next chapter, the full-blown, central model of optimal growth as it has been known for more than 40 years.

Exercises

9.1 Suppose that the rate of preference for the present is variable through time. This implies, for instance, that the present value (at time t) of a utility flow received at time τ is $U'_C(\tau)e^{-\int_t^\tau i(z)dz}$.[6] Using economic arguments, derive the Ramsey rule either with a finite or an infinite horizon.

9.2 In this exercise you can show that the time of reference chosen for the evaluation of costs and rewards is arbitrary, and that valuing those flows at any other arbitrary time than present time (t) would also lead to the Ramsey rule. Verify that this indeed is true by considering time T ($\neq t$) as the time of reference.

9.3 When we showed the results of optimal growth theory using optimal control theory, we considered investment ($I_t = \dot{K}_t$) as the control variable. In this exercise, you are invited to obtain those results using consumption ($C_t = F(K_t) - \dot{K}_t$) as the control variable. Apply first the Hamiltonian, and then the Dorfmanian.

Answers

9.1 Suppose we consider the infinite horizon approach. The equilibrium equation now reads:

$$U'_C(t) = \int_t^\infty U'_C(\tau)F'_K(\tau)e^{-\int_t^\tau i(z)dz}d\tau. \tag{1}$$

Differentiating (1) with respect to t yields:

$$\dot{U}'_C(t) = \int_t^\infty U'_C(\tau)F'_K(\tau)e^{-\int_t^\tau i(z)dz} \cdot i(t)d\tau - U'_C(t)F'_K(t). \tag{2}$$

In the right-hand side of (2), factor $i(t)$ out of the integral and replace the integral by $U'_C(t)$. The Ramsey equation results, where the constant i is now replaced by $i(t)$.

---

[6] This exercise implies that the reader is familiar with the concept of instantaneous forward interest rate. If not, he will find a detailed exposition of the concept in chapter 11.

If we consider the finite horizon approach, the equilibrium condition evaluated at time t is:

$$U'_C(t) = \int_t^T U'_C(\tau)F'_K(\tau)e^{-\int_t^\tau i(z)dz}d\tau + U'_C(T)e^{-\int_t^T i(z)dz}. \quad (3)$$

Taking the derivative with respect to t gives:

$$U'_C(t) = \int_t^T U'_C(\tau)F'_K(\tau)e^{-\int_t^\tau i(z)dz} \cdot i(t)d\tau$$
$$- U'_C(t)F'_K(t) + U'_C(T)e^{-\int_t^T i(z)dz} \cdot i(t). \quad (4)$$

The limiting process works like the one described in this chapter. When $T \to t$, the integral vanishes, and the last term converges towards $U'_C(t)i(t)$, from which the Ramsey equation results.

9.2 The cost and rewards equation, expressed in future value of time T, now reads

$$U'_C(t)e^{i(T-t)} = \int_t^T U'_C(\tau)F'_K(\tau)e^{i(T-\tau)}d\tau + U'_C(T). \quad (5)$$

Taking the derivative of (5) with respect to t gives:

$$\dot{U}'_C(t)e^{i(T-t)} + U'_C e^{i(T-t)} \cdot (-i) = -U'_C(t)F'_K(t)e^{i(T-t)}. \quad (6)$$

Dividing (6) throughout by $U'_C(t)e^{i(T-t)}$ leads to

$$i = F'_K + \frac{\dot{U}'_C(t)}{U'_C(t)}.$$

9.3 Let us consider C_t as the control variable. Then we have $\dot{K}_t = F(K_t) - C_t$. The Hamiltonian is

$$H = U(C_t)e^{-it} + \lambda(t)[F(K_t) - C_t].$$

Equation (I) of the Pontryagin maximum principle becomes

$$\frac{\partial H}{\partial x_t} = \frac{\partial H}{\partial C_t} = U'_{C_t}e^{-it} - \lambda(t) = 0. \quad (I)$$

Equation (II) is:

$$\frac{\partial H}{\partial K_t} = \lambda(t)F'_{K_t} = -\dot{\lambda}(t). \quad (II)$$

From (II), the growth rate of $\lambda(t)$ is $-F'_{K_t}$. Taking $\dot{\lambda}/\lambda$ in (I) and replacing its value by $-F'_{K_t}$ yields the Ramsey equation.

Alternatively, we can form the Dorfmanian

$$H^* = U\,[C_t]\,e^{-it} + \lambda(t)\dot{K}_t + \dot{\lambda}(t)K_t$$
$$= U\,[C_t]\,e^{-it} + \lambda(t)\,[F(K_t) - C_t] + \dot{\lambda}(t)K_t.$$

Equate to zero the partial derivatives of H^* with respect to C_t and K_t:

$$\frac{\partial H^*}{\partial C_t} = U'_{C_t}e^{-it} - \lambda(t) = 0$$

$$\frac{\partial H^*}{\partial K_t} = \lambda(t)F'_{K_t} + \dot{\lambda}(t) = 0.$$

These equations correspond to (I) and (II) and yield the same result.

CHAPTER 10

Optimal growth and the optimal savings rate

The fall in the savings rate observed in most OECD countries in recent years propounds the perennial question of optimal savings, and foremost the problem of defining an optimality criterion. For nearly eighty years – since Frank Ramsey's seminal contribution (1928) – the fundamental problem of optimal savings policy has been to find the time path of capital accumulation maximizing, over a finite or an infinite horizon, the sum of discounted *utility* flows pertaining to consumption.

The Ramsey problem was a problem in the theory of optimal growth; unfortunately however, it remained in the realm of theory. No serious attempt to compare an optimal strategy of investment to the amounts actually invested in a given nation was ever carried out. In our opinion, this is due to the fact that the optimal paths resulting from the differential equations governing the motion of the economy were simply inapplicable because they implied unrealistic policies, in particular exceedingly high savings rates.

We hold that a fundamental reason for such a lack of applicability of the traditional model is the use of an arbitrary utility function. However, the idea of introducing a concave utility function cannot be dismissed outright because it has considerable intuitive appeal. Indeed, one could well envision (as many writers did) a benevolent planner for whom adding one more unit to consumption when total consumption is low has more value for society than when total consumption is high, and who therefore would have a bias toward giving more consumption to poorer generations; hence, one could feel well justified to use a concave utility function. But the outcome of those models is, as we will see, exactly the contrary of what intuition would dictate. A few warning lights had been flashed in the sixties: in a two-sector model, Goodwin (1961) had obtained "optimal" savings rate in excess of 60%; and Stoléru (1970), in the only numerical solution of the Ramsey problem ever given, was led to savings rates in the order of 90%.

We feel that the time has come to make a systematic analysis of the role played by utility functions upon optimal trajectories of the economy. We have known since the sixties that the model exhibited only saddle-point stability, implying that, given an initial capital–labour ratio, one and only one initial value of consumption (or saving) would eventually lead to a steady state, the slightest departure from this initial value entailing the collapse of the economy. But we still possess only scant indications about the exact properties and the implications of the rare transition path eventually leading to the steady state.

In this chapter our preliminary aim is to take a close look at optimal growth paths implied by the families of utility functions commonly referred to in the literature, the power function and the negative exponential function. A first surprise with power functions will be to discover that for all acceptable initial values of consumption the economy collapses almost immediately – in fact within a couple of years, thus revealing the extreme instability of the model. We will then show that if we want to set foot on the stable path leading to the steady state, we have to adopt outrageously low initial values of consumption. As a consequence, we will address the inverse problem: if we want optimal policies to imply reasonable initial consumption values, what should be the corresponding utility functions? We will discover that the relevant utility functions have perfectly unacceptable properties, implying typically that massive increases in consumption per person, even starting from a low level, carry no significant increase in society's welfare. As to the negative exponential, the situation deteriorates even further: in addition to the drawback just mentioned, an equilibrium point does not exist any more.

This evidence alone would be ample reason to dispense with the services of a utility function. But we will argue that there are other reasons as well to do so. We will then suggest to focus on maximizing a welfare objective for society defined by the sum of discounted consumption flows. This will have many rewards. Most prominently, the optimal savings rate will turn out to have reasonable, very reachable values.

I   The central model of optimal growth theory

We will briefly recall the features of the mainstream model of optimal growth theory that has been in existence in the last forty years. We suppose that the economy is driven by a homogeneous of degree one production function, namely a CES production function exhibiting labour augmenting progress at constant rate g. The function is

$$Y_t = F(K_t, L_t, t) = [\delta K_t^p + (1 - \delta)(L_t e^{gt})^p]^{1/p} \tag{1}$$

where Y_t, K_t and L_t are indices of income, capital and labour respectively. Y_t is *net* income (net of capital depreciation[1]) at constant prices. Y_t is a general mean

---

[1] Assuming that capital decays exponentially would not lead to any additional insights.

of order p of K_t and $L_t e^{gt}$; $p = 1 - 1/\sigma$ $(\sigma \neq 1)$ where σ is the elasticity of substitution; thus, because of properties of general means, Y_t is an increasing function of σ. When $\sigma \to 1$, $p \to 0$ and Y_t becomes the geometric mean

$$Y_t = K_t^\delta (L_t e^{gt})^{(1-\delta)}. \tag{2}$$

The work force increases exponentially at rate n; so $L_t = L_0 e^{nt}$; without loss of generality, we can take $L_0 = 1$. Since the labour augmenting technical progress property has the effect of multiplying the labour force at any instant t by $\exp(gt)$, the production function is

$$Y_t = F(K_t, L_t, t) = \left[\delta K_t^p + (1-\delta)e^{(n+g)tp}\right]^{1/p} \tag{3}$$

when $p \neq 0$ (or $\sigma \neq 1$), and

$$Y_t = K_t^\delta e^{(1-\delta)(n+g)t} \tag{4}$$

when $p = 0$ (or $\sigma = 1$).

Denote C_t society's consumption flow at any time t; since Y_t is net income, we have $C_t = Y_t - \dot{K}$. Let now $c_t \equiv C_t/L_t$ be consumption per person, and $U(c_t)$ be a standard utility function in the sense that $U(.)$ is twice differentiable, increasing and strictly concave, so that $U'(C_t) > 0$ and $U''(C_t) < 0$. The classic problem is then to maximize the integral

$$\int_0^\infty L_t U\left(\frac{C_t}{L_t}\right) e^{-it} dt \tag{5}$$

where i is a discount rate, subject to the constraint

$$C_t = Y_t - \dot{K} = F(K_t, L_t, t) - \dot{K}. \tag{6}$$

In the literature on optimal growth theory, two families of utility functions have been declared fit for service so far. Both are strictly increasing and concave in c. The most frequently used and referred to is an affine transform of a power function, with the logarithmic function as a particular case:

$$\begin{cases} U(c) = \dfrac{c^\alpha - 1}{\alpha}, & \text{with } 0 < \alpha < 1 \\ & \text{or} \quad \alpha < 0 \\ U(c) = \log c, & \text{corresponding to } \alpha = 0. \end{cases} \tag{7a}$$

Innocuous as the case $\alpha < 0$ may look, it has deep consequences for the properties of the utility function. Indeed, whereas the cases $0 < \alpha < 1$ correspond to a utility level that tends to infinity when $c \to \infty$, $\alpha < 0$ implies that $U(c)$ tends to a finite number $(1/\alpha)$ when $c \to \infty$. We will see the importance of this in applications.

The second family of utility functions is the negative exponential:

$$U = -\frac{1}{\beta}e^{-\beta c}, \quad \beta > 0. \tag{7b}$$

Our analysis will first focus on the first family of utility functions (equations (7a)). We will then examine the implications of the second family (7b).

2   The consequences of using power utility functions

As is usually done, it will be convenient to work in a time-independent framework by using the following transformed variables. Define the ratio of capital to effective labour force as

$$r_\gamma \equiv \frac{K_t}{e^{gt} L_t}. \tag{8}$$

Using the homogeneity of degree one property of $F(.)$, we can then write:

$$y_\gamma \equiv \frac{Y_t}{e^{gt} L_t} = F\left(\frac{K_t}{e^{gt} L_t}, 1\right) = \varphi(r_\gamma).$$

We then have:

$$\varphi(r_\gamma) = [\delta r_\gamma^p + (1 - \delta)]^{1/p} \tag{9}$$

if $p \neq 0$ (or $\sigma \neq 1$), and

$$\varphi(r_\gamma) = r_\gamma^\delta \tag{10}$$

if $p = 0$ (or $\sigma = 1$).

Denoting $r \equiv K_t/L_t$, $y \equiv Y_t/L_t$, $c \equiv C_t/L_t$, we know that the equation of motion of the capital–labour ratio r is

$$\dot{r} = y - c - nr. \tag{11}$$

We can then write from (8):

$$\frac{\dot{r}_\gamma}{r_\gamma} = \frac{\dot{r}}{r} - g, \tag{12}$$

and, using (11):

$$\dot{r}_\gamma = \frac{\dot{r}}{r} r_\gamma - g\, r_\gamma = \dot{r}e^{-gt} - g\, r_\gamma$$
$$= (y - c - nr)e^{-gt} - g\, r_\gamma.$$

Denoting $c_\gamma \equiv ce^{-gt}$, the equation of motion of capital to effective labour force is

$$\dot{r}_\gamma = \varphi(r_\gamma) - c_\gamma - (n + g)r_\gamma, \tag{13}$$

so that

$$c_\gamma = \varphi(r_\gamma) - \dot{r}_\gamma - (g+n)r_\gamma. \tag{14}$$

The problem defined by (5) and (6) will now turn into a time-autonomous one. Using the fact that L_t is just e^{nt}, we can write:

$$\underset{r_\gamma}{\text{Max}} \int_0^\infty U(c)e^{-(i-n)t} dt \tag{15}$$

subject to the constraint

$$c = c_\gamma e^{gt} = [\varphi(r_\gamma) - \dot{r}_\gamma - (g+n)r_\gamma]e^{gt}. \tag{16}$$

There are at least three methods of solving this problem. The first is to substitute the constraint (16) into the functional (15) and apply the Euler–Lagrange equation of the calculus of variations. The second is to form a Hamiltonian $H = U(c)e^{-(i-n)t} + \lambda(t)\dot{r}_\gamma$ and use the Pontriaguine principle by writing $H_{c_\gamma} = 0$ and $H_{r_\gamma} = -\dot{\lambda}$. The third is to form, following Robert Dorfman's remarkable interpretation of optimal control theory (1969), a modified Hamiltonian, or Dorfmanian $H^* = U(c)e^{-(i-n)t} + \frac{d}{dt}[\lambda(t)r_\gamma]$ and take $H^*_{c_\gamma} = 0$ and $H^*_{r_\gamma} = 0$. The first method immediately leads to a pair of first-order differential equations in (r_γ, c_γ). The remaining two methods yield a system of three differential equations in $(r_\gamma, c_\gamma, \lambda)$, from which the former system in (r_γ, c_γ) can be recovered. We will choose the most direct route, i.e. the Euler–Lagrange method.

Replacing (16) into (15) leads to:

$$\underset{r_\gamma}{\text{Max}} \int_0^\infty U\{[\varphi(r_\gamma) - (g+n)r_\gamma - \dot{r}_\gamma]e^{gt}\}e^{-(i-n)t} dt. \tag{17}$$

Designating the integrand in (17) as $G(r_\gamma, \dot{r}_\gamma, t)$, the Euler–Lagrange equation $\frac{\partial G}{\partial r_\gamma} - \frac{d}{dt}\frac{\partial G}{\partial \dot{r}_\gamma} = 0$ leads, after simplification, to:

$$\varphi'(r_\gamma) + \frac{\dot{U}'_c}{U'_c} - i = 0. \tag{18}$$

From (7a), the growth rate of U'_c is:

$$\frac{\dot{U}'_c}{U'_c} = c\frac{U''_c}{U'_c}\frac{\dot{c}}{c} = (\alpha-1)\frac{\dot{c}}{c} = (\alpha-1)\left(\frac{\dot{c}_\gamma}{c_\gamma} + g\right). \tag{19}$$

Replacing (19) into the Euler–Lagrange equation (18) yields the equation of motion of c_γ; $\dot{c}_\gamma$ is the following function of (c_γ, r_γ):

$$\dot{c}_\gamma = \frac{c_\gamma}{1-\alpha}[\varphi'(r_\gamma) - i + (\alpha-1)g], \alpha \neq 1 \tag{20}$$

where

$$\varphi'(r_\gamma) = [\delta r_\gamma^p + (1-\delta)]^{\frac{1-p}{p}} \delta r_\gamma^{p-1} \tag{21}$$

if $p \neq 0$ (or equivalently if $\sigma \neq 1$), and

$$\varphi'(r_\gamma) = \delta r_\gamma^{\delta-1} \tag{22}$$

if $p = 0$ (or $\sigma = 1$).[2]

We now have to check whether the Euler equation (18) leads to a global maximum of the functional defined in (17). From Takayama's theorem, we know that the concavity of the integrand of (17), together with the Euler equation, does constitute a set of necessary and sufficient conditions for such a maximum. In order to check the concavity of the integrand, notice it is a composite function of r_γ and $\dot{r}_\gamma$ through a function which is itself an increasing and concave function of its argument. Indeed, the integrand in (17) can be denoted $e^{-(i-n)t}U(c)$, and $U(c)$ is such that $U'(c) > 0$ and $U''(c) < 0$. Let us now check whether c is concave in r_γ and $\dot{r}_\gamma$. We have

$$\frac{\partial c}{\partial r_\gamma} = e^{gt}[\varphi'(r_\gamma) - (g+n)]; \qquad \frac{\partial c}{\partial \dot{r}_\gamma} = -e^{gt}$$

and

$$\frac{\partial^2 c}{\partial r_\gamma^2} = e^{gt}\varphi''(r_\gamma) < 0; \qquad \frac{\partial^2 c}{\partial \dot{r}_\gamma^2} = 0; \qquad \frac{\partial^2 c}{\partial r_\gamma \partial \dot{r}_\gamma} = 0.$$

As a result, c is concave in $(r_\gamma, \dot{r}_\gamma)$ and we can apply theorem 17.6 in Sydsaeter and Hammond (1995): the integrand is concave in $r_\gamma, \dot{r}_\gamma$. From Takayama's theorem, the Euler equation (18) does yield a global maximum.

The steady-state value of r_γ, obtained by setting $\dot{c}_\gamma = 0$ in (20) and by using (21) and (22), is:

$$r_\gamma^* = \left\{ \frac{1-\delta}{\left[\frac{\delta}{i+(1-\alpha)g}\right]^{1-\sigma} - \delta} \right\}^{\frac{\sigma}{\sigma-1}} \qquad \text{if} \quad \sigma \neq 1 \tag{23}$$

---

[2] It is to be noted that (18) is a second-order non-linear differential equation in r_γ, in accordance with the general character of Euler equations. This can be verified by replacing, in (20), c_γ and $\dot{c}_\gamma$ from (14) (see exercise 10.1); the second derivative of r_γ will appear in $\dot{c}_\gamma$. Neither the resulting second-order differential equation, nor the corresponding system of first-order equations (13), (20) lead to an analytic solution. This is the reason we concentrate on the system (13), (20) in order to understand, with the phase diagram, the fundamental instability of the system, as we have done in chapter 9.

and

$$r_\gamma^* = \left[\frac{\delta}{i + (1-\alpha)g}\right]^{\frac{1}{1-\delta}} \quad \text{if} \quad \sigma = 1, \tag{24}$$

which now enables to determine the steady-state values of the saving-investment rate s^*.

First we obtain the steady-state income per efficiency labour unit $\varphi(r_\gamma^*)$ by plugging (23) and (24) into (9) and (10), respectively. Setting $\dot{r}_\gamma = 0$ in (13) and dividing throughout by $\varphi(r_\gamma^*)$, we get

$$s^* = (n+g)\left[\frac{\delta}{i + (1-\alpha)g}\right]^\sigma \tag{25}$$

which is valid both for $\sigma \neq 1$ and $\sigma = 1$.

Time has now come to make a thorough examination of the actual time paths that may or may not lead to this steady state.

2.1 A close look at optimal growth paths

We will now determine numerically the time paths corresponding to the pair of non-linear differential equations

$$\dot{r}_\gamma = \varphi(r_\gamma) - c_\gamma - (n+g)r_\gamma \tag{13}$$

and

$$\dot{c}_\gamma = \frac{c_\gamma}{1-\alpha}\left[\varphi'(r_\gamma) - i + (\alpha - 1)g\right] \tag{20}$$

where $\varphi(r_\gamma)$ and $\varphi'(r_\gamma)$ are given respectively by

$$\varphi(r_\gamma) = [\delta r_\gamma^p + (1-\delta)]^{1/p} \tag{9}$$

and

$$\varphi'(r_\gamma) = \delta[\delta r_\gamma^p + (1-\delta)]^{\frac{1-p}{p}} r_\gamma^{p-1} \tag{21}$$

if $p \neq 0$ or $\sigma \neq 1$, and by

$$\varphi(r_\gamma) = r_\gamma^\delta \tag{10}$$

and

$$\varphi'(r_\gamma) = \delta r_\gamma^{\delta-1} \tag{22}$$

if $p = 0$ or $\sigma = 1$.

Since we are dealing first with functional forms $U = (c^\alpha - 1)/\alpha$, we need to choose a number of values for the parameter α. A first natural choice, among many, would to be to start with $\alpha = 1/2$, implying for $U(c)$ an affine transform of the square root of c (we know from general principles of the calculus of variations that

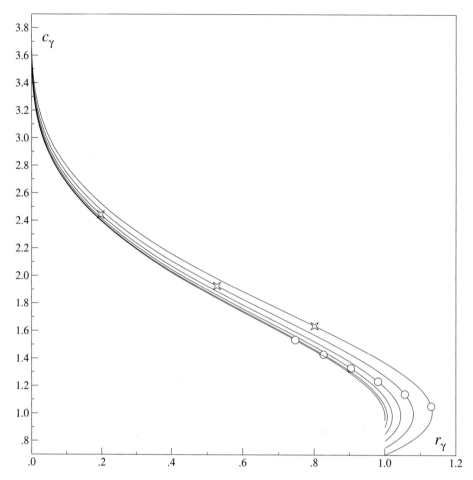

Figure 10.1a Optimal time paths for $\alpha = 0.5$. This diagram depicts the time paths of r_γ and c_γ when the initial value $r_\gamma(0) = r(0)$ is equal to 1, for 6 initial values $c_\gamma(0) = c(0)$ from 0.7 to 0.95 by steps of 0.05. The circles denote the position of the economy after 1 year; the stars: after 2 years. The economy crashes after 1.61 years if it starts at $c(0) = 0.95$ and after 2.61 years if $c(0) = 0.7$. Notice that the increasing length of the paths between the circles and the stars – if any – denotes the acceleration of the economy toward its doom. This acceleration is an increasing function of $c(0)$.

any affine transformation of the integrand of the functional will have no bearing on the solution).

Also, we have to choose values for the other parameters. We will first opt for the following middle-of-the-road values: $i = 0.07$; $\delta = 0.3$; $\sigma = 1$; $n = 0.01$; $g = 0.015$. Variations from this central scenario will be considered in a systematic way.

Assume that at time 0 the capital stock is equal to one unit, and therefore, from our previous hypotheses, that $r_\gamma(0) = 1$; accordingly, $\varphi[r_\gamma(0)] = y(0) = 1$. It is natural to ask what will happen to the economy if the initial consumption rate

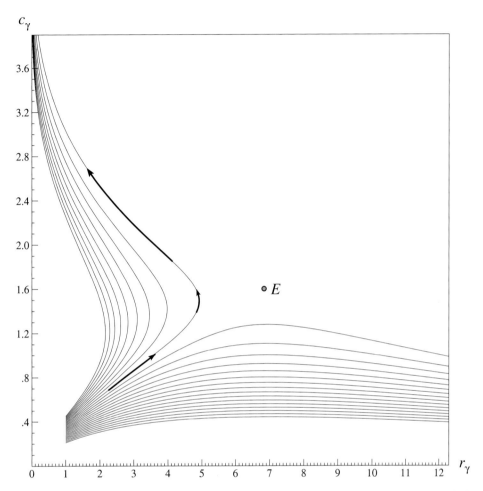

Figure 10.1b Optimal time paths for $\alpha = 0.5$. An initial savings rate of $\sim$63.3% (!) is necessary to put us on the stable arm of the phase diagram. Only the initial value $c_0 = 0.36663293269\ldots$ will lead to the equilibrium point $E \equiv (r_\gamma^*, c_\gamma^*)$. Any departure from this razor's edge will lead to the collapse of the economy. The inner upper curve starts at $c(0) = 0.372$. After 13 years, the curve veers away, and the economy crashes after 20 years. The arrows on the curve correspond to a duration of exactly 3 years.

of the economy $c(0) = c_\gamma(0)$ is chosen within an interval of frequently observed values. We will then choose the six following values for $c(0)$, namely $c(0) = 0.70$ to 0.95 by increments of 0.05.

The first shocking answer is in figure 10.1a. The six time paths in (r_γ, c_γ) space are depicted for each initial value of $c(0)$. The circles denote the position of the economy after exactly one year, and the stars denote its position after two years. Remembering that the capital stock after one year is $K(1) = r_\gamma(1)e^{g+n}$ (1.0253 $r_\gamma(1)$ in this case), we can see from the diagram that if the initial consumption rate is between 85% and 95% society will start eating up its own capital stock after

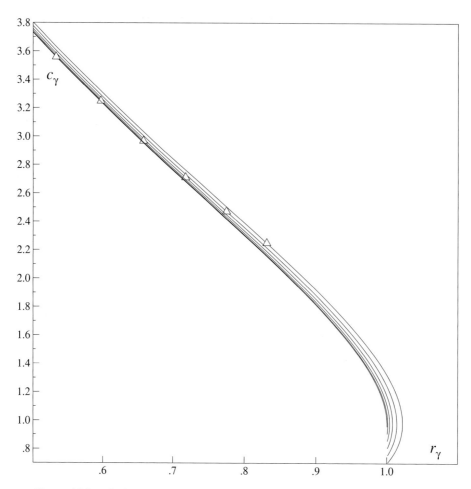

Figure 10.2a **Optimal time paths for $\alpha = 0.9$. The situation deteriorates further if we look for less concavity in the utility function. This time, with the same initial values of $c(0)$ (0.7 to 0.95 by steps of 5%), the economy collapses before one year (the triangles on each curve denote the position of the economy after 6 months only).**

less than one year. There are no stars on those paths: this means that the economy has collapsed *before* two years (since σ is equal to one in this example, $K = 0$ entails $Y = 0$).

Very high initial savings rates $s_0 = 0.25$ and 0.20 (corresponding to $c_0 = 0.75$ and 0.80), do not help much: in those cases, more than 40% of the initial capital is depleted after two years. If c_0 is 0.75, the economy collapses after 2.32 years. On any path the economy is accelerating toward its doom; this acceleration is itself an increasing function of c_0. For the six time paths corresponding to $c_0 = 0.7 \ldots 0.95$, K becomes zero after 2.61; 2.32; 2.09; 1.9; 1.74; 1.61 years respectively. (Notice that, contrary to the qualitative treatments of the phase diagram in the literature, the collapse of the economy is never along concave paths throughout; at some points

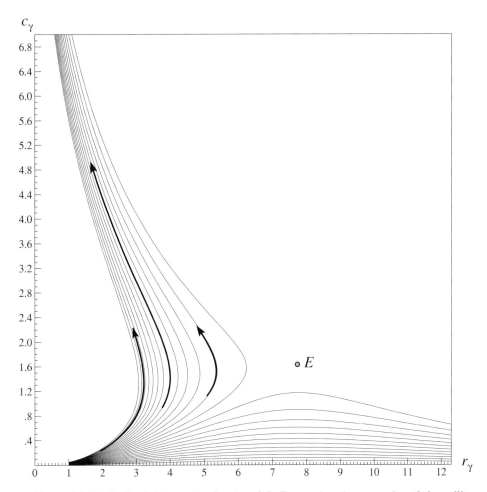

Figure 10.2b **Optimal time paths for $\alpha = 0.9$. Decreasing the concavity of the utility function only makes things worse. Only an initial consumption rate c_0 of 3% (or an initial saving rate of 97%) can put us on the stable path.**

in time, the paths always become convex, although the crash ($K = 0$) happens in finite time.)

What then is the initial value c_0 that would lead to the steady state? Calculations show the dreadful result that it lies between 0.366632 and 0.366633, implying an investment-savings rate of about 63%! Figure 10.1b displays the trajectories that start in the vicinity of the required value for c_0 (on the diagram, the length of an arrow corresponds to a duration of exactly 3 years). The equilibrium point $E \equiv (r_\gamma^*, c_\gamma^*)$ is indicated on the diagram. It is a testimony to the highly unstable nature of the model that initial values of c_0 as close to the stable arm value as 0.372 and 0.362 will lead to the two inner time paths on Figure 10.1b; after 13 years they will start to diverge violently from the stable arm; if the economy is on the upper path, it will collapse within 20 years.

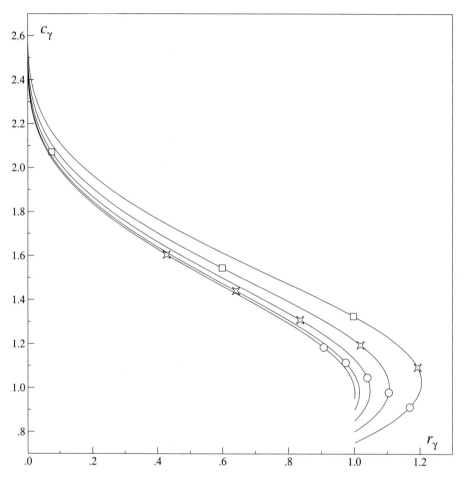

Figure 10.3a   Optimal trajectories for $\alpha = 0$ ($U = \log c$). The economy stays alive a little longer, although not by much, for reasonable initial values of $c(0)$. The circles give the position of the economy after 1 year; stars: 2 years; squares: 3 years.

Facing this disquieting news, the experimenter may wonder whether something has gone astray in his selection of the utility function. He may then opt for more prudent concavity, and choose an alpha closer to one, say $\alpha = 0.9$. To his dismay, he will see that the situation deteriorates even further: this time, an initial value of consumption c_0 equal to 0.9 will make the whole capital stock of the economy collapse after little more than 3 months (see figure 10.2a). As to the initial value of consumption that will put him on the stable arm, its order of magnitude is a paltry 3%, implying that the savings rate should be 97%! (figure 10.2b).

This is definitely not the direction to take; at that point our experimenter will probably rush all the way down to $\alpha = 0$ (corresponding to $U = \log c$). This hardly improves the situation. Indeed, for the very reasonable $c_0 = 0.8$, for instance, the whole capital stock vanishes in about three years and a half. For the same initial

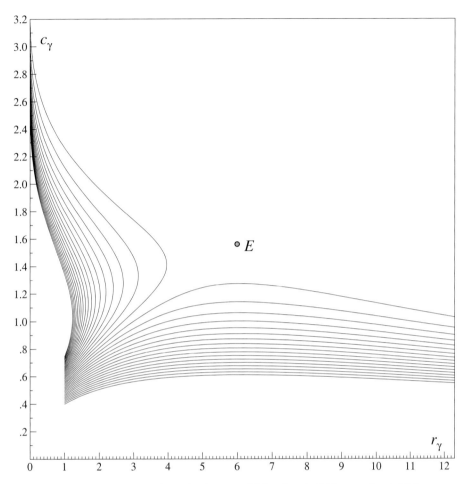

Figure 10.3b **Optimal trajectories for $\alpha = 0$ ($U = \log c$). Still a very low initial consumption rate $c(0) \approx 0.56$ is necessary to put us on the stable arm leading to the steady state.**

values c_0 between 0.7 and 0.95 the time paths are given in figure 10.3a. What is, then, for $U = \log c$, the initial value c_0 that would lead to the steady state? It is still a very low 56.5%, implying an initial savings rate of 43.5% (figure 10.3b).

2.2 The initial value of c_0 leading the economy to the steady state as a function of α

We definitely need now a general picture of the initial values c_0 that are necessary to put us on the stable arm of the phase diagram, as a function of parameter α ($\alpha \in [0, 1)$). Figure 10.4a gives the initial value of consumption

$$c_0 = c_0(\alpha; \sigma; \overline{i}, \overline{\delta}, \overline{n}, \overline{g}) \tag{26}$$

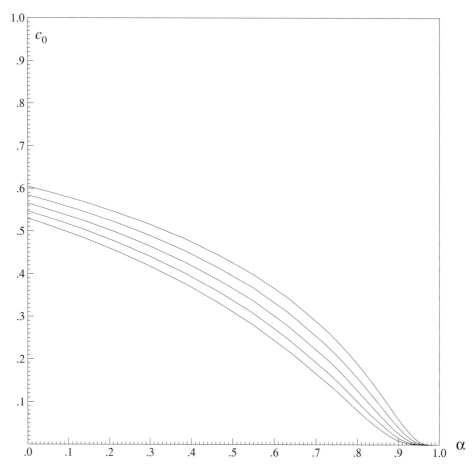

Figure 10.4a The initial value c_0 leading to the study state, as a function of α $(0 \le \alpha < 1)$ for $\sigma = 0.8$ (lower curve) to $\sigma = 1.2$ (upper curve) by steps of 0.1. No positive value of α entailing a concave utility function permits an acceptable initial value c_0. Even $\alpha = 0$ implies an initial savings rate close to or in excess of 40%.

leading to the steady state as a function α $(\alpha \in [0, 1))$, for the same parameters $\bar{\delta}, \bar{i}, \bar{n}$ and $\bar{g}$ as before, and for five different values of σ : $\sigma = 0.8, 0.9, 1, 1.1$ and $1.2.$[3]

Clearly, increasing or decreasing the concavity of the utility function will never enable us to reach acceptable values for the initial value of consumption leading to a steady state. Something much more dramatic has to be found. The solution is to consider that α becomes negative, thus entailing a utility level tending toward $1/\alpha$ when $c \to \infty$. Figure 10.4b depicts the initial value of c_0 for all values of α such that $\alpha \in [-4, +1)$, and for the five values of σ mentioned above. Note that if $\alpha \to -\infty$ each curve $c_0(\alpha; \sigma; \bar{i}, \bar{\delta}, \bar{n}, \bar{g})$ tends toward 1.

---

[3] We owe to the generosity and the competence of our colleague Ernst Hairer the construction of the program to determine c_0 as a function of α and the other parameters of the system.

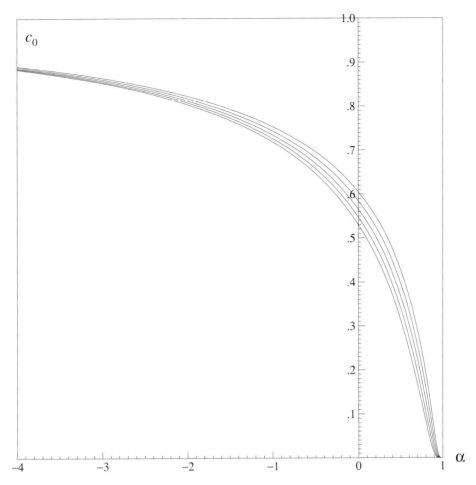

Figure 10.4b   Stable arm initial values of c_0 for $-4 \le \alpha < 1$ and for $\sigma = 0.8$ to 1.2 by steps of 0.1; other parameters: same as in central case. Only strongly negative values of α lead to acceptable initial values c_0.

We may wonder how the shape and position of the curves $c_0(\alpha; \sigma; .)$ depend on the parameters other than σ. For $\sigma = 1$, diagrams 10.5, 10.6, 10.7 and 10.8 show those curves when i, δ, g and n depart from their central values 0.07, 0.3, 0.015 and 0.01 respectively. In figure 10.5, the discount rate moves from $i = 5\%$ (upper curve) to 9% (lower curve). In figure 10.6, the lower curve corresponds to $\delta = 0.25$, the upper curve to $\delta = 0.35$. Figures 10.7 and 10.8 display the c_0 curves when n and g move up and down from their central values by 0.5%. The curves $c_0(\alpha; .)$ are little sensitive to rather substantial changes in the parameters.

2.3   Questioning the relevance of power utility functions

Coming back to the case of the central values of the parameters, what should then be the value of α for a very acceptable initial savings rate $s(0)$ of, say, 14%? It

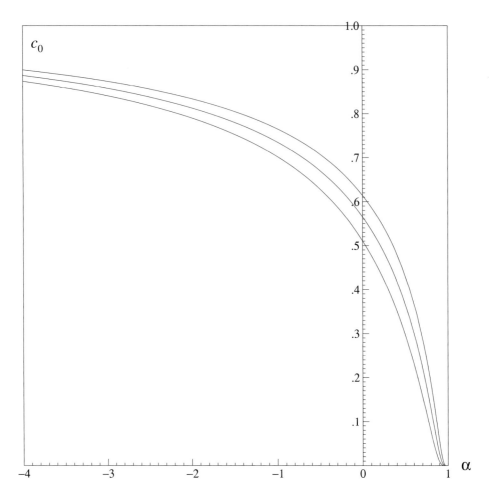

Figure 10.5 The initial values of c_0 leading to the steady state for $-4 \le \alpha < 1, \sigma = 1$ and different values of i : 0.05 (upper curve); 0.07 and 0.09 (lower curve); other parameters: same as in central case.

should be in the vicinity of $\alpha = -3$. Now we should take a close look at the utility function entailed by an alpha equal to -3, i.e.

$$U(c) = \frac{c^{-3} - 1}{-3} = \frac{1}{3}(1 - c^{-3})$$

Its shape is depicted in figure 10.9 as the strangest utility curve anybody would ever come up with, since for values of consumption per person above 2.4 or so, it has no slope to speak of. This comes from the fact that $U(c)$ tends asymptotically toward $-1/\alpha$ (1/3 in this case), and very quickly at that because of the power -3 in $U(c)$. Not surprisingly, for $\alpha = -3$ the steady-state value of the savings-investment rate, given by (25), is a very weak 5.77%, leading to a long-term weak economy.

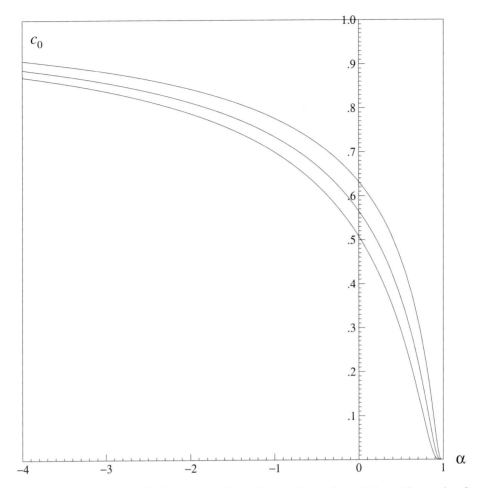

Figure 10.6 The initial values of c_0 leading to the steady state for $-4 \le \alpha < 1, \sigma = 1$ and different values of δ : 0.25 (lower curve); 0.3 and 0.35 (upper curve); other parameters: same as in central case.

Thus, the only way to set foot on the stable path leading to the steady state is either to force society to save an exceedingly high share of its income or to give no value to additional consumption per person beyond abnormally low levels.

3   The consequences of using exponential utility functions

Having recourse to the negative exponential $U(c) = -\frac{1}{\beta} e^{-\beta c} (\beta > 0)$ turns out to be even more disastrous. Indeed, if in the case of the power utility function there existed a saddle-point equilibrium – however unstable and unreachable with reasonable initial conditions – now equilibrium does *not* exist any more. As we will show, whatever the initial conditions, the economy is doomed in finite time either by a collapse of its capital stock or by a zero consumption rate.

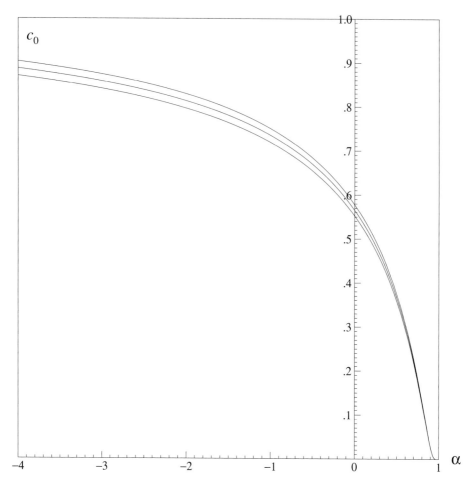

Figure 10.7 **The initial values of c_0 leading to the steady state for $-4 \leq \alpha < 1, \sigma = 1$ and different values of g : 0.01 (lower curve); 0.015 and 0.02 (upper curve); other parameters: same as in central case.**

The pair of differential equations now becomes

$$\dot{r}_\gamma = \varphi(r_\gamma) - c_\gamma - (n + g)r_\gamma \tag{27}$$

$$\dot{c}_\gamma = \frac{1}{\beta e^{gt}}\left[\varphi'(r_\gamma) - i\right] - g c_\gamma \tag{28}$$

i.e. a non-autonomous system.[4] Numerical analysis shows that it does *not* have an equilibrium point any more in the positive space (r_γ, c_γ). The divergent solutions are also extremely sensitive to initial conditions, and much more complex than in the case of power functions.

---

[4] See exercise 10.2.

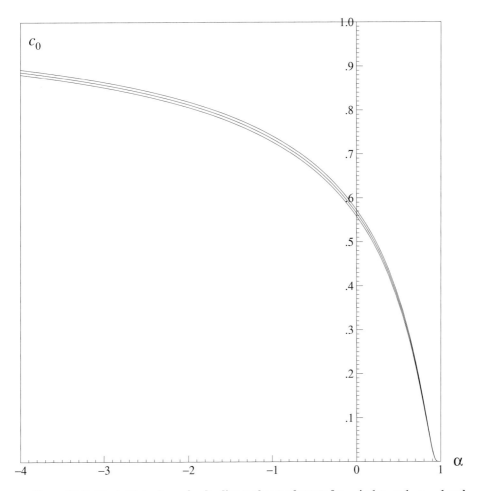

Figure 10.8 **The initial values of c_0 leading to the steady state for $-4 \le \alpha < 1, \sigma = 1$ and different values of n : 0.005 (lower curve); 0.01 and 0.015 (upper curve); other parameters: same as in central case.**

Typical of such divergent solutions are those which correspond to $\beta = 1$. All time paths reach both axes in finite time, with one trajectory having a cusp[5] (point C in figure 10.10). When the c_γ axis is reached (when r_γ is equal to zero),

---

[5] This cusp $(\hat{r}_\gamma, \hat{c}_\gamma)$ and the time at which the trajectory reaches it can be determined numerically as follows. Let $\dot{r}_\gamma = h_1(r_\gamma, c_\gamma)$ and $\dot{c} = h_2(r_\gamma, c_\gamma, t)$, and let $r(t, c_0)$ and $c_\gamma(t, c_0)$ be time paths with initial conditions $r(0, c_0) = 1$ and $c_\gamma(0, c_0) = c_0$. The cusp implies a curve non-differentiable in (r_γ, c_γ) space, but differentiable in (r_γ, c_γ, t) space, with $\dot{r}_\gamma = 0$ and $\dot{c}_\gamma = 0$. So the initial value $\hat{c}_0$ of the trajectory and the time $\hat{t}$ at which the cusp is reached are determined by solving numerically the system in (t, c_0):

$$h_1[r_\gamma(t, c_0), c_\gamma(t, c_0)] = 0$$
$$h_2[r_\gamma(t, c_0), c_\gamma(t, c_0), t] = 0$$

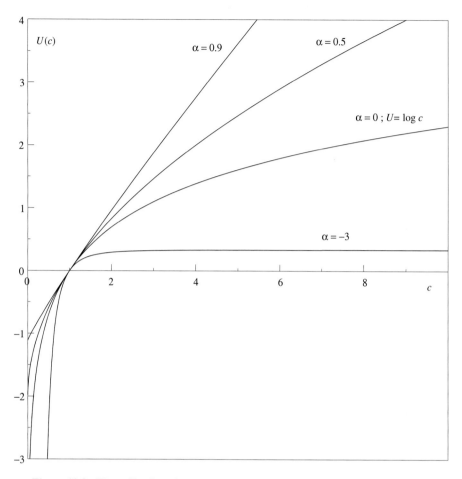

Figure 10.9 The utility function

$$U = \frac{c^\alpha - 1}{\alpha}, \alpha < 1, \alpha \neq 0; \; U = \log c (\alpha = 0)$$

The utility function corresponding to $\alpha = -3$, $U = -(1/3)(c^{-3} - 1)$, has no slope to speak of above $c = 2.4$.

$\dot{r}_\gamma < 0$, but the system is not defined any more for negative values of r_γ – and of course such negative values do not make economic sense. On the other hand, when the r_γ axis is reached, c_γ becomes negative, which is devoid of economic sense as well; mathematically, time paths still exist, converging toward point E corresponding to $c_\gamma = 0$ and to an r_γ value such that $0 = \varphi(r_\gamma) - (n + g)r_\gamma$ (figure 10.11).

Insight into the surprising complexity of the time paths may be gained by the enlargement of the cusp area (figure 10.12) and by the extreme difficulty of

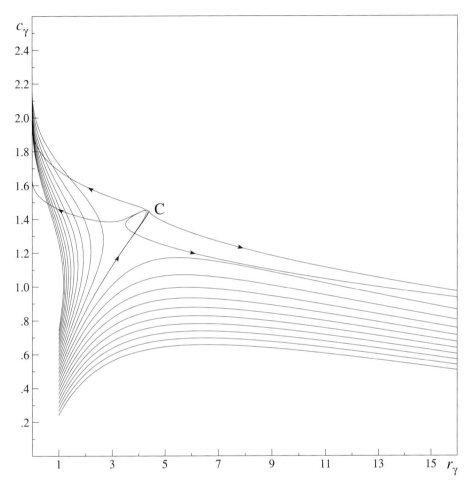

Figure 10.10 **With the negative exponential utility function, no equilibrium point exists any more for positive (r_γ, c_γ). One trajectory has a cusp (point C); it ultimately veers toward $c_\gamma = 0$.**

determining the initial value of c_0 leading to divergence toward either axis. The value $\hat{c}_0$ leading to the cusp is definitely not this separating value.

The initial value $\hat{c}_0$ leading to the cusp is $\hat{c}_0 = 0.4917672367$ (this precision is required by the sensitivity of the trajectories); the time $\hat{t}$ at which the cusp C is reached is somewhat above 34 years. The 20 trajectories to the right or to the left of the cusp have their initial values separated by 0.5×10^{-5} only; the complexity of the trajectories is illustrated by the fact that immediately to the left of the cusp what appears as one trajectory veering to the left is in fact *eleven* (!) trajectories, all starting in the vicinity of 0.4917972963 (this is a little above $\hat{c}_0$) and separated by 10^{-10}. All those time paths will ultimately separate; seven of them will diverge toward the r_γ axis; the remaining four will end up on the c_γ axis.

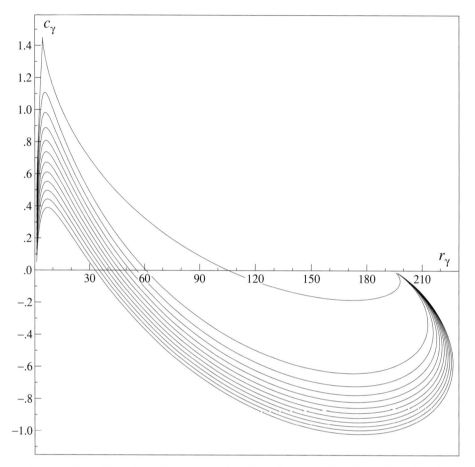

Figure 10.11 **The only equilibrium point implies** $\lim\limits_{t\to\infty} c_\gamma = 0$ **and** *negative* **values for** c_γ.

Finally, it is to be noticed that contrary to what might be inferred by a casual look at figure 10.10, time paths in the vicinity of the cusp cross other curves and may curl upon themselves, thereby passing through the same point at two different times (see figure 10.13).

From the above analysis, we conclude that making use of a utility function leads invariably to perfectly unacceptable growth policies and therefore should be very seriously questioned. This would be ample reason to discard it when searching for an optimal growth policy. But we will argue that the use of such a function should be questioned for the following reasons as well.

A first reason is the very arbitrary character of a utility function at the aggregate level of a society. Secondly, this arbitrariness is compounded by an additional difficulty: for the sum of utility flows to converge, the utility flows must be discounted at a rate whose value is no less arbitrary. Furthermore, it is difficult to imagine

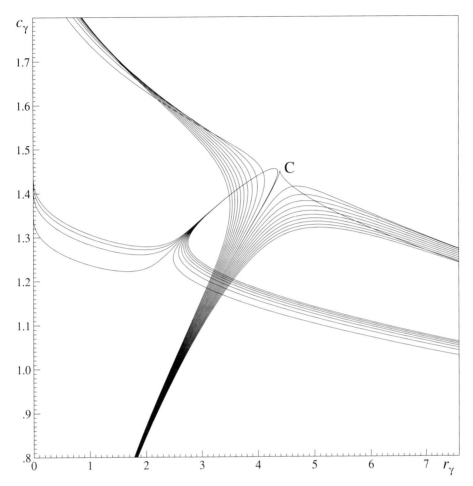

Figure 10.12 Enlargement of the cusp area. The cusp point C does *not* separate diverging time paths toward either axis. The separating initial point C_0 is just above $\hat{C}_0$, the initial value leading to the cusp. The trajectory immediately to the left of the cusp is in fact 11 time paths; 7 ultimately diverge toward the r_γ axis; 4 diverge toward the c_γ axis.

why a nation should be viewed as valuing its capital stock in an entirely different, arbitrary way from what individuals and firms have done until now and presumably always will. Indeed, when individuals or firms are making investment decisions, they try to rely on carefully forecast cash flows (or so they say is their intent) as well as on appropriate discount factors, but they would never come up with the odd idea of transforming their cash flows through some utility function. Finally, at the international level, it is hardly conceivable that comparisons of growth performances would ever be carried out with utility rescalings. For all these reasons, we will search for an optimal savings policy based upon the maximization of the

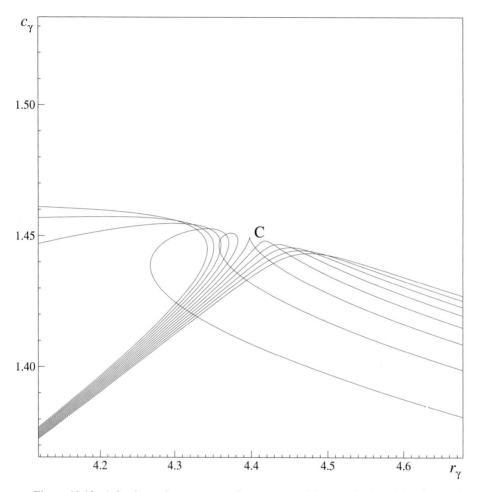

Figure 10.13 A further enlargement or the cusp area. The complexity of the time paths is illustrated by the fact that not only trajectories cross each other, but that some will curl upon themselves. The line ending vertically just below 1.45 depicts the first phase of the 11 trajectories in Figure 10.12, 7 of which diverge toward the r_γ axis, and 4 of which end up on c_γ.

sum of discounted consumption flows. This will be done in the third part of this text (chapter 13).

Exercises

10.1 Show that the Euler equation (18) is a second-order non-linear differential equation in r_γ. (Hint: Once you get the value of $\dot{U}'_c/U'_c$ as a function of c, express it as a function of c_γ, as in (19). Then use (14).)

10.2 Show that in the case of the negative exponential function the system of differential equations governing the economy is given by (23), (24).

10.3 This problem can be considered as a project. Using software such as Maple 9, for instance, verify the fundamental instability of the system of differential equations in (r_γ, c_γ) of this chapter. In particular, check the order of magnitude of the initial values c_0 leading to equilibrium in the case of the power utility function $U(c) = (c^\alpha - 1)/(1 - \alpha)$ for the parameter values we have chosen. In the case of the negative exponential utility function $U = -(1/\beta)c^{-\beta}$, $\beta > 0$, verify that no equilibrium point exists any more. In this last case, you will have to be careful: there exists a "middle" time path in (r_γ, c_γ) space that will *seem* to be heading toward an equilibrium point. In fact, it does not. One time path leads to a cusp point, from which divergence always results. Thus the model with a negative exponential utility function does not even exhibit saddle-point equilibrium as in the case of the power utility function; it is entirely unstable.

Answers

10.1 In the Euler equation

$$\varphi'(r_\gamma) + \frac{\dot{U}'_c}{U'_c} - i = 0$$

we derive $\dfrac{\dot{U}'_c}{U'_c}$ as $c\dfrac{U''_c}{U'_c}\dfrac{\dot{c}}{c} = (\alpha - 1)\dfrac{\dot{c}}{c}$. Indeed from equation (7a), the marginal utility of consumption is $U'_c = c^{\alpha-1}$, and the elasticity of U'_c with respect to c is $\alpha - 1$. Also, since $c = c_\gamma e^{gt}$, $\dot{c}/c = \dot{c}_\gamma/c_\gamma + g$. Then $\dfrac{\dot{U}'_c}{U'_c}$ is equal to $(\alpha - 1)(\dot{c}_\gamma/c_\gamma + g)$. Now use equation (14) to determine

$$\dot{c}_\gamma = \varphi'(r_\gamma) \cdot \dot{r}_\gamma - \ddot{r}_\gamma - (g + n)\dot{r}_\gamma = [\varphi'(r_\gamma) - (g + n)]\dot{r}_\gamma - \ddot{r}_\gamma.$$

Therefore the Euler–Lagrange equation is

$$(\alpha - 1)\frac{[\varphi'(r_\gamma) - (g + n)]\dot{r}_\gamma - \ddot{r}_\gamma}{\varphi(r_\gamma) - \dot{r}_\gamma - (g + n)r_\gamma} + \varphi'(r_\gamma) - i = 0, \qquad (1A)$$

a second-order non-linear differential equation in r_γ, where $\varphi(r_\gamma)$ is given either by (9) or (10) depending upon $\sigma \neq 1$ or $\sigma = 1$ respectively. In consequence, the equation has no more analytical solutions than the first-order, non-linear system (13), (20). But the numerical solutions of (13), (20) in (r_γ, c_γ) will be much simpler to read and interpret than the numerical solutions of (1A).

10.2 With $U = -(1/\beta)e^{-\beta c}$, the marginal utility and its derivative are:

$$U'_c = e^{-\beta c}$$

and

$$U_c'' = -\beta e^{\beta c},$$

so that the term $\dot{U}_c'/U_c$ of the Ramsey equation is

$$\dot{U}_c'/U_c' = U_c'' \cdot \dot{c}/U_c' = -\beta \dot{c}.$$

This last term can also be written

$$\dot{U}_c'/U_c' = -c\beta(\dot{c}/c).$$

Since $c = c_\gamma e^{gt}$, $\dot{c}/c = \dot{c}_\gamma/c_\gamma + g$, and $\dot{U}_c'/U_c'$ can be expressed in terms of c_γ as

$$\dot{U}_c'/U_c' = -c_\gamma e^{\gamma t}\beta \left(\frac{\dot{c}_\gamma}{c_\gamma} + g \right).$$

This can be plugged into equation (18) in the text to yield:

$$c_\gamma e^{\gamma t}\beta \left(\frac{\dot{c}_\gamma}{c_\gamma} + g \right) = \varphi'(r_\gamma) - i$$

from which the following differential equation in c_γ results:

$$\dot{c}_\gamma = \frac{1}{\beta e^{gt}}[\varphi'(r_\gamma) - i] - g c_\gamma,$$

which is equation (28). Equation (27) stays the same as (13).

PART III

A unified approach

Bethe[1] had found out that if you do just the right things,
if you kind of forget some things and don't forget other
things, do it just right, you can get the right answers.
Richard Feynman[2]

In this book we have presented the theory of economic growth along the lines it followed in the twentieth century: in Part I, we considered positive, or descriptive growth theory. Assumptions were made about the functioning of the economy (income was generated through a production function); the savings rates *s* chosen by society; and finally the growth rate of population. In Part II, we discussed the normative approach, whereby society chooses a savings rate so as to meet a long-term objective such as the maximization of welfare over a long horizon. This was the heart of optimal growth theory.

We will now show, in the third part of this book, that both approaches can, and should, be unified. If, as Robert Solow pointed out in his path-breaking essay, we are in a competitive economy, the wage rate *and the real rental rate* are determined by the traditional marginal productivity equations. We underline the second relationship, namely the equality between the real rental rate and the marginal productivity of capital because, as we will show, it determines a savings rate leading to an optimal, dynamic, allocation of capital.

Thus, the 1956 essay by Robert Solow is a major landmark not only because it freed the theory of rigid production constraints adopted in the literature of the first part of the twentieth century, but also because it carries all the seeds of *optimal* economic growth. In our opinion, this has not yet been recognized. Indeed, if the Solow growth model has been the subject of innumerable descriptions, the part of his paper where he discusses the roles of the capital rental rate and the

---

[1] Hans Bethe (1906–2005) received the 1967 Nobel Prize in Physics.
[2] Richard Feynman, *The pleasure of finding things out*, Penguin Books, London, New York, 1999, p. 235.

rate of interest in the growth process has received amazingly short shrift; more importantly, to the best of our knowledge their fundamental link to optimal growth has never been uncovered.

In order to emphasize the importance of Solow's analysis, we cannot do better than to quote it in its entirety. In the following extract, the reader will find a central piece on the basis of which we will set out to unify the two major strands of economic growth theory.

> In a competitive economy the real wage and real rental are determined by the traditional marginal-productivity equations:

(10)
$$\frac{\partial F}{\partial L} = \frac{w}{p}$$

and

(11)
$$\frac{\partial F}{\partial K} = \frac{q}{p}.$$

> Note in passing that with constant returns to scale the marginal productivities depend only on the capital-labor ratio r, and not on any scale quantities.

> The real rental on capital q/p is an own-rate of interest – it is the return on capital in units of capital stock. An owner of capital can by renting and reinvesting increase his holdings like compound interest at the variable instantaneous rate q/p, i.e., like $e^{\int_0^t q/p\,dt}$. Under conditions of perfect arbitrage there is a well-known close relationship between the money rate of interest and the commodity own-rate, namely

(12)
$$i(t) = \frac{q(t)}{p(t)} + \frac{\dot{p}(t)}{p(t)}.$$

> If the price level is in fact constant, the own-rate and the interest rate will coincide. If the price level is falling, the own-rate must exceed the interest rate to induce people to hold commodities. That the exact relation is as in (12) can be seen in several ways. For example, the owner of $1 at time t has two options: he can lend the money for a short space of time, say until $t + h$ and earn approximately $i(t)h$ in interest, or he can buy $1/p$ units of output, earn rentals of $(q/p)h$ and then sell. In the first case he will own $1 + i(t)h$ at the end of the period; in the second case he will have $(q(t)/p(t)h + p(t + h)/p(t))$. In equilibrium these two amounts must be equal

$$1 + i(t)h = \frac{q(t)}{p(t)}h + \frac{p(t + h)}{p(t)}$$

> or

$$i(t)h = \frac{q(t)}{p(t)}h + \frac{p(t + h) - p(t)}{p(t)}.$$

Dividing both sides by h and letting h tend to zero we get (12). Thus this condition equalizes the attractiveness of holding wealth in the form of capital stock or loanable funds.

Another way of deriving (12) and gaining some insight into its role in our model is to note that $p(t)$, the transfer price of a unit of capital, must equal the present value of its future stream of net rentals. Thus with perfect foresight into future rentals and interest rates:

$$p(t) = \int_t^\infty q(u)e^{-\int_t^u i(z)dz}du.$$

Differentiating with respect to time yields (12).[3]

A number of remarks are now in order. First, we need to be familiar with the concepts of instantaneous rate of return and forward rate used by the author, as well as with the concept of continuous time discounting with forward rates. Secondly, we must explain how the mechanism of arbitrage may work in order to establish the equality between the real rate of interest and the marginal productivity of capital. Finally, it may be useful to show how these relationships can be extended to conditions of uncertainty.

This is why a detailed exposition of these concepts is given in the next two chapters. In chapter 11, the continuously compounded spot rate, the instantaneous forward rate and the intimate links between those two concepts are discussed. In chapter 12, we describe the arbitrage process that may bring equilibrium between the capital goods market and the market for loanable funds. We will then be on firm ground to show, in chapter 13, how the fundamental equation of interest – the Fisher equation – is in fact a Euler equation, implying optimal growth paths for the capital stock and for investment, and therefore an optimal savings rate. Another surprise is in store for us: we will show that this optimal savings rate implies that the economy is on its equilibrium path.

---

[3] Extract from Robert Solow, "A Contribution to the Theory of Economic Growth", *The Quarterly Journal of Economics*, Vol. 70, No 1 (February 1956), 79–81.

CHAPTER 11

Preliminaries: interest rates and capital valuation

Throughout this book, we have underlined the role of investment in the growth process. Until now, however, we have considered that the decision to invest was either exogenous (independent of any variable in the system) or driven by the general aim of maximizing a sum of discounted utility flows, as we have described it in our chapters on optimal growth theory. But so far we have left aside the essential role played by the rate of interest, the price of loanable funds which is both a cost to investors in capital goods and a reward to those agents who are willing to supply those funds. For investors, we know from general economic principles that their decision to invest depends both on expected future rewards and on the rate of interest.

Along a growth process, four prices are in search of an equilibrium: the spot price of any capital good, its future price, the rental rate, and the rate of interest. Those four prices are linked in a fundamental equation developed formally for the first time by Irving Fisher (1896). This equation will turn out to be of central importance: it has far reaching, surprising consequences. In particular, we will demonstrate that if competitive equilibrium enforces it, society maximizes the sum of all future discounted *consumption* flows it can acquire.

Before showing this, we have to be very precise about the nature of the interest rates and the process by which equilibrium can be reached simultaneously on the capital goods market and on the loanable funds market. But even before doing so, we should ask the question: "Why do interest rates exist in the first place?" We will also explain how both lenders and borrowers alike benefit from the very existence of an equilibrium interest rate. We will then turn to the various concepts of interest rates, their fundamental properties, and their intimate links.[1]

---

[1] To do this we have relied in the first part of this chapter on some of our previous work. Section 1 borrows from chapter 1 of our book *Bond Pricing and Portfolio Analysis – Protecting investors in the Long Run*, MIT Press, Cambridge, Mass., 2003, pp. 10–13; section 2 is adapted from our chapter

I   The reason for the existence of interest rates

Most people, when asked the innocuous-looking question about the reason why interest rates should exist in the first instance, respond that since inflation is a pervasive phenomenon common to all places and times, it is therefore only natural that lenders will want to protect themselves against rising prices; borrowers might well agree with that, therefore establishing the existence of an equilibrium rate of interest.

It is rather strange that inflation is so often the first explanation given for the existence of interest rates. In fact, positive interest rates have always been observed in countries where there was practically no inflation – or even a slight decrease in prices. Although inflation is certainly a contributor to the magnitude of interest rates, it is in no way their primary determinant. There are two other principal causes.

First, and foremost, an interest rate exists because one monetary unit can be transformed, through fixed capital, into more than one unit after a certain period of time. Some people are able, and willing, to perform that rewarding transformation. On the other hand, other people are willing to lend the necessary amount, and it is only fitting that a price for that monetary unit be established between the borrowers and the lenders. Let us add that on any such market *both* borrowers and lenders will find a benefit in this transaction. We will soon discover this.

Second, an interest rate exists because people usually prefer to have a consumption good now rather than later. For that they are prepared to pay a price; and as before, others may consider they could well part with a portion of their income or their wealth today if they are rewarded for doing so. There again, borrowers and lenders will come to terms that will be rewarding for both parties, in a way entirely similar to what we have seen in the case of productive investments.

Together with *expected* inflation, these reasons explain the existence of interest rates. The level of interest rates will depend on the attitudes of the parties regarding each kind of transaction, and of course on the perceived risk of the transactions involved.

An important point now should be made, which is particularly relevant in the context of economic growth. We know how central the level of the interest is in the investment decision and hence in the growth process. We may then view the interest rate as a *cost* to investors, mitigated from the point of view of society as a whole by the fact that it is a gain for those who loan funds. But there is much more to this. Indeed, provided that the loanable funds is competitive, the whole society benefits from the very existence of such a market; those benefits have, to the best of

"Protecting Investors against Changes in Interest Rates", in *Asset and Liability Management*, W. Ziemba and S. Zenios, eds., Elsevier North-Holland, 2006, pp. 69–138. Authorizations from the editors are gratefully acknowledged.

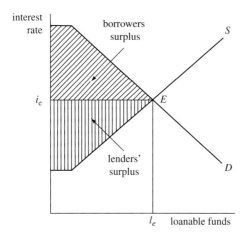

Figure 11.1   An equilibrium rate of interest on any financial market maximizes the sum of the lenders' and the borrowers' surpluses, as well as the amount of loanable funds at society's disposal.

our knowledge, received short shrift until now. As in any commodity market, the mere existence of an equilibrium interest rate set at the intersection of the supply and demand curves for loanable funds entails two major consequences: first, the surplus of society (the surplus of the lenders and the borrowers) is maximized (shaded area in figure 11.1); second, the amount of loanable funds that can be used by society is also maximized.[2]

Suppose that at its equilibrium the interest rate sets itself at 6%. Generally, lots of borrowers would have accepted a transaction at 7%, or even at much higher levels, depending on the productivity of the capital good into which they would have transformed their loan. The difference between the rate a borrower would have accepted and the rate established in the market is a benefit to him. On the other hand, consider the lenders: they lend at 6%, but many of them might well have settled for a lower rate of interest (perhaps 4.5%, for instance). Both borrowers and lenders derive benefits (what economists call *surpluses*) from the very existence of a financial market, in the same way that buyers and suppliers derive surpluses from their trading at an equilibrium price on markets for ordinary goods and services.

Let us now consider that for some reason interest rates are fixed at a level different from the equilibrium level (i_e). Two circumstances, at least, can lead to such fixed interest rates. First, government regulations could prevent interest rates from rising above a certain level (for instance i_0, below i_e). Alternatively, a monopoly or a cartel among lenders could fix the interest above its equilibrium value i_e (for instance, at i_1).

---

[2] For the reader who is not familiar with the concepts of surplus, a brief presentation is given in section 1 of chapter 1.

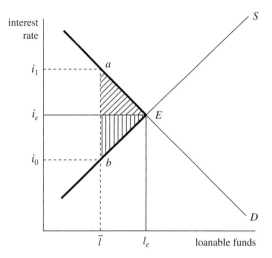

Figure 11.2 Any artificially fixed interest rate reduces both the amount of loanable funds at society's disposal and the surplus of society (the hatched area).

If interest rates are fixed in such a way, the funds actually loaned will always be the smaller of either the supply or the demand. Indeed, the very existence of a market supposes that one cannot force lenders to lend whatever amount the borrowers wish to borrow if interest rates are below their equilibrium value – and vice versa if interest rates are above that value. We can then draw the curve of effective loans when interest rates are fixed – the kinked, dark line in figure 11.2. Should the interest rate be fixed either at i_0 or at i_1, the loanable funds will be $\bar{l}$ (less than l_e), and the loss in surplus for society will be the shaded area abE. Innocuous as these properties of financial markets may seem, they are either unknown or ignored by governments when they nationalize banks – or when they close their eyes to cartels established among banks, nationalized or not.

But the consequences of a competitive equilibrium in the loanable funds market extend even beyond the benefits which we have just described. Indeed, in chapter 13 we will show that, together with competitive equilibrium on the capital market, such equilibria constitute a necessary and sufficient condition for society to achieve quite a surprising result: the maximization of the sum of all discounted consumption flows it can acquire in the future, and, at any point of time the maximization of the value of society's activity, measured as consumption plus the rate of increase in the capital stock's value.

2   The various types of interest rates and their fundamental properties

The concept of an interest rate compounded once a year, or a finite number of times per year, is a familiar one. For instance, some savings accounts may carry a 4%

yearly rate of interest, with interest paid quarterly. This implies that $1 invested into such an account and left there for one year will become more than $1.04 at the end of the year, because the contract between the bank and the depositor stipulates that at the end of the first quarter $1 + 0.04(\frac{1}{4})$ is due; this new amount, $1.01, is to be remunerated at the rate of 4% for the next quarter, thus becoming $(1.01)(1.01) = 1.0201$ after 6 months; this process will be repeated until the end of the year, yielding not 1.04 to its owner, but $\left[1 + 0.04\left(\frac{1}{4}\right)\right]^4 = 1.0406$. It turns out that in the economic or financial literature, ample use is made of interest rates that are not compounded a finite number of times a year, but an infinitely high number of times a year. This process is called "continuous compounding". The reason is two-fold: first it greatly simplifies calculations, because, as we will see, products will be transformed into sums, and geometric means become arithmetic means. Furthermore, when we deal with interest rates or growth rates as random variables, this very transformation enables us to apply one of the most important and powerful theorems ever found in statistics, the central limit theorem – we have done this in chapter 6.

The concept of continuous compounding applies to the *two* main types of interest rates, depending on the type of contract signed between the lender and the borrower.

First, a contract may be signed at time t for a loan starting in the future at time τ, for a time span $\Delta\tau$. Such a contract is a forward contract, and defines a *forward* interest rate, which may be denoted $f(t, \tau, \Delta\tau)$. Sometimes, to simplify notation, the first and the last arguments of $f(\cdot)$ are omitted, and the forward rate is denoted simply as $f(\tau)$. It is understood that the contract is signed at some date t ($t < \tau$), which depends upon the context, for a loan to start at time τ; the loan is supposed to be paid back $\Delta\tau$ later.

Second, an important special case of the forward rate is the *spot* rate, whereby the starting point in time of the contract is t. Thus $s(t, \Delta t) \equiv f(t, t, \Delta t)$ denotes an interest rate decided upon at time t, for a loan starting immediately (at time t), with a duration Δt. Often, instead of designating the *duration* Δt of the contract specified in the spot rate, it is simpler to designate as v, for instance, the time of reimbursement. Then, with $\Delta t = v - t$, the spot rate is often denoted $s(t, v)$. Since the concept of the forward rate generalizes the concept of the spot rate, we will start with the forward rate. We emphasize that, in what follows, those rates will always be measured *per year*.

2.1 The forward rate with discrete and continuous compounding

Consider a time span $[u, v]$ subdivided into n intervals $\Delta z_1, \ldots, \Delta z_j, \ldots, \Delta z_n$. This partitioning of $[u, v]$ is arbitrary in the following sense: each Δz_j interval ($j = 1, \ldots, n$) has arbitrary length; two given intervals, say Δz_1 and Δz_2, may

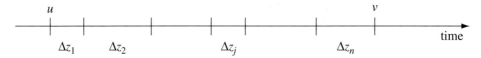

Figure 11.3   An arbitrary partitioning of the time span $[u, v]$.

or may not be equal. Such an arbitrary partitioning of the time span $[u, v]$ is represented in figure 11.3.

Suppose that to each interval Δz_j corresponds a forward rate. Such a forward rate is defined as the *yearly* interest rate for a loan agreed upon at time u; the loan is to start at the beginning of the Δz_j interval, and is to be paid back at the end of Δz_j. Call f_j this forward rate. For instance, f_j may be equal to 5% per year.

If \$1 is lent at the beginning of this time interval Δz_j, what will be the amount to be reimbursed at the end of Δz_j? There are many ways of answering this question. For instance, one could agree that it is

- either $(1 + f_j)^{\Delta z_j}$, in conformity with annual interest compounding if Δz_j is typically equal to a few years;
- or $1 + f_j \Delta z_j$, following what is usually done if the interval Δz_j is smaller than one year, which will be justified below.

Until now, we have said nothing of the length of the time span $[u, v]$. In fact, inasmuch as the partitioning of $[u, v]$ is arbitrary, so is its length: it could be a non integer number of years or days. It turns out that, whatever this length may be, we will at one point consider that the number n of intervals Δz_j tends toward infinity, and that at the same time the largest of those intervals tends toward zero. Therefore, we can assume already at this stage that Δz_j is small. We will now show why it is both natural and legitimate to use the second formula, i.e. $1 + f_j \Delta z_j$, although it is not necessary to do so; the first formula would work as well for our purposes.

We could first observe that, for any fixed value Δz_j, $1 + f_j \Delta z_j$ is a first-order approximation of $(1 + f_j)^{\Delta z_j}$ at point $f_j = 0$. This can be shown by taking the first-order Taylor expansion of $(1 + f_j)^{\Delta z_j}$ around $f_j = 0$. But there is more to it. It turns out that $1 + f_j \Delta z_j$ is an excellent, *second-order*, approximation of the function $(1 + f_j)^{\Delta z_j}$ around point $(f_j, \Delta z_j) = (0, 0)$. Indeed, consider the latter expression as a function of the two variables f_j and Δz_j, denoted momentarily, for convenience, as f and h respectively. Let $\varphi(.)$ be the function

$$\varphi(f, h) = (1 + f)^h \equiv (1 + f_j)^{\Delta z_j}. \tag{1}$$

Expand (1) in Taylor series around point $(f, h) = (0, 0)$. The second-order approximation is

$$\varphi(f, h) \approx \varphi(0, 0) + \frac{\partial \varphi}{\partial f}(0, 0)f + \frac{\partial \varphi}{\partial h}(0, 0)h$$

$$+ \frac{1}{2}\left[\frac{\partial^2 \varphi}{\partial f^2}(0, 0)f^2 + 2\frac{\partial^2 \varphi}{\partial f \partial h}(0, 0)fh + \frac{\partial^2 \varphi}{\partial h^2}(0, 0)h^2\right]. \quad (2)$$

Immediate calculations show that of the six terms in the right-hand side of (2), all are equal to zero except the first one, equal to 1, and the fifth (involving the cross second-order derivative), equal to fh. Therefore, we may write

$$1 + fh \approx (1 + f)^h \quad (3)$$

as a *second-order* approximation. From a geometric point of view, $1 + fh$ is a surface which has a high (second-order) degree of contact with surface $(1 + f)^h$ at point $(0, 0)$ because all partial derivatives up to the second order are equal for each function (as for the tangent plane at $(0, 0)$, or the first-order contact surface, it is just $\varphi(f, h) = 1$). To get some sense of this closeness, suppose that f_j is 5% per year and Δz_j is one month, or $0.08\bar{3}$ year. On the one hand, $(1 + f_j)^{\Delta z_j} = 1.0041$, while $1 + f_j \Delta z_j = 1.0042$ on the other.

Consider now that the rate of interest f_j is compounded not once within interval Δz_j, but m times. Using this approximation, one dollar invested at the beginning of this interval thus becomes $(1 + f_j \Delta z_j / m)^m$ where $\Delta z_j / m$ is the length of time over which the interest is compounded. Now set $f_j \Delta z_j / m = 1/k$; thus $m = k f_j \Delta z_j$ and one dollar becomes $(1 + 1/k)^{k f_j \Delta z_j}$. Take the limit of this amount when the number of compoundings m within Δz_j tends towards infinity – equivalently, when $k \to \infty$, since the $f_j \Delta z_j$'s terms are finite. We get

$$\lim_{k \to \infty}\left(1 + \frac{1}{k}\right)^{k f_j \Delta z_j} = e^{f_j \Delta z_j}. \quad (4)$$

This result could have been reached without recourse to the second-order approximation $(1 + f_j)^{\Delta z_j} \approx 1 + f_j \Delta z_j$. From formula $(1 + f_j)^{\Delta z_j}$, when interest is compounded m times within Δz_j, we get $(1 + f_j/m)^{m \Delta z_j}$ at the end of interval Δz_j. Now set $f_j/m = 1/k$, so that $m = k f_j$. One dollar becomes $(1 + 1/k)^{k f_j \Delta z_j}$, and we get the above result.

If the same limiting process is taken for each interval Δz_j $(j = 1, \ldots, n)$, an investment C_u at time u becomes

$$C_v = C_u e^{\sum_{j=1}^{n} f_j \Delta z_j} \quad (5)$$

at time v.

Suppose now that, whatever the initial partitioning of the time span $[u, v]$, the sum $\sum_{j=1}^{n} f_j \Delta z_j$ tends towards a unique limit when the number of time intervals n tends toward infinity, and when the maximum interval length Δz_j tends towards zero. The forward rate function is then said to be integrable, and the limit is the definite integral of f_j over $[u, v]$. We have

$$\lim_{\substack{n \to \infty \\ \max \Delta z_j \to 0}} \sum_{j=1}^{n} f_j \Delta z_j = \int_{u}^{v} f(z)dz. \tag{6}$$

We are now ready for a definition of the instantaneous forward rate.

DEFINITION   Let $[u, v]$ be a time span. Let z be any point of time within this interval. The *instantaneous forward rate* $f(z)$ is the yearly interest rate decided upon at time u for a loan starting at time z, $z \in [u, v]$, for an infinitesimally small trading period dz.

Sometimes, as noted earlier, to recall the time (u) at which this instantaneous forward rate is agreed upon, the forward rate is denoted $f(u, z)$. If, for instance, the time of inception of the contract is 0 and the time at which the loan starts is t (with an infinitesimal trading period), the instantaneous forward rate is denoted $f(0, t)$, and so forth.

From (5) and (6) a sum C_u invested during $[u, v]$ at the infinite number of instantaneous forward rates $f(u, z)$ – or $f(z)$ for short – becomes

$$C_v = C_u e^{\int_u^v f(z)dz}. \tag{7}$$

A final word about (6) and (7) is in order. Notice the dimension of the infinitesimal element $f(z)dz$ in the integral: since $f(z)$ is in (1/time) units, and since dz is in time units, $f(z)dz$ is dimensionless; and so are $\int_u^v f(z)dz$ and $\exp[\int_u^v f(z)dz]$.

2.2   The continuously compounded spot rate

Consider the following, particular, rate of interest:

- the time of signing of the contract and the starting point of the loan are the same: u;
- the length of the loan is the time span $[u, v]$ or $v - u$; and
- the amount loaned is C_u; the amount due is C_v.

There are a number of ways of defining the rate of interest on such a loan. If this rate is calculated once only over the whole period $[v - u]$ (which may or may not be an integer number of years), one could define this rate as the *spot* rate (because it corresponds to a loan starting at the very signing of the contract) compounded *once* over $[v - u]$. Denote such a spot rate as $s_{u,v}^{(1)}$. The lower indices of s are self-explanatory; the superscript (1) refers to the fact that the rate of interest is calculated once over $[u, v]$. We have

$$s_{u,v}^{(1)} = \frac{C_v - C_u}{C_u}/(v - u) \tag{8}$$

and equivalently

$$C_v = C_u\big[1 + s_{u,v}^{(1)}(v - u)\big]. \tag{9}$$

Suppose now that our spot interest is compounded m times over interval $(v - u)$ instead of once only. It implies that the length of time between any two successive compoundings is $(v - u)/m$. The spot rate is now written $s_{u,v}^{(m)}$, and equation (9) becomes

$$C_v = C_u\big[1 + s_{u,v}^{(m)}(v - u)/m\big]^m. \tag{10}$$

In order for the contracts to be equivalent (that is, to yield the same amount due C_v), the right-hand sides of (9) and (10) must be equal. Hence

$$1 + s_{u,v}^{(1)}(v - u) = \big[1 + s_{u,v}^{(m)}(v - u)/m\big]^m \tag{11}$$

or

$$s_{u,v}^m = \frac{m}{v - u}\left\{\big[1 + s_{u,v}^{(1)}(v - u)\big]^{1/m} - 1\right\}. \tag{12}$$

Replacing m by 1 in the right-hand side of (12) yields $s_{u,v}^{(1)}$ as it should.

Consider now what happens to (10) when the number of compoundings m tends toward infinity. Similarly to what we did before (§2.1), we can replace $s_{u,v}^{(m)}(v - u)/m$ by $1/k$; therefore, with $m = k\, s_{u,v}^{(m)}(v - u)$, we can write

$$C_v = C_u \left(1 + \frac{1}{k}\right)^{k\, s_{u,v}^{(m)}(v-u)}. \tag{13}$$

Taking the limit of C_v when $m \to \infty$ and $k \to \infty$

$$\lim_{\substack{m \to \infty \\ k \to \infty}} C_v = C_u e^{s_{u,v}^{(\infty)}(v-u)}. \tag{14}$$

This leads to the following definition.

DEFINITION   Let $[u, v]$ be a time span. The *continuously compounded spot rate* is the yearly interest rate, denoted $s(u, v)$ that transforms an investment C_u at time u into C_v at time v, the rate being compounded over infinitesimally small time intervals between u and v.

Denote for simplicity $s_{u,v}^{(\infty)} \equiv s(u, v)$. Equation (14) is

$$C_v = C_u e^{s(u,v)(v-u)}. \tag{15}$$

From (15), we deduce

$$s(u, v) = \frac{\log(C_v/C_u)}{v - u}. \tag{16}$$

Notice that there is another way of deriving the continuously compounded rate of interest, which proceeds directly from equation (10). Indeed, we can write from (10), denoting $w = 1/m$

$$s_{u,v}^{(m)} = \frac{m}{v - u}\left[\left(\frac{C_v}{C_u}\right)^{1/m} - 1\right] = \frac{\left(\frac{C_v}{C_u}\right)^{1/m} - 1}{\frac{v-u}{m}} = \frac{\left(\frac{C_v}{C_u}\right)^w - 1}{w(v - u)}. \tag{10a}$$

When the number of compoundings m within the period $v - u$ tends to infinity (or when $w = 1/m$ tends to zero), both numerator (N) and denominator (D) in (10a) tend to zero. Therefore we can apply the Marquis de L'Hospital's rule to get

$$\lim_{m \to \infty} s_{u,v}^{(m)} = \lim_{w \to 0} \frac{N'(w)}{D'(w)} = \lim_{w \to 0} \frac{(C_v/C_u)^w \log(C_v/C_u)}{v - u} = \frac{\log(C_v/C_u)}{v - u} \tag{10b}$$

as before.

There is an all-important relationship between the continuously compounded spot rate $s(u, v)$ and the forward rate $f(z)$ (a function defined over the interval $[u, v]$). Arbitrage without transaction costs guarantees that the right-hand sides of (7) and (15) must be identical. Thus, from

$$e^{\int_u^v f(z)dz} = e^{s(u,v)(v-u)}$$

we get

$$\boxed{s(u, v) = \frac{\int_u^v f(z)dz}{v - u}.} \tag{17}$$

Therefore the spot rate $s(u, v)$ is nothing else than the average value of the forward rate function $f(z)$ over the interval $[u, v]$. In this average the infinitely large number of elements $f(z)$ are all weighted by the infinitely small quantities $dz/(v - u)$ whose sum is equal to one.

On the other hand, it is always possible to express a forward rate as a function of a spot rate. Write (17) as

$$\int_u^v f(z)dz = (v - u)\, s(u, v) \tag{18}$$

and take the derivative of (18) with respect to v. This yields

$$f(v) = s(u, v) + (v - u)\frac{\partial s(u, v)}{\partial v}. \tag{19}$$

It is important to consider the spot rate as a function of two variables (u and v). The partial derivatives of the spot rate are, using (17):

$$\frac{\partial s}{\partial u} = \frac{1}{v - u} [s(u, v) - f(u)] \tag{17a}$$

and

$$\frac{\partial s}{\partial v} = \frac{1}{v - u} [f(v) - s(u, v)]. \tag{17b}$$

The instantaneous forward rate and the continuously compounded spot rate play respectively exactly the roles of a marginal and an average quantity, in economics parlance. This fact does not seem to be well known, and for that reason we will now introduce what we feel to be the missing link between the two concepts, namely the continuously compounded *total* return.

2.3   Introducing the missing link: the continuously compounded total return

Let us first simplify our notation. Without loss of generality, call 0 instant u, and t instant v. Our time span $[u, v]$ is now $[0, t]$. The simplification comes from the fact that t stands both for an *instant* of time and for the *length* of the time span $[0, t]$.

2.3.1   Definition of the continuously compounded total return

Let $f(0, z)$ be an instantaneous forward rate agreed upon at 0 for a loan starting at z ($0 \leq z < t$), for an infinitesimal trading period. Define the *continuously compounded total return* at time t as the integral sum of the forward rates between 0 and t, equal to $\int_0^t f(0, z)dz$. Denoted $S(0, t)$, it is a pure (dimensionless) number. The continuously compounded total return will now be abbreviated as the "total return", the continuously compounded spot rate $s(0, t)$ will be called the "spot rate", and "forward rate" will stand for the instantaneous forward rate $f(0, t)$.

From what precedes, we have the following equalities:

$$S(0, t) = \int_0^t f(0, z)dt = s(0, t)t = \log(C_t/C_0). \tag{20}$$

We can see that the total return, defined by the integral sum of the forward rates, is nothing else than the product of the spot rate and the investment horizon.

This implies that the relationship between the amount invested C_0 and the amount collected C_t can be expressed in either of the following ways:

$$\boxed{C_t = C_0 e^{S(0,t)} = C_0 e^{\int_0^t f(z)dz} = C_0 e^{s(0,t)t}.} \tag{21}$$

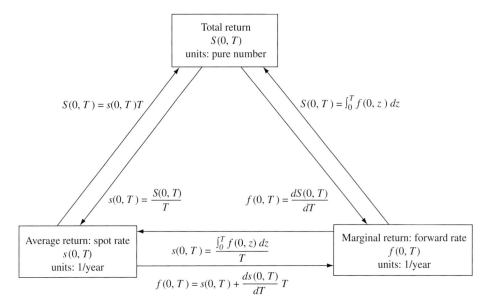

Figure 11.4 Summary of the relationships between the total return $S(0,t)$, the spot rate $s(0,t)$ and the forward rate $f(0,t)$.

Figure 11.4 summarizes all the relationships between the total return, the spot rate and the forward rate. Each of these three concepts are set at the corner of a triangle to underscore the fact that each of them can be derived from the two others in the following way:

$$
\begin{aligned}
&\bullet \text{ Total return} \equiv S(0,t) && = \int_0^t f(0,z)dz \\
&&& = s(0,t)t \\
&\bullet \text{ Spot rate} \equiv s(0,t) && = \frac{S(0,t)}{t} \\
&&& = \frac{\int_0^t f(0,z)dz}{t} \\
&\bullet \text{ Forward rate} \equiv f(0,t) && = \frac{d}{dt}\int_0^t f(0,z)dz \\
&&& = s(0,t) + t\frac{ds(0,t)}{dt}
\end{aligned}
$$

As an illustration, consider that the continuously compounded total return is $S(0,t) = S(0,20) = 1.2$, or 120% after 20 years. This means that, equivalently:

- the spot rate (continuously compounded) is 6% per year
- the forward rates $f(0,z)$, denoted $f(z)$ between 0 and t are given by *any* function $f(z)$ such that its average value over t is equal to 0.06. In other

words, we can choose any function $f(z)$ from the infinity of functions $f(\cdot)$ such that $\int_0^t f(z)dz = 1.2$, or $\int_0^t f(z)dz/20 = 0.06$. How can we do this? It is enough to choose *any* spot rate curve $s(0, t)$ that goes through point $(20, 0.06)$, take the derivative of $s(0, t)$ with respect to t, $s'(0, t)$, and finally write $f(t) = s(0, t) + ts'(0, t)$ (from equation (19)). An example may be useful: consider the spot rate defined by the arc of parabola

$$s(0, t) = 0.01(-0.005\, t^2 + 0.2^t + 4) \tag{22}$$

for $t = 0$ to $t = 20$, and by $s(0, t) = 0.06$ for $t \geq 20$.

This curve increases from point $(0, 0.04)$ to $(20, 0.06)$. At this last point, it goes through a maximum; it then remains constant at level 0.06 for $t \geq 20$.

The forward rate curve is then (from (19) and (22)):

$$f(t) = s(0, t) + s'(0, t)t = 0.01(-0.015t^2 + 0.4t + 4)$$

for $t = 0$ to $t = 20$, and by $f(t) = 0.06$ for $t \geq 20$.[3]

This is just one of the infinitely large number of forward curves that would correspond to a spot rate $s(0, 20) = 0.06$. We can verify that the total return is 1.2. We have indeed:

$$S(0, 20) = \int_0^{20} f(z)dz = \int_0^{20} 0.01(-0.015t^2 + 0.4t + 0.04)dz = 1.2,$$

which is also equal to $s(0, 20) \cdot 20 = (0.06)20 = 1.2$ as it should.

The spot rate and the forward rate in this example are represented in figure 11.5a. Notice that the forward rate curve goes through a maximum at $\hat{t} = 13.\bar{3}$ years before decreasing to reach the maximum of the spot rate at $t = 20$ years. The fact that the forward rate goes through a maximum when the spot rate curve is concave, increasing toward a plateau as we have described in this example, is a general property about which more will be said very soon.

The total return, $S(0, t) = s(0, t) \cdot t$, is the third-order polynomial $0.01(-0.005t^3 + 0.2t^2 + 4t)$ from $t = 0$ to $t = 20$; it goes through a point of inflection at $t = 13.\bar{3}$ (see figure 11.5b). For $t \geq 0$, the total return becomes the linear function $S(0, t) = 0.06t$.

2.4   *An economic interpretation of e*

We will now use the above relationships to give an economic interpretation of the number e. From (21), we can write equivalently the future value of the

---

[3] Note that another method of getting the forward curve would have been to multiply $s(0, t)$ by t (to obtain the total return $S(0, t) = \int_0^t f(z)dz$) and take the derivative of $S(0, t)$ with respect to t.

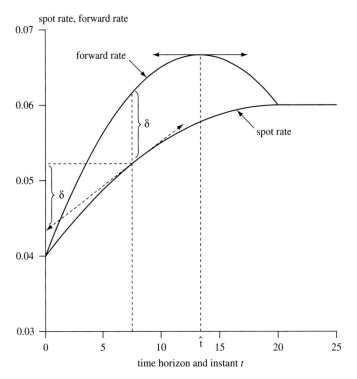

Figure 11.5a The spot rate curve $s(0,t)$ (lower curve) and the corresponding forward rate curve $f(0,t)$ (upper curve). The forward curve is $f(0,t) = s(0,t) + t\frac{ds(0,t)}{dt}$ and is constructed geometrically in the diagram.

investment as

$$C_t = C_0 e^{\frac{\int_0^t f(z)dz}{t}\cdot t} = C_0 e^{s(0,t)\cdot t} \tag{23}$$

In order to isolate the number e, it suffices to set $C_0 = 1$ and $[\int_0^t f(z)dz]/t = s(0,t) = 1/t$; in other words we just choose a spot rate equal to the inverse of the investment period. Thus we have the following interpretation of e:

$e = 2.71828\ldots$ is equal to the future value of \$1 at time t when, equivalently:

• the average of the instantaneous forward rates is $1/t$
• the continuously compounded spot rate is $1/t$

Suppose, for instance, that $t = 20$ years. Then $1/t$ is 0.05/year, or 5% per year. One dollar will become $e = 2.718\ldots$ if the *average* of the forward rates over 20 years is 5% per year, or if the spot rate is 5% a year.

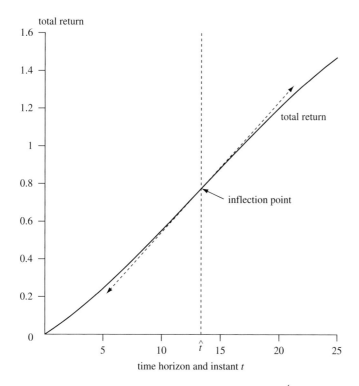

Figure 11.5b **The total return $S(0,t) = s(0,t) \cdot t = \int_0^t f(0,z)dz$.**

2.5   An economic interpretation of $\log x$

Let x designate the future value of a \$1 investment after any fixed period of time, one year for example. (The analysis can be made much more general than this; at the end of this section 2.5 we will give a general interpretation of $\log x$ corresponding to *any* time period Δz.) Equivalently, x designates the ratio between the future value of an investment after one year, C_1, and the value of that investment at time 0, C_0. So $x = C_1/C_0$, which we may call the yearly growth factor of C; it is equal to the growth rate of C plus one.

Then $\log x$ is the corresponding continuously compounded spot rate that transforms 1 into x after one year. This comes from our equation (21), $C_t = C_0 e^{s(0,t)t}$, where we replace C_0 and t by 1, and take logs.

For instance, if an investment increases by 20% over one year (\$1 becomes \$1.2 after one year), the corresponding continuously compounded spot rate is $\log(1.2) = 0.1823$. It is useful to picture the relationship between $x = C_1/C_0$, on the one hand, and $R_{0,1} \equiv (C_1 - C_0)/C_0 \equiv s_{0,1}^{(1)}$ and $\log(C_1/C_0) \equiv s(0,1)$, on the other. $R_{0,1} = s_{0,1}^{(1)} = x - 1$ is the linear approximation of $s(0,1) = \log x$ at $x = 1$ (see figure 11.6a).

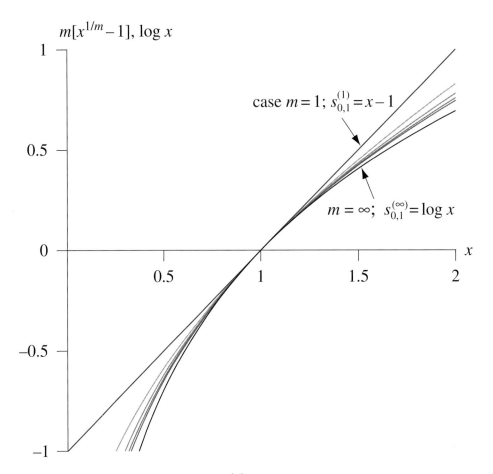

Figure 11.6a The growth rate of C, $s_{0,1}^{(m)}$, compounded m times per period, as a function of the growth factor $x = C_1/C_0$; $s_{0,1}^{(m)} = m[(C_v/C_u)^{1/m} - 1]$. The cases from $m = 1$ $((C_v/C_u) - 1 = x - 1)$ to $m = 5$ have been depicted, as well as the case $m \to \infty$ ($\log x$).

This economic interpretation of $\log x$ is also useful to get the order of magnitude of $\log x$ when x is close to 1. For instance, we can estimate $\log(0.8)$ in the following way. We just need to figure out the continuously compounded rate of return that would decrease the value of an investment by 20% after one year. We can figure that it will be somewhat *less* than -0.2 for the following reason. Suppose that the rate is compounded twice over one year at rate -20% per year. After 6 months, the investment becomes 0.9; after one year, it has lost again 10% and thus becomes 0.81. For the investment to be 0.8 only after one year, the rate of interest compounded twice a year should therefore be *less* than -20%; the argument holds of course for interest rates compounded more than twice per year, in particular for the continuously compounded rate of interest, which is $\log(0.8) \approx -0.223$.[4]

It is also useful to picture the relationship between the yearly growth factor of C, i.e. $C_1/C_0 \equiv x$ – or what \$1 becomes after one year – and the corresponding rate of return or growth rate $s_{0,1}^{(m)}$ when the number of compoundings within one year is m. From equation (12) we know that, with $v - u = 1$ year, $u = 0$, $v = 1$ we have

$$s_{0,1}^{(m)} = m\left[\left(\frac{C_v}{C_u}\right)^{1/m} - 1\right] = m[x^{1/m} - 1] \qquad (24)$$

(we verify that $s_{0,1}^{(1)}$ is equal to $x - 1 = (C_1 - C_0)/C_0$). This parametric relation between the growth factor and $s_{0,1}^{(m)}$ is represented in figure 11.6a, for values of m equal to 1 (the case corresponding to $s_{0,1}^{(1)} \equiv R_{0,1} = \frac{C_1 - C_0}{C_0}$), 2, 3, 4, 5 and ∞ (this last case corresponds to $s_{0,1}^{(\infty)} = \log(C_1/C_0)$. It can be seen how the family of curves $m[(x - 1)^{1/m} + 1]$ converges toward $\log x$ when $m \to \infty$. For relatively low values of m, the curves cluster relatively quickly; but the convergence toward $\log x$ is relatively slow; the vicinity of $\log x$ is reached only with high values of m. This is made clear by enlarging the areas of the diagram in the vicinity of $x = 0.8$ (figure 11.6b) and $x = 1.2$ (figure 11.6c).

The above interpretation of $\log x$ can be made much more general. Indeed, we should not restrict ourselves to a "one year" framework; *any* time period can be used as we will now demonstrate.

Let Δz be a period of any length; it may be a year, a month, a day, a fraction or a multiple – not necessarily an integer – of any of those time spans. Let $r_{\Delta z}^{(1)}$ be the growth rate of C defined *over that period*, compounded once over that same period.[5] Then, by definition: $r_{\Delta z}^{(1)} = \frac{C_{u+\Delta z} - C_u}{\Delta z}$, or $C_{u+\Delta z} = C_u(1 + r_{\Delta z}^{(1)})$. For instance, if Δz is one day, $r_{\Delta z}^{(1)}$ is the daily growth rate compounded once per day.

Let $r_{\Delta z}^{(m)}$ designate the growth rate of C compounded m times over the interval Δz. We then have

$$C_{u+\Delta z} = C_u\left(1 + r_{\Delta z}^{(m)} \cdot \frac{1}{m}\right)^m = C_u\left(1 + \frac{r_{\Delta z}^{(m)}}{m}\right)^m$$

---

[4] From a geometric point of view, we may observe that $\log x$ being a convex function, $\log(0.8)$ must be somewhat smaller than its first order (linear) approximation $x - 1 = -0.2$.

[5] Note that, as we mentioned at the end of the introduction of section 2, the spot rate and the forward rates are always defined *per year* (i.e. on a yearly basis). Now the rate $r_{\Delta z}^{(1)}$ is defined *over period* Δz.

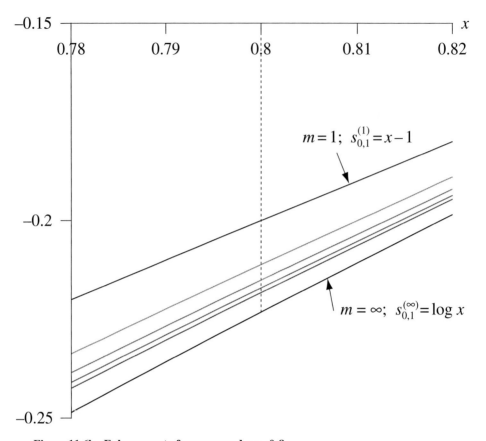

Figure 11.6b   Enlargement of area around $x = 0.8$.

from which we deduce $r_{\Delta z}^{(m)}$ as a function of $C_{u+\Delta z}/C_u$:

$$r_{\Delta z}^{(m)} = m\left[\left(\frac{C_{u+\Delta z}}{C_u}\right)^{1/m} - 1\right].$$

In order to determine $\lim_{m\to\infty} r_{\Delta z}^{(m)}$, we just write

$$r_{\Delta z}^{(m)} = \frac{\left(\frac{C_{u+\Delta z}}{C_u}\right)^{1/m} - 1}{1/m}$$

and apply L'Hospital's rule. Denoting $\lim_{m\to\infty} r_{\Delta z}^{(m)} = r_{\Delta z}^{(\infty)} \equiv r_{\Delta z}$ the continuously compounded growth rate over period Δz, we get

$$\lim_{m\to\infty} r_{\Delta z}^{(m)} \equiv r_{\Delta z} = \log(C_{u+\Delta z}/C_u).$$

We can call $C_{u+\Delta z}/C_u \equiv x$ the growth factor of C over period Δz, and we have the following interpretation of $\log x$:

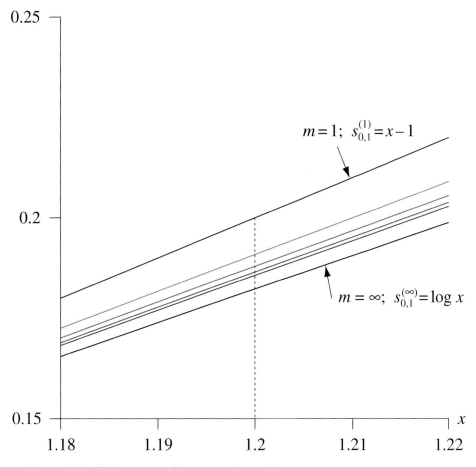

Figure 11.6c   Enlargement of area around $x = 1.2$.

Let x be the growth factor of a variable during *any* time period; $\log x$ is the corresponding continuously compounded growth rate defined over the same period.

For example, suppose an asset increases by 2% over one day. The growth factor is then $x = C_1/C_0 = \frac{C_1 - C_0}{C_0} + 1 = 1.02$. Then $\log x = \log 1.02 \approx 0.0198 = 1.98\%$ is the corresponding continuously compounded daily growth rate. If C had grown by 2% over one month or over one year, $\log 1.02\ x \approx 1.98\%$ would have been the corresponding continuously monthly or yearly growth rate.

2.6 *Fundamental properties*

From the very definition of the forward and spot rates we can deduce the following properties.

(1) The forward rate is above (below) the spot rate if and only if the spot rate is increasing (decreasing). It is equal to the spot rate if and only if the spot rate is constant at least over an infinitesimally small interval.

PROOF Using $f(0, t) = s(0, t) + t\,ds(0, t)/dt$, $ds(0, t)/dt \gtreqless 0$ implies $f(0, t) \gtreqless s(0, t)$, and conversely.

(2) If the spot rate $s(0, t)$ is an increasing, concave function of t, levelling off at $s(0, \bar{t}) = \bar{s}$ for an abscissa t, and equal to level $\bar{s}$ beyond t, then:

(a) the forward rate goes through a maximum in the interval $(0, \bar{t})$ and is decreasing in an interval to the level of $\bar{t}$. If $t \geqslant \bar{t}$, the forward rate is equal to the spot rate $\bar{s}$.

(b) the total return is an increasing function of t with at least one inflection point for $0 < t < \bar{t}$. For $t \geqslant \bar{t}$, the total return becomes a linear function of $\bar{t}$.

PROOF See exercise 11.5; (detailed answers to each exercise appear at the end of the chapter).

(3) At the origin, the slope of the forward curve is twice that of the spot rate curve (exercise 11.6).

3 Applications to the model of economic growth

We are now able to apply those concepts to some central issues in the valuation of capital as presented by Robert Solow in his path-breaking essay.

We will first consider the future value of a dollar invested in a capital good when returns are measured in continuous time and when those returns are variable through time. Then we will measure the value of capital in the same framework. Finally, we will derive the Fisher equation, which will play a central role in unifying the approaches to economic growth theory.

3.1 The future value of a dollar invested in a capital good

Let us first explain why, as Robert Solow writes, one dollar invested in capital earning a real rental $q(\tau)/p_0$ becomes, after a time period t, $e^{\int_0^t [q(\tau)/p_0]d\tau}$ (we use the letter τ to distinguish the integration variable from the upper bound of the integral). Let us check the units of this expression. If $q(\tau)$ denotes the rental rate of capital at time τ, it is expressed in \$ per unit of capital, per unit of time. We have, in units:

$$q(\tau) = \frac{\text{"dollars"}}{\text{"unit of capital} \cdot \text{unit of time"}} \quad \text{at time } \tau.$$

The price of capital p_0 is expressed as

$$p_0 = \frac{\text{``dollars''}}{\text{``unit of capital''}} \text{ at time } \tau.$$

The inverse of p_0, $1/p_0$, is also a price: it is the price of one dollar expressed in units of capital

$$\frac{1}{p_0} = \frac{\text{``units of capital''}}{\text{``dollar''}} \text{ at time } \tau.$$

Therefore the ratio $q(\tau)/p_0$ is expressed as

$$\frac{q(\tau)}{p_0} = \frac{1}{\text{``unit of time''}} \text{ at time } \tau;$$

it is a pure number divided by a unit of time – which may very well be a year. Therefore, as Solow writes, it plays exactly the role of an interest rate. $q(\tau)$ can be decided upon at time τ; it is then the current rate existing at time τ. Alternatively, it may be decided upon already at time 0. It is then a forward rate, applying at the future date τ. In both cases the rate applies over an infinitesimal period $d\tau$. The formula $e^{\int_0^t [q(\tau)/p_0]d\tau}$ in Solow's essay is just an illustration of the formula

$$C_v = C_u e^{\int_u^v f(z)dz} \tag{25}$$

which applies directly here: we just replace C_u by 1, u by 0 and v by t; and the forward rate is replaced by $q(\tau)/p_0$, with $\int_0^t [q(\tau)/p_0]d\tau$ being the (unitless) continuously compounded total return over period $[0, t]$.

It is important to observe that if the formula $e^{\int_0^t [q(\tau)/p_0]dz}$ gives indeed the value of \$1 invested in capital when the real rental rate is $q(\tau)/p_0$, the investor will, in addition, also benefit – or suffer – from any changes in the value of capital. Therefore, at any point of time τ we have to consider the real rental rate $q(\tau)/p_0$ as well as any relative change in the value of capital $\dot{p}(\tau)/p(\tau)$; the total *rate* of return received by an investor of \$1 in capital stock is then $q(\tau)/p_0 + \dot{p}(\tau)/p(\tau)$, and the *total return* over a period t is $\int_0^t [q(\tau)/p_0 + \dot{p}(\tau)/p(\tau)]dz$. Hence when the total *rate* of return is considered, one dollar becomes $\exp\{\int_0^t [q(\tau)/p_0 + \dot{p}(\tau)/p(\tau)]dz\}$ after a time period t. We will make use of this fact very soon.

3.2 Evaluating one unit of capital

We can now easily understand the valuation of capital as the indefinite integral

$$p(t) = \int_t^\infty q(\tau) e^{-\int_t^\tau i(z)dz} d\tau. \tag{26}$$

The left-hand side is expressed in \$ (it is the value of one unit of capital at time t, equal to (\$/unit of capital) times (1 unit of capital). One such unit of capital generates, during an infinitesimal period of time $d\tau$, a cashflow equal to $q(\tau)d\tau$, expressed in dollars. We have indeed:

$$\text{units of } q(\tau)d\tau = \frac{\text{``dollars''}}{\text{``unit of capital'' } \cdot \text{ ``unit of time''}} \times 1 \text{ ``unit of capital''}$$

$$\times \text{ duration } d\tau = \text{dollars} \tag{27}$$

Since $d\tau$ is infinitesimally small, there is an infinite number of cashflows within any finite time interval $[t_1, t_2]$, and of course there is an infinity of such cashflows in the infinite interval $[t, \infty)$. Let us now use equation (7) to evaluate the present value C_u: it is $C_v = C_u e^{-\int_u^v i(z)dz}$. Therefore, the present value at time t of the cashflow $q(\tau)d\tau$ received at time τ during the infinitesimally small interval $d\tau$ is $q(\tau)e^{-\int_t^\tau (i(z)dz}d\tau$, and the price of capital at time t is just the integral sum of this infinite number of cashflows, i.e. $\int_t^\infty q(\tau)e^{-\int_t^\tau i(z)dz}d\tau$.

Note that there is no need to express the present value of the cashflow $q(\tau)d\tau$ by using the forward rate function $i(z)$. Indeed, the very existence of this forward rate function implies the existence of a spot rate that applies over any interval $\tau - t$, denoted $s(t, \tau)$ and equal to $\left(\int_t^\tau i(z)dz\right) / (\tau - t)$. Therefore, we could have written the value of capital equivalently as:

$$p(t) = \int_t^\infty q(\tau)e^{-s(t,\tau).(\tau-t)}d\tau. \tag{28}$$

3.3 Deriving the Fisher equation

There are many ways to obtain the Fisher equation

$$i(t) = \frac{q(t)}{p(t)} + \frac{\dot{p}(t)}{p(t)}. \tag{29}$$

Robert Solow gives two of them (see the extract at the beginning of Part III of this book). The first cleverly uses approximations of the returns an investor would receive over a finite horizon either on the financial market or on the capital market; it then applies conditions of arbitrage leading to the equality of those returns and finally takes the limit of the equality when the horizon goes to zero. The second equates the cost of one unit of capital to its discounted returns; differentiating this equality with respect to t yields the Fisher equation.

How would the first Solow approach work without recourse to any approximation? The answer to this question will enable us to show the intimate links between the two methods. After a period h, one dollar invested at the variable rate $i(\tau)$ becomes $e^{\int_t^{t+h} i(\tau)d\tau}$. On the other hand one dollar enables, at time t, to buy a quantity $1/p(t)$ of the capital good, which can be rented at a rate $q(\tau)$ at any time τ between t and $t + h$, thus earning over an infinitesimal period a rental $\frac{q(\tau)}{p(t)}d\tau$.

Each of those rentals can be invested on the financial market at the variable rate $i(z)$, yielding, at time $t + h$, $\frac{q(\tau)}{p(t)}e^{\int_\tau^{t+h} i(z)dz}d\tau$. The total of those returns will be $\int_t^{t+h} \frac{q(\tau)}{p(t)}e^{\int_\tau^{t+h} i(z)dz}d\tau$. In addition the investor holds at time $t + h$ a capital stock $1/p(t)$ whose value is $p(t + h)/p(t)$. Arbitrage will lead to the equality

$$e^{\int_t^{t+h} i(z)dz} = \int_t^{t+h} \frac{q(\tau)}{p(t)}e^{\int_\tau^{t+h} i(z)dz}d\tau + \frac{p(t + h)}{p(t)}. \tag{30}$$

Differentiating (30) with respect to h gives

$$e^{\int_t^{t+h} i(z)dz} \cdot i(t + h)$$
$$= i(t + h)\int_t^{t+h} \frac{q(\tau)}{p(t)}e^{\int_\tau^{t+h} i(z)dz}d\tau + \frac{q(t + h)}{p(t)} + \frac{\dot{p}(t + h)}{p(t)}. \tag{31}$$

Taking the limit when $h \to 0$ yields the Fisher equation.

Notice how Solow's second method is linked to the first one by going through the following steps. Use the fact that the price of capital can always be expressed as the sum of discounted cashflows received until some future time $t + h$ and the present value of the residual value of capital at time $t + h$. From equation (26) corresponding to Solow's second method, write:

$$p(t) = \int_t^\infty q(\tau)e^{-\int_t^\tau i(z)dz}d\tau$$
$$= \int_t^{t+h} q(\tau)e^{-\int_t^\tau i(z)dz}d\tau + \int_{t+h}^\infty q(\tau)e^{-\left[\int_t^{t+h} i(z)dz+\int_{t+h}^\tau i(z)dz\right]}d\tau. \tag{32}$$

In the second integral of the right-hand side of (32), the exponential $e^{-\int_t^{t+h} i(z)dz}$ does not depend upon τ and hence can be factored out, leaving $e^{-\int_t^{t+h} i(z)dz}\int_{t+h}^\infty q(\tau)e^{-\int_{t+h}^\tau i(z)dz}d\tau$, which is nothing else than the present value of one unit of capital at time $t + h$. Thus (32) can be written as

$$p(t) = \int_t^{t+h} q(\tau)e^{-\int_t^\tau i(z)dz}d\tau + e^{-\int_t^{t+h} i(z)dz}p(t + h). \tag{33}$$

Multiplying through (33) by $e^{\int_t^{t+h} i(z)dz}$ and dividing by $p(t)$ leads to equation (30), corresponding to the first method.

3.4 Deriving the value of an asset from the Fisher equation

Until now we have shown multiple ways of deriving the fundamental equation of interest theory from the value of an asset. We will now explain how to do the reverse, i.e. determine the value of a unit of capital stock from the Fisher equation.

Observe that the Fisher equation (29) is a first-order non-linear differential equation in $p(t)$. Integrating it will not prove difficult, but care should be exercised when identifying the constant of integration. Two options at least are open to us. The first is to suppose that when time tends to infinity our capital stock tends to a value $p(\infty)$ which, large as it may be, is such that $\lim_{t\to\infty} p(t)/e^{\int_0^t i(z)dz} = 0$. In other words, we will assume that $p(\infty)e^{-\int_0^\infty i(z)dz} = 0$. The second is to suppose that we know the residual value of capital at some future date $t+h$, $p(t+h)$.

In the appendix of chapter 2, we had shown that the solution of the first-order non-linear differential equation

$$a(t)y'(t) + b(t)y(t) = g(t),$$

with initial condition $y(t_0) = y_0$ was

$$y(t) = e^{-\int_{t_0}^t \frac{b(z)}{a(z)}dz}\left(y_0 + \int_{t_0}^t \frac{g(\tau)}{a(\tau)}e^{\int_{t_0}^\tau \frac{b(z)}{a(z)}dz}d\tau\right). \tag{34}$$

Here our differential equation (29) can be written

$$\dot{p}(t) - i(t)p(t) = -q(t). \tag{35}$$

The functions $y(.)$, $a(.)$, $b(.)$ and $g(.)$ are, in this case, $p(.)$, 1, $-i(.)$ and $-q(.)$ respectively. Depending upon the context, the time variable will be denoted t, τ or z.

3.4.1 *First solution: identification of t_0 with ∞ and y_0 with p_∞*

We first set

$$\lim_{t\to\infty} p(t) = p_\infty \tag{36}$$

with one proviso: $p_\infty e^{-\int_t^\infty i(z)dz} = 0$. This implies that p_∞ and $i(z)$ are such that p_∞ is of smaller order than $\exp[\int_0^\infty i(z)dz]$. Applying now (34), we get:

$$p(t) = e^{\int_\infty^t i(z)dz}\left(p_\infty + \int_\infty^t -q(\tau)e^{-\int_\infty^\tau i(z)dz}d\tau\right). \tag{37}$$

In view of our hypothesis, the first term in the right-hand side of (37) multiplied by p_∞ cancels. Also, the exponential term $e^{-\int_t^\infty i(z)dz}$ depends upon t only; it can therefore be inserted in the integral of the right-hand side; (37) then becomes

$$p(t) = \int_t^\infty q(\tau)e^{-[\int_t^\infty i(z)dz+\int_\infty^\tau i(z)dz]}d\tau$$

$$= \int_t^\infty q(\tau)e^{-\int_t^\tau i(z)dz}d\tau \tag{38}$$

which is the capital valuation equation over a horizon of infinite length; this was the first form of evaluation used by Solow (equation 26).

3.4.2 Second solution: identification of t_0 with $t + h$ and y_0 with $p(t + h)$

We now set the "initial" conditions as follows: when $t_0 = t + h$, the residual value of capital is $p(t + h)$. So, in (34) we replace y_0 by $p(t + h)$. Applying (34) gives

$$p(t) = e^{\int_{t+h}^{t} i(z)dz} \left(p(t + h) - \int_{t+h}^{t} q(\tau)e^{-\int_{t+h}^{\tau} i(z)dz} d\tau \right). \qquad (39)$$

Carrying out the multiplication and, as before, introducing the first exponential term into the integral, we end up with our second form of capital valuation (33)

$$p(t) = \int_{t}^{t+h} q(\tau)e^{-\int_{t}^{\tau} i(z)dz} d\tau + e^{-\int_{t}^{t+h} i(z)dz} p(t + h).$$

Until now, we have simply assumed that arbitrage would enforce equality between a return on the financial market and a return on the capital good market. Our task is now to show the mechanisms and the forces at play that will lead to this equilibrium. This will be done in our next chapter.

Exercises

11.1 What is the yearly, continuously compounded, growth rate which makes an interest rate decrease from 7% to 4% over 250 years? What would be the corresponding yearly rate compounded once a year?

11.2 Can you give economic interpretations of the exponential function $y = e^x$? (Hint: You can give three of them if you think of the continuously compounded total return, spot rate and forward rate.)

11.3 Demonstrate the following proposition (its importance stems from the fact that the spot rate most often has the general outlook described hereafter).

Let the spot rate $s(0, t)$ be represented by an increasing, concave function of maturity t, levelling off at $s(0, \bar{t}) = \bar{s}$ for an abscissa $\bar{t}$, and equal to level $\bar{s}$ beyond $\bar{t}$. Then:

(a) the forward rate goes at least through one maximum in the interval $(0, \bar{t})$ and is decreasing in an interval to the left of $\bar{t}$. If $t \geq \bar{t}$, the forward rate is equal to the spot rate $\bar{s}$.

(b) the total return is an increasing function of t, with at least one inflection point for $0 < t < \bar{t}$. If $t \geq \bar{t}$, the total return becomes a linear function of t.

11.4 The reason why practitioners use third-order polynomials for splines is little known, and merits mentioning here. It stems from the following important property. If a polynomial represents a curve joining a given set of points, a third-order polynomial minimizes both its curvature and its deformation energy. Indeed, either of these concepts is basically represented – within the confines of affine transformations – by the functional

$$I[s(z)] = \int_a^b [s''(z)]^2 dz$$

where $s''(z)$ is the second derivative of the spot rate – or of the spline (denoted $s(z)$ for convenience). Show that minimizing I leads to a third-degree polynomial. (Hint: use the Euler–Poisson equation; see chapter 7).

11.5 In this chapter, we obtained the Fisher equation from the valuation of capital expressed as

$$p(t) = \int_t^\infty q(\tau) e^{-\int_t^\tau i(z)dz} d\tau,$$

by taking the derivative of both sides of the above equation with respect to t. Derive the Fisher equation when cashflows are discounted with the spot rate. (Hint: you have to be careful and consider the spot rate as the two-variable function $s(t, \tau)$).

11.6 Derive the Fisher equation by equating the cost of one unit of capital to its discounted future rewards, evaluated as the present value of income streams for a period h plus the present value of its residual value at time $t + h$.

Answers

11.1 Let i_0 be the initial interest rate and i_{250} the interest rate after 250 years. Let x be the yearly, continuously compounded, rate; x must be such that

$$i_{250} = i_0 e^{x.250}$$

$$\text{or} \qquad x = \frac{1}{250} \log\left(\frac{i_{250}}{i_0}\right).$$

In the example, $x = -0.002238 = -0.2238\%$ per year.

Let $x^{(1)}$ be the corresponding growth rate compounded once a year. $x^{(1)}$ must be such that

$$i_{250} = i_0(1 + x^{(1)})^{250}$$

or

$$x^{(1)} = \left(\frac{i_{250}}{i_0}\right)^{\frac{1}{250}} - 1 = -0.2236\%.$$

Equivalently, $x^{(1)}$ could have been determined from what we have seen as $x_1 = e^x - 1$.

(This example illustrates the fact that continuously compounding implies very little difference in results if the rates are very small; also, we will use these numbers in chapter 15.)

11.2 $y = e^x$ is what \$1 becomes if the continuously compounded total return is x, for any investment horizon T we may want to choose. It means that the spot rate, $s(0, T)$ (the average of the instantaneous forward rates $\int_0^T f(z)dz/T$), is equal to x/T. For example, $e^{0.5}$ is what \$1 becomes if $T = 10$ years, $s(0, T) = \int_0^T f(z)dz/T = \int_0^{10} f(z)dz/10 = 0.05$ per year. Equivalently it is what \$1 becomes after 10 months if the *monthly* continuously compounded spot rate is 0.05; it is also what \$1 becomes after 10 days if the daily continuously compounded spot rate is 0.05.

11.3 Let us first consider the behaviour of the slope of the forward rate curve at the origin, i.e. when $t \to 0$. The above assumptions imply $ds(0, 0)/dt > 0$. On the other hand, taking the derivative of $f(0, t) = s(0, t) + t\,ds(0, t)/dt$ with respect to t, we deduce

$$\frac{df(0, t)}{dt} = \frac{ds(0, t)}{dt} + \frac{d^2s(0, t)}{dt^2}t + \frac{ds(0, t)}{dt} = 2\frac{ds(0, t)}{dt} + \frac{d^2s(0, t)}{dt^2}t$$

and therefore, with $t = 0$

$$\frac{df(0, 0)}{dt} = 2\frac{ds(0, 0)}{dt}.$$

Notice how surprisingly simple this intermediate result is: *whatever* the spot rate curve, and in particular *whatever the sign* of the spot curve slope at the origin, the initial slope of the forward rate curve will *always* be twice that of the spot curve.

This result can be generalized while retaining its simplicity. At the origin the nth derivative of the forward rate is $(n + 1)$ times the nth derivative of the spot rate, i.e. $d^n f(0, 0)/dt^n = (n + 1)d^n s(0, 0)/dt^n$.

Coming back to (30), we know that for $t = \bar{t}$, $ds(0, \bar{t})/dt = 0$ and its left-hand side second derivative is negative $(d^2s(0, \bar{t}_-)/dt^2 < 0)$, as implied in our concavity hypothesis. This leads to a left-hand side derivative of $f(0, \bar{t})$ equal to

$$\frac{df(0, \bar{t}_-)}{dt} = \frac{d^2s(0, \bar{t}_-)}{dt^2}\bar{t} < 0$$

and therefore the forward rate is *decreasing* in an interval on the left-hand side of $\bar{t}$.

We know that $df(0, 0)/dt$ is strictly positive and that $df(0, \bar{t}_-)/dt$ is strictly negative. It follows that $df(0, t)/dt$ changes sign from positive to negative at least once within the interval $[0, t]$, and therefore that $f(0, t)$

goes through a local maximum at least for one value of the maturity. We denote such a value $\hat{t}$ ($\hat{t} \in (0, \bar{t})$) – assuming it is unique.

The final part of part a) of the property is evident: if $ds(0, t)/dt = 0$ for $t > \bar{t}$, then $f(0, t) = s(0, t)$.

Part (b) is just a direct consequence of (a). If $f(0, t)$ goes through a unique maximum in the interval $[0, t]$ (at $t = \hat{t}$), its integral (the total return $S(0, t)$) has an inflection point at $\hat{t}$; it is a convex function between 0 and $\hat{t}$ and a concave function between $\hat{t}$ and $\bar{t}$. Finally, if (for $t \geq \bar{t}$) $f(0, t)$ is equal to a constant $s(0, t) \equiv \bar{s}$, then

$$S(0, t)|_{t \geq \bar{t}} = \int_0^t f(0, z)dz \bigg|_{t \geq \bar{t}}$$

$$= \int_0^{\bar{t}} f(0, z)dz + \int_{\bar{t}}^t f(0, z)dz \bigg|_{t \geq \bar{t}}$$

$$= \bar{s}\bar{t} + \bar{s}t - \bar{s}\bar{t}|_{t \geq \bar{t}} = \bar{s}t|_{t \geq \bar{t}},$$

a *linear* function of maturity t. The proof is thus complete.

These properties allow for the following interpretation. Consider the continuous maturity as a discrete variable, albeit with infinitesimally short increments. First, let us explain the property that at the origin the forward rate is equal to the spot rate, and that the forward curve has twice the slope of the spot curve. Let $\varepsilon(\varepsilon \to 0)$ be the first maturity, 2ε the second one. For only one maturity, the spot rate is the average of one forward rate only; therefore it is equal to it. So $s(0, 1) = f(0, 0)$. Suppose now that the spot rate for maturity 2ε has increased by an amount Δs. If an average increases by Δs for one additional element, it implies that the second element has increased by twice the increase of the average, i.e. by $2\Delta s$. (The same argument applies, of course, to the case where the average *decreases* by Δs.) Therefore at the origin the slope of the forward rate must be twice the slope of the spot rate. Furthermore, at the point where the spot rate (the average of the forward rates) reaches a maximum, the last forward rate must equal the spot rate. The fact that between the origin and that point the forward rate goes at least through one maximum is just a consequence of Rolle's theorem applied to the difference between the forward rate and the spot rate.

The property that the forward rate must be decreasing just before the spot rate has reached its maximum (or its plateau) has the following interpretation. Consider an increasing spot rate. It means that the last forward rate is *above* it: this is what has made the spot rate increase. If the spot rate, for the next maturity, does *not* change (because it has reached a maximum, or a plateau), the forward rate *must* be decreasing. Indeed, suppose the contrary: if the forward rate increases *or* stays constant, the spot rate will still increase, entailing a contradiction with our hypothesis. Therefore, the forward rate can only decrease.

This property could be generalized in a natural way to the relationship between the derivative of a function $f'(x)$ and the unit value of that function, $f(x)/x$.

A corollary of this property is the following:

Let the spot rate be represented by a decreasing, convex function of maturity t, levelling off at $s(0, \bar{t}) = \bar{s}$ for an abscissa $\bar{t}$, and equal to level $\bar{s}$ beyond $\bar{t}$. Then:

(a) the forward rate goes at least through one minimum in the interval $(0, t)$ and is increasing in an interval to the left of $\bar{t}$. If $t \geq \bar{t}$, the forward rate is equal to the spot rate $\bar{s}$.

(b) the total return is an increasing function of t, with at least one inflection point for $0 < t < \bar{t}$. If $t \geq \bar{t}$, the total return becomes a linear function of t.

The proof follows the same lines as above.

11.4 Minimizing the integral I is a particular case of minimizing a functional

$$J[s(z)] = \int_a^b F[z, s(z), s'(z), s''(z)]dz.$$

Such a problem is solved by the Euler–Poisson fourth-order differential equation

$$\frac{\partial F}{\partial s}(z, s, s', s'') - \frac{d}{dz}\frac{\partial F}{\partial s'}(z, s, s', s'') + \frac{d^2}{dz^2}\frac{\partial F}{\partial s''}(z, s, s', s'') = 0.$$

In our case, the arguments z, s and s' are missing in F, which depends solely upon s''. So the Euler–Poisson equation becomes

$$\frac{d^2}{dz^2}\frac{\partial F}{\partial s''}(s'') = 0. \tag{A1}$$

In the case of $I = \int_a^b [s''(z)]^2 dz$, we have $F(s'') = [s'']^2$; therefore

$$\frac{\partial F}{\partial s''}(s'') = 2s''(z);$$

thus a first-order condition for $s(z)$ to minimize the functional I is that it solves the fourth-order differential equation

$$\frac{d^2}{dz^2}[2s''(z)] = 2s^{(4)}(z) = 0,$$

which leads to the third-order polynomial

$$s(z) = \alpha_3 z^3 + \alpha_2 z^2 + \alpha_1 z_1 + \alpha_0.$$

11.5 The value of capital is expressed as

$$p(t) = \int_t^\infty q(\tau) e^{-s(t,\tau).(\tau-t)} d\tau;$$

application of the Leibniz formula yields

$$\dot{p}(t) = \int_t^\infty q(\tau) e^{-s(t,\tau).(\tau-t)} \left\{ -\frac{\partial}{\partial t} [s(t,\tau).(\tau-t)] \right\} d\tau - q(t).$$

To evaluate the partial derivative inside the integral, use (17a). You end up with $-f(t)$, equal to $-i(t)$. Factoring $i(t)$ out of the integral gives

$$\dot{p}(t) = i(t)p(t) - q(t)$$

and the Fisher equation follows as before.

The economic interpretation of the property $\frac{\partial}{\partial t}[s(t,\tau).(\tau-t)] = -i(t)$ is the following: the rate of *loss* of the total return when investment is postponed from time t by an infinitesimal amount of time is just the forward rate for a loan starting at t, i.e. $i(t) = f(t) = s(t,t)$.

11.6 The cost is $p(t)$; in present value, the rewards are $\int_t^{t+h} q(\tau) e^{-\int_t^\tau i(z)dz} d\tau + p(t+h)e^{-\int_t^{t+h} i(z)dz}$. The equality reflecting equilibrium is

$$p(t) = \int_t^{t+h} q(\tau) e^{-\int_t^\tau i(z)dz} d\tau + p(t+h) e^{-\int_t^{t+h} i(z)dz}.$$

Differentiating this equality with respect to h:

$$0 = q(t+h) e^{-\int_t^{t+h} i(z)dz} + \dot{p}(t+h)e^{-\int_t^{t+h} i(z)dz}$$
$$-p(t+h).i(t+h)e^{-\int_t^{t+h} i(z)dz}.$$

Taking $h \to 0$ yields the Fisher equation.

CHAPTER 12

From arbitrage to equilibrium

In chapter 11, we described outcomes of investing either on the financial market or the capital goods market. We had also made the hypothesis that market forces would be at play to establish an equilibrium between those outcomes. Our aim in this chapter is to describe those forces. We begin with the case of a risk-free world in the sense that the existence of forward markets enables some investors to protect themselves against uncertainty (section 1). We then introduce uncertainty (section 2).

I The case of risk-free transactions

We have considered four prices in the Fisher–Solow equation of interest: $p(t)$ is the price of the capital good at time t; $p(t + h)$ is the forward price for time $t + h$, decided upon at time t; $q(t + h)$ is the forward rental rate of the capital good, to be received at time $t + h$; and $i(t)$, the interest rate, is the price of loanable funds at time t. Until now, we have just supposed that an equilibrium would exist between these four prices, stemming from an equality between the available returns on the financial market and on the capital goods market. We will now describe the forces that come into play to establish this equilibrium.

Two types of forces should be distinguished. The first is arbitrage; we define arbitrage as the action of individuals who will earn benefits without committing their own resources. The second is investing, i.e. the action of agents who buy capital goods (or assets) with their own resources. In order to simplify the exposition, we suppose that the capital good may be borrowed, and also that we are able to sell it on a forward market.

Suppose that at time 0 we *observe* the four following prices: p_0, p_1, q_1, and i_0, resulting from supply and demand curves as described in figure 12.1. The question now is: can these four prices be considered in equilibrium in the sense that, if nothing else is disturbed in the economy, these numbers will remain constant

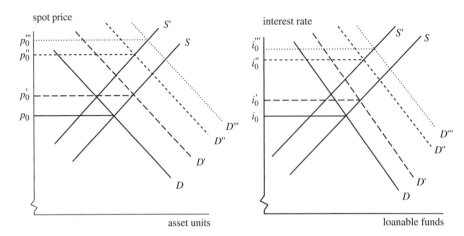

Figure 12.1a   (Spot) asset market.   **Figure 12.1b   Financial market.**

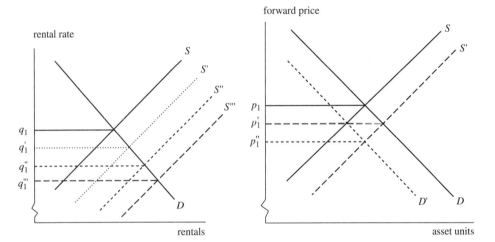

Figure 12.1c   Rentals market.   **Figure 12.1d   Forward asset market.**

Figure 12.1a–d   The consequences of arbitrageurs' actions and investors' behaviour.

at least for a short time? To answer this question, let us retrace the steps of Solow's first method, supposing that h is one year. An investor of \$1 on the risk-free financial market will earn $1 + i_0$ after one year. If he invests in the capital good, he will buy $1/p_0$ units of the capital good; in order to protect himself against any uncertainty, he does two things: he sells his capital good on the forward market at price p_1, and rents it for one year at rate q_1, with such guarantees that the contract is riskless.

Table 12.1 The gain of arbitrageurs in the case of an undervalued capital good or asset; $1 + i_0 < \frac{q_1}{p_0} + \frac{p_1}{p_0}$

Time 0		Time 1	
Action	Cashflow	Action	Cashflow
1. Borrow \$1	+1	1. Receive rentals	$+\dfrac{q_1}{p_0}$
2. Buy $1/p_0$ units of asset	−1	2. Receive value of asset sold on the forward market	$+\dfrac{p_1}{p_0}$
3. Sign rental contract	0	3. Reimburse loan	$-(1+i_0)$
4. Sell $1/p_0$ units of asset on forward market at prices p_1	0		
Net cashflow: 0		Net cashflow: $\dfrac{q_1+p_1}{p_0} - (1+i_0) > 0$	

1.1 The case of an undervalued asset

Suppose now that the proceeds of investing in the capital good are higher than those on the financial market; this translates as the inequality

$$1 + i_0 < \frac{q_1}{p_0} + \frac{p_1}{p_0}. \tag{1}$$

Two sets of forces will come into play to establish equilibrium. The first is due to the appearance of arbitrageurs. The second results from the behaviour of investors who were operating initially on these markets.

1.1.1 Arbitrageurs

We describe in table 12.1 the actions taken by arbitrageurs and the resulting cashflows.

First, arbitrageurs will borrow \$1 at rate i_0 (cashflow: +1). They will buy $1/p_0$ units of capital, for a cashflow equal to −1. Also they will sign a rental contract at a rate q_1, to be paid at time 1. No cashflow at time 0 results from that action. Finally, they will sell $1/p_0$ units of capital on the forward market; this does not generate either any cashflow. In total, their net cashflow at time 0 will be nil.

At time 1, they will collect q_1/p_0 in rentals and will sell the capital good for p_1/p_0, implying a cashflow of $(q_1 + p_1)/p_0$, and will reimburse $1 + i_0$. This translates into a positive, net profit equal to

$$\frac{q_1 + p_1}{p_0} - (1 + i_0) = \frac{q_1}{p_0} + \frac{p_1 - p_0}{p_0} - i_0$$

although arbitrageurs have not committed one cent of their own money. Notice that, per dollar invested, the arbitrageurs manage to reap exactly the difference between the observed total rate of return on the capital good and the existing rate of interest.

These actions will trigger changes in the four markets considered. The fact that arbitrageurs start borrowing will displace to the right the demand curve of loanable funds on the financial market (figure 12.1b). This will lead to an increase of i_0, perhaps to i'_0. Their willingness to buy the asset will lead as well to an increase of its price, to p'_0 (figure 12.1a). Also, the market for rentals will also be modified in the sense that the supply curve will move to the right, therefore entailing a decrease of q_1 to q'_1 (figure 12.1c). Finally, the fact that arbitrageurs start selling the asset on the forward market will push down the price p_1 on that market to p'_1 (figure 12.1d). This is a first series of forces that will tend to increase the left-hand side of inequality (1), and to decrease its right-hand side.

1.1.2 *Investors' behaviour*

Other forces will be at play as well to establish equilibrium. Indeed, there is no reason why investors initially on the four markets should continue behaving as described in the diagrams of figure 12.1. First, consider the suppliers of loanable funds. Since investing in the asset market is more rewarding, investors will decrease their supply of loanable funds (S moves to S' in figure 12.1b), and they will start investing on the asset market (the demand curve will move once more to the right, to D'' – figure 12.1a), and finally they will displace once more the supply curve on the rentals market (to S''). The outcome of those actions will be to accentuate the increase of i_0 and p_0 (to i''_0 and p''_0 respectively) and the decrease of q_1 (to q''_1). Finally, consider the behaviour of those agents who wanted to buy the asset on the forward market. Since the initial price on the forward market, p_1, is such that $p_1 > p_0(1 + i_0) - q_1$, their interest is to buy the asset on the spot market. The demand on the forward market will shrink to D', triggering a lower price p''_1. To buy one unit of the asset they may borrow on the financial market, entailing D''' and i'''_0. On the asset market, demand will be displaced to D''', leading to a spot price p'''_0. They will sign a rental contract, displacing the rentals supply curve to S''', and driving the price to q'''_1. Their actions will thus have the same effect as described earlier: an increase in the interest rate and in the spot price; a decrease in the rental rate and in the forward price.

It is to be noted that the actions described above do not exhaust all possibilities of establishing equilibrium. For instance, we may think of the behaviour of suppliers of the asset on the spot market. They may soon discover that rather than selling the asset at the spot price p_0, they should sell on the forward market, and borrow – precisely because what they will have to reimburse, $p_0(1 + i)$, is smaller than what they will receive at time 1 $(p_1 + q_1)$. They will thus displace to the left the supply curve on the spot market, and to the right the supply curve on the forward market, and so forth.

Of course the presentation here is voluntarily simplified; the actions of arbitrageurs and investors will take place simultaneously, and some agents may very well be playing both roles at the same time. Nevertheless, barring any indivisibilities, lack of information and transactions costs, those actions as described above are bound to lead to the equilibrium characterized by the Fisher equation.

1.2 The case of an overvalued asset

Suppose now that we observe the reverse inequality:

$$1 + i_0 > \frac{q_1}{p_0} + \frac{p_1}{p_0}$$

and therefore that it is more rewarding to invest in the financial market than to commit funds in the capital good. We will describe how arbitrageurs and investors alike will re-establish equilibrium. Care must be exercised, because the actions to be taken are not exactly symmetrical to those described in section 1.1, although the outcomes on prices will be.

1.2.1 Arbitrageurs' actions

The asset being overvalued (p_0 is too high for the equality between $1 + i_0$ and $(q_1 + p_1)/p_0$ to hold), it should be sold. Arbitrageurs will step in and borrow the asset for a year; this will not lead to any (positive or negative) cashflow. They will sell the asset for a positive cashflow p_0, then lend the proceeds, implying a negative cashflow of $-p_0$. At the same time, they will buy on the forward market the asset at price p_1 in order to be able to give it back to its owner at time 1. Buying the asset on the forward market does not entail any cashflow. In total the net cashflow at time 0 for arbitrageurs is zero, as it should.

At time 1, the arbitrageur receives the proceeds of the loan, $p_0(1 + i_0)$. This enables him to buy the asset which he had committed at time 0 to buy at price p_1 (cashflow: $-p_1$). He then returns the asset to its owner; also, he has to pay the owner the rentals the latter could not collect (cashflow: $-q_1$). In all, his net cashflow at time 1 will be $p_0(1 + i_0) - p_1 - q_1$, a positive amount by the very fact that we had observed the inequality $1 + i_0 > q_1/p_0 + p_1/p_0$. The effects of

Table 12.2 *The gain of arbitrageurs in the case of an overvalued capital good or asset;* $1 + i_0 > \frac{q_1}{p_0} + \frac{p_1}{p_0}$

Time 0		Time 1	
Action	Cashflow	Action	Cashflow
1. Borrow asset	0	1. Receive proceeds of loan	$+p_0(1+i)$
2. Sell asset on spot market	$+p_0$	2. Buy asset	$-p_1$
3. Loan proceeds	$-p_0$	3. Give back asset to owner	0
4. Buy asset on forward market at price p_1	0	4. Pay forgone rentals to owner	$-q_1$
Net cashflow: 0		Net cashflow: $p_0(1+i_0) - p_1 - q_1 > 0$	

the arbitrageur's behaviour on prices will be the following: a decrease in p_0 and i_0; an increase in p_1.

1.2.2 Investors' behaviour

Naturally, traditional investors will not remain inactive; demand for the asset will shrink on the spot market and will expand on the forward market, thus reinforcing the decrease of p_0 and the increase in p_1. Consider now the behaviour of those owners of the asset who intended to sell on the forward market; they will now sell on the spot market, invest; they will earn $p_0(1 + i_0) > q_0 + p_1$; their action will reinforce the movements in prices described earlier. Other investors' behavior can easily be inferred.

2 Introducing uncertainty and a risk premium

Until now we have supposed that investments were risk free. There was no possibility of default from the borrowers' part, and the existence of forward markets enabled some investors to have perfect foresight on the future cashflows generated by their investments. This of course is a simplification of reality. The purpose of this section is to show how equilibrium prices may be modified by the introduction of uncertainty.

It can be safely assumed that an investor is unwilling to undertake a risky project if his expected return is not above the risk-free rate $i(t)$ we have referred to until now. Symmetrically, lenders will definitely want to receive a higher return on a risky loan. Neither of these claims prevents, however, an equilibrium to

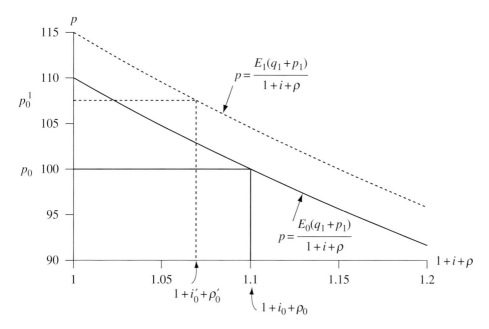

Figure 12.1b   The equilibrium price of capital as a function of $E(q_1 + p_1)$, i and ρ.

be established in such markets where investments are at risk. Both lenders and borrowers may agree on a price of loanable funds that may be separated from the risk-free rate by a risk premium, which may be variable through time, and which we denote $\rho(t)$. The Fisher equation would read

$$i(t) + \rho(t) = \frac{E[q(t)]}{p(t)} + \frac{E[\dot{p}(t)]}{p(t)}$$

Thus, the risk-free rate $i(t)$ would be augmented by the risk-premium $\rho(t)$; and instead of certain rental rates $q(t)$ and capital gains $\dot{p}(t)$, the investor would take into consideration their expected values $E[q(t)]$ and $E[\dot{p}(t)]$.

In order to have a precise view of the way a risk-premium diminishes the price of capital, let us carry out our analysis in discrete time and consider as before an investment horizon of one year. $E[q(t)]$ would simply be $E(q_1)$, the expected value of the rental rate to be paid in one year. $E[\dot{p}(t)]$ would be $E[p_1 - p_0] = E(p_1) - p_0$. So the Fisher equation reads, with $t = 0$

$$i_0 + \rho_0 = \frac{E(q_1 + p_1)}{p_0} - 1 \tag{2}$$

Equivalently, the equilibrium value of capital is given by

$$p_0 = \frac{E(q_1 + p_1)}{1 + i_0 + \rho_0}, \tag{3}$$

i.e. by the discounted value of the asset's expected rental and future price.

The price of capital is thus represented by the hyperbola in $(p, 1 + i + \rho)$ space (figure 12.2). It can be easily seen either from figure 12.2 or equation (3) how the equilibrium price of the asset may change if any of the four parameters in the right-hand side of (3), $E(q_1)$, $E(p_1)$, i_0 or ρ_0 receives a shock of any kind. For instance, an increase in $E(q_1)$, $E(p_1)$ or a decrease in i_0 or ρ_0 will lead to an increase in the equilibrium price of the asset.

The difficult question now is to know how the market determines the risk-premium of an asset. Indeed, should we have that knowledge, together with the market's expected values $E(q_1)$ and $E(p_1)$, we would immediately know whether an asset is undervalued or overvalued, and act in consequence.

The first attempt to determine the risk-premium for financial assets was carried out by William Sharpe in 1964; it built upon the optimal diversification principles enunciated in 1952 by Harry Markovitz. Both authors received in 1990 the Nobel Prize in economics for those outstanding contributions, which find a detailed exposition in all textbooks in finance.

Here, in this highly aggregated model of the economy, what is the risk-premium? The expected rental rate, denoted $E(q/p)$, is just the expected marginal productivity of capital, which we write as $E(F_K)$. So we have

$$i(t) + \rho(t) = E(F_K) + E(\dot{p}/p)$$

The risk-premium, in *real* terms, is simply $\rho(t) - E(\dot{p}/p) = E(F_K) - i(t)$; so it is the difference between the expected value of the marginal productivity of capital and the risk-free rate. How we can evaluate this risk premium will be described in our next chapter.

CHAPTER 13

Optimal savings: a general approach

Enrich the time to come with smooth-faced peace,
with smiling plenty and fair prosperous days
Richmond (King Richard III)

In chapter 10 we described the serious difficulties entailed by the use of utility functions in the definition of optimal savings policies. We then suggested to look for optimal investment paths that would maximize the sum of time-discounted consumption flows. This is what we will now do.

We will be led to show that the theory of economic growth should not be separated into two strands: positive, or descriptive theory on the one hand, and normative theory on the other. Traditionally, the literature has indeed asked two different types of questions: what would be the evolution of the economy if the investment-savings rate were a given, exogenous, rate s? And another question was: what should be the savings rate if some global welfare objective were to be attained? It is essential here to understand that when asking the first question, we assume the economy to be competitive, and in consequence the basic marginal equalities apply: the marginal productivity of labour is equal to the wage rate; the marginal productivity of capital is equal to the real rate of interest. But those very hypotheses *are* in fact the *answer* to the apparently unrelated question: how can a society maximize the sum of the discounted consumption flows it can acquire? We will show that the optimal savings rate is *endogenous* to a competitive economy.

In this chapter, we will deal in detail with this important issue. The main result is that the optimal savings rate will now have reasonable, very reachable values. We will then be able to carry out comparative dynamics. A change in the elasticity of substitution will be shown to have more impact on the optimal savings rate than a change in any other parameter. And, even more surprising, the ultimate benefits that society can derive from an increase in the elasticity of substitution are considerably larger than those which would be generated by the same increase in the rate of technical progress.

I Competitive equilibrium and its resulting savings rate

Our starting point is the fundamental equation of equilibrium on the competitive financial and capital goods markets. We can express it either in differential form or in integral form.

In differential form, it is

$$i(t) = F_K(t) + \frac{\dot{p}(t)}{p(t)}. \tag{1}$$

In integral form, it can be written equivalently as

$$p(t) = \int_t^\infty F_K(\tau) e^{-\int_t^\tau i(z)dz} d\tau \tag{2}$$

or

$$p(t) = \int_t^{t+h} F_K(\tau) e^{-\int_t^\tau i(z)dz} d\tau + p(t+h) e^{-\int_t^{t+h} i(z)dz}, \tag{3}$$

depending upon the constant of integration we have chosen, as we have seen in chapter 11. In equation (2) the price of capital is valued as the sum of discounted cashflows over an infinitely long horizon. In equation (3), $p(t)$ is equal to the sum of discounted cashflows over a time span of length h, plus the discounted residual value of capital at time $t + h$.

Since our analysis will always be in *real* terms, we will consider that i is the *real* interest rate (net of $\dot{p}/p$) and keep the same notation

$$i(t) = F_K \tag{4}$$

in the differential form (1), where $i(t)$ now designates the *real* rate of interest. In integral form therefore, we can consider p as a constant that can be normalized to one (as we did in chapter 8). Our equations (2) and (3) become

$$1 = \int_t^\infty F_K(\tau) e^{-\int_t^\tau i(z)dz} d\tau \tag{5}$$

if cashflows are counted over an infinite horizon or equivalently

$$1 = \int_t^{t+h} F_K(\tau) e^{-\int_t^\tau i(z)dz} d\tau + e^{-\int_t^{t+h} i(z)dz} \tag{6}$$

if cashflows are received over a horizon of length h, with a residual value of capital (equal to 1) at time $t + h$ – remember that F is net income (net of depreciation). Differentiating (6) with respect to h and taking h to zero yields (4).

Let us now concentrate on the Fisher–Solow equation in real terms (4) which we may write, with the dependent variables, as

$$i(t) = F_K(K_t, L_t, t). \tag{7}$$

The dependency of the marginal productivity of capital on the time variable may reflect the hypothesis of factor-augmenting technical progress, a hypothesis we will retain throughout.

Before going any further, let us think about the meaning of "the interest rate" in this highly aggregated model of the economy. We will always consider it as the society's rate of preference for the present in real terms. Its dependency on time reflects possible changes in its very long term trend. It might be measured, in a first approximation, as a moving average of real interest rates over a very long time span (perhaps a century). We may venture to think that the rate of preference for the present has slowly declined in those societies which experienced an increase in their welfare over the centuries.

It definitely does not reflect the daily or yearly movements of the short-term or long-term interest rates, because the capital stock of a society does not and could not adjust to the stochastic behaviour of interest rates. In chapter 8, we had supposed, as a simplification, that $i(t)$ was a constant – in a way, an average, long-term rate. But we should definitely examine in detail the consequences of a variable rate of preference for the present. This will be done in due course in this chapter.

Consider the very definition of the savings rate: it is the ratio of (net) investment to net income, and it can be written

$$s = \frac{I_t}{Y_t} = \frac{\dot{K}_t}{F(K_t, L_t, t)}. \tag{8}$$

The savings rate resulting from competitive equilibrium will thus be determined as the solution of the system of equations (7) and (8):

$$i(t) = F_{K_t}(K_t, L_t, t) \tag{7}$$

$$s = \frac{\dot{K}_t}{F(K_t, L_t, t)} \tag{8}$$

Depending upon the structure of the production $F(.)$, many ways to solve this system are available, as will be demonstrated. But more fundamentally we will now show that the above system exactly corresponds to the maximization of the sum of the discounted consumption flows, and henceforth to an optimal growth policy for society.

2   The optimal savings rate: derivation from optimal growth

The general problem of finding the optimal savings rate of an economy can be written as follows: determine the optimal trajectory of capital K_t^* that maximizes the functional

$$V = \int_0^\infty C_t e^{-\int_0^t i(z)dz} dt \tag{9}$$

under the constraint

$$C_t = Y_t - I_t = F(K_t, L_t, t) - \dot{K}_t \tag{10}$$

where $F(K_t, L_t, t)$ is a concave function in K and L.

Straightforward substitution of (10) into (9) leads to maximize

$$\int_0^\infty [F(K_t, L_t, t) - \dot{K}_t] e^{-\int_0^t i(z)dz} dt \tag{9a}$$

without any constraints. If $G(K, \dot{K}, t)$ denotes the integrand of (10), the Euler equation

$$\frac{\partial G}{\partial K}(K, \dot{K}, t) - \frac{d}{dt}\frac{\partial G}{\partial \dot{K}}(K, \dot{K}, t) = 0$$

leads to the Fisher–Solow equation in real terms (7), $i(t) = F_K(K_t, L_t, t)$.

Furthermore, since $G(K, \dot{K}, t)$ is concave[1] in $(K, \dot{K})$, we know from Takayama's theorem – see chapter 7 – that (7) constitutes a condition which is both necessary and sufficient for a global maximum of the functional (9).

On the other hand the savings rate s is defined by the ratio $s_t = I_t/Y_t$, and the optimal savings rate is given by $s_t^* = I_t^*/Y_t^* = \dot{K}_t^*/Y_t^*$ where K_t^* is the optimal time path of capital. So the solution of the problem is given by the very system of equations

$$i(t) = F_K(K_t, L_t, t) \tag{7}$$

$$s_t^* = \frac{\dot{K}_t}{F(K_t, L_t, t)}; \tag{8}$$

(7) is entailed *either* by competitive equilibrium, *or* by the intertemporal maximization of 9a as we wanted to ascertain. Figure 13.1 summarizes this result.

Notice the structure of this system (7),(8). The first equation gives K_t in implicit form; the second equation includes both K_t in implicit form and its derivative $\dot{K}_t$. Therefore two general methods can be pursued to solve this system. The first method consists in differentiating equation (7) with respect to time, solve it in terms of $\dot{K}_t$ and replace $\dot{K}_t$ into equation (8). In the second method, we would determine K_t^* from (7), then calculate $Y^* = F(K_t^*, L_t, t)$, $I_t^* = \dot{K}_t^*$ and finally $s^* = I_t^*/Y_t^*$. Furthermore, if the production function is homogeneous of degree

---

[1] From chapter 7 we remember that $G(K, \dot{K}, t)$ is concave in $(K, \dot{K})$ if and only if the following set of three conditions is met: $G_{KK} \leqq 0$; $G_{\dot{K}\dot{K}} \leqq 0$; $G_{KK}G_{\dot{K}\dot{K}} - G_{K\dot{K}}^2 \geqq 0$. Here $G_K = F_K e^{-\int_0^t i(z)dz}$; $G_{\dot{K}} = -e^{-\int_0^t i(z)dz}$. Thus $G_{KK} = F_{KK}e^{-\int_0^t i(z)dz} < 0$; $G_{\dot{K}\dot{K}} = 0$; $G_{K\dot{K}} = 0$. Hence G is concave in $(K, \dot{K})$. Another way of checking the concavity of G is to use the concavity of F in $(K, \dot{K})$, and Sydsaeter and Hammond's theorem: since G is an increasing and concave function of F, G is concave in $(K, \dot{K})$.

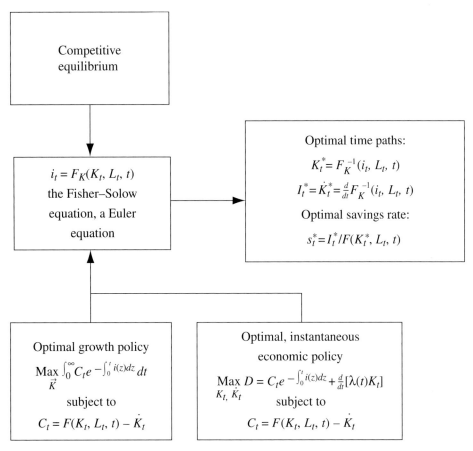

Figure 13.1   The common outcome of competitive equilibrium, optimal growth policy and optimal, instantaneous economic policy.

one, both methods will apply as well when the central variable of interest K_t is replaced by the capital–labour ratio $r_t = K_t/L_t$.

Another point is worth noting. We had noticed that the Euler equation (18) in chapter 10 led to a second-order non-linear differential equation, or equivalently to a system of two first-order, non-linear differential equations which did not have an analytic solution. Now equation (7) of this chapter – or its equivalent $i(t) = f'_r(r_t, t)$ if $F(.)$ is homogeneous of degree one in K_t, L_t – becomes an ordinary equation[2] which usually yields a unique, closed-form solution.

Let us determine s^* if hypotheses of the central model of economic growth apply. We will suppose that $F(.)$ is a CES function with labour-augmenting technical progress at variable rate $g(t)$; also, the work force will be increasing at the variable rate $n(t)$. These last two hypotheses mean that L_t is

[2] This is due to the fact that the integrand of the functional (9a) is an affine function of $\dot{K}$ (see appendix of chapter 7).

$L_0 \exp\{\int_0^t [n(\tau) + g(\tau)]d\tau\}$, and the growth rate of L_t is $\dot{L}_t/L_t = n_t + g_t$. The production function (where L_0 is normalized to 1) is then

$$Y = F(K_t, L_t, t) = \left[\delta K_t^p + (1-\delta)e^{p \int_0^t [n(\tau)+g(\tau)]d\tau}\right]^{1/p}. \qquad (11)$$

We now use the homogeneity of degree one of F with respect to K and L to determine the optimal savings rate. Denoting $r_t = K_t/L_t$, equation (7) can be written

$$i(t) = f'(r_t) \qquad (12)$$

and equation (8) becomes

$$s^* = \frac{\dot{K}_t}{Y_t} = \frac{\dot{K}_t}{K_t}\frac{K_t/L_t}{Y_t/L_t} = \left(\frac{\dot{r}_t}{r_t} + n_t + g_t\right)\frac{r_t}{f(r_t)}. \qquad (13)$$

On the other hand, differentiating (12) gives

$$\frac{i'(t)}{i(t)} = \frac{f''(r)r}{f'(r)} \cdot \frac{\dot{r}}{r} \qquad (14)$$

and, denoting for simplicity $r_t \equiv r$ and $f(r_t) \equiv y$,

$$\frac{\dot{r}}{r} = \frac{i'(t)}{i(t)}\frac{y'}{y''(r)r} \equiv \frac{i'(t)}{i(t)}\frac{y'}{y''r}. \qquad (15)$$

(Notice that if i_t is increasing, the growth rate of r will be negative, as it should since $y'' = f''(r) < 0$).

From the expression of the elasticity of substitution

$$\sigma = -\frac{y'(y - ry')}{ryy''}$$

we deduce

$$\frac{y'}{y''r} = -\sigma\frac{y}{y - ry'} = -\sigma\frac{1}{1 - ry'/y} = -\sigma\frac{1}{1 - \pi(r)} \qquad (16)$$

where $\pi(r) = F_K \cdot K/Y = f'(r)r/y$ is the capital share.

So we have

$$\frac{\dot{r}}{r} = -\frac{\sigma}{1 - \pi}\frac{i'(t)}{i(t)}. \qquad (17)$$

The value of $\dot{r}/r$ given by equation (17) can now be replaced in (13); also, using (12) we can write

$$s^* = \frac{r}{f(r)}\frac{f'(r)}{i_t}\left[n_t + g_t - \frac{\sigma}{1 - \pi(r)}\frac{i'(t)}{i(t)}\right]$$

$$= \frac{\pi(r)}{i_t}\left[n_t + g_t - \frac{\sigma}{1 - \pi(r)}\frac{i'(t)}{i(t)}\right]. \qquad (18)$$

But we know from chapter 4, equation (35), that $\pi(r)$ is equal to the geometric average of δ and i, with weights σ and $1 - \sigma$ respectively, where i is now a function of time i_t:

$$\pi(r) = \delta^\sigma i_t^{1-\sigma};\tag{19}$$

so finally the optimal savings rate s^* is

$$s^* = \left(\frac{\delta}{i_t}\right)^\sigma \left[n_t + g_t - \frac{\sigma}{1 - \delta^\sigma i_t^{1-\sigma}} \cdot \frac{i_t'}{i_t}\right]\tag{20}$$

which depends solely on the parameters of the model.

This result can be verified by focusing on the K_t^* variable and applying the second method we referred to (see exercise 2 at the end of this chapter).

Note that if $\sigma = 1$ (the Cobb–Douglas case, with $y = f(r) = r^\delta$) the formula remains directly applicable and reduces to

$$s^* = \left(\frac{\delta}{i_t}\right)\left[n_t + g_t - \frac{1}{1 - \delta}\frac{i_t'}{i_t}\right].\tag{21}$$

In line with what we stated at the beginning of this chapter, let us now consider that $i(t)$ is society's very long term rate of preference for the present, and that it has been slowly decreasing over the last centuries, presumably because of the increase in living standards. Suppose for instance that France's rate of preference for the present decreased from 7% in Turgot's century to 4% today. Such a decrease of 300 basis points over, say, a 250-year time span means that the corresponding average continuously compounded growth rate of i, denoted ξ, is such that $0.04 = 0.07 \exp(\xi 250)$, or $\xi = (1/250) \int_0^{250} [i'(t)/i(t)]dt = (1/250)\log(4/7) = -0.00224$. It is thus in the order of minus 0.2 per cent per year. Let us now examine the order of magnitude of the coefficient multiplying $i'(t)/i(t)$ in the formula of the optimal savings rate (this coefficient is $\sigma/(1 - \delta^\sigma i^{1-\sigma})$). We will consider that σ is within the range where it has been observed (between 0.7 and 1.1 – see chapter 5) and that i_t is between 3% and 6%. Tables 13.1a and 13.1b give the values of this coefficient for $\delta = 0.3$ and $\delta = 0.25$ respectively. It can be observed that the values of the coefficient remain between 0.81 and 1.77 (it is 1 for $\delta = 0.3$, $i_t = 0.04$ and $\sigma = 0.8$), so that in the optimal savings rate formula $n_t + g_t$ would be reduced by a number between a minimum of $0.81 \times 0.2\% = 0.16\%$ and a maximum of $1.77 \times 0.2\% = 0.35\%$, a number well within the margin of error of our estimate of $n_t + g_t$ (we have taken $n_t + g_t = 2.5\%$ as a central value throughout this text). We feel therefore entitled to consider the rate of preference for the present as a constant, given at time t. In the same vein, we can consider also the population growth rate n_t and the coefficient of technical progress g_t as fixed at

Table 13.1   Values of $\sigma/(1 - \delta^{\sigma}i^{1-\sigma})$, the coefficient multiplying $i'(t)/i(t)$ in the optimal savings rate s^*

(a) $\delta = 0.3$

i_t \ σ	0.7	0.8	0.9	1	1.1
0.03	0.82	0.99	1.18	1.43	1.77
0.04	0.84	1.00	1.19	1.43	1.74
0.05	0.85	1.01	1.20	1.43	1.72
0.06	0.86	1.02	1.21	1.43	1.70

(b) $\delta = 0.25$

i_t \ σ	0.7	0.8	0.9	1	1.1
0.03	0.81	0.96	1.13	1.33	1.60
0.04	0.81	0.97	1.14	1.33	1.59
0.05	0.83	0.98	1.14	1.33	1.56
0.06	0.84	0.99	1.15	1.33	1.55

long term values, n and g. The optimal savings rate, if $F(.)$ is a CES function with labour-augmenting technical progress, is then given by

$$s^* = \left(\frac{\delta}{i}\right)^{\sigma}(n + g). \tag{22}$$

We will now show how this optimal, competitive equilibrium savings rate can be constructed geometrically.

3   A geometric construction of the optimal savings rate

Suppose that the parameters of our model are constant and that the rate of technological progress g is zero (if g had a positive value, we would just work in (r_γ, y_γ) space as we have done before). The equation $i = f'(r)$ implies that we must stay at an equilibrium point r^*, $f(r^*)$, with $r^* = f'^{-1}(i)$. From this we know that the optimal savings rate s^* must be such that $s^* f(r^*) = nr^*$, or $s^* = nr^*/f(r^*)$. On figure 13.2, draw $f(r)$ and nr. From the curve $f(r)$, determine abscissa r^* such that $f'(r^*) = i = \operatorname{tg}\alpha$. Normalizing $f(r^*)$ to one, the optimal savings rate is just the distance nr^*.

Consider now changes in the long-term values of i and n. From the diagram it can be immediately seen why the optimal savings rate is a decreasing function of i and an increasing function of n. When i decreases (for instance from i_0 to i_1), the equilibrium capital–labour ratio increases from r_0^* to r_1^*. The optimal savings

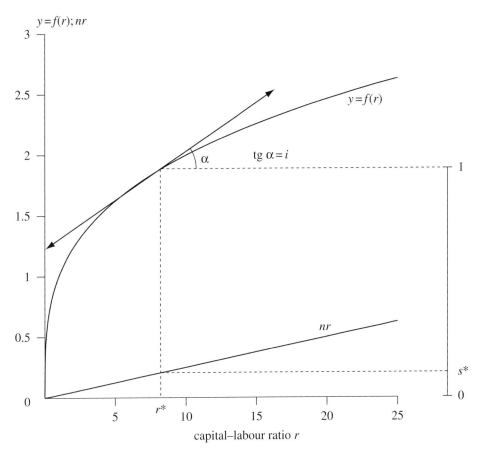

Figure 13.2 A geometrical construction of the optimal savings rate s^* **implied by competitive equilibrium. From the curve** $y = f(r)$ **determine the abscissa** r^* **for which** $f'(r^*) = i(t)$**. Since** r^* **has to be maintained at that level,** s^* **must be such that** $s^* f(r^*) = nr^*$**. So** $s^* = nr^*/f(r^*)$**. If** $y = f(r^*)$ **is normalized to 1,** s^* **is just the height** nr^***. The existence of competitive equilibrium enforces an equilibrium capital–labour ratio as well as an optimal savings rate.**

rate is then $s_1^* = nr_1^*/f(r_1^*)$, which is obviously larger than $s_0^* = nr_0^*/f(r_0^*)$. The fact that s^* is increasing with n is also evident from the diagram.

4 Values of the optimal savings rate and its sensitivity to parameter changes

Table 13.2 gives an overview of the values of s_t^* when σ is between 0.7 and 1.2, and for values of i between 2% and 10%; δ, n and g have the central values used before: $\delta = 0.3$; $n = 0.01$ and $g = 0.015$.

Contrary to the values of s^* we had in chapter 10, these are reasonable, very reachable numbers.

Table 13.2 *The optimal investment-savings rate* s^* *as a function of the rate of interest i and the elasticity of substitution* σ *(in per cent; $n + g = 2.5\%$; $\delta = 0.3$)*

i_t σ	4%	5%	6%	7%	8%	9%	10%
0.7	10.2	8.9	7.7	6.9	6.3	5.8	5.4
0.75	11.3	9.6	8.4	7.4	6.7	6.2	5.7
0.8	12.5	10.5	9.1	8.0	7.2	6.6	6.0
0.85	13.9	11.5	9.8	8.6	7.7	7.0	6.4
0.9	15.3	12.5	10.6	9.3	8.2	7.4	6.7
0.95	17.0	13.7	11.5	10.0	8.8	7.8	7.1
1	18.8	15	12.5	10.7	9.4	8.3	7.5
1.05	20.7	16.4	13.5	11.5	10.0	8.9	7.9
1.10	22.9	17.9	14.7	12.4	10.7	9.4	8.4
1.15	25.4	19.6	15.9	13.3	11.4	10.0	8.8
1.20	28.1	21.5	17.2	14.3	12.2	10.6	9.3

For example, suppose that the values of n and g are 1% and 1.5% respectively. Suppose also that the rate of preference for the present is 6% (this value may be the addition of a 4% risk premium and a riskless real interest rate of 2%); finally, suppose that $\sigma = 0.9$ and $\delta = 0.3$; then the optimal savings-investment rate is 10.6%.

We are now able to carry out comparative dynamics with the optimal savings rate s^*. We will want to know the sensitivity of s^* to changes in the parameters of the system. Denoting by $e_{z,x}$ the partial elasticity of z with respect to x ($e_{z,x} \equiv \partial \log z / \partial \log x$), we have the following partial elasticities with respect to i, n, g and σ, and their values when the parameters take their central values $\delta = 0.3$; $i = 6\%$; $\sigma = 0.9$; $n = 1\%$; $g = 1.5\%$:[3]

$$e_{s*,i} = -\sigma = -0.9$$

$$e_{s*,n_t} = \frac{n_t}{n_t + g_t} = 0.4$$

$$e_{s*,g_t} = \frac{g_t}{n_t + g_t} = 0.6$$

$$e_{s*,\sigma} = \sigma \log \left(\frac{\delta}{i} \right) = 1.8$$

By far the parameter whose change has the greatest impact upon the optimal savings rate is the elasticity of substitution. This confirms the importance of that parameter in the growth process we had underlined in chapter 4.

---

[3] Notice that δ being the partial elasticity of output with respect to capital at the base year used to measure the indexes Y, K and L, we have not considered changes in this normalizing constant.

In section 7, we will take a step still further and examine the impact of σ on the ultimate variable of optimal growth, i.e. the maximum value of the discounted consumption flows obtained by society. Before doing so, we will address the issues of estimating the risk premium of an economy, and transition growth.

5   Estimating the risk premium of the economy

In chapter 6, we underlined the fact that an economy operates in a fundamentally uncertain environment. Therefore, either at a micro- or macro-economic level, an equilibrium Fisher equation must incorporate, on the side of the rate of interest, a risk premium. In this section we will apply this very principle: we will consider that the rate of preference for the present, which we called $i(t)$, includes a risk premium. Society may very well continue to equate the marginal productivity of capital to the rate of preference for the present; but what society takes into consideration is the *expected* value of the marginal productivity of capital. For that very reason its preference for the present that would be prevalent in a risk-free world, which we could denote as r_f, is naturally augmented by a risk premium ρ.

As we have done earlier with the rate of preference for the present, we view its component, the risk premium of the economy, as a long-term variable. We may also conjecture that, likewise, it decreased through the centuries, perhaps with somewhat higher variability. It is conceivable that in the Europe of the Middle Ages the rate of preference for the present was much higher than today, and that it reached its peak in the fourteenth century, when society was devastated by the great plague and never-ending conflicts. It may have then decreased in the Renaissance. War, the fear of war, and peace may have been prime factors for its fluctuations in the last few centuries.

Let us now suppose that for some decades society has benefited from a state of competitive equilibrium, and let us try to estimate the risk premium ρ of its economy. If we make the assumption of competitive equilibrium, we will not need the expected marginal productivity of capital to estimate ρ. Indeed, the equilibrium, optimal savings rate s^* only will be needed. To see that, consider both r_f and ρ as constant. Then, replacing i_t by $r_f + \rho$ in (22) we have

$$s^* = \left(\frac{\delta}{r_f + \rho} \right)^{\sigma} (n_t + g_t) \tag{23}$$

from which the *equilibrium* risk premium, in real terms, of the economy, can be deduced:

$$\rho = \delta \left(\frac{n_t + g_t}{s^*} \right)^{1/\sigma} - r_f. \tag{24}$$

For example, consider our central case of $\delta = 0.3, \sigma = 1, n_t + g_t = 0.025$; suppose also that $r_f = 0.03$ and $s^* = 0.1.$[4] Then $\rho = 4.5\%$, a result which makes quite some of sense. Also, note that ρ is a decreasing function of the optimal savings rate s^*.

6 Growth in disequilibrium

We have shown earlier that competitive equilibrium implied an optimal savings rate. Suppose now that, for some reason, the Fisher equation does not apply any more, for instance because the marginal productivity of capital is above the social rate of preference for the present, including its risk premium. We know that to re-establish equilibrium the capital stock per person should increase. But at what speed? Variational principles would dictate that the gap between existing capital and the optimal capital stock should be filled as quickly as possible, i.e. by investing all income, which is plainly indefensible.

There is no clear-cut solution to such a problem; however, it seems appropriate to revert to the values of optimal savings s^* that correspond to equilibrium, and examine what would be the consequences of applying them. Remember that we had observed in chapter 8 that those values were always in a very reasonable, acceptable range. Let us now examine the consequences of applying s^* when $F_K > i$. If we draw $s^* f(r)$ in the phase diagram (figure 13.2) we can see that the equilibrium r^* will be reached asymptotically. For r^* to be reached in finite time the savings rate should be marginally above s^*. We observe that s^* is the *minimum* value of the savings rate for the economy to converge toward its equilibrium, optimum point. But how much above s^* should a nation save and invest remains an open question.

Symmetrically, if the rate of preference for the present were above the marginal productivity of capital, we have no clear-cut rule to determine what would be the optimal policy to be pursued. We can say however that a savings rate of s^* is the *maximum* savings rate which enables the economy to direct itself toward its competitive, optimal equilibrium. We conclude from those observations that the rate s^* is a useful benchmark if, in case of disequilibrium, we still try to define what an optimum path for the economy should be.

7 Consequences for our future

We have supposed that society tries to maximize its discounted consumption flows over an infinite horizon. The maximum value of the functional, denoted V^*, is

$$V^* = \int_0^\infty C^*(t)e^{-it}dt \tag{25}$$

---

[4] Remember that s^* is the *net* savings rate, net of depreciation.

where $C^*(t)$ is the optimal time path of consumption, which we will now determine. There are several ways to do this. We will indicate the method that looks the simplest. We first consider $\sigma \neq 1$.

Coming back to equation (7) and using the production function (11), we can determine the optimal time path of capital K_t^* as

$$K_t^* = e^{(n+g)t} \left[\frac{1-\delta}{\left(\frac{\delta}{i}\right)^{1-\sigma} - \delta} \right]^{\frac{\sigma}{\sigma-1}}. \qquad (26)$$

From this optimal path, we can deduce the optimal time path of income Y_t^* by plugging K_t^* into the production function (11). We obtain

$$Y_t^* = F(K_t^*, L_t, t) = e^{(n+g)t} \left\{ \delta \left[\frac{1-\delta}{\left(\frac{\delta}{i}\right)^{1-\sigma} - \delta} \right] + (1-\delta) \right\}^{\frac{\sigma}{\sigma-1}}. \qquad (27)$$

The optimal path of consumption C_t^* is just the difference $Y_t^* - I_t^* = Y_t^* - \dot{K}_t^*$. Here we can either calculate the derivative of (26) with respect to time, and determine the difference $Y_t^* - \dot{K}_t^*$, or, more directly since we know the optimal savings rate s^*, calculate $C^* = (1-s^*)Y_t^*$. We then obtain

$$C_t^* = \left[1 - \left(\frac{\delta}{i}\right)^{\sigma} (n+g) \right] \left\{ \delta \left[\frac{1-\delta}{\left(\frac{\delta}{i}\right)^{1-\sigma} - \delta} \right] + (1-\delta) \right\}^{\frac{\sigma}{\sigma-1}} e^{(n+g)t}. \qquad (28)$$

The calculation of V^* is now almost immediate. With

$$V^* = \int_0^\infty C_t^* e^{-it} dt$$

$$= \left[1 - \left(\frac{\delta}{i}\right)^{\sigma} (n+g) \right] \left\{ \delta \left[\frac{1-\delta}{\left(\frac{\delta}{i}\right)^{1-\sigma} - \delta} \right] + 1 - \delta \right\}^{\frac{\sigma}{\sigma-1}} \int_0^\infty e^{(n+g-i)t} dt \qquad (29)$$

we get V^* which depends upon the parameters σ, i, δ, n and g:

$$V^*(\sigma, i, \delta, n, g) = \frac{1 - \left(\frac{\delta}{i}\right)^{\sigma} (n+g)}{i - (n+g)} \left\{ \delta \left[\frac{1-\delta}{\left(\frac{\delta}{i}\right)^{1-\sigma} - \delta} \right] + 1 - \delta \right\}^{\frac{\sigma}{\sigma-1}}. \qquad (30)$$

If $\sigma = 1$, we just replace $F(K_t, L_t, t)$ by the Cobb–Douglas with labour augmenting technical progress at rate g and follow the same procedure. We then obtain

$$V^*(i, \delta, n, g) = \frac{1 - \left(\frac{\delta}{i}\right)(n+g)}{i - (n+g)} \left(\frac{\delta}{i}\right)^{\frac{\delta}{1-\delta}}. \tag{31}$$

We will now measure the sensitivity of this optimal value V^* to changes in i, σ and g. In particular we will want to know how a change in the elasticity of substitution σ compares to a change in the rate of technical progress from the point of view of society's welfare. But before that we should have a look at the speed of convergence of the integral in (25).

7.1   The (in)significance of an infinite time horizon

Let us now ask how much time is needed to be very close to the value V^*. "Very close" will be defined as within 5 per thousand or less. Denoting the sum of the discounted consumption flows from time 0 to time T as V_T^*, we have

$$V^* = \lim_{T \to \infty} V_T^*$$

and V_T^* is equal to

$$V_T^* = (1 - s_t^*) \int_0^T Y_t^* e^{-it}. \tag{32}$$

In the case $\sigma \neq 1$, an immediate calculation, replacing by T the infinite upper bound of the integral in (25), yields

$$V_T^* = \frac{1 - \left(\frac{\delta}{i}\right)^\sigma (n+g)}{i - (n+g)} \left\{ \delta \left[\frac{1 - \delta}{\left(\frac{\delta}{i}\right)^{1-\sigma} - \delta} \right] + 1 - \delta \right\}^{\frac{\sigma}{\sigma-1}}$$

$$\times \left\{ 1 - e^{-[i-(n+g)]T} \right\} \tag{33}$$

so that the relationship between V_T^* and its limiting value V^* is simply

$$V_T^* = V^* \left\{ 1 - e^{-[i-(n+g)]T} \right\}. \tag{34}$$

(The same result applies if $\sigma = 1$). Thus, the ratio V_T^*/V_T is just $1 - \exp\{-[i - (n+g)T]\}$, and does not depend on the parameters δ and σ. Table 13.3 and figure 13.3 indicate the ratio V_T^*/V^* for values of $i - (n+g)$ between 2% and 5% by steps of 0.5%, and for various values of horizon T.

It is clear that V_T^* reaches 0.995 V^* quickly. For any practical purpose, we could replace "infinity" by 265 years for such a low discount rate $i - (n+g)$ as 2%.

Table 13.3 *Ratio of the definite integral V_T^* to the indefinite integral V^* for various values of $i - (n + g)$ and T; $V_T^*/V^* = 1 - e^{-[i-(n+g)]T}$.*

	$i - (n + g)$	0.02	0.025	0.03	0.035	0.04	0.045	0.05
T								
50		0.63	0.71	0.78	0.83	0.86	0.89	0.92
100		0.86	0.92	0.95	0.97	0.98	0.99	0.99
200		0.98	0.99	1	1	1	1	1
265		1*	1	1	1	1	1	1

* A value of 1 indicates a ratio V_T^*/V^* closer to 1 than to 0.99.

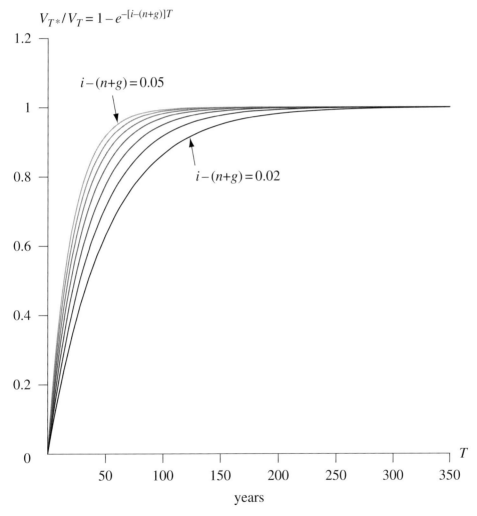

Figure 13.3 Ratio of the definite integral V_T^* to the indefinite integral $V^* (V_T^*/V_T = 1 - e^{-[i-(n+g)]T})$ for values of $i - (n + g)$ ranging from **0.02 (lower curve)** to **0.05 (upper curve)** by steps of **0.005.**

7.2 The optimal value V^* as a function of i and σ

We first give the general picture of V^* for various values of i and σ, supposing that δ and $n + g$ are fixed at 0.3 and 0.025 respectively. Table 13.4a summarizes the results. Note that the numbers are expressed in units of net national product of the initial year.

We all know that increasing interest rates spell bad news. The surprise here is the amount of the damage done to society by such increases. Suppose, for instance, that the elasticity of substitution is 0.95 and that the interest rate is 5%. Should this rate become 6% and stay there, the total consumption flows of society as measured by their maximum value V^* would fall from 78.7 to 53.6, i.e. by no less than 32%! An increasing rate of interest is indeed paid dearly. This is quite paradoxical. Indeed, if society's rate of preference for the present increases, we might think (and society might think) that its additional gain in today's consumption is just matched by a decrease in consumption of the same magnitude in the future. As this example shows, this is far from true: there is a *net loss* for society.

How could society be compensated, at least partially for a loss in total welfare entailed by a permanent increase in i? Clearly either by an increase in the elasticity of substitution σ, or by an increase in the rate of technical progress g. Which way would be more efficient is what we are now set to discover.

7.3 Is a change in the elasticity of substitution preferable to a change in the rate of technical progress?

Consider first the effects of a change in the elasticity of substitution. The elasticity of the optimal value of the functional V^* with respect to the elasticity of substitution is, assuming $\sigma \neq 1$:[5]

$$e_{V^*,\sigma} \equiv \frac{\partial \log V^*}{\partial \log \sigma} = -\sigma \frac{\left(\frac{\delta}{i}\right)^{\sigma} (n+g) \log\left(\frac{\delta}{i}\right)}{1 - \left(\frac{\delta}{i}\right)^{\sigma} (n+g)}$$

$$-\frac{\sigma}{(\sigma-1)^2} \log\left[\delta \frac{1-\delta}{\left(\frac{\delta}{i}\right)^{1-\sigma} - \delta} + 1 - \delta\right] + \frac{\sigma^2 \delta}{\sigma - 1} \cdot \frac{1-\delta}{\left[\left(\frac{\delta}{i}\right)^{1-\sigma} - \delta\right]^2}$$

$$\cdot \left(\frac{\delta}{i}\right)^{1-\sigma} \cdot \log\left(\frac{\delta}{i}\right) \cdot \left[\delta \frac{1-\delta}{\left(\frac{\delta}{i}\right)^{1-\sigma} - \delta} + (1-\delta)\right]^{-1}. \tag{35}$$

---

[5] In the case $\sigma = 1$, $e_{V^*,\sigma}$ is determined numerically.

Table 13.4a *Optimal value* $V^*(i, \sigma; \delta, n, g) = \int_0^\infty C_t^* e^{-it} dt$ *as a function of the rate of interest i and the elasticity of substitution σ; $\delta = 1/3$ and $n + g = 0.025$*

i	0.04	0.05	0.06	0.07	0.08	0.09
σ						
0.7	97.1	57.3	40.2	30.7	24.6	20.5
0.75	102.5	60.2	42.1	32.0	25.6	21.2
0.8	108.9	63.7	44.3	33.6	26.8	22.1
0.85	116.6	67.8	46.9	35.3	28.0	23.1
0.9	126.0	72.7	49.9	37.4	29.5	24.2
0.95	137.6	78.7	53.6	39.8	31.2	25.4
1	152.4	86.1	58.0	42.7	33.2	26.9
1.05	179.6	95.4	63.4	46.2	35.6	28.6
1.10	197.2	107.5	70.3	50.5	38.5	30.6
1.15	233.1	123.6	79.1	55.8	42.0	32.9
1.2	286.1	146.0	90.7	62.6	46.3	35.8

Table 13.4b *Elasticity of the optimal value* $V^* = \int_0^\infty C_t^* e^{-it} dt$ *with respect to the elasticity of substitution $\sigma (\delta = 1/3; n + g = 2.5\%)$*

i	4%	5%	6%	7%	8%	9%	10%
σ							
0.7	0.72	0.67	0.62	0.57	0.53	0.49	0.45
0.75	0.85	0.69	0.73	0.67	0.62	0.57	0.52
0.8	1.03	0.94	0.86	0.79	0.72	0.65	0.60
0.85	1.23	1.12	1.01	0.92	0.83	0.75	0.69
0.9	1.48	1.33	1.20	1.08	0.97	0.87	0.78
0.95	1.80	1.69	1.42	1.26	1.12	1.01	0.90
1	2.19	1.92	1.68	1.48	1.31	1.16	1.03
1.05	2.69	2.32	2.01	1.74	1.53	1.34	1.19
1.10	3.34	2.83	2.41	2.07	1.79	1.56	1.37
1.15	4.23	3.49	2.92	2.47	2.11	1.82	1.58
1.2	5.46	4.37	3.57	2.96	2.50	2.12	1.82

It can be seen from table 13.4b (where $\delta = 0.33$; $n = 0.01$ and $g = 0.015$) that this elasticity is a strongly increasing function of the elasticity of substitution. When $\sigma = 0.9$ and $i = 0.04$, $e_{V^*,\sigma} = 1.48$. For the same interest rate, when $\sigma = 1$, $e_{V^*,\sigma} = 2.19$ and it is 3.34 when σ is 1.1.

Notice also that this elasticity is a decreasing function of i. There is always a penalty to pay when interest rates increase.

Table 13.4c   Elasticity of the optimal value $V^* = \int_0^\infty C_t^* e^{-it} dt$ with respect to the rate of technical progress $g(\delta = 1/3; n = 0.01; g = 0.015)$

σ \ i	4%	5%	6%	7%	8%	9%	10%
0.7	0.93	0.54	0.37	0.29	0.23	0.19	0.16
0.75	0.92	0.53	0.37	0.28	0.23	0.19	0.16
0.8	0.91	0.52	0.36	0.28	0.22	0.18	0.16
0.85	0.89	0.51	0.36	0.27	0.22	0.18	0.16
0.9	0.88	0.50	0.35	0.27	0.21	0.18	0.15
0.95	0.86	0.49	0.34	0.26	0.21	0.18	0.15
1	0.84	0.48	0.33	0.25	0.20	0.17	0.15
1.05	0.82	0.47	0.32	0.24	0.20	0.16	0.14
1.10	0.79	0.45	0.31	0.24	0.19	0.16	0.14
1.15	0.76	0.43	0.30	0.23	0.19	0.15	0.13
1.2	0.72	0.41	0.28	0.22	0.18	0.15	0.13

Table 13.4d   The ratio of the sensitivities of V^* to a change in the elasticity of substitution σ and to a change in the rate of technical progress g: $e_{V^*,\sigma}/e_{V^*,g} = \dfrac{\partial \log V^*}{\partial \log \sigma} \Big/ \dfrac{\partial \log V^*}{\partial \log g} (\delta = 1/3;\ n = 0.01;\ g = 0.015)$

σ \ i	4%	5%	6%	7%	8%	9%	10%
0.7	0.8	1.2	1.7	2	2.3	2.6	2.8
0.75	0.9	1.5	2	2.4	2.7	3.0	3.2
0.8	1.1	1.8	2.4	2.8	3.2	3.5	3.8
0.85	1.4	2.2	2.8	3.4	3.8	4.2	4.4
0.9	1.7	2.6	3.4	4.1	4.5	4.9	5.2
0.95	2.1	3.2	4.2	4.9	5.4	5.8	6.1
1	2.6	4.0	5.1	5.9	6.5	6.9	7.1
1.05	3.3	5.0	6.2	7.1	7.8	8.2	8.4
1.10	4.2	6.3	7.8	8.8	9.4	9.8	9.9
1.15	5.6	8.1	9.8	10.9	11.5	11.8	11.8
1.2	7.6	10.7	12.6	13.7	14.2	14.3	14.1

Let us now turn to the effects of a change in the rate of labour-augmenting technical progress. The elasticity of V^* with respect to g is

$$e_{V^*,g} = \frac{\partial \log V^*}{\partial \log g} = g \left[\frac{\left(\frac{\delta}{i}\right)^\sigma}{\left(\frac{\delta}{i}\right)^\sigma (n+g) - 1} + \frac{1}{i - (n+g)} \right]. \tag{36}$$

Its values for various i and σ, and for the same values of the parameters δ, n and g as previously are in table 13.4c.

As is obvious by comparing tables 13.4b and 13.4c, the elasticity of substitution is a long winner over the rate of technological change. Apart from extremely low – and rather irrealistic – values of σ and i, the sensitivity of V^* to a change in σ is significantly higher than the sensitivity of V^* to a change in g. Table 13.4d gives the ratio of both elasticities.

The results are compelling. For instance, if $\sigma = 0.95$ and $i = 8\%$, the ratio is 5.4. While it is quite natural that the advantage of σ over g increases with σ, it is striking that this advantage also increases with i. This tells a lot about the benefits a society can derive from an increase in the elasticity of substitution in face of possible higher interest rates or higher risk.

8 Conclusion

In our introduction we had mentioned the observed decline of the savings rate in most OECD countries. A natural step is now to suggest an explanation of this phenomenon in light of what we have just seen. We may then offer the following conjecture. Suppose that throughout all these years during which a declining savings rate has been witnessed, countries have been following optimal savings policies, equating their marginal productivity to the rate of preference for the present. We have shown that the optimal savings rate was inversely related to that rate, and an increasing function of the elasticity of substitution (equation (40)). Furthermore, there is evidence that the elasticity of substitution has increased in all OECD countries. If the parameters n and g can be considered as fairly constant during that period, we can conclude that the observed decline in savings may well be due to a significant increase in the rate of preference for the present.

Confidence in this explanation implies that we can answer the question of optimal savings. To do that, we must agree on three issues, significant hurdles in their own right: first, the production process that drives the economy today and will drive it in the future; and secondly, the rate of preference for the present. A final hurdle is perhaps the most formidable one: do we have any assurance that large investment expenditures reflect the consent of the governed? Such assurance requires democracy, the same condition for the existence of competitive equilibrium, which we have shown to be at the very heart of optimal growth. In the last millennium, the evolution of democracy has looked like a fractal process, with sudden, unexpected downfalls, sometimes identified as "accidents of history". Nevertheless, its upward trend has carried with it economic growth. Because of the first hurdles we mentioned, we will perhaps never know how much a nation should save. But we have one certainty: progress in civilization, slow as it may seem, cannot fail to drive actual saving rates toward their optimal values.

Exercises

13.1 The following exercises are designed to show the many ways that can be used to determine the optimal investment-savings rate s^* maximizing $\int_0^\infty C_t e^{-it} dt$ subject to $C_t = F(K_t, L_t, t) - \dot{K}_t$. Suppose labour grows at rate n and $F(.)$ is Cobb–Douglas, with labour-augmenting technical progress at rate g. Determine s^*, using the fact that $F_K(K_t, L_t, t) = f'_r(r_t, t)$. You can get the answer by determining s^* such that (1) $i = f'(r_t, t)$ is maintained, and (2) $\dot{r}$ and s^* are related by the fundamental equation of motion of the economy (equation (14) of chapter 2). You should end up with $s^* = \frac{\delta}{i}(n + g)$ (the particular case of equation (22) where $\sigma = 1$).

13.2 Verify the formula for the optimal savings rate s^* as given by equation (21) by determining s^* through the second method we indicated in this chapter (you can deduce from $i(t) = F(K_t, L_t, t)$ the optimal trajectory K_t^*, and then compute $\dot{K}_t^* = I_t^*$, $Y_t^* = F(K_t^*, L_t, t)$ and $s^* = I_t^*/Y_t^*$).

Answers

13.1 If $F(K_t, L_t, t)$ is Cobb–Douglas with labour-augmenting technical progress at rate g, income Y is, with $L_t = L_0 e^{nt}$,

$$Y_t = K_t^\delta (L_t e^{gt})^{1-\delta} = K_t^\delta (L_0 e^{nt} \cdot e^{gt})^{1-\delta};$$

normalizing L_0 to 1, we get

$$Y_t = K_t^\delta e^{(n+g)(1-\delta)t} \tag{A1}$$

and income per person Y_t/L_t, denoted y_t is

$$\frac{Y_t}{L_t} \equiv y_t = K_t^\delta e^{(n+g)(1-\delta)t} \cdot e^{-nt} = K_t^\delta e^{nt-\delta nt+g(1-\delta)t-nt}$$

$$= K_t^\delta e^{-\delta nt+g(1-\delta)t} = \left(\frac{K_t}{L_t}\right)^\delta e^{g(1-\delta)t} \equiv r_t^\delta e^{g(1-\delta)t} = f(r_t, t). \tag{A2}$$

Suppressing for convenience the time variable and subscript t, the marginal productivity of capital is

$$\frac{\partial F}{\partial K} = f'(r) = \delta r^{\delta-1} e^{g(1-\delta)t}. \tag{A3}$$

We know that maximizing $\int_0^\infty C_t e^{-it} dt$ subject to $C_t = F(K_t . L_t, t) - \dot{K}_t$ leads to the Fisher–Solow equation $i = \partial F/\partial K = f'(r)$. In this case the equation turns out to be

$$i = \delta r^{\delta-1} e^{g(1-\delta)t}, \tag{A4}$$

from which we deduce the optimal trajectory for r_t:

$$r^* = \left(\frac{\delta}{i}\right)^{\frac{1}{1-\delta}} e^{gt} \tag{A5}$$

as well as the corresponding optimal trajectory of income per person (using equation (A2)):

$$y^* = f(r^*) = \left(\frac{\delta}{i}\right)^{\frac{\delta}{1-\delta}} e^{gt}. \tag{A6}$$

In order to determine the value s^* that will maintain r at its optimal level r^*, remember that r is always governed by the fundamental equation of motion $\dot{r} = sf(r) - nr$. Here, the equation can be conveniently written in terms of $r's$ growth rate, $\dot{r}/r$. We have:

$$\frac{\dot{r}}{r} = \frac{sf(r)}{r} - n. \tag{A7}$$

From equation (A5), for r^* to be on its optimal trajectory, its growth rate must be equal to g. We must have then, using (A7):

$$\frac{sf(r^*)}{r^*} - n = g \tag{A8}$$

and finally

$$s^* = \frac{r^*}{f(r^*)}(n+g) = \frac{(\delta/i)^{1/(1-\delta)}}{(\delta/i)^{\delta/(1-\delta)}}(n+g) = \frac{\delta}{i}(n+g), \tag{A9}$$

which is indeed the optimal savings rate given by equation (22) when $\sigma = 1$.

13.2 If our production function is

$$Y_t = F(K_t, L_t, t) = \left[\delta K_t^p + (1-\delta)L_0^p e^{p \int_0^t [n(\tau)+g(\tau)]d\tau}\right]^{1/p}, \tag{A10}$$

normalizing L_0 to 1, equation $i(t) = F_K(K_t, L_t, t)$ leads to

$$i(t) = \left[\delta K_t^p + (1-\delta)e^{p \int_0^t [n(\tau)+g(\tau)]d\tau}\right]^{\frac{1}{p}-1} \delta K_t^{p-1} \tag{A11}$$

from which the optimal path of capital accumulation K_t^* results:

$$K_t^* = e^{\int_0^t [n(\tau)+g(\tau)]d\tau} \left[\frac{1-\delta}{\left(\frac{\delta}{i(t)}\right)^{1-\sigma} - \delta}\right]^{\frac{\sigma}{\sigma-1}}. \tag{A12}$$

The optimal time path of production, or income, Y^* is obtained by plugging (A12) into (A10). We then get:

$$Y_t^* = e^{\int_0^t [n(\tau)+g(\tau)]d\tau} \left\{ \delta \left[\frac{1-\delta}{\left(\frac{\delta}{i(t)}\right)^{1-\sigma} - \delta} \right] + (1-\delta) \right\}^{\frac{\sigma}{\sigma-1}}.$$

Differentiating K_t^* with respect to time results, after simplifications, in the optimal investment path

$$I_t^* = e^{\int_0^t [n(\tau)+g(\tau)]d\tau} \left[\frac{1-\delta}{\left(\frac{\delta}{i(t)}\right)^{1-\sigma} - \delta} \right]^{\frac{\sigma}{\sigma-1}}$$

$$\times \left\{ n_t + g_t - \frac{\sigma}{1 - \delta^\sigma i_t^{1-\sigma}} \frac{i_t'}{i_t} \right\}.$$

The optimal savings rate can now be determined by forming the ratio I_t^*/Y_t^*. After simplifications, this yields

$$s_t^* = \left(\frac{\delta}{i_t}\right)^\sigma \left[n_t + g_t - \frac{\sigma}{1 - \delta^\sigma i_t^{1-\sigma}} \frac{i_t'}{i_t} \right]$$

as in (21).

CHAPTER 14

Problems in growth: common traits between planned economies and poor countries

Planning the economy is just one manifestation of the perennial desire to mould society into a very precise, rigid, shape. All too often, unfortunately, that shape results from the whim of a few individuals. The problem with planning is two-fold: on the one hand its aims are intuitively appealing, since they are nothing less than society's future welfare. Also, the unfortunate appeal of planning is founded on the belief that private interests are fundamentally opposed to public interests. That belief is very deep, and may be traced as far back as we can go in history. Han Fei Tzu justifies this opposition by the very *way* "private" and "public" have first been written: "In ancient times when Ts'ang Chieh created the system of writing, he used the character for 'private' to express the idea of self-centeredness, and combined the elements for 'private' and 'opposed to' to form the character for 'public'. The fact that public and private are mutually opposed was already well understood at the time of Ts'ang Chieh. To regard the two as being identical in interest is a disaster which comes from lack of consideration".[1]

A further difficulty to dismissing planning offhand is that it is almost impossible to imagine that its consequences will be the exact opposite of its intent. A planned economy, as it will turn out, will achieve neither the objectives assigned to it, nor its potential.

In this chapter, we will describe some of the problems encountered by planned economies. We will then draw a parallel between those economies and countries whose fate is to remain poor unless they put together a number of conditions necessary for growth and development.

---

[1] See Han Fei Tzu in *Basic Writings of Mo Tzu, Hsün Tzu, and Han Fei Tzu*, translated by Burton Watson, in: Records of Civilization: Sources and Studies, Columbia University Press, New York, 1965. It is believed that Han Fei Tzu's work dates from the middle of the third century BC.

That society could acquire more of some essential goods or services at a lesser cost is a natural wish. Why shouldn't a central authority decide upon the amount of goods to be produced and the prices at which these should be sold? In the event of possible refusal, producers may be coerced to do so, for instance by turning private ownership of capital (land and all industrial equipment) into public, or state property.

I The consequences of planning

Among the most important characteristics of a planned economy is the fact that the capital stock (land, technical equipment) is public, not private, property. The state will decide what to produce, in which quantities, and at what prices output will be sold on markets. For instance, consider an agricultural market (figure 14.1). The state may urge farmers to produce an amount q_0. This amount will be bought from farmers by a state agency – that may be a "popular commune" – at a price $\bar{p}$. The commune will then decide upon the price at which it will sell the produce it has received from the farmers.

The first problem, of course, is that for a price $\bar{p}$ producers are willing to produce $\bar{q}$, and not more. So it is the amount $\bar{q}$ that the commune will receive from producers, and sell on the market. The commune has now a number of options: first, it can sell this amount for the high price, $\hat{p} = p_D(\bar{q})$ that consumers are prepared to pay for this relatively low quantity.[2] Another option is to sell at any other price below $\hat{p}$, for instance at a price below p_e. We will consider both cases, and their consequences.

1.1 *First possibility: the selling price is fixed at $\hat{p}$*

The commune has received a quantity $\bar{q}$ from the farmers. It may very well decide that it can sell this quantity at the price consumers are willing to pay for it, $p(\bar{q}) = \hat{p}$. Consequences for society are important, and can be analysed in a very precise way.

The commune will make a gross profit equal to the difference between the selling and the buying price, $\hat{p} - \bar{p}$, multiplied by the quantity $\bar{q}$, i.e. $(\hat{p} - \bar{p})\bar{q}$. This is equal to area $a + c$ in figure 14.1. Observe that this amount does not correspond to any value added by the commune; this amount is just the result of transfers in income: a is financed by consumers, who have to pay $\hat{p} - p_e$ in addition to what they would have paid before the institution of the commune and if, in a free market, the equilibrium price p_e had prevailed. The remainder of the commune's receipts, c, is transferred from producers who are paid $p_e - \bar{p}$ less on the quantity $\bar{q}$ which they could have sold for p_e.

---

[2] An additional reason for the amount at the communes' disposal to be small is that sometimes part of the production is confiscated by the state and sold or bartered abroad.

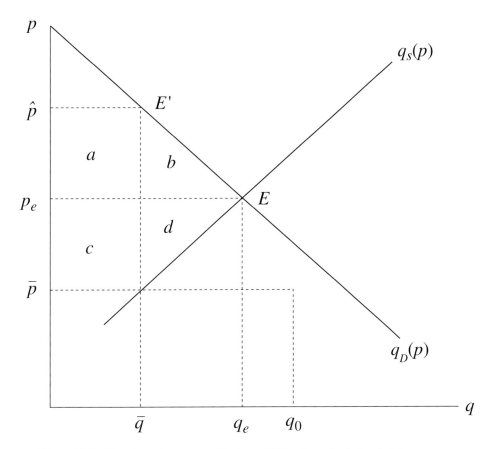

Figure 14.1 **The planned economy. First possibility: the price is fixed at $\hat{p}$.**

Comparing the situation of a free market, characterized by equilibrium point $E = (q_e, p_e)$, to the new equilibrium created by the commune (point $E' = (\bar{q}, \hat{p})$), we have:

- gain of the commune $= a + c$.

Consumers lose on two grounds: they are now able to buy $q_e - \bar{q}$ less of the good; and they have to pay $\hat{p} - p_e$ more for the quantity $\bar{q}$ they still buy. These losses translate for the first part into a loss in surplus equal to area b, and into the additional amount they have to disburse, a. Notice that if a, as we have observed, is a transfer from consumers to the commune, the area b is not transferred to anybody, it is merely lost; it will account as a net loss for society. In summary:

- loss for consumers : $a + b$.

Producers lose also on two grounds. First, they cannot earn the profits d they made before; on the other hand, their profit on $\bar{q}$ is reduced by c, the amount they transfer to the commune. Symmetrically to the consumers' fate, their loss is made of a transfer to the commune, c, and a net loss for society, d. We have

- loss for producers : $a + d$.

Let us now establish the global consequences for society from this sole, very restrictive, accounting point of view. It is restrictive because we envision a transfer of one monetary unit from one agent to another as neutral from society's point of view. We will come back to this point very soon.

Society is considered to be receiving the aggregate net gains of each agent in the economy. We have already seen that the commune's gains were just transfers from consumers and producers, and that both consumers and producers suffered net losses. We may well surmise that society will experience a net loss. This is confirmed by aggregating the results of the three agents:

- loss for society = consumers' loss + producers' loss
  − commune's gain : $(a + b) + (c + d) − (a + c) = b + d$.

As we mentioned earlier, society will experience losses that go far beyond those pure monetary losses. History amply documents the drama, including famine, experienced in the Soviet Union and China when collective farming was forced upon them. But those events are certainly not confined to those places or times. For instance, we should think of the famines endured by France under the dictatorships of the Terror and the Directoire. (On this see Pierre Gaxotte, *Histoire de la révolution française*.) The dramatic situation in France opened wide the door to a series of other disasters: a first war of conquest whose initial and foremost purpose, reckoned by the Directoire itself, was the pillage of Northern Italy, and the rise of other authoritarian regimes, namely the Consulate and the Empire, leading to the unending Napoleonic wars.[3]

Our purpose here is not to recall those events and their outcomes. We want to concentrate on the sole economic consequences of a command economy, using the example of an agricultural market. The first consequence is an impoverishment of the economy, due to the very decrease in the production of the good considered.

---

[3] It is estimated that they cost Europe four million lives – among which three million on the French side. From the far less important economic perspective, those events would cost France dearly. To illustrate, it would take 70 years for France to recover the level of foreign trade it experienced before the French revolution. In the meantime, England who at the time of the Seven Year War had an income per person about half that of France – see Turgot de l'Aulne, *Réflexions sur la formation et la distribution des richesses*, 1766 – took the lead after the Treaty of Vienna. A vivid illustration of the economic gap between France and Northern Europe in the middle of the nineteenth century is the map of the european railway network in existence in 1850. As David Landes expressed it very well, "the density of the railway networks is the best physical marker of the location and pattern of European industrial development" (*The Wealth and Poverty of Nations*, Norton, 1998, p. 260). While the network is dense in central Europe and extremely dense in Great Britain, Paris is not yet connected to Lyon, not to mention Bordeaux, Marseille or Milano.

A second series of consequences stems from the redistribution of income from consumers and producers, on the one hand, to the commune, on the other hand. They are important both for the present and the future of the economy.

First, the authoritarian regime will direct its income flow to areas which may be quite different from those that society would have chosen in a more democratic system. Second, the income transferred both by consumers and producers could have been spent in ways that would have shaped differently the future of the economy.

The consumers could have done two things with the income they lost. They could have used it to buy goods and services from sectors that were not to be those chosen by the state for development. Also, they could have saved part of it, and those savings could have been channelled through the financial system to sectors that might have been quite different from the areas privileged by the political power.

Producers are clearly deprived of profits which could have been used for investment, thereby enabling the introduction of technical progress. Marginal costs would have been pushed down, and the supply curve would have been displaced to the right, generating an increasing surplus, and thereby the growth process we described in chapter 2.

1.2 Second possibility: the selling price is fixed below $\hat{p}$

Suppose now that the planning authorities decide that the commodity should be sold at a price lower than $\hat{p}$. We will choose it to be at p_0, at a level lower than p_e (figure 14.2). This case was indeed frequently observed in planned economies: prices were often lower than the equilibrium prices which would have prevailed in free markets, or which could be observed in market economies with a similar level of technical development.

The situation on the market is the following. At price p_0, demand is now $q_D(p_0)$, considerably above the supply which remains fixed at $q_S(\bar{p}) = \bar{q}$. Thus an excess demand $q_D(p_0) - \bar{q}$ is created. Such an excess demand will entail a number of problems to be examined in turn. Two types of consequences may follow, depending on the policy adopted. The first is organized rationing; the second, in the absence of such a policy, is the appearance of a black market.

1.2.1 Consequences of rationing

Suppose that the state decides to ration the rare produce $\bar{q}$ by distributing an equal number of coupons to each individual, the total of coupons being equal to $\bar{q}$. On average each individual will receive a share $\bar{q}/q_D(p_0)$ of total demand. The new equilibrium is now E'', and we want to compare that situation to the previous one, characterized by equilibrium E.

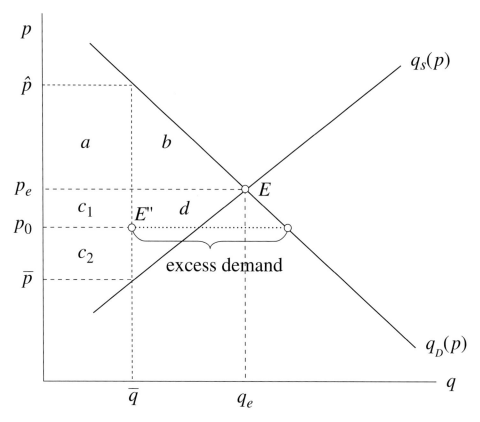

Figure 14.2   The planned economy. Second possibility: the price is fixed at p_0, below p_e.

Consumers lose area b and gain c_1; so their loss is $b - c_1$. For producers, they still lose $d + c_1 + c_2$, the same amount they lost when the commune sold their product at $\hat{p}$, since they still receive only $\bar{p}$ from the commune. The latter now gains only c_2. The final outcome is then:

- loss for society : $b - c_1 + d + c_1 + c_2 - c_2 = b + d$.

The loss is the same as the loss that prevailed when price was fixed at $\hat{p}$. This result was predictable: indeed, fundamentally society loses a quantity $q_e - \bar{q}$. Society values this amount by the area under the demand curve corresponding to this segment of the abscissa, and the cost of producing this amount is the area under the supply curve; the difference of those two areas, the net loss, is just $b + d$.

1.2.2   The black market

It is obvious that rationing is preferable to a system whereby a very high price may be fixed by the black market at $\hat{p}$. If the net loss for society is the same, at least the amount $\bar{q}$ is distributed more equitably among the population – while a price

$\hat{p}$ enables only a few to gain access to the product. However, a rationing system will seldom be successfully implemented and might soon be replaced by the black market, driven by the very existence of an excess demand.

2   Common traits of centrally planned economies and poor countries

After World War II, planning the economy was an idea that was by no means confined to Eastern European countries, Russia or China. It was pervasive in Western Europe as well – but with a fundamental difference: the principle of private property was kept enforced, and the final step of collectivizing the capital stock was never taken. Thus Europe embarked for almost half a century upon one of the most remarkable – and perhaps unique – economic experiments in history, its eastern part choosing the road of collectivization.

We may now draw a parallel between the main characteristics of planned economies and poor countries. Common features are a closed economy, a broken growth process, the absence of equality of chances, and the stability of the system.

2.1   A closed economy

Planned economies and poor countries are usually closed to foreign competition; they levy high duties on imports, or suppress imports altogether. The reasons may differ: in poor countries, customs duties are an easy way of levying taxes; and planned economies will tend to shun exchanges with the outside world for political reasons. The result will be comparable to what we just saw: net losses will be suffered by society compared to an economy that is open to the world. It is possible to determine with precision those losses, in a manner similar to what we have just done to measure the impact of fixed prices (see exercises 14.1, 14.2 at the end of this chapter).

2.2   A broken growth process; the potential of the economy is not achieved

The second striking common feature is a broken growth process. Indeed, what is called investment does not enhance the capital stock of the nation ($I \neq dK/dt$). Throughout this text on growth, we assumed that the capital stock and labour combined with technological progress to generate an output which was desired by society, divided into consumption and investment in carefully calculated proportions: society invested an amount such that the present sacrifice would be exactly matched by its rewards. In planned economies and in poor countries, investment has been conducted on premises which have little in common with those objectives.

The potential of the economy is not achieved for other reasons as well, which differ however. In poor countries, the reason is the insufficient public spending on health and education; planned economies do not achieve their potential because the state chooses its own areas of development.

2.3 Absence of equality of chances

A problem common to planned and poor countries is that their societies are not truly egalitarian in the sense that we defined earlier. This inequality will take a form somewhat different in each system. In planned economies, success is bestowed upon those close to the political power, or who work in activities privileged by the power. In poor countries, inequalities, particularly those based upon age and gender, are forced upon society by tradition and particular interests.

2.4 Stability of the system

Some poor countries remained so for centuries; and the experiment of planning dragged on not for a few years, but for decades. The reason for such stability seems to be, in each case, the weakness or the altogether absence of democracy. The non-separation of the three powers: legislative, executive and judicial may be self-perpetuating for a long time.

We are now led naturally to try to define the fundamental, necessary, conditions for economic growth. This will be the object of our next and concluding chapter.

Exercises

14.1 On a given market demand and supply are given respectively by:

$$q_D = -p + 7$$

and

$$q_S = p/2 - 1/2$$

where q is the quantity (in millions of tons), and p is the price (in hundreds of dollars per ton).

Initially, this market is in competitive equilibrium.
(a) Determine the equilibrium price and quantity.
(b) Determine the consumers' surplus and the producers' surplus.
(c) Suppose that a State agency intervenes on this market, forcing producers to sell to the said agency their produce at price $p = 3$. Determine the quantity produced and the price at which the agency will sell this product,

supposing that this price corresponds to the maximal level that consumers are willing to pay.

(d) Indicate the losses incurred by consumers and producers; the profit made by the agency; the transfers within society; the net loss suffered by society.

14.2 Use the same data as in question 14.1 Suppose now that the State agency aims at maximizing its profit (defined by the difference between its income and its costs).

(a) Which quantity will it buy from producers? At which price? What will be the price at which the agency will sell this quantity? What will be its profits?

(b) In a figure under the supply and demand diagram set in abscissa the quantity of the good considered and in ordinate the profit made by the agency. Draw the curve corresponding to that profit. Indicate the point where this profit is maximum and those where it is equal to zero.

Answers

14.1 (a) quantity: 2 million tons; price $500/ton

(b) consumers' surplus: $200 million; producers' surplus: $400 million

(c) quantity: 1 million tons; price $600/ton

(d) in $millions: losses incurred by consumers: 150; losses incurred by producers: 300; profit made by the agency: 300; transfers from consumers to the agency: 100; transfers from producers to the agency: 200; net loss incurred by society: 150.

14.2 100 million tons at price $300/ton; this quantity will be sold at $600/ton; the agency's prifit will be $300. The profit curve is the parabola $\pi = -3q^2 + 6q$, with a maximum at $q = 3$, and zeroes at 0 and 2.

CHAPTER 15

From Ibn Khaldun to Adam Smith, and a proof of Smith's conjecture

Our first aim in this concluding chapter is to bring together the fundamental conditions of economic growth. As we mentioned at the outset of Part I, we believe they were laid out in a definitive, masterly way by Ibn Khaldun in his *Muqaddimah* (*Introduction to History*, 1377).

Western civilization had to wait four centuries for those conditions to be formulated independently. One of them would be expressed in a most daring and powerful conjecture: we owe it to Adam Smith. It is intimately linked to the very engine of growth we have described in this text: investment, or the accumulation of capital. Smith wrote that whenever individuals try to find the most advantageous use of their capital, they are led to prefer that employment which is most advantageous to society. By doing so, the individual "intends his own gain, and he is in this as in many other cases, led by an invisible hand to promote an end which was no part of his intention".[1]

Here is what Kenneth Arrow and Frank Hahn had to say about Smith's conjecture: "The notion that a social system moved by independent actions in pursuit of different values is consistent with a final coherent state of balance, and one in which the outcomes may be quite different from those intended by the agents, is surely the most important intellectual contribution that economic thought has made to the general understanding of social processes".[2]

The conjecture is daring: it is not in the least supported by intuition. It is also far reaching because it can steer society away from what might appeal to many: the centralization of decisions, or planning. Our second aim in this chapter will be to convert Smith's conjecture into a theorem.

---

[1] A. Smith, *An Inquiry into the Nature and the Causes of the Wealth of Nations* (1776). This edition: Dent & Sons, London and Toronto, 1975, p. 400.

[2] Kenneth Arrow and Frank Hahn, *General Competitive Analysis*, Holden-Day, San Francisco, Oliver and Boyd, Edinburgh, 1971, p. 1.

The power and similarity of the messages of Ibn Khaldun and Adam Smith will induce us in a natural way to ask the question of the convergence of ideas and values among civilizations.

1   Ibn Khaldun's message

Ibn Khaldun built his theory of economic growth on a deep understanding of fundamental economic mechanisms which would come to be comprehended only very slowly, centuries later, in the Western world.[3] We should cite here the idea of the gains society can derive from the division of labour and specialization; the mutual advantages received by two parties in an exchange process, an outcome that was casually denied not only by Aristotle but also, two millennia later, by some thinkers of the mercantilist school.

We will now indicate the five fundamental factors of the growth process as they were expounded by Ibn Khaldun in his *Introduction to History*. They are:

- demographic growth
- technical progress
- the search for individual profit
- the principle of private property
- the soundness of political and legal institutions.

Let us examine each of these factors in turn. Some of them (the first and the third) might come as a surprise to the reader; all have profound implications on the organization of society. The way they are presented is not random. On the contrary, as the reader will discover, there are logical links between them.

---

[3] The first arabic edition of the *Muqaddimah* appeared in Egypt in 1857, published by Nasr al-Hûrînî. Almost simultaneously, another arabic edition was published in France by Etienne Marc Quatremère, under the title *Les Prolégomènes d'Ibn Khaldun* (Firmin Didot Frères, Paris, 1858).

   The *Muqaddimah* was first translated, partially, into Turkish in 1730 by Pirizade Effendi. This Turkish translation of the first five chapters remained in manuscript form until 1859 when it was published in Cairo. The first complete translation was made in French, and is due to William de Slane, who based his work on the Quatremère arabic edition, on the manuscripts used by Quatremère, the Egyptian edition, as well as on the Turkish translation. The three volumes of the *Prolégomènes* appeared in 1862, 1865 and 1868 in the *Notices et Extraits des manuscrits de la Bibliothèque impériale.*

   The first English translation is due to Franz Rosenthal. It was published in 1958 by Routledge and Kegan Paul, London and Henley, under the title *The Muqaddimah – An Introduction to History*. We have used here the second edition (1967).

   Ibn Khaldun has been a precursor of innumerable economic ideas that would be independently rediscovered only centuries later. The fascinating life of Ibn Khaldun is beautifully related both in Slane (1862) and Rosenthal (1958).

1.1   First factor: demographic growth

This first factor may sound surprising to anybody who is accustomed to measuring growth – as we all do – by an increase in income per person, and who would therefore conclude that since the growth rate of income per person is the difference between the growth rate of income and the growth rate of population, demographic growth may impede economic progress. Ibn Khaldun's idea is much more subtle: an increase in the population will enhance the division of labour, and hence all the gains that a society can derive from specialization and exchange. This was certainly a remarkable observation, which could explain some of the advantages a civilization would derive when transforming its living mode from nomadic to sedentary.

1.2   Second factor: technical progress

Not only will demographic growth enhance the division of labour, but the concomitant increase in the division of labour will improve the chances of innovation from the very fact that an individual will be able to concentrate more of his time to a given task. Therefore, odds are that he will perfect it, or that he will be able to find entirely new means of obtaining a given result.

1.3   Third factor: the search for individual profit

What will be the motivation for seeking to improve the way things are produced? Possibly curiosity; but most certainly the search for profit. If only for that reason, the search for profit would thus play a major role in economic growth. But Ibn Khaldun, like Adam Smith four centuries later, goes much further. They will assert that the mere search for profit is conducive to enhanced welfare for the whole society. Let us first hear Ibn Khaldun.

> Civilization and its well-being as well as business prosperity depend on productivity and people's efforts in all direction in their own interest and profit. When people no longer do business in order to make a living, and when they cease all gainful activity, the business of civilization slumps, and everything decays. People scatter everywhere in search of sustenance, to places outside the jurisdiction of their present government. The population of the particular region becomes light. The settlements there become empty. The cities lie in ruins. The disintegration of (civilization) causes the disintegration of the status of dynasty and ruler, because (their peculiar status) constitutes the form of civilization and the form necessarily decays when its matter (in this case, civilization) decays.[4]

---

[4] Ibn Khaldun, *The Muqaddimah – An Introduction to History* (1377), Translated from the Arabic by Franz Rosenthal, Routledge and Kegan Paul, London and Henley; first printing, 1958; this edition, 1986, p. 104. The parentheses have been added for clarity by the translator.

Those words were echoed, independently, four centuries later by Adam Smith in his *Inquiry into the Nature and Causes of the Wealth of Nations* (1776):

> Every individual is continually exerting himself to find out the most advantageous employment for whatever capital he can command. It is his own advantage, indeed, and not that of the society, which he has in view. But the study of his own advantage naturally, or rather necessarily, leads him to prefer that employment which is most advantageous to the society...
>
> He generally, indeed, neither intends to promote the public interest, nor knows how much he is promoting it ... He intends only his own gain, and he is in this, as in many other cases, led by an invisible hand to promote an end which was no part of his intention.[5]

This is perhaps the most surprising among the factors determining economic growth as proposed by Ibn Kahldun and Adam Smith. Indeed, how could one imagine that in the event that some odd person (whom we do not even know) tries to increase his own profit, his very action will benefit you or me? Neither Ibn Khaldun, nor Adam Smith, four centuries later, would demonstrate that proposition. Theirs was an intuition, and it became their conviction.

Both Ibn Khaldun and Smith have been very clear about the means that are not permissible to increase profit, and among these are the creation of monopolies: Ibn Khaldun opposed private or state monopolies; Smith denounced the large-scale cartels that employers had formed on the labour markets.

We will show in sections 2 and 3 how this remarkable conjecture – perhaps the most important that was ever made in economics or the social sciences – can find a proof and how it can be illustrated.

1.4 Fourth factor: the principle of private property

The logical consequence of the search of profit as a fundamental factor of economic growth is the principle of private property. In a section headed "Injustice brings about the ruin of civilization", Ibn Khaldun writes

> It should be known that attacks on people's property remove the incentive to acquire and gain property. People, then, become of the opinion that the purpose and ultimate destiny of (acquiring property) is to have it taken away from them. When the incentive to acquire and obtain property is

---

5 Adam Smith, *An Inquiry into the Nature and Causes of the Wealth of Nations* (1776); this edition: Dent: London, 1975, pp. 398–400. This quotation is extracted from Book Four, "Of Systems of Political Economy," Chapter II, "Of Restraints upon the Importation from Foreign Countries of such Goods as can be produced at Home." In this chapter, while advocating free trade, Smith held the view that, by investing domestically (rather than abroad), individuals would maximize the "annual revenue of society."

gone, people no longer make efforts to acquire any. The extent and degree to which property rights are infringed upon determines the extent and degree to which the efforts of the subjects to acquire property slacken. When attacks (on property) are extensive and general, extending to all means of making a livelihood, business inactivity, too, becomes (general), because the general extent of (such attacks upon property) means a general destruction of the incentive.

Ibn Khaldun analyses in detail the principle of private property, not only from a legal but also from an economic point of view. In particular, he gives three examples, or situations, in which the principle is violated, with dramatic consequences for society: first, slavery, which was unequivocally condemned by Ibn Khaldun – to the best of our knowledge, he was the first writer ever to do so. Also the principle of private property is violated by the constitution of private or state monopolies, as well as by excessive taxation.

1.4.1   The first transgression: slavery

Here is what Ibn Khaldun had to say about slavery:

> One of the greatest injustices and one which contributes most to the destruction of civilization is the unjustified imposition of tasks and the use of the subjects for forced labor. This is so because labor belongs to the things that constitute capital, as we shall explain in the chapter on sustenance. Gain and sustenance represent the value realized from labor among civilized people. All their efforts and all their labors are (means) for them (to acquire) capital and (to make a) profit. They have no other way to make a profit except (through labor). Subjects employed in cultural enterprises gain their livelihood and profit from such activities. Now, if they are obliged to work outside their own field and are used for forced labor unrelated to their (ordinary ways of) making a living they no longer have any profit and are thus deprived of the price of their labor, which is their capital (asset). They suffer, and a good deal of their livelihood is gone, or even all of it. If this occurs repeatedly, all incentive to cultural enterprise is destroyed, and they cease utterly to make an effort. This leads to the destruction and ruin of civilization.[6]

1.4.2   The second transgression: private and public monopolies

Ibn Khaldun goes on by showing how the principle of property is violated by the state when it organizes public monopoly, monopsony, or both: "An injustice even

---

[6] Ibn Khaldun, *op. cit.*, p. 108–9.

greater and more destructive of civilization and the dynasty than (the one just mentioned) is the appropriation of people's property by buying their possessions as cheaply as possible and then reselling the merchandise to them at the highest possible prices by means of forced sales and purchases."[7] In section 2.1 we will show how this scheme exactly applied six centuries later when China organized, under Mao Tse Tung, the popular communes.

1.4.3 The third transgression: excessive taxation

The last infringement on property is high taxes, which lead ultimately to the disappearance of the dynasty:

> [The] customs and needs [of the dynasty][8] become more varied because of the prosperity and luxury in which they are immersed. As a result, the individual imposts and assessments upon the subjects, agricultural laborers, farmers, and all the other taxpayers, increase. Every individual impost and assessment is greatly increased, in order to obtain a higher tax revenue. Customs duties are placed upon articles of commerce and (levied) at the city gates, as we shall mention later on. Then, gradual increases in the amount of the assessments succeed each other regularly, in correspondence with the gradual increase in the luxury customs and many needs of the dynasty and the spending required in connection with them. Eventually, the taxes will weigh heavily upon the subjects and overburden them. Heavy taxes become an obligation and tradition, because the increases took place gradually, and no one knows specifically who increased them or levied them. They lie upon the subjects like an obligation and tradition. The assessments increase beyond the limits of equity.
>
> The result is that the interest of the subjects in cultural enterprises disappears, since when they compare expenditures and taxes with their income and gain and see the little profit they make, they lose all hope. Therefore, many of them refrain from all cultural activity.[9] The result is that the total tax revenue goes down, as (the number of) the individual assessments goes down. Often, when the decrease is noticed, the amounts of individual imposts are increased. This is considered a means of compensating for the decrease. Finally individual imposts and assessments reach their limit. It would be of no avail to increase them further. The costs of all cultural enterprise are now too high. The taxes are too heavy, and the

---

[7] *Ibid.*, p. 109.

[8] The brackets and parentheses have been added for clarity by the translator, Franz Rosenthal.

[9] The translation "cultural activity" and, further, "cultural enterprise" can be considered as synonymous with "enterprise".

profits anticipated fail to materialize. Thus the total revenue continues to decrease, while the amounts of individual imposts and assessments continue to increase, because it is believed that such an increase will compensate (for the drop in revenue) in the end. Finally, civilization is destroyed, because the incentive for cultural activity is gone. It is the dynasty that suffers from the situation, because it (is the dynasty that) profits from cultural activity. If (the reader) understands this, he will realize that the strongest incentive for cultural activity is to lower as much as possible the amounts of individual imposts levied upon persons capable of undertaking cultural enterprises. In this manner, such persons will be psychologically disposed to undertake them, because they can be confident of making a profit from them.

1.4.4 Consequences

The consequences of such acts by the ruler are described by Ibn Khaldun:

> If no trading is being done in the markets, [the subjects] have no livelihood, and the tax revenue of the ruler decreases or deteriorates, since, in the middle (period) of a dynasty and later on, most of the tax revenue comes from customs duties on commerce, as we have stated before. This leads to the dissolution of the dynasty and the decay of urban civilization. The disintegration comes about gradually and imperceptibly. This happens whenever the ways and means of seizing property described above are used. On the other hand, if (the property) is taken outright and if the hostile acts are extended to affect the property, the wives, the lives, the skins, and the honor of people, it will lead to sudden disintegration and decay and the quick destruction of the dynasty. It will result in disturbances leading to complete destruction. On account of these evil (consequences), all such (unfair activities) are prohibited by the religious law. The religious law legalizes the use of cunning in trading, but forbids depriving people of their property illegally. The purpose is to prevent such evil (consequences), which would lead to the destruction of civilization through disturbances or the lack of opportunity to make a living.[10]

1.5 Fifth factor: soundness of political and legal institutions

We have already mentioned that the ideas contained in the *Introduction to History* would be rediscovered in Western civilization only centuries later. This is true also of Ibn Khaldun's view of an ideal political system in which individuals should be protected. The idea would finally re-emerge in Europe in the eighteenth

---

[10] *Ibid.*, pp. 110–11.

century; it would appear in the US Declaration of Independence; very slowly, the principle would be written down in Western constitutions, and even more slowly implemented in every citizen's life. For Ibn Khaldun, not abiding by this principle would lead to decadence. Let us now see how he defended this principle.

1.5.1 The all-important letter from Tâhir b. al-Husayn (821)

It is highly illuminating to see how Ibn Khaldun defined the optimal political and legal system that should be set up. He refers to a famous letter addressed more than five centuries before, in the year 821, by Tâhir b. al-Husayn, al-Ma'mûn's general, to his son Abdallâh b. Tâhir, when the latter had just been appointed governor of an Egyptian province. Ibn Khaldun quotes here important parts of the text, whereby Tâhir b. al-Husayn tells his son on which principles he must establish his power:

> God has been benevolent to you. He has made it obligatory for you to show kindness to those of His servants whom He has made your subjects. He has made it your duty to be just to them, to see to it that His rights and punishments are observed in connection with them, to defend them and protect their families and women, to prevent bloodshed, to make their roads safe, and to enable them to live in peace.[11]

And further:

> Consider it your most important task to take personal charge of the affairs of (your) officials and to protect your subjects by looking after their needs and providing for their requirements.[12] ... Do not be greedy. Let the treasures and riches you gather and hoard up be piety, the fear of God, justice, the improvement of your subjects, the cultivation of their country, the supervision of their affairs, the protection of the mass of them, and support of the unfortunates. You should know that property, once it is gathered and stored in treasuries, does not bear fruit, but if it is invested in the welfare of the subjects and used for giving them what is due to them and to prevent them from need, then it grows and thrives. The common people prosper[13] ... Devote yourself to looking after the affairs of the poor and indigent, those who are not able to bring before you complaints about injustices they have suffered, and other lowly persons who do not know that they may ask for their rights. Inquire about these people in all secrecy, and put good men from among your subjects in charge of them. Command them to report to you their needs and conditions, so that you will be able to look into the measures through which

[11] *Ibid.*, p. 141.   [12] *Ibid.*, pp. 143–4.   [13] *Ibid.*, pp. 145–6.

God might improve their affairs. Have regard also for people who have suffered accidents, and for their widows and orphans. Give them stipends from the treasury, following the example of the Commander of the Faithful. . . . Set up houses for muslims who are ill, shelter them, (appoint) attendants in these houses who will handle them kindly, and (appoint) physicians who will treat their diseases. Comply with their desires so long as it does not lead to waste in the treasury.[14]

In the mind of Tâhir b. al-Husayn, God has endowed the ruler with power and responsibilities he is strictly accountable for. The letter, as quoted by Ibn Khaldun, adds: "God will punish you in connection with the duties He has placed upon you (if you do not take care of them properly). He will make them your concern and hold you responsible for them and reward you for (the good deeds) you have done or (the evil deeds you have) not done."[15]

1.5.2 Ibn Khaldun's valuation of the Tâhir b. al-Husayn letter

Highly significantly, Ibn Khaldun reports that according to historians

the people liked the letter when it appeared, and it found wide circulation. Al-ma'mûn heard about it. When it had been read to him, he said: "Tâhir did not omit any of the matters that concern this world, the religion, administration, (the formation of) opinion, politics, the improvement of the realm and the subjects, the preservation of the government, obedience to the caliphs, and maintenance of the caliphate. He has dealt very well with all these matters, and has given directions (how to handle) them." Al-ma'mûn then ordered the letter to be sent to all officials in the various regions, so that they might use it as a model and act accordingly.[16]

A final quote of Ibn Khaldun is essential: it shows how much the famous Tâhir b. al-Husayn letter epitomizes the ideal political system he could ever conceive: "This is the best treatment of this type of politics that I have found".[17]

2 Two illustrations of the message of Ibn Khaldun and Adam Smith

The reader will easily be convinced of the soundness of each of Ibn Khaldun's propositions as fundamental causes of the growth process. There might be, however, one exception: it may be tricky, indeed, to prove the third proposition, i.e. the search for individual profit.

---

[14] *Ibid.*, p. 153.   [15] *Ibid.*, p. 141.   [16] *Ibid.*, p. 156.   [17] *Ibid.*, p. 156.

As we mentioned earlier, neither Ibn Khaldun nor Adam Smith gave a formal proof of the idea. Our intent here is to offer two illustrations, which are proofs in particular but important cases, before giving a proof of Adam Smith's conjecture.

Let us already note that we can understand easily that the profit motive is certainly a sufficient condition for growth in the sense that it may be a strong incentive both to investment (not necessarily accompanied by technical progress) *and* to the introduction of technical progress which will in turn induce investment in capital goods of a new type. Both sources of investment would definitely contribute to the enhancements of the capital stock of the nation, and therefore to its growth. But the message of Ibn Khaldun and Smith goes well beyond that: what they say is that not only the economy will grow as a result of the actions of some individuals, but *the whole society* will benefit from those actions; Smith will even add that individuals' independent decisions will lead to the *maximization* of advantages received by society. This is the part which is very far from obvious, where a proof is required; it will be the object of section 3.

We will first give two illustrations of Smith's conjecture. Each of them applies independently of time or place. However, the first builds upon one of the most momentous events in the political and economic history of the second part of the twentieth century: the suppression of the popular communes in China in 1978, after Mao Tse Tung's death. The second one shows how firms, when introducing technical progress for their own benefit, end up increasing society's welfare – although this may occur at the expense of an ultimate decrease in their own profits.

2.1 First illustration: the consequences of suppressing popular communes and (partially) liberalizing markets

Consider now the initial situation of a planned economy; as an example, we can envision the situation of the popular communes in China under Mao Tse Tung. The commune buys the production of farmers at price $\bar{p}$, and the farmers have to remit all their product to the commune; so they produce $\bar{q}$, which is then sold by the commune at the high price that consumers are prepared to pay for this relatively scarce commodity, i.e. $\hat{p}$. Thus, the commune gains the difference between its selling price $\hat{p}$ and its buying price $\bar{p}$, times the quantity $\bar{q}$, i.e. $(\hat{p} - \bar{p})\bar{q}$, which is area $a + c$ in figure 15.1.

It is a good place to note that this scheme by which the state buys some good (usually an agricultural good) to resell at a higher price is common to all times and places. Remember also that these schemes had been denounced by Ibn Khaldun in very precise terms – see the above quote in section 1.4.2.

Let us briefly see what the welfare loss to society such a system entails. Consumers lose $a + b$; a is the additional amount they have to pay in order to buy

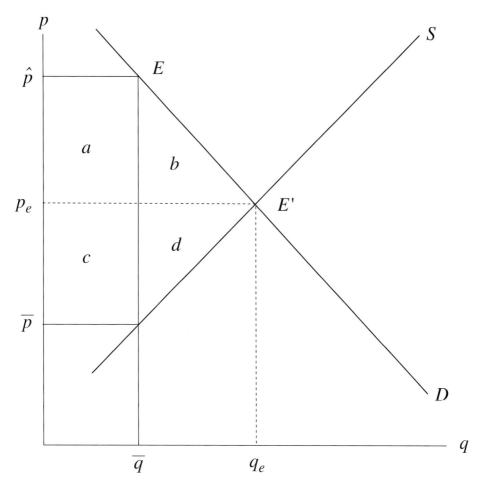

Figure 15.1 The net gain of society from the suppression of the popular communes. When farmers receive the right to produce and sell on the market more than what they have to remit to the cooperative ($\bar{q}$), the equilibrium point moves from $E(\bar{q}, \hat{p})$ to $E'(q_e, p_e)$. The consumers' net gain is $a + b$; the producers' net gain is d; the loss of the popular commune is a, which is transferred to consumers. Society's net gain is $b + d$, part of which will be invested, both in agriculture and in other sectors, leading to a growth process.

the quantity $\bar{q}$; b is the surplus they would enjoy on quantity $q_e - \bar{q}$ if the price was p_e. Producers lose $c + d$; indeed, c is lost on quantity $\bar{q}$ because their price is reduced by $p_e - \bar{p}$; and d is the profit they would be making if they produced the additional quantity $q_e - \bar{q}$.

Suppose now that the system is partially liberalized in the following sense (as it was a few years after Mao Tse Tung's death). Farmers are still required to sell a quota $\bar{q}$ of their production to a cooperative, at price $\bar{p}$. However, they are free to produce more than $\bar{q}$ and sell it at the price they can find on the market. Farmers do not take long to discover that they can charge, for their additional production, a price far superior to the one they currently receive ($\bar{p}$); in fact, they could sell some units at a price very close to $\hat{p}$. To be precise, at price $\hat{p}$ they would be prepared to supply much more than the quantity the consumers are prepared to buy ($\bar{q}$). Thus at price $\hat{p}$ they immediately create an excess supply whose effect is two-fold: first the price is driven down (the cooperative is now competing with the farmers and has to lower its price as well); second, demand increases. The adjustment takes place until the new equilibrium point E is reached.

Let us now measure the benefits to society of such a partial liberalization scheme. Consumers gain $a + b$; producers gain d. The popular commune (now transformed into a cooperative) loses a; in all, society's welfare increases by $a + b + d - a = b + d$.

Ibn Khaldun and Smith are once more vindicated. The producers' intent was to increase their profit: this they certainly achieved (by the amount d); but in addition – and this was definitely *not* part of their intention – they have given consumers a net surplus (b). How did this happen? The reason is that competition has forced the producers to lower the initial price $\hat{p}$ – and this has resulted in a gain for the consumers.

We should now recall what the effects of that liberalization policy were in China in the last 25 years. The surplus thus entailed in the agricultural sector generated a huge demand both in the form of consumption and investment goods. A remarkable growth process was thus set in motion, to an extent which has hardly been observed anywhere else, or at any time.

2.2 Second illustration: the advantages derived by society from technical progress introduced by firms for their own profit

Consider a given market characterized by a demand from many consumers, and by a supply from a few – or many – competing firms. Suppose that, spurred by the profit motive, some firms introduce technical progress in the production process. For instance, we could imagine that these new production techniques are energy saving.

The effect of this is to reduce the marginal costs in those firms that have introduced those techniques; the ultimate outcome is to move the supply curve to the right (see figure 15.2). The equilibrium point of the market thus moves from E to E'. Let us now draw a picture of the gains made by consumers and producers after this process has been completed.

Let us consider first the consumers' gain. It is equal to the areas $a + b + c$. This result can be derived in two different ways: first, it can be determined as the difference between the new consumers' surplus and the former one. Second, we can see that the consumers' gain is made of two parts: the saving they make by paying less for the initial quantity they bought q_0; this saving amounts to

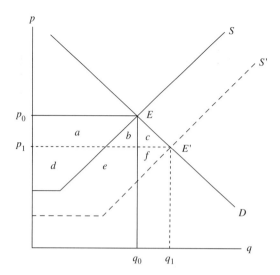

Figure 15.2 The net gain of society from introducing technical progress. Technical progress has the effect of reducing the marginal costs of firms, thus displacing the supply curve from S to S' and the equilibrium point from E to E'. Consumers gain $a + b + c$. The producers' gain is $e + f - a$ (due to the price decrease, this may turn out to be negative). However the net gain of society is $e + b + c + f$, always positive. The area $e + b$ is the cost reduction in the quantity initially produced; $c + f$ is the net gain of society corresponding to the increase in the quantity at society's disposal.

$q_0(p_1 - p_0)$, which is equal to the area $a + b$; in addition, they receive a surplus on the additional quantity they buy at the new price p_1: this additional surplus is area c; in total, they receive $a + b + c$.

Turn now to the producers. Initially their profits were $a + d$; their new profits are $d + e + f$; so their gain is $d + e + f - a - d = e + f - a$; here we have a surprise: their gain is *not* necessarily positive; it may well be the case that $a > e + f$, and thus introducing technical progress might well entail *lower* profits for firms. The reader may easily figure out a diagram where that would be the case.

Consider finally society's gains. They are just the sum of the consumers' and the producers' gains (that may be negative). So they are $a + b + c + e + f - a = b + c + e + f$. This area is always positive: hence society will *always* find an advantage in technical progress being introduced by producers, although producers as a set of individuals will not necessarily gain from it.

Let us now give an economic interpretation of the net advantage received by society. We had simply calculated it as the sum of the gains made by consumers and by producers. But the a priori odd-looking shape made by the $b + c + e + f$ area can be interpreted directly from the diagram, and makes a lot of economic sense. Consider first the area $b + e$: this is what society saves on the initial quantity q_0, which is now produced at a lower cost. Secondly, society reaps another advantage by the fact that it receives an increase in quantity $(q_1 - q_0)$ which it values by the area under the demand curve, while it costs the area under the supply curve to produce; the net benefit is precisely the area $c + f$. So the gain made by society is partly made on the former quantity at its disposal, in terms of lower costs (to the amount of $b + e$) and in a surplus on an additional amount it acquires (that surplus is $c + f$). We thus understand why the gain of society is always positive.

Let us now examine the fundamental cause of the potential miscalculation of producers, and of the necessary decrease in price. At the initial equilibrium point, any firm that manages to reduce its marginal cost is not any more in equilibrium, because its marginal revenue (the initial price p_0) becomes larger than its marginal cost (which has been reduced following the innovation in the production technique). The firm has now a strong incentive to increase its production, precisely to reap those marginal profits, until its new marginal cost curve meets the horizontal p_0. This is true for *all* firms who have managed to reduce their marginal cost. The effect of this, of course, is to displace the supply curve S to its new positions S', thus entailing an excess supply at the initial price level. Firms will compete to put on the market the additional quantity they would like to sell. They will lower the price; demand will increase, and supply will fall along the new supply curve S' until the new equilibrium point E' is reached.

We observe finally that society will benefit from the introduction of technical progress in an initially competitive market only if competition is maintained. This gives striking significance to the position that both Ibn Khaldun and Smith had taken against monopolies.

3 A proof of Smith's conjecture

We will now take one step further. As we have seen, both Ibn Khaldun and Adam Smith had stressed individual profit searching as a potent explanatory variable of growth, Smith adding that not only would it be to society's benefit, but that it would maximize it. We will now prove Smith's conjecture in a general setting.

What is, for society, the purpose of building up a capital stock in the amount of $K(t)$ at time t? It is only to receive, ultimately, consumption flows from it. Let us then determine the whole trajectory of capital $K(t)$, denoted $\vec{K}$, such that society maximizes the sum of the discounted cashflows it can acquire from now (time 0) to infinity.

Any consumption flow at time t is discounted via a rate of preference for the present, equal to a risk-free rate plus a risk premium. Indeed, we may consider that all future production, and hence future consumption, will be obtained with a degree of uncertainty which is captured by including a risk premium in the discount factor. Let $\exp(-\int_0^t i(z)dz)$ be the discount factor that applies to any cashflow received at time t, as we have seen in chapter 9. Production at time t, Y_t, is obtained via a production function depending upon three arguments: capital K_t, labour L_t and the state of technological progress, as we supposed throughout this book; thus $Y_t = F(K_t, L_t, t)$; Y_t is society's *net* income (net of capital depreciation).

The problem can be written

$$\underset{\vec{K}}{\text{Max}} \int_0^\infty C_t e^{-\int_0^t i(z)dz} dt \tag{1}$$

subject to

$$C_t = F(K_t, L_t, t) - \dot{K}_t. \tag{2}$$

We have shown in chapters 9 and 10 the many ways in which problems of this kind can be solved, using the calculus of variations or the Pontryagin maximum principle either with the Hamiltonian or the Dorfmanian. We choose here to use the latter, together with the Dorfmanian, for the following reason. Using the Dorfmanian leads to quite a remarkable conclusion: as we will show, it is not only one, but *two* magnitudes that society maximizes through competitive equilibrium on the capital market. First, society maximizes the sum, *calculated over an infinite horizon*, of the discounted consumption flows which it can enjoy. Second, it maximizes *at any point of time* the benefits of its activity. It is our strong belief that the Dorfman approach best mirrors the thinking of Ibn Khaldun and Adam Smith – and who knows? – they might have approved of it.

Let us introduce as $\lambda(t)$ the *present value*, as measured as of today (time 0) of one additional unit of capital received at time t. This is defined as the present value of the rate of increase of the optimal value of the functional per additional unit of capital received at time t. This value will be determined as soon as the optimization has been carried out. So $\lambda(t)K(t)$ is the present value of the quantity of capital in existence at time t, and $\frac{d}{dt}[\lambda(t)K(t)] = \lambda(t)\dot{K}_t + \dot{\lambda}(t)K_t$ is the rate at which the *value* of capital in existence at time t increases.

On the other hand, the direct benefit received by society is the consumption flow C_t, expressed in present value, i.e. $C_t e^{-\int_0^t i(z)dz}$. So our Dorfmanian is:

$$D = C_t e^{-\int_0^t i(z)dz} + \frac{d}{dt}[\lambda(t)K(t)]. \tag{3}$$

It is indeed the total benefit society can receive at any time t if an optimal policy in the form of an optimal trajectory of capital $\vec{K}$ is pursued. This total benefit can be written

$$D(K_t, \dot{K}_t, t) = [F(K_t, L_t, t) - \dot{K}_t]e^{-\int_0^t i(z)dz} + \lambda(t)\dot{K}_t + \dot{\lambda}(t)K_t. \tag{4}$$

Let us now maximize D with respect to K_t and $\dot{K}_t$. Equating the gradient of D to zero leads to

$$\frac{\partial D}{\partial K_t} = F_{K_t}(K_t, L_t, t)e^{-\int_0^t i(z)dz} + \dot{\lambda}(t) = 0 \tag{5}$$

and

$$\frac{\partial D}{\partial \dot{K}_t} = -e^{-\int_0^t i(z)dz} + \lambda(t) = 0 \tag{6}$$

which, together with the concavity of the Dorfmanian with respect to K and $\dot{K}$ gives a necessary and sufficient condition for a global maximum of D.

Differentiating (6) with respect to t and replacing $\dot{\lambda}(t)$ into (5) yields the Fisher–Solow equation

$$F_K(K_t, L_t, t) = i(t) \tag{7}$$

which is at the very core of the individual's objective in Ibn Khaldun's and Smith's messages: the search of each individual's advantage means that capital is employed in such a way that its marginal productivity is equal to the rate of preference for the present.

We should now verify that the value of $\lambda(t)$, given by equation (6) as $\lambda(t) = \exp(-\int_0^t i(z)dz)$, is indeed the present value of the rate of increase of the functional's optimal value with respect to one additional unit of capital received at time t. Let $\vec{K}$ designate the optimal path of capital accumulation from time t to infinity, and $V^*(K_t, t)$ the maximum value of the functional. We have

$$V^*(K_t, t) = \underset{\vec{K}}{\mathrm{Max}} \int_t^\infty C_\tau e^{-\int_t^\tau i(z)dz} d\tau, \tag{8}$$

and the rate of increase of $V^*(K_t, t)$ with respect to K_t is

$$\frac{\partial V^*}{\partial K_t} = \frac{\partial}{\partial K_t} \int_t^\infty [F(K_\tau, L_\tau, \tau) - \dot{K}_\tau] e^{-\int_t^\tau i(z)dz} d\tau$$

$$= \int_t^\infty F_K(K_\tau, L_\tau, \tau) e^{-\int_t^\tau i(z)dz} d\tau. \tag{9}$$

Since K_τ follows the optimal path $\vec{K}$, equation (7) applies at all instants τ, and the marginal productivity of capital $F_K(K_\tau, L_\tau, \tau)$ in equation (9) can be replaced by $i(\tau)$. The rate of increase of V^* with respect to K_t is then:

$$\frac{\partial V^*}{\partial K_t} = \int_t^\infty i(\tau) e^{-\int_t^\tau i(z)dz} d\tau. \tag{10}$$

The indefinite integral of $i(\tau) \exp[-\int_t^\tau i(z)dz]$ is $-\exp[-\int_t^\tau i(z)dz]$ plus an arbitrary constant. We then have:

$$\frac{\partial V^*}{\partial K_t} = -e^{-\int_t^\tau i(z)dz} \Big|_t^\infty = 1 \tag{11}$$

and hence $\lambda(t)$, the present value of $\partial V^*/\partial K_t$, is

$$\lambda(t) = e^{-\int_0^t i(z)dz} \frac{\partial V^*}{\partial K_t} = e^{-\int_0^t i(z)dz} \tag{12}$$

as stated in equation 6.

The economic interpretation of this result is the following. Since the decay of capital is systematically taken into account (F designates *net* income – net of depreciation), receiving one additional unit of capital at time t implies that from that point of time onward this unit is at society's disposal. Keeping it as such has an opportunity cost, measured by the consumption society could have enjoyed instead of having that unit of capital. So the value of one additional unit of capital *at time t* must be exactly one unit of consumption, and its present value is therefore $\exp(-\int_0^t i(z)dz)$.

We can thus convert Smith's conjecture into the following theorem:

THEOREM   *If individuals find out the most advantageous employment for whatever capital they can command by equating the marginal productivity of capital to the rate of preference for the present, society maximizes simultaneously two magnitudes:*

(1) the sum of the discounted consumption flows society can acquire from now to infinity

(2) the benefits of society's activity at any point of time t; those benefits are the sum of the consumption flows received at time t plus the rate of increase in the value of the capital stock at that time.

This result is both surprising and powerful. It means that competitive equilibrium entails the maximization of society's advantages measured by (1) as well as by (2). It implies that the capital stock trajectory K_t and its derivative, the investment time path $\dot{K}_t$, are definitely not goals in themselves, but appear as the mere instruments of achieving society's welfare – which they should be.

Another striking result is the following. In uncertainty, we have no idea of the functional relationship that might prevail between the production factors and output in the future. For instance, we do not know what kind or level of technological progress will be achieved thirty years from now, nor do we know the very structure of the resulting production function. The growth process may, and probably will, be changing in a way that we can little imagine today. But in the far future, people will know the entire history of those variables and relationships and they may ask the question: "What *should* have been the optimal time path of K_t such that society had maximized the integral of the discounted consumption flows and at the same time its benefits at any point of time?" The answer of course is that the Fisher–Solow equation applied at all times, and this is exactly the essence of Smith's conjecture.

IN CONCLUSION: ON THE CONVERGENCE OF IDEAS AND VALUES THROUGH CIVILIZATIONS

In the last chapter, we have shown how a conjecture of tremendous import for the future of our societies, namely Ibn Khaldun's and Adam Smith's idea that our well-being is driven by competitive equilibrium, is vindicated today by economic theory.

Their conjecture came from two different worlds, four centuries apart. Nevertheless, their works were linked in more ways than one. William Letwin had these words to conclude his "Introduction" to Adam Smith's magnum opus: "Far from being a hymn in praise of anarchic greed, the *Wealth of Nations* is a reasoned argument for justice, order, liberty and prudent plenty".[1] It would certainly be difficult to find a better way to characterize the *Muquaddimah* by Ibn Khaldun.

We can pursue the examples of the convergence of ideas and values among civilizations on the normative level. Remember how Ibn Khaldun had relied on the Tâhir b.al-Husayn letter, written in 821, to define what in his mind was the optimal form of government, and how its responsibilities were to be defined. It turns out that Tâhir's letter found an exact echo four centuries later, in Thomas Aquinas' letter to Hugues II, King of Cyprus (*De Regno ad Regem Cypri*, 1265).[2] We will never know if Thomas Aquinas had known of Tâhir's letter. It is most likely that he had not. This convergence toward a common political and social ethic is then nothing short of remarkable.

Some of the most cherished values of Western civilization were independently formulated in the ancient chinese philosophical writings of Mo Tzu[3] (later half of the fifth century BC). Mo Tzu spent a good part of his life trying to advocate the principle of defensive wars, and condemning offensive warfare. But this is not the only way he announces the Augustinian precepts. His message of universal love is based upon the fundamental principle of equality among individuals, families,

---

[1] William Letwin, in the *Introduction* of A. Smith, *op. cit.*, p. xxii.

[2] See the profound analysis of Aquinas' *De Regno ad Regem Cypri* (1265) by Patrick de Laubier, in *Pour une civilisation de l'amour*, Fayard, Paris, 1990.

[3] See *Basic Writings of Mo Tzu, Hsün Tzu and Han Fei Tzu*, translated by Burton Watson, Columbia University Press, New York, 1963. I am very grateful to my colleague Patrick de Laubier for bringing to my attention Mo Tzu's work.

cities and States – they are all equal under the Heavens. This principle would take thousands of years to be slowly, very imperfectly implemented in law and societal behaviour.

Mo Tzu announced values that we recognize today as belonging to civilization – a rich, complex concept designed to characterize the multi-faceted development of society. A civilization grows in step with the degree by which individuals, being considered as equal, are respected in their persons and in their ideas. Progress takes many forms; it means progress in equality of rights, in tolerance, as well as in the respect of nature. The concept is intertemporal in the sense that it requires to heed the interests not only of the current, but of the future generations as well. The Mo Tzu principle applies: from one generation to another, society transmits more than it has received.

Economic growth is just one of those facets; it is only one of the interdependent processes which make up civilization. Like natural phenomena, they do not follow smooth paths, and defy prediction. In each of those fractal-like processes, tiny and apparently harmless events may lead to momentous, unpredictable consequences, often referred to as "accidents of history". Not only the economic development of societies, but also the evolution of ideas may experience steep, sustained downfalls marked by the strangest of ideologies, carrying down civilization with them. Those downfalls were endured in China after Mo Tzu's time, during and after Europe's Renaissance, and throughout the French revolution; they doomed our twentieth century, in China and on the Western and the Eastern sides of the Danube alike.

Nevertheless, how could we not see an upward trend in the paths that are slowly shaping civilization? When we hear the voices of Mo Tzu, Tâhir b. al-Husayn, Ibn Khaldun, Thomas Aquinas, Adam Smith, those voices from a distant past and at the same time so close to each of us, how could we ever doubt that civilizations will converge toward a system of common, elevated values? This is the message of hope I want to convey to you.

FURTHER READING, DATA ON GROWTH AND REFERENCES

An excellent companion of this book, illustrating the difficulties and challenges of growth and development, is William Easterly, *The Elusive quest for growth: an economist's adventures in the tropics*, MIT Press, 2001. The reader may also want to pursue the subject of growth in two broad directions: empirical observations and theory. They will find tremendous help in a website opened and maintained by Jonathan Temple of Bristol University. The site is www.bris.ac.uk/Depts/Economics/Growth.

Available at this address is also a list of the sites which carry the most detailed and accurate data on economic growth, for a very large number of countries. Those are:

- Penn World Table (Summers–Heston data set)
- Barro–Lee (1993) growth data set
- Barro–Lee (2000) education data set
- Political instability and growth data set
- Sachs and Warner data sets
- Social Indicators of Development
- Trends in Developing Economies
- World Bank Growth Research
- World Bank World Tables

Most economic journals publish research on growth and development; some are even specialized in each of these fields: the *Journal of Economic Growth*, the *Journal of Economic Development*. A wealth of recent books and papers is also available on line through Jonathan Temple's website.

The reader who would like to refresh his calculus, especially on subjects directly relevant to economic dynamics, has many excellent texts at his disposal; we indicate four of those, which he may find particularly helpful:

Chiang, A., *Fundamental methods of mathematical economics*, 3rd edn, McGraw-Hill, New York, 1985.
Gandolfo, G., *Economic dynamics*, 3rd edn, Springer, Berlin, New York, 1997.
Hammond, P. J. and K. Sydsaeter, *Mathematics for economic analysis*, Prentice Hall, Englewood Cliffs, NJ, 1995.

Takayama, A., *Mathematical economics*, Cambridge University Press, Cambridge, New York, 1994.

If the reader wants to enter the subject of the calculus of variations and optimal control, the following references are particularly recommended:

- for the calculus of variations per se:

Elsgolc, L., *Calculus of variations*, International Series of Monographs in Pure and Applied Mathematics, Pergamon Press, Reading, MA, 1962.
Gelfand, I. and S. Fomin, *Calculus of variations*, Englewood Cliffs, NJ, Prentice Hall, 1963.

- for optimal control and its applications to growth, a good introduction is:

Chiang, A., *Elements of dynamic optimization*, McGraw-Hill, New York, 1992.

In-depth and very clear presentations are in:

Arrow, K. J., "Applications of control theory to economic growth", in G. B. Dantzig and A. F. Veinott, eds., *Mathematics of the decision sciences*, American Mathematical Society, Providence, RI, 1968.
Arrow, K. J. and M. Kurz, *Public investment, the rate of return, and optimal fiscal policy*, Johns Hopkins Press, Baltimore, 1971.

The best known textbooks and collected papers in growth theory, often from very different perspectives, and at different levels are:

Acemoglu, D. (ed.), *Recent developments in growth theory*, Edward Elgar, 2004.
Aghion, P. and P. Howitt, *Endogenous growth theory*, MIT Press, Cambridge, MA, 1998.
Aghion, P. and S. N. Durlauf, *Handbook of economic growth*, North-Holland, Amsterdam, 2005.
Aghion, P. and R. Griffith, *Competition and growth, reconciling theory and evidence*, MIT Press, Cambridge, MA, 2005.
Barro, Robert J. and Xavier Sala-i-Martin, *Economic growth* (2nd edition), Boston: MIT Press, 2004.
Bertola, Giuseppe, Foellmi, Reto and Zweimuller, Josef, *Income distribution in macroeconomic models*, Princeton University Press, Princeton, 2006.
Eicher, T. and C. Garcia-Peñalosa, (eds.), *Institutions, development and economic growth*, MIT Press, Cambridge, MA, 2006.
Eicher, T. and S. Turnovsky, (eds.), *Inequality and growth, theory and policy implications*, MIT Press, Cambridge, MA, 2007.
George, Donald A. R., Oxley, Les and Carlaw, Kenneth I., *Surveys in economic growth: theory and empirics*, Oxford: Blackwell, 2004.
Gylfason, Thorvaldur, *Principles of economic growth*, Oxford University Press, Oxford, 1999.
Helpman, Elhanan, *The mystery of economic growth*, Cambridge, Harvard University Press, 2004.
Jensen, B. S., *The dynamic systems of basic economic growth models*, Dordrecht: Kluwer Academic Publishers, 1994.
Jones, Charles I., *An introduction to economic growth*, Norton, 1997.
Klundert, Theo van de, *Growth theory in historical perspective: selected essays of Theo van de Klundert*, Edward Elgar, Cheltenham, UK. Edited by Sjak Smulders, 2001.

Lucas, Robert E., Jr., *In search of prosperity: analytic narratives on economic growth*, Princeton: Princeton University Press, 2002.

Malinvaud, E., *Macroeconomic theory: a textbook on macroeconomic knowledge and analysis*, translated into English by Fenella Kirman, Elsevier, Amsterdam, 1998.

Parker, Philip M., *Physioeconomics: the basis for long-run economic growth*. MIT Press, Cambridge, MA, 2000.

Rodrigo, G. Chris, *Technology, economic growth and crises in East Asia*. Edward Elgar, Cheltenham, UK, 2001.

Rodrik, Dani (ed.), *In search of prosperity: analytic narratives on economic growth*, Princeton: Princeton University Press, 2003.

Rogers, Mark, *Knowledge, technological catch-up and economic growth*. Edward Elgar, 2003.

Romer, David, *Advanced macroeconomics*, 2nd edition. McGraw-Hill, Boston, MA, 2001.

Ros, Jaime, *Development theory and the economics of growth*, University of Michigan Press, 2000.

Solow, Robert M., *Growth theory: an exposition* (2nd edition), Oxford University Press, Oxford, 2000.

Thirlwall, Tony, *The nature of economic growth: an alternative framework for understanding the performance of nations*, Edward Elgar, forthcoming. Mexico lectures, 2002.

Weil, David N., *Economic growth*, Pearson, Addison-Wesley, 2005.

An excellent synthesis of the research presently conducted on the all-important environmental issues is in:

Brock, William A. and M. Scott Taylor, "Economic growth and the environment: a review of theory and empirics", in Aghion, P. and Durlauf, S., *op. cit.*, 2005.

Other references, quoted in this book

Antras, P., "Is the U.S. aggregate production function Cobb-Douglas? New estimates of the elasticity of substitution", Harvard University and NBER Working Paper, September 2003.

Arrow, K., H. Chenery, B. Minhas and R. M. Solow, "Capital-labour substitution and economic efficiency", *Review of Economics and Statistics*, 43, No 4, pp. 225–50.

Arrow, K. J. and F., Hahn, *General competitive analysis*, Holden-Day, San Francisco, Oliver and Toyd, Edinburgh, 1971.

Byström J., L. E. Persson and F. Strömberg, http://www.sm.luth.se~johanb/applmath/chap.en/part7.htm.

Dorfman, R., "An economic interpretation of optimal control theory", *American Economic Review*, Vol. 59, No 5, December, 1969, 817–31.

Elsgolc, E., *Calculus of variations*, International Series of Monographs in Pure and Applied Mathematics Pergamon Press, Reading, MA, 1962.

Feynman, R., *The pleasure of finding things out*, Penguin Books, London, New York, 1999.

Fischer, I., *Appreciation and interest*, Vol. XI, No 4, New York, American Economic Association, 1896, pp. 331–442.

Goldstine, H., *A History of the calculus of variations*, Springer Verlag, New York, 1981.

Goodwin, Richard M., "The optimal growth path for an underdeveloped economy", *The Economic Journal*, 1961, 71 (284), 756–74.

Hairer, E., and G. Wanner, *L'analyse au fil de l'histoire*, Springer Verlag, Berlin, Heidelberg, New York, 2000.

Hairer, E., S. P. Nørsett and G. Wanner, *Solving ordinary differential equations*, Volume I, Second Edition, Springer Verlag, New York, 2000.

Hardy, G., J. E. Littlewood and G. Polya, *Inequalities*, Cambridge University Press, Cambridge, 1952.

Hicks, J., *Theory of wages*, Macmillan, London, 1932.

Ibn Khaldun, *The Muqaddimah – An Introduction to History* (1377), translated from the Arabic by Franz Rosenthal, Routledge and Kegan Paul, London and Henley; First printing, 1958; this edition, 1986.

Ivanov, A., http://home.ural.ru/~iagsoft/BrachJ2.html.

Jones, R., "The structure of simple general equilibrium models", *The Journal of Political Economy*, 73, No 6, 557–72, 1965.

Johnston, L. and S. Williamson, "The annual real and nominal GDP for the United States, 1790–Present", *Economic History Services*, October 2005, URL: www.eh.net/hmit/gdp/.

Klump, R. and H. Preissler, "CES production functions and economic growth", *Scandinavian Journal of Economics*, 102, 41–56, 2000.

Klump, R. and O. de La Grandville, "Economic growth and the elasticity of substitution: two theorems and some suggestions", *American Economic Review*, 90, No 1, 282–91, 2000.

Klump, R. P. McAdam and A. Willman, "A supply-side diagnosis of growth in the euro area: factor substitution, productivity and unemployment", Paper presented at the C.E.S. Conference, University of Frankfurt, October 20–22, 2006.

La Grandville, O. de, "Capital theory, optimal growth and efficiency conditions with exhaustible resources", *Econometrica*, Vol. 48, No 7, November 1980, 1763–76.

"In Quest of the Slutsky Diamond", *American Economic Review*, 79, No 3. 468–81, 1989.

"New Hamiltonians for high-order equations of the calculus of variations: a generalization of the Dorfman approach", *Archives des Sciences*, Vol. 45, May 1992, 51–8.

"Curvature and the elasticity of substitution: straightening it out", *Journal of Economics*, Vol. 66, No 1, 1997, 23–34.

Bond pricing and portfolio analysis – protecting investors in the long run, MIT Press, Cambridge, MA, 2002.

"Protecting investors against changes in interest rates", in *Asset and liability management*, W. Ziemba and S. Zenios, eds., Elsevier North Holland, Amsterdam, New York, 2006, pp. 69–138.

"The 1956 contribution to theory of economic growth by Robert Solow: a major landmark and some of its undiscovered riches", *Oxford Review of Economic Policy*, no. 1, 2006, 1–10.

La Grandville, O. de, and Robert M. Solow, "A conjecture on general means", *Journal of Inequalities in Pure and Applied Mathematics*, Vol. 7, no. 1, 2006.

Laubier, Patrick de, *Pour une civilisation de l'amour*, Fayard, Paris, 1990.

Leung, H.M., "Endogenizing the aggregate elasticity of substitution", Paper presented at the C.E.S. Conference, University of Frankfurt, October 20–22, 2006.

Malinvaud, E., "Sur l'aggrégation des demandes de travail non-qualifié", *Annales d'Economie et de Statistique*, 66, 41–80, 2002.

Malinvaud, E., "An aggregation problem", Working Paper, 2003.

Pitchford, J., "Growth and the elasticity of substitution", *Economic Record*, 36, 491–504, 1960.

Pitman, J., *Probability*, Springer Verlag, New York, 1993.

Ramsey, F., "A mathematical theory of saving", *The Economic Journal*, Vol. 38, No 152, December, 1928, 543–59.

Rutherford, T., *Lecture notes on constant elasticity functions*, University of Colorado, November 2003.

Smith, A., *An inquiry into the nature and causes of the wealth of nations* (1776); this edition: Dent: London, 1975, pp. 398–400.

Solow, R., "A contribution to the theory of economic growth", *The Quarterly Journal of Economics*, Vol. 70, No 1, February, 1956, 65–94.

Srinivasan, T. N., "Optimal savings in a two-sector model of growth", *Econometrica*, Vol. 32, No 3, July, 1964, 358–73.

Stoléru, L., *L'équilibre et la croissance économique, Principes de macroéconomie*, Paris, Dunod, 1970.

Sussman, H. J., and J. C. Willems, "300 years of optimal control: from the brachistochrone to the Maximum principle," *IEEE Control Systems*, June 1997, pp. 33–44.

Swan, T., "Economic growth and capital accumulation," *Economic Record*, 32, 340–61, 1956.

Sydsaeter, J., and P. Hammond, *Mathematics for economic analysis*, Prentice Hall, 1995.

Uzawa, H., "Optimal Growth in a Two-Sector Model of Capital Accumulation", *Review of Economic Studies*, XXXII, 90, April, 1965, 85–104.

Watson, Burton (transl.), *Basic writings of Mo Tzu, Hsün Tzu and Han Fei Tzu*, Columbia University Press, New York, 1963.

Young, L., "The Tao of markets: Sima Quian and the invisible hand", *Pacific Economic Review*, Vol. 1, No 2, September 1996.

Yuhn, K.H., "Economic Growth, Technical Change Biases, and the Elasticity of Substitution: a Test of the de La Grandville Hypothesis", *The Review of Economics and Statistics*, LXIII, No 2, 1991, pp. 340–6.

INDEX